face2face

Advanced Teacher's Book

Nick Robinson, Lindsay Warwick, Johanna Stirling, Craig Thaine and Helen Naylor
with Gillie Cunningham and Jan Bell

CAMBRIDGE
UNIVERSITY PRESS

CAMBRIDGE UNIVERSITY PRESS

Cambridge, New York, Melbourne, Madrid, Cape Town, Singapore, São Paulo, Delhi

Cambridge University Press
The Edinburgh Building, Cambridge CB2 8RU, UK

www.cambridge.org
Information on this title: www.cambridge.org/9780521712804

First published 2009

Printed in the United Kingdom at the University Press, Cambridge

A catalogue record for this publication is available from the British Library

ISBN 978-0-521-71280-4 Teacher's Book
ISBN 978-0-521-71278-1 Student's Book with CD-ROM
ISBN 978-0-521-71279-8 Workbook with Key
ISBN 978-0-521-71282-8 Class Audio CDs

Contents

Welcome to face2face!

face2face	p4
face2face Advanced Components	p4
The face2face Approach	p5
The Student's Book	p6
The CD-ROM: Instructions	p11
The Common European Framework (CEF)	p15
Teaching Tips for Advanced Classes	p20

Teaching Notes

1	Let's talk	p24
2	Remarkable!	p34
3	Well-being	p44
4	Civilised	p54
5	It's just a job!	p64
6	Ask the public	p73
7	Laying down the law	p82
8	What's stopping you?	p92
9	Cash	p100
10	The key to success	p109

Photocopiable Materials

Class Activities

	Instructions	p118
1A	Getting to know you	p133
1B	Student survey	p134
1C	In other words, …	p135
2A	The great brain game	p136
2B	Survival at sea	p137
2C	Tourism role play	p138
3A	Connotation crossword	p139
3B	This is my life	p140
3C	Tactful or tactless?	p141
1–3 Review	Board game	p142
4A	No comment!	p143
4B	Guess the word	p144
4C	The powers of persuasion	p145
5A	Prefix Pelmanism	p146
5B	Picture story	p147
5C	Carry on talking	p148
6A	Anti-social behaviour	p149
6B	Grab a word game	p150
6C	What a joke!	p151
4–6 Review	Cash quiz	p152
7A	You said it!	p154
7B	Fact or fiction?	p155
7C	Crime circle	p156
8A	The council meeting	p157
8B	The thrill-seekers	p159
8C	What a dilemma!	p160
9A	Verb dominoes	p161
9B	My partner	p162
9C	Entrepreneur enterprises	p163
7–9 Review	Across the board	p164
10A	Secret auction	p166
10B	Give me the sentence	p167
10C	A problem shared	p168

Vocabulary Plus

	Instructions	p169
1	Vague language	p172
2	Guessing the meaning of unknown words	p173
3	Health idioms	p174
4	Words used in newspaper headlines	p175
5	Phrasal verbs with out, back and down	p176
6	New words from the Internet	p177
7	Law and crime	p178
8	Stress patterns in long words	p179
9	Formal and informal money expressions	p180
10	Idioms about success and failure	p181

Help with Listening

	Instructions	p182
1	Monologues	p189
2	Taking part in a conversation	p190
3	Leaving things out	p191
4	Disagreeing	p192
5	Talking about problems and solutions	p193
6	Asides	p194
7	Opinions	p195
8	Small words	p196
9	Different uses of that	p197
10	Presenting information	p198

Progress Tests

Instructions	p199
Answer Key and Recording Scripts	p199
Progress Test 1	p204
Progress Test 2	p206
Progress Test 3	p208
Progress Test 4	p210
Progress Test 5	p212
Progress Test 6	p214
Progress Test 7	p216
Progress Test 8	p218
Progress Test 9	p220
Progress Test 10	p222

Welcome to face2face!

face2face

face2face is a general English course for adults and young adults who want to learn to communicate quickly and effectively in today's world.

face2face is based on the communicative approach and it combines the best in current methodology with special new features designed to make learning and teaching easier.

The face2face syllabus integrates the learning of new language with skills development and places equal emphasis on vocabulary and grammar.

face2face mainly uses a guided discovery approach to learning, first allowing students to check what they know, then helping them to work out the rules for themselves through carefully structured examples and concept questions.

All new language is included in the interactive *Language Summaries* in the back of the face2face Student's Book and is regularly recycled and reviewed.

There is a strong focus on listening and speaking throughout face2face.

At Advanced level, face2face has authentic listening texts which help students to understand natural spoken English in context and there are numerous opportunities for communicative, personalised speaking practice. The *Real World* lesson (lesson C) in each unit focuses either on the functional language students need for day-to-day life or on integrated reading and listening tasks which provide a stimulus for spoken and written communication.

The face2face Student's Book provides approximately 80 hours of core teaching material, which can be extended to 120 hours with the photocopiable resources and extra ideas in this Teacher's Book. Each self-contained lesson is easily teachable off the page with minimal preparation.

The vocabulary selection in face2face has been informed by the *Cambridge International Corpus* and the *Cambridge Learner Corpus*.

face2face is fully compatible with the *Common European Framework of Reference for Languages* (CEF) and gives students regular opportunities to evaluate their progress. face2face Advanced covers C1 (see p15).

face2face Advanced Components

Student's Book with free CD-ROM

The Student's Book provides 30 lessons in 10 thematically linked units. Each unit also contains a *Review, Accurate Writing* and *Preview* section to revise and consolidate students' knowledge of grammar and vocabulary, and help students become better writers.

The free CD-ROM is an invaluable resource for students, with over 200 exercises in all language areas, plus video, recording and playback capability, a fully searchable *Grammar Reference* section, a link to the *Cambridge Advanced Learner's Dictionary*, all the sounds in English, customisable *My Activities* and *My Test* sections, and *Progress* sections where students evaluate their own progress. Help students to get the most out of the CD-ROM by giving them the photocopiable instructions on p11–p14.

Class Audio CDs

The three Class Audio CDs contain all the listening material for the Student's Book, including conversations, drills, songs and the listening sections of the *Progress Tests* for units 5 and 10.

Workbook

The Workbook provides further practice of all language presented in the Student's Book. It also includes a 30-page *Reading and Writing Portfolio* based on the *Common European Framework of Reference for Languages*, which can be used either for homework or for extra work in class.

Teacher's Book

This Teacher's Book includes *Teaching Tips for Advanced Classes, Teaching Notes* and photocopiable materials: 33 *Class Activities*, 10 *Vocabulary Plus* and 10 *Help with Listening* worksheets, and 10 *Progress Tests*.

Website

Visit the face2face website www.cambridge.org/elt/face2face for downloadable activities, sample materials and more information about how face2face covers the language areas specified by the CEF.

The face2face Approach

Listening

A typical listening activity in **face2face** Advanced checks understanding of gist and then asks questions about specific details. In other activities students guess the meanings of words or phrases from the context and interpret the speaker's attitudes. The authentic recordings in every unit expose students to natural connected speech and a range of accents.

The 10 *Help with Listening* worksheets in this Teacher's Book use authentic recordings from the Student's Book, and focus on how fluent speakers of English structure their discourse in a variety of genres.

For *Teaching Tips* on Listening, see p20.

Speaking

All the lessons in **face2face** Advanced and the *Class Activities* worksheet provide students with numerous speaking opportunities, which focus on both accuracy and fluency.

Even at advanced level, students may need time to formulate their ideas before they speak. Therefore this preparation stage is incorporated into the *Get ready ... Get it right!* activities at the end of each A and B lesson.

For *Teaching Tips* on Speaking, see p20.

Reading

In the **face2face** Advanced Student's Book, there is a wide range of authentic texts covering a variety of genres. As well as developing the reading skills of skimming and scanning, there are activities which focus on other sub-skills such as interpretation of attitude, and awareness of text structure.

For classes that require more practice, there is the 30-page *Reading and Writing Portfolio* in the **face2face** Advanced Workbook. This section contains 10 stand-alone lessons, one for each unit of the Student's Book, which are designed for students to do at home or in class. The topics and content of these lessons are based closely on the CEF reading and writing competences for level C1. At the end of this section there is a list of 'can do' statements that allows students to track their progress.

For *Teaching Tips* on Reading, see p21.

Writing

face2face Advanced recognises the importance of accuracy in writing, and includes sections which focus on spelling, punctuation and the accurate use of discourse markers.

For students who need more practice of writing skills, there is the *Reading and Writing Portfolio* and the *Accurate Writing* exercises in the **face2face** Advanced Workbook.

For *Teaching Tips* on Writing, see p21.

Vocabulary

There is lexical input in most lessons, all of which is consolidated for student reference in the interactive *Language Summaries* in the back of the Student's Book. The areas of vocabulary include: collocations, sentence stems (e.g. *There's*

no way I'd ...), connotation, informal and formal language, phrasal verbs and phrasal nouns (e.g. *go down with, onset*), word building, fixed and semi-fixed phrases (e.g. *hit and miss, in phases*).

When students meet a new vocabulary area, they are often asked to tick the words they know before doing a matching exercise or checking in the *Language Summaries*. This is usually followed by communicative practice of the new vocabulary. They are also encouraged to deduce the meaning of new words, either from the context or from the prefix, suffix, etc. In addition, each unit in **face2face** Advanced includes at least one *Help with Vocabulary* section, designed to guide students towards a better understanding of the lexical systems of English. The information in these sections is in the *Language Summaries* for students to refer to.

For longer courses and/or more able students, this Teacher's Book also contains one *Vocabulary Plus* worksheet for each unit. These worksheets introduce and practise new vocabulary that is **not** included in the Student's Book.

For *Teaching Tips* on Vocabulary, see p22.

Grammar

Examples of the new grammar are taken from the listening and reading texts in the lesson and there is a strong focus on appropriacy of language in both spoken and written contexts.

In most of the *Help with Grammar* sections there is a guided discovery approach to grammar in which students work out the rules before checking their answers in the *Language Summaries*. However, at Advanced level, because some of the grammatical rules are so complex, we sometimes use a more deductive approach where students are given the rule before they look at examples and practise the new grammar forms.

For *Teaching Tips* on Grammar, see p22.

Real World

At this level, students need to think about the subtleties of effective communication in more depth. Therefore, some units practise strategies such as paraphrasing, ways of being tactful, etc., whereas other units focus on developing fluency by encouraging students to react personally to topics which they have read and heard about.

Reviewing and Recycling

face2face Advanced includes *Preview* sections designed to give students an opportunity to test themselves on areas of grammar and vocabulary which they have probably already studied, before they go on to explore new aspects of that particular language area.

Opportunities for review are also provided in the *Quick Review* sections at the beginning of lessons, the comprehensive *Review* sections at the end of each unit, the 10 photocopiable *Progress Tests* and three of the *Class Activities* worksheets in this Teacher's Book.

For *Teaching Tips* on Reviewing and Recycling, see p23.

The Student's Book

Lessons A and B in each unit introduce and practise new language and develop Advanced skills.

Menu boxes list the language taught and reviewed in each lesson.

Help with Grammar sections combine both inductive and deductive approaches to grammar. Either the rules of form and use are given or students are encouraged to work them out for themselves before checking their answers in the interactive *Language Summary* for the unit.

There are practice activities immediately after the presentation of vocabulary to help consolidate the new language.

Students can learn and check the meaning of new vocabulary in the interactive *Language Summary* for the unit in the back of the Student's Book.

---

4 Civilised

4A Society and the media

QUICK REVIEW ● ● ●
Make a list of six euphemisms (*getting on a bit*, etc.). Work in pairs. Swap lists. Take turns to make sentences with phrases from your partner's list.

Vocabulary News collocations

1 a) Match the verbs in A to the words/phrases in B. Check in V4.1 p127.

A	B
read	publicity
seek	a press conference
hold	the tabloids/glossy magazines
receive	the headlines
sue	for libel
hit	a lot of coverage
make	a press release
issue	the front page
run	a story

b) Fill in the gaps with a word from 1a).

1 Do you ever read _____ magazines? If so, which ones?
2 Which celebrities in your country actually _____ publicity?
3 What type of news regularly receives a lot of _____ in your country?
4 What's the latest story to _____ the front page of the newspaper you read?
5 Do you know of any famous people who have _____ a newspaper for libel?
6 Do newspapers in your country often _____ stories about TV celebrities?

c) Work in pairs. Ask and answer the questions in 1b). Ask follow-up questions.

Reading and Grammar

2 a) Work in pairs. Discuss these questions.

1 How do you find out what's in the news?
2 How much time do you spend each day watching, reading, listening to or discussing news stories?

b) Check the meaning of these words/phrases.

> a bugging device   go through the roof   axe something
> a lawsuit   a defendant   a spouse

c) Read news items 1–4. Then match four of these headlines to the news items. Which headline does not belong to any of the stories?

a) New airport 'green' tax due to be introduced
b) Driving age set to rise
c) Sale of bugging devices about to go through roof
d) New TV boss on the verge of axing reality TV shows
e) Dry cleaner's to face lawsuit over pair of trousers

d) Read news items 1–4 again. Then complete these sentences in your own words.

1 a) The government is bringing in a new airport tax because ...
   b) Parents will be upset about it because ...
2 a) The Chungs' story is extraordinary because ...
   b) Judge Pearson's basing his case on ...
3 a) The government is increasing the legal driving age because ...
   b) Another new restriction to be introduced is ...
4 a) Judge Benini concluded that the 22 defendants were ...
   b) The current law in Italy on invasion of privacy is restricted to ...

36

Vocabulary news collocations
Grammar phrases referring to the future
Review euphemisms

① The cost of an average family holiday abroad is likely to increase under current government plans. The Department of Transport proposals emerged at the height of the holiday season, when more than five million people a month fly from British airports. The Department is looking for ways in which aviation can meet its 'full climate change costs'. However, this decision is sure to annoy parents, particularly in the summer when they already pay a high premium for flying during school holidays.

② An immigrant family from South Korea first went into business seven years ago and believed they had found their American dream. However, the Chungs, who own a dry cleaner's in Washington, are being sued for $65 million by Roy Pearson, a District of Columbia judge. The judge is suing the Chung family over a missing pair of trousers, despite the fact that they were later found! The family have been living with this legal nightmare for over two years and they are unlikely to stay in America if they lose their case. Much of Judge Pearson's lawsuit rests on two signs that Custom Cleaners had on its walls: 'Satisfaction Guaranteed' and 'Same Day Service'. Pearson claims the signs amount to fraud.

③ The government has announced new measures aimed at reducing the number of road deaths. The minimum legal driving age is shortly to rise and ministers are proposing that learner drivers should undergo a training period of no less than 12 months; a measure which they claim is certain to reduce the number of accidents caused by young drivers. The same proposal, to be published this autumn, will also recommend a no-alcohol limit for newly qualified drivers of any age for a year after they pass their test.

④ From now on people in Italy would be wise not to use their cars for 'secret meetings'. According to a judge's ruling yesterday, married people can now legally bug their spouse's car if they believe their husband or wife is being unfaithful. However, when 22 of these bugging devices were recently found by police, the people involved were charged with 'invasion of privacy'. However, Lorenzo Benini, a judge in Brescia, ruled that installing bugging devices in a car "was not a criminal offence". He pointed out that the law forbidding bugging only applies to homes. Many fear the judge's ruling is bound to result in an increased use of these devices.

4A

3 Work in groups. Discuss these questions.

1 What measures are being taken in your country to fight global warming?
2 What would happen in your country if a dry cleaner's lost or damaged an item of clothing?
3 At what age do you think people should be allowed to drive? Give reasons.
4 What legitimate reasons, if any, are there for using bugging devices?

Help with Grammar phrases referring to the future

See Preview, p35.

4 a) Change headlines a)–e) in 2c) into sentences by adding the correct form of *be* and using an article where necessary.
A new airport 'green' tax is due to be introduced.

TIP! ● Many newspaper headlines are not written as complete sentences.

b) Look at the words/phrases in **pink** in headlines a)–e) and in **blue** in news stories 1–4. Which group of words/phrases tells us:

1 that something is ready to happen, probably in the near future?
2 the speaker or writer's opinion of how certain they are that this will happen?

c) Look again at the words/phrases in **pink** and **blue**. Which phrase is followed by verb+*ing* (or noun)? What verb form follows the other phrases?

TIP! ● *due to* is usually used when we are talking about a particular time: *Building work is due to start in March.*

d) Check in G4.2 p127.

5 Fill in the gaps with these prompts. Use the correct form of the verb.

> set / rise   verge / turn back   due / retire
> about / sign   settle for

1 Interest rates *are set to rise* by a half a percent.
2 Liverpool's chief of police _____ after 40 years of service.
3 Everest's youngest climbers _____ because of poor weather conditions.
4 The singer, Migs, _____ a new recording deal for £10 million.
5 The Workers' Union _____ a 10% pay rise.

37

Reduced sample pages from **face2face** Advanced Student's Book

> *Quick Reviews* at the beginning of each lesson recycle previously learned language and get the class off to a lively, student-centred start.

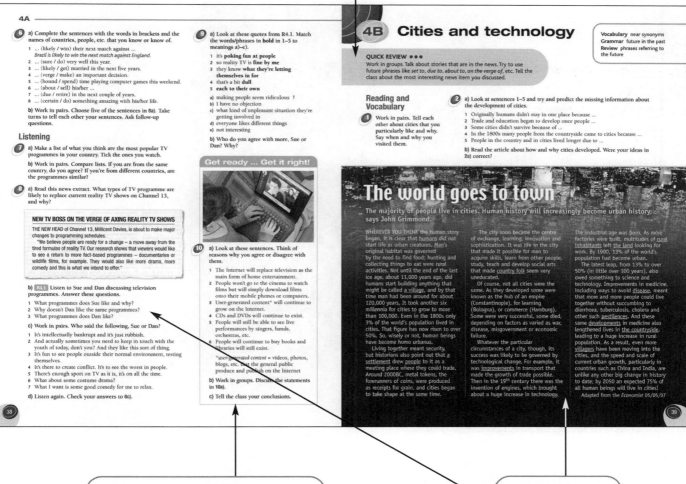

4A

6 a) Complete the sentences with the words in brackets and the names of countries, people, etc. that you know or know of.

1 ... (likely / win) their next match against ...
Brazil is likely to win the next match against England.
2 ... (sure / do) very well this year.
3 ... (likely / get) married in the next five years.
4 ... (verge / make) an important decision.
5 ... (bound / spend) time playing computer games this weekend.
6 ... (about / sell) his/her ...
7 ... (due / retire) in the next couple of years.
8 ... (certain / do) something amazing with his/her life.

b) Work in pairs. Choose five of the sentences in 6a). Take turns to tell each other your sentences. Ask follow-up questions.

Listening

7 a) Make a list of what you think are the most popular TV programmes in your country. Tick the ones you watch.

b) Work in pairs. Compare lists. If you are from the same country, do you agree? If you're from different countries, are the programmes similar?

8 a) Read this news extract. What types of TV programme are likely to replace current reality TV shows on Channel 13, and why?

NEW TV BOSS ON THE VERGE OF AXING REALITY TV SHOWS

THE NEW HEAD of Channel 13, Millicent Davies, is about to make major changes to programming schedules.

"We believe people are ready for a change – a move away from the tired formulas of reality TV. Our research shows that viewers would like to see a return to more fact-based programmes – documentaries or wildlife films, for example. They would also like more drama, more comedy and this is what we intend to offer."

b) **R4.1** Listen to Sue and Dan discussing television programmes. Answer these questions.

1 What programmes does Sue like and why?
2 Why doesn't Dan like the same programmes?
3 What programmes does Dan like?

c) Work in pairs. Who said the following, Sue or Dan?

1 It's intellectually bankrupt and it's just rubbish.
2 And actually sometimes you need to keep in touch with the youth of today, don't you? And they like this sort of thing.
3 It's fun to see people outside their normal environment, testing themselves.
4 It's there to create conflict. It's to see the worst in people.
5 There's enough sport on TV as it is, it's on all the time.
6 What about some costume drama?
7 What I want is some good comedy for me to relax.

d) Listen again. Check your answers to 8c).

9 a) Look at these quotes from R4.1. Match the words/phrases in **bold** in 1–5 to meanings a)–c).

1 it's **poking fun at people**
2 so reality TV is **fine by me**
3 they know **what they're letting themselves in for**
4 that's a bit **dull**
5 **each to their own**

a) making people seem ridiculous *1*
b) I have no objection
c) what kind of unpleasant situation they're getting involved in
d) everyone likes different things
e) not interesting

b) Who do you agree with more, Sue or Dan? Why?

Get ready ... Get it right!

10 a) Look at these sentences. Think of reasons why you agree or disagree with them.

1 The Internet will replace television as the main form of home entertainment.
2 People won't go to the cinema to watch films but will simply download films onto their mobile phones* or computers.
3 User-generated content* will continue to grow on the Internet.
4 CDs and DVDs will continue to exist.
5 People will still be able to see live performances by singers, bands, orchestras, etc.
6 People will continue to buy books and libraries will still exist.

user-generated content = videos, photos, blogs, etc. that the general public produce and publish on the Internet

b) Work in groups. Discuss the statements in 10a).

c) Tell the class your conclusions.

38

4B **Cities and technology**

Vocabulary near synonyms
Grammar future in the past
Review phrases referring to the future

QUICK REVIEW ●●●
Work in groups. Talk about stories that are in the news. Try to use future phrases like *set to, due to, about to, on the verge of*, etc. Tell the class about the most interesting news item you discussed.

Reading and Vocabulary

1 Work in pairs. Tell each other about cities that you particularly like and why. Say when and why you visited them.

2 a) Look at sentences 1–5 and try and predict the missing information about the development of cities.

1 Originally humans didn't stay in one place because ...
2 Trade and education began to develop once people ...
3 Some cities didn't survive because of ...
4 In the 1800s many people from the countryside came to cities because ...
5 People in the country and in cities lived longer due to ...

b) Read the article about how and why cities developed. Were your ideas in 2a) correct?

The world goes to town

The majority of people live in cities. Human history will increasingly become urban history, says John Grimmond.

WHEREVER YOU THINK the human story began, it is clear that humans did not start life as urban creatures. Man's original habitat was governed by the need to find food; hunting and collecting things to eat were rural activities. Not until the end of the last ice age, about 11,000 years ago, did humans start building anything that might be called a village, and by that time man had been around for about 120,000 years. It took another six millennia for cities to grow to more than 100,000. Even in the 1800s only 3% of the world's population lived in cities. That figure has now risen to over 50%. So, wisely or not, human beings have become homo urbanus.

Living together meant security, but historians also point out that a settlement drew people to it as a meeting place where they could trade. Around 2000BC, metal tokens, the forerunners of coins, were produced as receipts for grain, and cities began to take shape at the same time.

The city soon became the centre of exchange, learning, innovation and sophistication. It was life in the city that made it possible for man to acquire skills, learn from other people, study, teach and develop social arts that made country folk seem very uneducated.

Of course, not all cities were the same. As they developed some were known as the hub of an empire (Constantinople), for learning (Bologna), or commerce (Hamburg). Some were very successful, some died, depending on factors as varied as war, disease, misgovernment or economic failure.

Whatever the particular circumstances of a city, though, its success was likely to be governed by technological change. For example, it was improvements in transport that made the growth of trade possible. Then in the 19th century there was the invention of engines, which brought about a huge increase in technology.

The industrial age was born. As more factories were built, multitudes of rural inhabitants left the land looking for work. By 1900, 13% of the world's population had become urban.

The latest leap, from 13% to over 50% (in little over 100 years), also owed something to science and technology. Improvements in medicine, including ways to avoid disease, meant that more and more people could live together without succumbing to diarrhoea, tuberculosis, cholera and other such pestilences. And these same developments in medicine also lengthened lives in the countryside, leading to a huge increase in rural population. As a result, even more villagers have been moving into the cities, and the speed and scale of current urban growth, particularly in countries such as China and India, are unlike any other big change in history to date; by 2050 an expected 75% of all human beings will live in cities!

Adapted from the *Economist* 05/05/07

39

> *Get ready ... Get it right!* sections are structured communicative speaking tasks that focus on both accuracy and fluency. The *Get ready ...* stage provides the opportunity for students to plan the language and content of what they are going to say before *Getting it right!* when they do the communicative stage of the activity.

> New language is introduced in context in authentic listening or reading texts.

The *Pair and Group Work* section on p108–p116 of the Student's Book provides further communicative speaking practice activities.

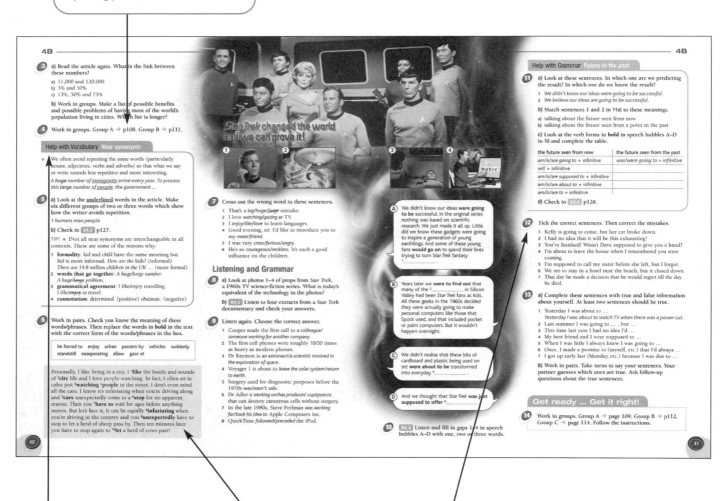

Help with Vocabulary sections encourage students to work out the rules of form and use of new vocabulary themselves before checking in the interactive *Language Summary* for the unit.

Controlled practice exercises check students have understood the meaning and form of new language.

Reduced sample pages from **face2face** Advanced Student's Book

Lesson C in each unit provides students with opportunities to work with different types of authentic listening and reading texts, and then to develop their speaking and writing skills. In the even-numbered units these lessons focus on integrated skills practice. In the odd-numbered units they focus on functional language.

Real World sections focus on the functional language students need for day-to-day life.

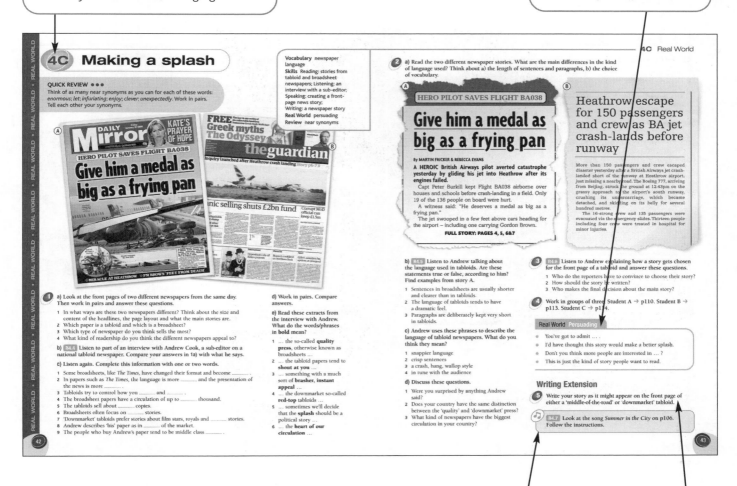

The *Songs* section on p106–p107 of the Student's Book contains fun activities based on popular songs appropriate for Advanced students.

Writing Extension activities offer creative writing practice based on the theme of the lesson. Each activity encourages students to write in a different genre, for example, a report, a short story or a personal action plan.

Reduced sample pages from **face2face** Advanced Student's Book

The Student's Book

The *Review* sections at the end of every unit provide revision of key language from the unit. These exercises can be done in class or for homework and will help students prepare for the *Progress Test* for the unit.

The *Preview* sections revise and consolidate grammar and vocabulary students have probably studied before, and help students prepare for the next unit. These activities can be done in class or for homework.

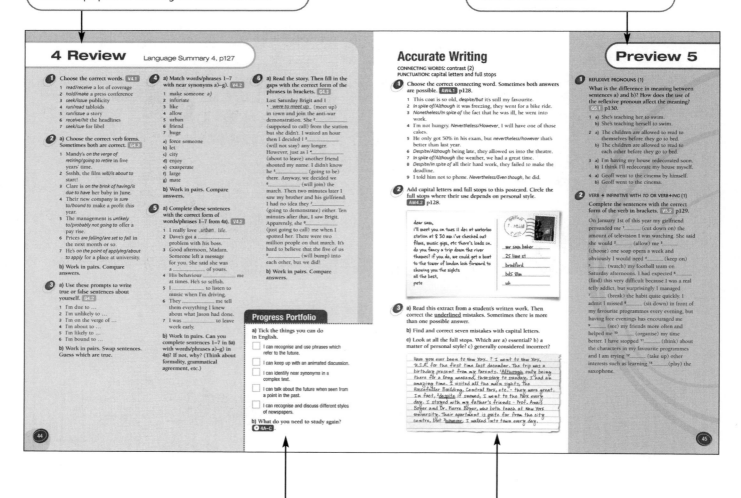

Based on the requirements of the *Common European Framework of Reference for Languages* (see p15), the *Progress Portfolios* allow students to monitor their own language development by checking what they can remember from the unit. Students are then directed to the CD-ROM for further practice of areas they are unsure about.

The *Accurate Writing* sections help students by focusing on punctuation, spelling and discourse markers.

Reduced sample pages from **face2face** Advanced Student's Book

The CD-ROM: Instructions

- Use the CD-ROM in your computer to practise language from the Student's Book.

Look at the *Language Summary* reference for the *Grammar* and *Real World* language you have learned in the lessons. You can also add your own notes.

Find the meaning of any word in the activities on the CD-ROM using the Cambridge Dictionaries Online website.

Learn the phonemic symbols and practise saying the sounds.

Check your progress.

Make your own *Tests* from over 600 questions.

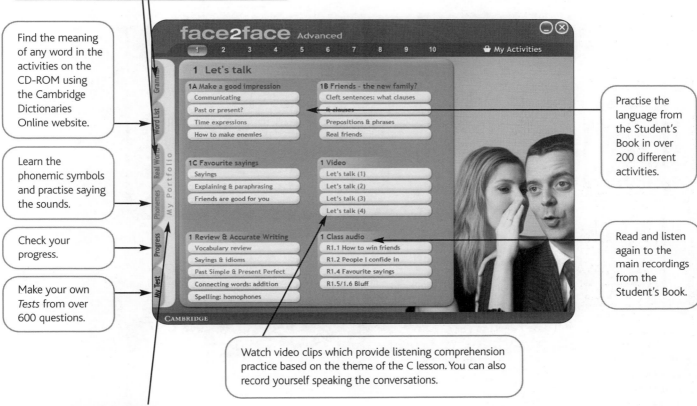

Practise the language from the Student's Book in over 200 different activities.

Read and listen again to the main recordings from the Student's Book.

Watch video clips which provide listening comprehension practice based on the theme of the C lesson. You can also record yourself speaking the conversations.

How to use *My Portfolio*

Grammar

Click on the *Grammar* tab to open the *Grammar* screen. It gives all the information from the *Language Summaries* in the Student's Book so you don't need to have the Student's Book to hand when you are working.

Click on the name of a grammar area to find the information you need.

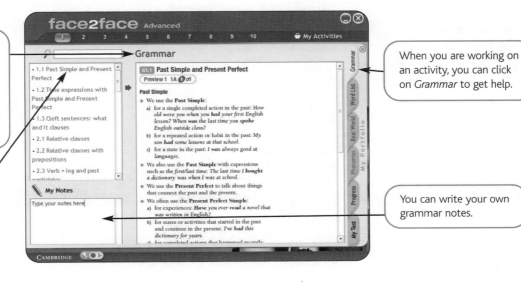

When you are working on an activity, you can click on *Grammar* to get help.

You can write your own grammar notes.

Two screen grabs from **face2face** Advanced CD-ROM

Phonemes

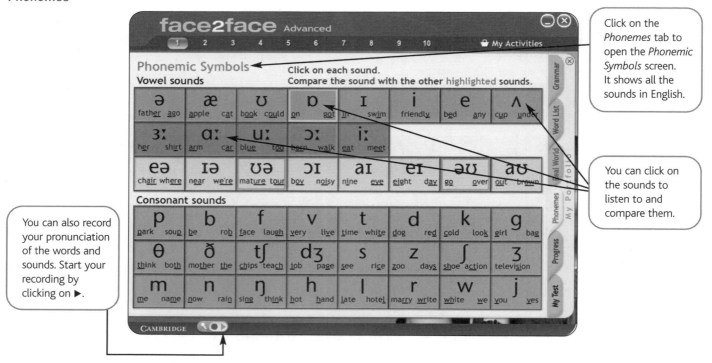

Click on the *Phonemes* tab to open the *Phonemic Symbols* screen. It shows all the sounds in English.

You can click on the sounds to listen to and compare them.

You can also record your pronunciation of the words and sounds. Start your recording by clicking on ▶.

Progress

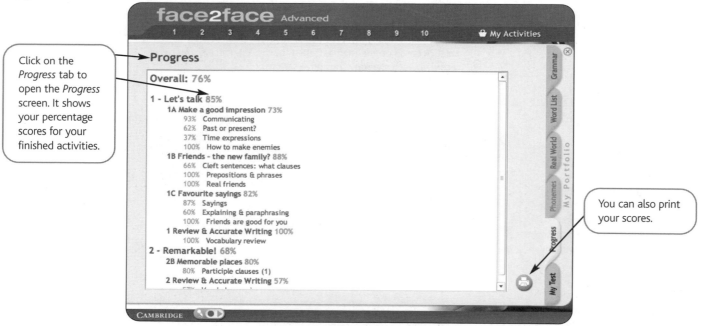

Click on the *Progress* tab to open the *Progress* screen. It shows your percentage scores for your finished activities.

You can also print your scores.

Two screen grabs from **face2face** Advanced CD-ROM

face2face Advanced Photocopiable

My Test

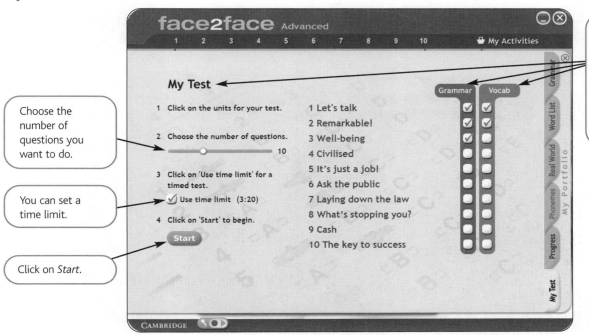

Choose the number of questions you want to do.

You can set a time limit.

Click on *Start*.

Click on the *My Test* tab to open the *My Test* screen. You can choose the grammar and vocabulary that you want to be tested on.

How to practise new language

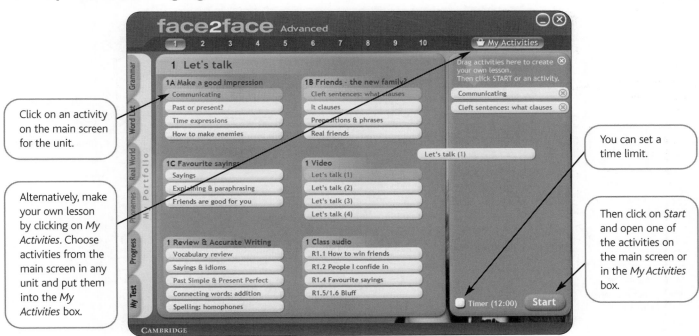

Click on an activity on the main screen for the unit.

Alternatively, make your own lesson by clicking on *My Activities*. Choose activities from the main screen in any unit and put them into the *My Activities* box.

You can set a time limit.

Then click on *Start* and open one of the activities on the main screen or in the *My Activities* box.

Two screen grabs from **face2face** Advanced CD-ROM

Read the instructions for the activity.

Move the words/phrases to the gaps.

Click on ▶ to hear the recording of the sentence.

When you have finished, check which answers you got right/wrong.

You can do the activity again and correct your wrong answers.

You can click for help with how to do the activity.

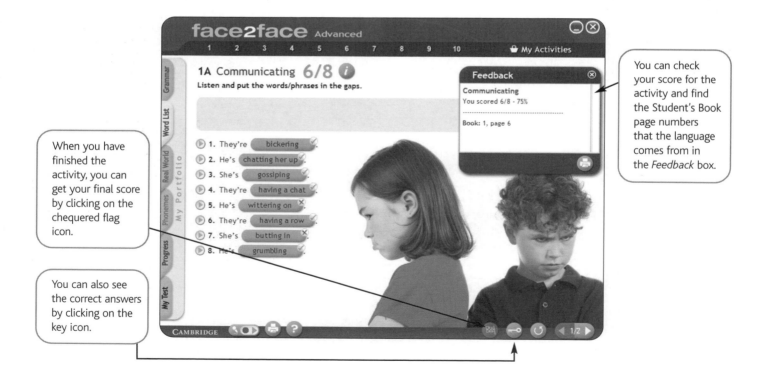

When you have finished the activity, you can get your final score by clicking on the chequered flag icon.

You can check your score for the activity and find the Student's Book page numbers that the language comes from in the *Feedback* box.

You can also see the correct answers by clicking on the key icon.

Two screen grabs from **face2face** Advanced CD-ROM

The Common European Framework (CEF)

What is the Common European Framework (CEF)?

Since the early 1970s, a series of Council of Europe initiatives has developed a description of the language knowledge and skills that people need to live, work and survive in any country or environment where the main language of communication is different from their own language. *Waystage 1990*[1], *Threshold 1990*[2] and *Vantage*[3] detail the knowledge and skills required at different levels of ability.

The contents of these language specific documents served as the basis for the more general *Common European Framework of Reference for Languages: Learning, teaching, assessment* (CEF)[4], which was officially launched by the Council of Europe in 2001 and includes sets of 'can do' statements or 'competences'. A related document, *The European Language Portfolio*, encourages learners to assess their progress by matching their competence against the 'can do' statements.

The **face2face** series has been developed to include comprehensive coverage of the requirements of the CEF. The table above right shows how **face2face** relates to the CEF and the examinations which can be taken at each level through University of Cambridge ESOL Examinations (Cambridge ESOL), which is a member of ALTE (The Association of Language Testers in Europe).

face2face Advanced and CEF level C1

The table on the right describes the general degree of skill required at C1 of the CEF. The 'can do' statements for C1 are listed in the *Common European Framework of Reference for Languages: Learning, teaching, assessment*.

face2face Advanced covers level C1. The Listening, Reading, Speaking and Writing tables on p16–p19 show where the required competences for level C1 are covered in **face2face** Advanced.

More information about how **face2face** Advanced covers the grammatical, lexical and other areas specified by the CEF can be found on our website: www.cambridge.org/elt/face2face/cef

face2face Student's Book	CEF level	Related examinations	Council of Europe document
Starter	A1		*Breakthrough*
Elementary	A2	KET Key English Test	*Waystage*
Pre-intermediate Intermediate	B1	PET Preliminary English Test	*Threshold*
Upper Intermediate	B2	FCE First Certificate in English	*Vantage*
Advanced	C1	CAE Cambridge Advanced Certificate	

In the spirit of *The European Language Portfolio* developed from the CEF, **face2face** provides a *Progress Portfolio* at the end of every Student's Book unit. Students are encouraged to assess their ability to use the language they have learned so far and to review any aspects by using the CD-ROM. In the Workbook there is a 30-page *Reading and Writing Portfolio* section linked to the CEF and a comprehensive list of 'can do' statements in the *Reading and Writing Progress Portfolio*, which allows students to track their own progress.

U N D E R S T A N D I N G	Listening	I can understand extended speech even when it is not clearly structured and relationships are only implied and not signalled explicitly. I can understand television programmes and films without too much effort.
	Reading	I can understand long and complex factual and literary texts, appreciating distinctions of style. I can understand specialised articles and longer technical instructions, even when they do not relate to my field.
S P E A K I N G	Spoken Interaction	I can express myself fluently and spontaneously without much obvious searching for expressions. I can use language flexibly and effectively for social and professional purposes. I can formulate ideas and opinions with precision and relate my contribution skilfully to those of other speakers.
	Spoken Production	I can present clear, detailed descriptions of complex subjects integrating sub-themes, developing particular points and rounding off with an appropriate conclusion.
W R I T I N G	Writing	I can express myself in clear, well-structured text, expressing points of view at some length. I can write about complex subjects in a letter, an essay or a report, underlining what I consider to be the salient issues. I can select a style appropriate to the reader in mind.

[1] *Waystage 1990* J A van Ek and J L M Trim, Council of Europe, Cambridge University Press ISBN 978-0-521-56707-7
[2] *Threshold 1990* J A van Ek and J L M Trim, Council of Europe, Cambridge University Press ISBN 978-0-521-56706-0
[3] *Vantage* (2001) J A van Ek and J L M Trim, Council of Europe, Cambridge University Press ISBN 978-0-521-56705-3
[4] *Common European Framework of Reference for Languages: Learning, teaching, assessment* (2001) Council of Europe Modern Languages Division, Strasbourg, Cambridge University Press ISBN 978-0-521-80313-7 © Council of Europe

Listening

A language user at level C1 can:	1	2	3
follow extended speech on abstract and complex topics beyond his/her own field	1C	2A 2B 2C	3A
follow extended speech which is not clearly structured and when the message is not given explicitly	1B		3A 3B
recognise a wide range of idiomatic expressions and colloquialisms, appreciating shifts in register	1A 1C	2A	3A 3B
easily follow complex interactions in group discussions and debates, even when the topic is complex and unfamiliar	1A 1C	2B	3B
easily follow most lectures, discussions and debates		2C	
understand complex technical information			
understand a wide range of recorded and broadcast audio material, including some which uses non-standard language, and identify finer points of detail such as implicit attitudes and relationships between speakers	1C	2A	
	This competence is practised throughout		

Reading

A language user at level C1 can:	1	2	3
understand in detail lengthy or complex texts, whether or not they relate to his/her own area of speciality, provided he/she can reread difficult sections	1A 1B WBP1	2A WB2A WBP2	3A WBP3
understand any correspondence given the occasional use of a dictionary		WBP2	WB3B
identify finer points of detail including attitudes and implied as well as stated opinions	1A 1B WBP1	2B	
understand in detail lengthy, complex instructions or procedures			
scan quickly through long or complex texts, locating relevant details	1A 1B WBP1	2A 2B WBP2	3A WBP3
quickly identify the content and relevance of texts on a wide range of topics, deciding whether closer study is worthwhile		2A 2C	3B

1A = **face2face** Advanced Student's Book unit 1 lesson A
WB1A = **face2face** Advanced Workbook unit 1 lesson A
WBP1 = **face2face** Advanced Workbook Reading and Writing Portfolio 1

4	5	6	7	8	9	10
4B 4C	5A 5B	6A 6B 6C	7A 7B	8A 8B	9B 9C	10A 10B
4A	5B	6A 6B	7B	8A 8C		10C
	5B 5C	6A 6B	7C	8C		10C
	5C	6A			9A	
4A 4B 4C	5C	6C	7A		9B 9C	
4B		6C	7A			
4B		6C	7A 7C	8B	9B	10A

the course on the interactive CD-ROM.

4	5	6	7	8	9	10
4A 4B 4C WB4B WB4C WBP4	5A 5B WB5A WB5B WBP5	6A 6B WB6B WB6C	7A 7B WBP7	8A 8B WBP8	9A 9B WB9B WBP9	10A 10B 10C WB10C WBP10
		WBP6		WBP8	WB9A	
4B 4C WB4C WBP4	5A WBP5	6A WB6C WBP6	7A WBP7	8A 8B 8C WBP8	9A 9B	10B WB10C WBP10
					WBP9	
4A 4B WBP4	5A WBP5	6A 6B 6C WBP6	7A 7B		WBP9	10A WBP10
4C WB4C	5B					

The CEF

Speaking

A language user at level C1 can:	1	2	3
contribute to complex interactions between third parties in group discussions even on abstract, complex unfamiliar topics	1B	2A 2B	3A 3B
argue convincingly, responding to questions and answering complex counter arguments fluently, spontaneously and appropriately	1B	2A	3A 3B
give clear, detailed descriptions and presentations of complex subjects	1C	2A 2B	
backtrack when he/she encounters a difficulty, and reformulate what he/she wants to say without interrupting the flow of speech	1C		
use language flexibly and effectively for social purposes, including emotional, allusive and joking usage			3C
give elaborate descriptions and narratives, developing particular points and rounding off with an appropriate conclusion		2C	
handle interjections well, responding spontaneously and almost effortlessly			
participate fully in an interview, as either interviewer or interviewee	1A		
select from a wide range of discourse functions in order to get the floor, or to gain time and keep the floor whilst thinking			
vary intonation and place sentence stress correctly in order to express finer shades of meaning	1B		3C
ask follow-up questions for clarification	1A 1B	2B	3A
adjust what he/she says to the situation and the recipient and adopt a level of formality appropriate to the circumstances			
plan what is to be said and the means to say it, considering the effect on the recipients	This competence is practised in all the		
	1C	2C	3C
relate his/her own contribution to those of other speakers	This competence is practised throughout		
produce well-structured speech, using organisational patterns, connectors and cohesive devices		2B	

Writing

A language user at level C1 can:	1	2	3
write clear, detailed, well-structured and developed descriptions and imaginative texts in an assured, personal, natural style appropriate to the reader in mind		2C WBP2	
write clear, well-structured expositions of complex subjects, highlighting the relevant important issues	WBP1		WBP3
expand and support points of view at some length with subsidiary points, reasons and relevant examples	WBP1	WBP2	WBP3
express him/herself with clarity and precision, relating to the addressee flexibly and effectively		WBP2	WBP3
express him/herself with clarity and precision in personal correspondence			
use consistent and helpful layout, paragraphing and punctuation, and accurate spelling	This competence is practised in all the		
plan what is to be written and the means to express it, considering the reader	This competence is practised in all the		
use language effectively, including emotional, allusive and joking usage			
take detailed notes during a lecture		2C	

1A = **face2face** Advanced Student's Book unit 1 lesson A
WB1A = **face2face** Advanced Workbook unit 1 lesson A
WBP1 = **face2face** Advanced Workbook Reading and Writing Portfolio 1

4	5	6	7	8	9	10
4A	5B	6A 6B	7A 7B	8B 8C	9A 9B	10B 10C
4A 4C	5A 5B		7A 7B	8C	9C	10C
4B		6A	7A 7B	8A 8B 8C	9A 9C	10A 10C
	5C					
	5A 5C	6C	7C			
4C		6B 6C				10B
	5C					
			7C	8C		
	5C					
			7C			
4A 4B	5A 5B 5C	6A	7A 7C	8A 8B	9B	10A
			7C		9C	
Get ready ... Get it right! activities.						
4C	5C	6C	7C		9C	10C
the Student's Book.						
4B		6C			9C	

4	5	6	7	8	9	10
		6C		WBP8		WBP10
4C WBP4	WBP5		WBP7	8C	WBP9	10C
WBP4			WBP7			
4C WBP4	WBP5	WBP6				
		WBP6				
Accurate Writing exercises in the Student's Book and Workbook.						
Workbook Reading and Writing Portfolio writing exercises.						
		WBP6		WBP8		

Teaching Tips for Advanced Classes

Since we believe that one of the main aims of teaching Advanced students should be to prepare them to go out into the 'real world' and continue language learning on their own, the emphasis at this level needs to be on developing the skills and strategies which will help them to become autonomous. Being exposed to a wide range of authentic language and developing the strategies to cope with it must be priorities if students are to develop the confidence to read and listen outside the classroom. Issues of motivation are also very important at this level; one of the best ways of motivating students is for them to perceive that they are making progress in the productive skills of speaking and writing. By focusing on both linguistic accuracy and communication strategies and by giving students the opportunity to accept responsibility for monitoring their own language, this progress should soon be evident.

Listening

Students are exposed to both scripted and unscripted recordings, which are spoken at natural speed and in a range of accents. At this level, the main aim is to help students to develop confidence in listening for a communicative purpose, rather than expecting them to understand every word.

- Before asking students to listen to a recording, establish the context, the characters and what information you want them to listen for. This will help to prepare them for what they are about to hear.

- Give students time to read the comprehension questions in the Student's Book. Deal with any problems or new language in these questions before playing the recording.

- Be sensitive to the difficulties that students might be having. Authentic recordings may appear faster and more difficult to follow at first, and may have a vocabulary load that is heavier than usual, particularly if colloquial language is used. The key here is to be relaxed and supportive and not to expect too much at first. Since there is an authentic recording in nearly every lesson, students will soon begin to get accustomed to them.

- Be flexible about how many times you play the recording. You may want to play it two or even three times. However, sometimes you may not need to play it more than once if the students have comprehended sufficiently well from the first listening.

- If you play a recording for a second or third time, you can ask students to read the *Recording Scripts* at the back of the Student's Book while they listen. This helps them to 'tune in' to spoken English and connect what they hear with what they read.

- When students need to listen and write their answers, you can stop the recording at the appropriate moment, in order to give them time to write them down.

- Use the activities for the *Songs* on p106–p107 of the Student's Book at the points suggested in the course.

- Use the *Help with Listening* photocopiable worksheets in this Teacher's Book, which focus on how fluent speakers of English structure their discourse in a variety of genres.

Speaking

Although students at Advanced level may feel confident when speaking, they are often reluctant to take risks, which means they tend to keep on using the same grammar and vocabulary, rather than experimenting with a wider range of language. If they are to become truly Advanced-level speakers, students need to be encouraged to venture out of their 'comfort zone'.

- Make full use of all the communicative speaking activities in the Student's Book, which include the personal response questions after the reading and listening texts, the *Get ready … Get it right!* sections in the A and B lessons, and the fluency activities in all the C lessons.

- If students are to feel they can experiment and focus on the message they want to convey, rather than the accuracy of every word, the atmosphere in the class must be such that they feel relaxed and prepared to take risks without feeling that they will be laughed at or have every word corrected. Establish at the beginning of every speaking activity whether the aim is primarily accuracy or fluency.

- Depending on the main aim of the speaking activity, you may choose to focus your feedback on how well students have communicated, how accurate they have been, or both.

- Make it clear to students that the C lessons in the even-numbered units focus on integrated skills practice. This means that the reading and listening texts provide the stimulus for students to speak about their reactions to what they hear and read, and the emphasis is very much on fluency rather than accuracy.

- If you want your students to become genuinely independent, it is extremely important to encourage them to monitor themselves by asking them to reflect on how successful they were in getting their message across. You can do this by giving them a checklist of points against which they can assess their own or other students' performance. This may include questions such as: *Did you use a range of verb forms?*, *When you didn't know how to say something, did you try to explain in other words?*, *Did you include other students in the discussion?*

- Try to ensure that students work with a number of different partners during a class. If it is difficult for students to swap places in class, you can ask them to work with students in front of or behind them as well as on either side of them. However, since group dynamics are crucial to how well an activity will work, it is important to avoid putting students who do not get on well together in the same group if possible. It can sometimes be beneficial to put students with a similar personality type together, so that quieter students do not become overpowered by more dominant personalities. Many teachers find it useful to plan the composition of groups and pairs as much as possible before beginning the activity.

- Remember that students often find speaking activities much easier if they are personalised, as they don't need to think of ideas as well as language. You may like to adapt some activities so that they are relevant to your particular class.

- Go around the class and discreetly monitor students while

they are speaking in their pairs or groups. At this stage you can provide extra language or ideas as required and correct any language or pronunciation which is impeding communication.

- Avoid becoming too involved in speaking activities yourself unless you see students have misunderstood your instructions or you are asked for help. As soon as you join a group, students often stop talking to each other and talk to you instead.

- Write *banned words* up in the top corner of the board. Tell the students they are not allowed to use these words during the day's lesson. For example, write *good*, *bad* and *nice* on the board to encourage students to use adjectives such as *wonderful*, *amazing*, *excellent*, *fine*, etc.

- Alternatively, write *use these words today* on the board and acknowledge any students who use them. For example, write up adverbs such as *extremely*, *distinctly*, *highly*, *unusually* and *perfectly*. This technique can act as a form of revision for a lesson you have recently done with the class.

Correction

At this level students are likely to have fossilised errors which may be difficult to erase. It is still worth pointing them out to the student so that at least he/she is aware that they are mistakes and can make an effort to use the correct form if he/she chooses to. However, if these mistakes are impeding communication, you should definitely encourage the student to correct the mistake or offer an alternative way of saying the same thing. A good way of doing this is to make a general point at the end of the activity, rather than 'pointing the finger' at a particular student.

- When you hear a mistake, it is often useful to correct it immediately and ask the student to say the word or phrase again in the correct form. This is particularly effective if the mistake relates to the language you have been working on in the lesson.

- Alternatively, when you point out a mistake to a student you can encourage him/her to correct it before giving the correct version.

- Another approach to correction during a freer speaking activity or whole-class discussion is to simply reformulate what has been said:

STUDENT *We discussed about the advantages of being single.*

TEACHER *So, you discussed the advantages. Did you also discuss the disadvantages?*

This less intrusive approach to correction often results in the student repeating the correct version and answering your question.

STUDENT *Yes, we discussed the advantages and disadvantages.*

- Alternatively, you could note down any mistakes you hear during a fluency activity. Then at the end of the lesson, write the mistakes on the board and ask students to correct them in pairs. Making this into a game or competitive activity can be very motivating.

- Another type of feedback – particularly useful in the C lessons, where the focus is not so much on accuracy – is

to discuss how students could have improved in terms of appropriacy, or range of language. The students can then try doing part of the activity again, while another student listens to see if any of the suggestions are implemented.

- On the board, write a target area you want the students not to make mistakes in during the lesson. For example, *prepositions*. Then throughout the lesson pay particular attention to mistakes in this target area. This focuses students on an area, and can act as revision, for example, of verbs plus prepositions.

- Record or video your class doing communicative activities and then use this for feedback on communicative competence, accuracy or both.

Reading

It is important at Advanced level that students read as widely as possible in order to increase their range of vocabulary and consolidate language work. In addition, reading will enable them to develop the skills which they will need to continue reading authentic English texts outside the classroom.

- After a post-reading exercise, focus on how students arrived at the answer, not just what the answer was. It is useful for students to work in pairs or groups and justify their reasons for choosing their answers so that they can learn from each other and use these strategies in future.

- Encourage students to give their personal response to a text whenever possible. This is a good opportunity to encourage further speaking practice. However, if students are initially reluctant to do this, you could allow them to discuss this in their first language, since the focus is on comprehension rather than fluency.

- Give students a time limit to read a text for gist, so they get used to not worrying about every word.

- Encourage students to read the text from the lesson again at home and to record any vocabulary that they find useful in a vocabulary notebook. This is another very important way of encouraging independent learning.

- Encourage students to read outside the classroom. For example, you can set up a reading group for the class where the whole group reads the same book, or they tell each other about the book they have read. Stress that these need not be 'serious' books. Magazines and crime or romantic novels are an excellent source of up-to-date language.

- For homework, ask students to read an article from an online English newspaper, e.g. the *Guardian*. Then in the next lesson, ask one or two students to summarise a news item that they found interesting.

Writing

The *Accurate Writing* sections in Units 1–9 (and the *Accurate Writing* exercises in the Workbook) are intended to complement the skills work in the *Reading and Writing Portfolio* of the Workbook. They specifically focus on discourse markers, spelling and punctuation. Although students at this level will have already met most of the rules for discourse markers, spelling and punctuation, the aim here is to focus on their accurate use. A 'drip feed' approach has been adopted as the students are not expected to assimilate all the rules at once. So, for example, a unit may focus on discourse markers of addition plus one aspect of either spelling or punctuation.

- With more able classes, go directly to the exercise which asks students to correct a piece of work, rather than doing the practice exercises first. The correction exercise could then be used as a diagnostic tool, after which mistakes can be discussed and students subsequently referred to the *Language Summary*.

- In any other writing students may do in class or for homework, try to encourage them to check, correct and improve their own work, focusing particularly on the areas covered in this section of the book and in the *Help with Writing* sections in the *Reading and Writing Portfolio*. You may want to establish some kind of code, for example:

  sp (spelling)   p (punctuation)   vt (verb tense)

  so that students are able to correct their work more easily.

- Another technique is to ask students to exchange their work and try to correct each other's writing. This kind of assessment, as well as self-correction, helps to make learners more independent, as long as the correction is done sensitively.

- Obviously, there are occasions when it would be inappropriate to give feedback on accuracy – that is, if students are writing something personal, such as a diary entry or a poem. In this case you may prefer to write a personal response to what they have written, rather than comments on how it was expressed.

Vocabulary

It is obviously very important at this level to extend students' range of language and for them to become increasingly aware of different levels of formality in different situations. Encourage students to use the vocabulary they have learned in class but also any language they may have acquired outside the classroom from reading, listening to songs, etc.

- Give students time to work through the exercises in the *Help with Vocabulary* sections on their own or in pairs. This gives students the opportunity to try to work out the rules themselves before checking them in the *Language Summaries*. You can then check students have understood the main points with the whole class.

- Point out the stress marks (°) on all new words and phrases in the vocabulary boxes in the lessons and the *Language Summaries*. These show the main stress only on words and phrases.

- When you write a new vocabulary item on the board, make sure students know which syllable is stressed and which part of speech it is. Students then make a note of the new vocabulary item.

- Encourage students to buy a notebook in which they can note down new vocabulary both inside and outside the classroom. Suggest different techniques for noting down vocabulary, for example, word maps, illustration, examples and definitions. Point out that writing down words or phrases in isolation is often not very helpful, tend that they should, for example, include the dependent

preposition (e.g. *run the risk of doing something*). Encourage them to extend their vocabulary by including opposites or near synonyms where appropriate.

- Make sure students are aware of collocations in English (e.g. *heavy traffic*) by pointing them out when they occur and encouraging students to record them as one phrase.

- Encourage students to extend their vocabulary at every available opportunity, for example, in the reading and listening lessons, not just when they are 'doing vocabulary' in the lesson. It is equally important that they use the new vocabulary as much as possible in both their writing and speaking activities if they are going to be able to remember it and access it when they need it.

- Encourage students to work out new meanings for themselves as much as possible, either by using the context or by looking at the word itself.

- Encourage students to use monolingual or bilingual dictionaries as much as possible, and show them how to use them – that is, how to find whether a noun is countable or uncountable, where the stressed syllable is, how to find out whether a word is inappropriately formal or informal, etc.

- Review and recycle vocabulary at every opportunity in class, using the *Reviews*, the *Language Summaries* and the *Class Activities*.

- Use the *Vocabulary Plus* worksheets to introduce and practise vocabulary which is not included in the Student's Book. They can be used for self-study in class or as homework, or as the basis of a classroom lesson.

Grammar

At this level, although students may have covered a lot of the basic grammar, they still need practice in using it accurately and appropriately. They also need to extend their range by using more complex structures in appropriate situations.

- Work through the *Preview* exercise(s) first and do any revision necessary before starting on the related area(s) in the following unit. *Preview* exercise(s) can be done as a 'filler', or set for homework before doing the 'new' area of grammar.

- Give students time to work through the exercises in the *Help with Grammar* sections on their own or in pairs. This gives students the opportunity to try to work out the grammar rules, if that is appropriate, before checking their answers in the *Language Summaries*. You can then check students have understood the main points with the whole class, as shown in the *Teaching Notes* for each lesson.

- If your students don't already know grammatical terms (e.g. cleft sentences, past participle), it would be useful to teach them when the opportunity arises. This helps students become more independent and allows them to use grammar reference books more effectively.

- If you know the students' first language, highlight grammatical differences between their language and English. This raises their awareness of potential problems if they try to translate. It is also useful to highlight grammatical similarities to show students when a structure in English is the same as in their own language.

- Encourage students to notice how language is used when they are reading and listening, not just in dedicated 'grammar lessons'. Expect them to use a range of verb forms, modals, etc. in speaking and writing activities and refer back to work done in these areas. Point out that being an advanced learner means using all they have learned and self-monitoring and self-correcting at all times.

Pronunciation

Be aware that some students do not wish to sound like a native speaker of English and they are happy to retain their accent. As long as the student is comprehensible, this preference should be respected. To determine how much correction of pronunciation you should use with individual students it is wise to ascertain at the beginning of the course how 'English' they want to sound.

Helping students with sounds

- Consider teaching your students the phonemic symbols. This allows students to look up the pronunciation of the words and record difficult pronunciation themselves in their notebooks. It is often easier to take a 'little and often' approach to teaching these symbols, rather than trying to teach them all in one lesson.

- Encourage students to use the phonemes section of the CD-ROM at home. This will help them to learn the symbols and allow them to practise the sounds.

- Highlight the phonemic transcriptions in the *Language Summaries*. Note that transcriptions are given only for vocabulary that is particularly problematic.

- Write the phonemic transcription for difficult words on the board and ask students to work out the pronunciation.

- For any individual sounds which your students are having problems with (e.g. /θ/) try demonstrating the shape of the mouth (but not actually saying the sound) as sometimes students can't say certain sounds simply because they don't know the mouth position required.

- Draw students' attention to the English sounds which are the same in their own language(s) as well as highlighting the ones that are different.

Helping students with stress and intonation

- Emphasise that intonation and pitch level are important to meaning in English and often indicate the mood or attitude of the speaker. For example, whereas a high fall can often indicate enthusiasm (e.g. *great*), a low fall may appear ironic or sarcastic (e.g. *great*).

- People can often recognise a language by its intonation and rhythm (the 'music' of the language) even if they don't actually understand the language. In monolingual classes in particular, you can exploit this by comparing English to the students' native language. Play a short section (four to six lines) from a C lesson recording focusing on functional language. Ask the students to translate that into their language and, if possible, record them. Then play back and compare the two versions and ask students to identify similarities and differences. If you can't record the students, ask two students to say the conversation in their language and then play the recorded version for comparison.

Drilling

At Advanced level there is probably less need to drill words, phrases or sentences unless students are having particular problems. However, check a few students around the class to get an indication of how good their pronunciation is. This will help you assess whether you need to work on their pronunciation.

- If you decide to model a phrase or sentence, make sure that you speak at normal speed using natural stress, contractions and weak forms. Repeat the target language two or three times (you can beat the main stress with your hand), before asking the students to say it. Then again check a few students to see if there has been an improvement.

- If you drill students, correct them when they make a mistake, since the aim of any drill is accuracy. However, avoid making the students feel uncomfortable and don't spend too long with one student.

- When you write words or sentences on the board, mark the stress in the correct place or ask the students to tell you which syllables or words are stressed.

- Praise students for good/comprehensible pronunciation and acknowledge weaker students' improvement, even if their pronunciation is not perfect.

Reviewing and Recycling

- Use the *Quick Reviews* at the beginning of the lessons. They are easy to set up and should take no more than five to eight minutes. They are a good way of getting the class to speak immediately as well as reviewing what students learned in previous lessons.

- Exploit the *Review* sections at the end of the units. They can be done in class when students have finished the unit, or set for homework. Alternatively, individual exercises can be used as quick fillers at the beginning or end of a lesson, as the *Review* exercises are organised in lesson order.

- After a mid-lesson break, ask students to write down in one minute all the words or phrases they can remember from the first part of the lesson. These quick *What have we just learned?* activities are very important for helping students transfer information from their short-term memory to their long-term memory.

- Start a class vocabulary box. You or the students write each new vocabulary item on a separate card and put the cards in the box. The cards can be used for revision in later classes.

- Encourage students to use the **face2face** CD-ROM to look again at each lesson at home. Also encourage students to review new language by reading the *Language Summary* for the lesson.

- Set homework after every class. The **face2face** Advanced Workbook has a section for each lesson in the Student's Book, which reviews all the key language taught in that lesson.

1 Let's talk

Student's Book p6–p15

Preview 1 Past Simple and Present Perfect

This Preview section revises some of the time expressions used with the Past Simple and Present Perfect in preparation for the Help with Grammar box later in the lesson.

> **Vocabulary** communicating
> **Grammar** time expressions with Past Simple and Present Perfect

 1 **a)** Focus students on prompts 1–7. Remind students that we use the Present Perfect and Present Perfect Continuous to talk about things that connect the past and the present, and that we use the Past Simple for a single completed action in the past, a repeated action or habit in the past, a state in the past, and with certain time expressions.

Students make questions from the prompts.

b) Put students into pairs. Students take turns to ask each other the questions. Encourage students to ask follow-up questions.

Students check their answers in Language Summary 1 **G1.1** SB (Student's Book) p118.

> 2 How old were you when you had your first English lesson?
> 3 Have you seen any films in English recently?
> 4 When was the last time you spoke English outside class?
> 5 Did you have to write anything in English last month?
> 6 Have you ever read a novel that was written in English?
> 7 How long have you been coming to this school?

Vocabulary Communicating

 2 **a)** Focus students on sentences a)–j). Students work on their own and check the meaning of unknown words in **V1.1** SB p117.

Note that in **face2face** Advanced only the meanings of **new** words and phrases are shown in the Language Summaries. These words and phrases are highlighted by an asterisk (*) and the meanings are given in a dictionary box 📖. Also point out that only the **main** stress (•) in phrases is shown in vocabulary boxes and Language Summaries.

Check that students understand the difference between *overhear* and *hear*, and *chat* and *chat up*.

Point out that *witter on* is usually used in a disapproving way: *I'll go mad if I have to listen to him witter on all day*.

Highlight that *gossip*, *grumble* and *chat* can also be used as nouns and all collocate with the verb *have* (*have a gossip/grumble/chat*).

Point out that *chat-up* can also be used adjectivally, as in *chat-up line*.

Finally, point out that several of the phrases are quite informal: *butt in*, *have a row*, *witter on*, *chat* and *chat (sb) up*. Pay particular attention to the pronunciation of *row* /raʊ/.

b) Students do the exercise on their own.

c) Put students into pairs. Students compare their ideas and see if they agree. Ask each pair to share one or two of their ideas with the class.

Listening and Grammar

 3 **a)** Introduce the topic by asking students what they understand by the word *popular* (liked by many people). Ask students to think of someone they know who is popular and to write five personal qualities that make him/her popular.

> ── EXTRA IDEA ──
> * Before doing **3a)**, brainstorm with the class personal qualities that might make someone popular. For example, *kindness, generosity, gregariousness, sense of humour*. ✎ Write them on the board.

b) Students do the exercise in pairs and tell each other about the person they have chosen, comparing the personal qualities that make him/her popular.

c) Ask students to agree on the three most important qualities. ✎ When students have finished, elicit their suggestions and write them on the board.

 4 **a)** Focus students on the book cover and introduction. Be prepared with definitions, examples, etc. to pre-teach *print run* and *runaway success*. Students do the exercise on their own.

Check the answer with the class.

> They initially thought that very few people were going to be interested in the book.

b) Focus students on the photo of Ann, Sy, Dean and Amy.

Check students understand what a *book club* is (a club where members all read the same books and meet periodically to discuss their thoughts and opinions on them).

Tell students they are going to listen to part of a book club meeting where the members are discussing Carnegie's book.

R1.1 Play the recording (SB p148). Students listen and answer the question.

They compare answers in pairs.

Check answers with the class.

> Smile at people.
> Make the other person feel important.
> If you want people to like you, you've got to learn to really pay attention to what they're saying.
> Encourage the other person to talk about themselves, by asking questions – showing you're interested in them.
> Remember people's names.
> If you don't feel like smiling, force yourself to.

--- EXTRA IDEA ---

* Before doing **4b)**, ask students to make a list of things that they think can help you 'win friends and influence people'. Students then listen to the recording and see how many of their ideas are mentioned.

c) Play the recording again. Students listen and answer the questions.

They check their answers in pairs.

Check answers with the class.

> 1 a) Her brother has been telling her to read it for ages.
>   b) Because the advice it contains is quite basic.
> 2 a) No. This is the first time he's read a book like this.
>   b) That, as a rule, we aren't good listeners.
> 3 a) No, he didn't.
>   b) Because John is very good at remembering people's names.
> 4 a) Smiling at everyone you come into contact with for a week.
>   b) Very positively – he's been really chatty ever since.

d) Students discuss the questions in pairs. Ask each pair to share their ideas with the class.

--- EXTRA IDEAS ---

* Write these words from the recording on the board: *self-help, attentive, whatsoever, loo, scowl, chatty, mindset*. Ask students to look at R1.1, SB p148 and guess the meaning of the words from the context. Ask what helped them guess.
* Ask students to look at R1.1, SB p148 and underline all of the instances of *I mean*. Point out that people often say *I mean* before they start or continue a sentence in informal speech. The expression has no real meaning; it is used as a filler.

Help with Grammar Time expressions with Past Simple and Present Perfect

* Help with Grammar boxes help students to examine examples of language and discover the rules of meaning, form and use. Students should usually do the exercises on their own or in pairs, then check their answers in the Language Summaries. You can then check the main points with the class as necessary. For more information on the **face2face** approach to Grammar, see p5. Remind students of Preview 1, SB p6 if necessary.

 5 **a)–d)** Students do the exercises on their own or in pairs and check their answers in **G1.2** SB p118.

Check answers with the class.

* **a)** All of the sentences are talking about time up to and including now. The **Present Perfect Simple** (sentences 1, 2, 4) and **Present Perfect Continuous** (sentence 3) are used.
* **b)** 2 I've read about 150 pages <u>so far</u>.
  3 <u>During the last couple of weeks</u> I've actually been trying out some of Carnegie's suggestions.
  4 <u>Up until now</u>, I've never really had any contact with the guy in the ticket office.
* Remind students that we use the Past Simple with definite time expressions in the past (*yesterday, a few weeks ago, last year*, etc.).
* Remind students that the following time expressions are used with both the Present Perfect Simple and the Present Perfect Continuous: *for, since, just, yet, already, still, ever, never, recently* and *lately*.
* **c)** 2 Speaker A uses the **Past Simple** because the event (reading the book) was completed at a definite time in the past (during the summer holidays). Speaker B uses the **Present Perfect** because the time period (during the last month) is still continuing.
  3 Speaker A uses the **Past Simple** after *since* because the event (Ann's suggestion) was completed at a definite time in the past. Speaker B uses the **Present Perfect** because the event (being unemployed) is continuing to happen.
  4 Speaker A uses the **Past Simple** because the event (reading the book/magazine, etc.) was completed at a definite time in the past. Speaker B uses the **Present Perfect** because the event (reading the book) started in the past but is continuing to happen.
* Remind students that after *as soon as* the **Present Perfect** refers to future events.
* Point out that we can replace *as soon as* with *once/when/after*: *I'll lend it to you once I've finished it*.
* Tell students that we can use *during* or *in + the last few days/weeks*, etc.
* Highlight that we can use *up until now* and *until/till/ up to + now*: *I've written four pages **up to now***.

- Also highlight that we use *it's (not) the first time* with the Present Perfect to talk about the first instance of something happening: ***It's the first time** I've read a book like this, really.*
- Point out that we can also say *This is (not) / That's (not) the first (second, etc.) time … :* ***This is the fourth time** I've written a review of a book.*

EXTRA IDEA

- Write these time expressions on the board: *this week/month/year, during, since, as soon as.* Ask students to write a pair of sentences for each time expression, using both the Past Simple and the Present Perfect.

---

6 **a)–b)** Students do the exercises on their own and compare answers in pairs.

Check answers with the class.

---

1 Both are possible. *I spoke to him this morning* = the speaker considers the period of time (this morning) as finished – that is, it's now the afternoon or evening; *I've spoken to him this morning* = the speaker considers the period of time (this morning) as continuing – that is, it's still morning.
2 Both are possible. *I've seen her during the last few months* = the speaker considers the period of time (the last few months) as continuing; *I saw her during the last few months* = the speaker considers the period of time (the last few months) as finished (e.g. the period of someone's life or someone's stay somewhere). This is less likely than the Present Perfect, but possible.
3 Only *I'll call you as soon as she's arrived* is possible. After *as soon as* the Present Perfect, not the Past Simple, is used to refer to future events.
4 Only *She came here a lot last month* is possible. We use the Past Simple with a definite time in the past (last month).
5 Only *During last night's performance, several people walked out* is possible. As the event (last night's performance) is definitely completed, the Present Perfect is not possible here.
6 Both are possible. *There have been a lot of changes since I worked for them* = the event (working for them) was completed at a definite time in the past – that is, the speaker doesn't work for them any more; *There have been a lot of changes since I've worked for them* = the event (working for them) is continuing to happen – that is, the speaker still works for them.
7 Only *Once I met her, I really liked her* is possible. As the event (meeting her) is definitely complete, the Present Perfect is not possible here.
8 Only *I've been skiing twice since I saw you last* is possible. As the event (seeing you last) is definitely complete, the Present Perfect is not possible here.

Reading

7 **a)** Introduce the topic by asking students what they understand by *good/bad service* (being treated well/badly in customer service situations, such as shops or restaurants). Students do the exercise in pairs.

When students have finished, elicit their suggestions and write them on the board.

b) Focus students on the article. Be prepared with definitions, examples, etc. to pre-teach *fake, pushy, perfectly disgusting* and *turn-off*. Students do the exercise on their own or in pairs.
Check answers with the class.

Because she doesn't think that their niceness is sincere; she thinks that it's fake.

EXTRA IDEA

- Before students read the article, ask them to read the title and predict what they think it will be about. After students have read the article, they compare their predictions with the actual article.

---

c) Students do the exercise on their own or in pairs. Check answers with the class.

2T
3F She thought that it was 'perfectly disgusting' – that is, 'absolutely disgusting'.
4F She thought that it would make her friend feel uncomfortable if she told the waitress what she thought about the food.
5F She mentions other studies which have the same view as hers – that is, that customers find being treated as a friend by shop assistants a turn-off.
6T

EXTRA IDEA

- Write these words and phrases from the article on the board: *blissfully, every bit as (rude), perky, gritted teeth.* Ask students to guess the meaning of the words and phrases from the context. Ask what helped them guess.

---

8 **a)** Focus students on the words and phrases in bold in the article. Ask students what words are missing from each phrase. Check answers with the class and write them on the board.

In informal written and spoken English, unstressed words can be missed out at the start of a sentence, as long as the meaning is still clear; this is called *ellipsis.* Some of the most common words which can be left out are personal pronouns and auxiliary verbs, as shown in most of the examples from the article (*Having a good day? Been shopping all morning?*). Unstressed forms of *be* are sometimes left out, too (*Fine.*).

Are you having a good day?
Have you been shopping all morning?
So, **have you** got anything planned for this afternoon?
Is everything all right with your meal?
It's fine.
Do you need any help?
I'm just looking, thanks.

b) Check answers with the class.

9 Put students into groups. Students take turns to ask each other the questions. Encourage students to ask follow-up questions if possible.

Get ready ... Get it right!

- There is a Get ready ... Get it right! activity at the end of every A and B lesson. The Get ready ... stage helps students to collect their ideas and prepare the language they need to complete the task. The Get it right! stage gives students the opportunity to use the language they have learned in the lesson in a communicative (and often personalised) context. These two-stage activities help students to become more fluent without losing the accuracy they have

built up during the controlled practice stages of the lesson. For more information on the **face2face** approach to Speaking, see p5.

10 **a)** Focus students on the list of topics. Ask students to write three topics they would like to talk about.

b) Put students into pairs. Ask students to swap papers and then write six questions to ask their partner on one of the three topics.

11 Students do the activity in pairs. Encourage students to ask follow-up questions if possible. Finally, ask each student to tell the class one interesting thing they have found out about their partner.

┌─ EXTRA PRACTICE AND HOMEWORK ─
│ **Ph** **Class Activity** 1A Getting to know you p133
│ (Instructions p118)
│ **1 Review** Exercises 1, 2 and 3 SB p14
│ **CD-ROM** Lesson 1A
│ **Workbook** Lesson 1A p4
└─

1B Friends – the new family?

QUICK REVIEW ●●●
Quick Reviews begin lessons in a fun, student-centred way. They are short activities which review previously taught language and are designed to last about five or ten minutes. For more information on the **face2face** approach to Reviewing and Recycling, see p5.
This activity reviews time expressions used with the Past Simple and Present Perfect. Students do the first part of the activity on their own. Remind students that they should write a mix of true and false sentences. Put students into pairs. Students take turns to tell each other their sentences. They guess if their partner's sentences are true.

Listening and Grammar

1 Introduce the topic by asking students who would be the first person they talked to if they had a worry or problem.

Focus students on sentences 1–4. Students check the meaning of the phrases in bold. Be prepared with definitions to give students if necessary.

Students discuss the questions in pairs.
Point out that the underlined expressions are useful for making generalisations. Encourage students to use the expressions in other activities throughout the book.

> **Vocabulary** prepositions and phrases
> **Grammar** cleft sentences: *what* and *it* clauses
> **Review** time expressions with Past Simple and Present Perfect

2 **a)** Put students into pairs. Focus students on the photos and ask them how old they think the people in them are. (Dave and Helen are fortyish, Andrea is in her early twenties and Alex is a teenager.) Ask them who they would expect these people to confide in. ✍ Elicit ideas from the class and write them on the board.

b) Pre-teach *meaningful, put up with, degenerate into* /dɪˌdʒenəreɪt ˈɪntʊ/ and *break up with (someone)*.

R1.2 Play the recording (SB p148). Students listen and check their answers to **2a)**.

> **Dave** friends, especially older friends
> **Helen** both friends and family
> **Andrea** someone else (her hairdresser)
> **Alex** friends

Point out that when Dave refers to *older friends*, he means friends he has known for a long time.

c) Play the recording again. Students listen, tick the true sentences and correct the false ones.

Check answers with the class.

> 1F They usually start by talking about current affairs, but then talk about something much less serious, for example lists of favourite cars or films. 2T 3F They tend to meet about once a week. 4T 5T 6F She's unhappy that he's started confiding in her. 7T 8T

d) Students discuss the questions in pairs. Elicit ideas from the class.

> **EXTRA IDEA**
> - Write these words and phrases from the recording on the board: *snatch (about half an hour), go through, get in a flap*. Ask students to look at R1.2, SB p148 and guess the meaning of the words from the context. Ask what helped them guess.

Help with Grammar Cleft sentences: *what* and *it* clauses

Go through the introductory bullet with the class and check students understand what a cleft sentence is.

 3 **a)–c)** Students do the exercises on their own or in pairs and check their answers in **G1.3** SB p119.

- **a)** 1 (We'll have a drink and talk afterwards.) **What** we talk about **isn't** deep and meaningful, though. 2 *be/isn't*
- Highlight that in cleft sentences with *what*, the information that we already know comes after the word *what*, and the new information follows the verb *be*. If students are finding this concept difficult, underline the word *talk* in the example sentences. This will help highlight that we already know that they talk (it's explained in the first sentence); what we don't know is what they talk about.
- Point out that cleft sentences can focus on an action, using *what* + subject + *do* + *be* (+subject) + infinitive clause: *What I do if I get stressed is talk to my friends*.
- Point out that in order to focus on a whole sentence, we use *what* + *happens* + *be* + subject + infinitive clause: *What happens is we bottle things up*.
- Go through the **TIPS!** in the *WHAT* CLAUSES section in **G1.3** SB p119 with the class and check students understand them.
- **b)** 1 The speaker emphasises the information in the *it* clause.
  2 The verb that follows *it* is *be*.
- Go through the **TIPS!** in the *IT* CLAUSES section in **G1.3** SB p119 with the class and check students understand them.

 4 **a)** Students do the exercise on their own or in pairs.

> 2 It was after leaving my last job that I began to work freelance. 3 What you should do is write a letter and refuse to pay. 4 It's Tim who's/that's the problem, not Jo. 5 The person (who/that) I wanted to speak to was Ben. 6 What happened was I forgot the map.

b) **R1.3** Play the recording (SB p148). Students listen and check their answers.

Check answers with the class.

c) Play the recording again. Students listen and practise the sentences.

 5 **a)** Do the first question as an example, using information about yourself. Students do the exercise on their own.

b) Put students into groups. Students take turns to say their sentences. Encourage students to ask follow-up questions if possible. Ask groups to share one or two of their sentences with the class.

> **EXTRA IDEA**
> - If the class know each other well, ask each student to write one sentence on a piece of paper and give it you. Read the sentences out loud and see if the rest of the class can guess who wrote the sentence.

Reading and Vocabulary

6 **a)** Introduce the topic by asking students who their close friends are and where they met (at school, at work, etc.).

Put students into pairs and ask them to make a list of different types of friends they could meet at different stages of their life.

Ask students to share some of their ideas with the class.

b) Students discuss the questions in pairs.

Elicit ideas from the class and write them on the board.

c) Tell students they are going to read an article called 'Friendship overload'. Be prepared with definitions, examples, etc. to pre-teach *mate, confidant, second division* and *keep track of*. Pay particular attention to the pronunciation of *confidant* /kɒnfɪdænt/.

Students read the article and compare their ideas from **6b)**.

> 'Friendship overload' means having too many friends. The writer thinks that friendship overload might be a problem because it's impossible to keep in contact with everyone; some 'friendships' won't last long; other friends you barely ever meet; some you like a lot more than others; some are not really friends, just people you meet out of habit; you can feel out of your depth, or over-committed; your closest friends might be the people you see the least.

d) Students do the exercise on their own before checking in pairs. Check answers with the class.

1 Because we often live too far away from our families.
2 We see them regularly, help each other, are on the same wavelength, have kids at the same school and have a lot in common. 3 Friends we are not so close to, who are not our 'best' friends. 4 Because we travel more, and move jobs and houses more frequently.
5 They are split between people you see a lot in phases and those that you see regularly; those that you see regularly might include people that you like less than other friends, but who live very close.
6 Because a real friend recognises how stressful it is having so many friends and won't put pressure on you to see them.

e) Students do the exercise in pairs. Encourage students to give reasons.

Ask pairs to share some of their ideas with the class.

┌─ EXTRA IDEA ─────────────────────────────

• Turn this topic into a class debate. Create two teams and leave some of the class as the audience. The teams will debate the motion 'People these days have too many friends'.

• The rest of the class will be asked to vote at the end of the debate.

• Give the teams ten minutes to prepare their arguments. While they are doing that, the audience discusses the motion among themselves.

• The teams take turns to put forward their arguments. Set a time limit for each speaker. At the end, ask the audience to vote on the motion. The team with the most votes is the winner.

└───────────────────────────────────────

Help with Vocabulary Prepositions and phrases

• Help with Vocabulary boxes help students to explore and understand how vocabulary works, often by focusing on aspects of lexical grammar. Students should usually do the exercises on their own or in pairs, and then check their answers in the Language Summaries. Check the main points with the class as necessary. For more information on the **face2face** approach to Vocabulary, see p5.

Go through the introductory bullet with the class. Remind students what chunks are (groups of two or more words).

7 **a)** Students do the exercise on their own or in pairs and check their answers in **V1.2** SB p117.

Encourage students to try and guess the meaning of the phrases from the context of the article before looking at the definitions.

Check answers with the class.

1 on purpose 2 out of habit 3 in the long run
4 on the same wavelength 5 in phases
6 out of your depth

b) Students do the exercise on their own or in pairs and check their answers in **V1.2** SB p117.

Check answers with the class.

on	in	out of
good terms	control	control
a regular basis	fashion	fashion
average	touch	necessity
	common	touch
	contact	

c)–d) Students do the exercise in pairs and check their answers in **V1.2** SB p117.

Check answers with the class.

out of fashion being unpopular at a particular time, especially clothes, hair, etc.
on a regular basis happening or doing something often
in common sharing interests, experience or other characteristics with someone or something
on good terms have a good relationship with one another
on average typically
in touch in communication (with)
out of control not under the authority or power of someone
out of necessity because of a need
in contact communicating with someone

• Highlight that the following pairs of phrases are antonyms: *in control/out of control, in fashion/out of fashion, in touch/out of touch, on good/bad terms*. Also point out that *in touch/in contact* are synonyms.

• Check that students understand the difference in meaning between *on a regular basis* and *in phases*. (*I go to the gym on a regular basis* = I go to the gym regularly, e.g. once a week; *I go to the gym in phases* = I go to the gym regularly for periods of time and then don't go again for a while.)

┌─ EXTRA IDEA ─────────────────────────────

• Draw three circles, containing *in*, *on* and *out of*, on the board. Draw two lines radiating from each circle, and then write the phrases next to the lines; for example, *the long run* next to the *in* circle. Encourage students to record phrases with prepositions like this in their vocabulary notebooks.

└───────────────────────────────────────

8 **a)** Students do the exercise on their own before checking in pairs.

Check answers with the class.

1 in 2 in 3 out of 4 in 5 on 6 out of
7 out of 8 on

b) Students do the activity in pairs. They take turns to ask each other the questions. Encourage students to ask follow-up questions if possible.

Get ready ... Get it right!

9 Focus students on the list of sentences. Students do the exercise on their own.

10 a) Put students into groups. Ask students to discuss what they have written and to give reasons. Encourage students to ask follow-up questions if possible.

b) Finally, ask each group to tell the class three things that they agreed on.

EXTRA PRACTICE AND HOMEWORK

Ph Class Activity 1B Student survey p134 (Instructions p118)

Ph Vocabulary Plus 1 Vague language p172 (Instructions p169)

1 Review Exercises 4 and 5 SB p14

CD-ROM Lesson 1B

Workbook Lesson 1B p6

 Favourite sayings

Vocabulary sayings; idioms
Real World explaining and paraphrasing
Review prepositions and phrases

QUICK REVIEW ●●●

This activity reviews phrases which use the prepositions *in, on* and *out of*. Students do the first part of the activity on their own. Tell students that they should write at least five sentences, but that they can write more if they have time. Set a time limit of five minutes. Put students into pairs. Students take turns to tell each other their sentences without saying the preposition(s). Their partner has to say the sentence using the correct preposition(s).

 a)–b) Introduce the topic by asking students what they think a *saying* is (a well-known statement, which often has a metaphorical meaning). Ask students if they know any sayings in English and if they can explain what they mean.

Students do the exercise on their own before comparing their answers in pairs. Ask students what they think the sayings mean. Students check their answers in **V1.3** SB p117. Check answers with the class.

Point out that one good way of remembering sayings like this is to visualise them; for example, students could visualise the city of Rome being built.

2f) 3h) 4d) 5e) 6a) 7c) 8g)

c) Put students into pairs or groups. If you have a multilingual class, group students of the same nationality together. Ask students to think of a saying from their country and write down how they would explain it to a British person.

Ask each pair/group to explain their saying to you.

 a) Focus students on pictures A–E. Tell students they are going to listen to five people talking about sayings they like, which are illustrated by the five pictures.

Check that students understand *crow, peanuts* and *bark*. Pay particular attention to the pronunciation of *crow* /krəʊ/.

R1.4 Play the recording (SB p148). Students listen and put the pictures in order. They compare answers in pairs. Check answers with the class.

Point out that Claire says *even if you were wrong* when she meant to say *even if you weren't wrong*. Tell students that this is an authentic example of stumbling – saying the wrong thing without realising it. The correct word (*weren't*) is shown in brackets in R1.4, SB p148.

1B 2C 3A 4D 5E

b) Students do the exercise in pairs.

c) Play the recording again. Students listen and check their answers. Check answers with the class.

1B 2E 3D 4A 5C

d) Students discuss the sayings in pairs. Ask pairs to share their ideas with the class.

Real World Explaining and paraphrasing

- Real World boxes are designed to help students with functional language that they can use in real-life social situations, often by teaching fixed and semi-fixed phrases. Students should usually do the exercises on their own or in pairs, and then check their answers in the Language Summaries. Check the main points with the class as necessary. For more information on Real World boxes, see p5.

Introduce the topic by asking students what they understand by *paraphrasing* (repeating something using different words, often in a simpler way). Ask students when they might have to paraphrase something (if the listener hasn't understood what you've said, if you are explaining something new or complicated, etc.).

Go through the introductory bullet with the class and check students understand it.

3 **a)–d)** Students do the exercises on their own or in pairs and check their answers in **RW1.1** SB p119.

Check answers with the class.

- **a)** 1 Which 2 what 3 What 4 which 5 What 6 Which
- Ask students which word (*what* or *which*) can be replaced by *that* in the answers. (*which*)
- Point out that *it* and *this* can also precede *basically means*.
- **b)** 1 simply 2 That 3 way 4 other
- **c)** The speakers explain and paraphrase their ideas in the following ways:
  It basically means that you can't always plan ahead and you can't control everything.
  Well, **to put it simply**, you can't really worry about things that are way in the future.
  My favourite expression is "You pay peanuts, you get monkeys", **which kind of basically means that** the less money you pay, the worse the service.
  And, **what it means is that** if you hang about with the wrong crowd, …
  And **this basically means** there's no need to bother doing something difficult if someone around you can do it better than you.
- Go through the **TIP!** in **RW1.1** SB p119 with the class or ask them to read it for homework.

 4 **a)** Students do the exercise on their own or in pairs.

b) Students do the exercise in pairs. Check answers with the class.

2 by 3 which 4 which 5 words 6 simply
1d) 2a) 3b) 4e) 5f) 6c)

 5 **a)** Introduce the topic by asking students what *bluff* means (pretend). Tell students that they are going to listen to two teams playing a game called *Bluff*. Ask students to guess what they think the game will involve.

Give students time to read the questions.

R1.5 Play the recording (SB p149). Students listen and answer the questions. Check answers with the class.

1 The game is about sayings, or expressions.
2 Each person has to give a definition of an expression; however, only one of the three definitions is true.
3 The second team has to guess which of the three definitions is true.

b) Students discuss the question in pairs. Check answers with the class.

c) **R1.6** Play the recording (SB p149). Students listen and check their answers.

Check answers with the class.

It means don't worry, everything will be alright.

 6 Put students into two groups, A and B. Focus students on the idioms for their groups. Ask students to try and guess the meaning of the three idioms. Don't elicit answers.

— EXTRA IDEA —
- If any of the idioms are already known to students, suggest alternatives; for example, *it's a no-brainer* (= it's a decision or dilemma to which the answer is really obvious) or *it's gone pear-shaped* (= it's gone wrong).

 7 Group A turn to SB p108. Group B turn to SB p111.

a) Check that students understand the meaning of the idioms. With group A, pay particular attention to the pronunciation of *rave* /reɪv/.

b) Put students in group A into groups of three, and do the same with group B. Check that students understand that they have to write two false definitions and three example sentences (one correct and two false) for each idiom, so nine sentences in total.

c) Ask students to decide who is going to give each of the definitions. Ask them to practise giving their definitions, remembering that they are each trying to convince the other group that their definition is correct.

d) Put groups of three from each main group together. Ask students to follow the instructions 1–3.

e) Ask each group to tell the class how many correct definitions they got. The group who guessed the most correct definitions is the winner.

— EXTRA IDEA —
- Ask students to rate each other: did they come across as persuasive and convincing? If so, what were they good at? If not, how could they improve?

— EXTRA PRACTICE AND HOMEWORK —
Ph **Class Activity** 1C In other words … p135 (Instructions p119)
Help with Listening 1 Monologues p189 (Instructions p182)
1 Review Exercise 6 SB p14
CD-ROM Lesson 1C
Workbook Lesson 1C p8
Workbook Reading and Writing Portfolio 1 p54
Progress Test 1 p204
Preview 2 Exercises 1 and 2 SB p15

1 Review

- The Review section reviews the key language taught in the unit. It includes communicative and personalised speaking stages as well as controlled grammar and vocabulary practice.
- This section is designed to be used in class after students have finished lesson C, but individual exercises can be used as 'fillers' if you have a few minutes left at the end of a lesson. The Extra Practice and Homework boxes list which exercises are relevant to each lesson.
- The icons refer to the relevant sections in the Language Summary. Students can refer to these if they need help when doing the exercises.
- For more information on the **face2face** approach to Reviewing and Recycling, see p5.

> **1a)** 2 butt in 3 chat 4 bicker 5 come into contact with 6 overheard
> **2** 1b) 2a) 3b) 4a) 5a) 6b) 7a) 8b)
> **3** 2 moved 3 have seen 4 have already come 5 bumped into 6 worked/has been working/has worked 7 has always preferred/always preferred 8 was recently offered/has recently been offered 9 has tried 10 has moved
> **4** 2 What they did was sell the house. 3 It was us who were responsible. 4 The reason she's tired is because she didn't go to bed until 2 a.m. 5 It wasn't until I reached 40 that I started exercising. 6 It's fried food that I can't stand. 7 What really annoys me is when people talk during a film. 8 It was Julie who was brought up in Scotland.
> **5** 1 in 2 on 3 out of 4 out of 5 in 6 in
> **6** 1 day 2 shy 3 speak 4 meat 5 gained 6 late

Progress Portfolio

- Progress Portfolio boxes encourage students to reflect on what they have learned and help them decide which areas they need to study again. Note that the *I can …* statements reflect communicative competences as set out in the *Common European Framework of Reference for Languages* (CEF) for level C1. For more information on the CEF, see p15.

a) Students work through the list of *I can …* statements on their own and tick the things they feel they can do. They can refer to Language Summary 1 if they wish.
Students can also work in pairs or groups and compare which statements they have ticked.

b) Students work on their own or in pairs/groups and decide which areas they need to study again. Encourage students to use the CD-ROM lessons 1A–C to help them improve in these areas. For more information on the CD-ROM, see p11.

There is also further practice of all the key language taught in the Student's Book in the **face2face** Advanced Workbook.

Accurate Writing

CONNECTING WORDS: addition
SPELLING: homophones

- The Accurate Writing section helps students to fine-tune their writing, by focusing on discourse markers and common mistakes of spelling and punctuation.
- This section follows a 'test-teach-test' approach, which differs from the other grammar and vocabulary boxes in the course, which follow a guided discovery principle. Students do an initial exercise (the test) before reading a summary of the rules of that area (connecting words or spelling/punctuation) in the Language Summary (the teaching). They then do a final exercise, where they find and correct mistakes in a piece of student's work (the test).

1 Introduce the topic by asking students what the words in the box have in common (they are all connecting words used to add information).

Students do the exercise on their own or in pairs and check their answers in **AW1.1** SB p119.
Check answers with the class.
Point out that we do not usually use *also, too* or *as well* in negative clauses. Instead we use phrases such as *either*: *I haven't read the Harry Potter books either.*

> 1 as well/too 2 as well/too 3 Besides/What's more/Also
> 4 also 5 not only 6 Besides/What's more/Also

> — EXTRA IDEA —
> - Once students have read **AW1.1** SB 119, ask them to close their books. ✍ Write these headings on the board: *Used at the end of a clause, Used at the beginning of a clause* or *Used in the middle of a clause*. Students copy the headings onto a piece of paper and list the connecting words from **1** in the correct columns.

Focus students on the words in italics in sentences 1–5. Ask students if they notice anything about the pairs of words. Explain that the words are *homophones* – words which sound the same but have different spellings and different meanings.

Drill the homophones in sentences 1–5 chorally and individually.

Students do the exercise on their own or in pairs and check their answers in AW1.2 SB p119.

Check answers with the class.

> 1 who's 2 they're 3 've 4 your 5 their

— EXTRA IDEA —

- Divide the class into teams. Give each team five minutes to list as many homophones as they can. The team which lists the most is the winner. A fairly exhaustive list of English homophones can be found here: http://www.bifroest.demon.co.uk/misc/homophones-list.html

 a) Focus students on the extract. Explain that in addition to the two underlined mistakes, there are five common spelling mistakes involving homophones.

Students do the exercise on their own and check their answers in pairs.

Check answers with the class.

> 1 Besides/What's more/Also 2 as well/too

b) Students do the exercise on their own and check their answers in pairs.

Check answers with the class.

> ~~there~~ they're the kind of people …
> about ~~you're~~ your problems.
> ~~They're~~ Their names are …
> might ~~of~~ have/'ve lost contact …
> It's Jess ~~whose~~ who's my oldest friend …

┌─ EXTRA PRACTICE AND HOMEWORK ─
│ **Workbook** Accurate Writing Exercises 1 and 2 p84

Preview 2

RELATIVE CLAUSES
GRADABLE AND NON-GRADABLE ADJECTIVES; ADVERBS
VERB+*ING* AND PAST PARTICIPLES

The Preview section helps students prepare for some of the grammar and vocabulary which appear in the unit. It revises language from earlier levels of **face2face** with controlled grammar and vocabulary practice.

The Extra Practice and Homework boxes at the end of each lesson list which exercises in the Preview section relate to the following lesson. For example, the box in lesson 1C (p31) refers to **1** and **2** in Preview 2 as these exercises revise areas of grammar and vocabulary which are then covered in more depth in lesson 2A. The reference in the Extra Practice and Homework box in lesson 2A (p36) is to **3** in Preview 2 as this topic is covered in lesson 2B.

The icons refer to the relevant sections in the Language Summary for the unit. Students can refer to these if they need help when doing the exercises.

RELATIVE CLAUSES

 Students do the exercise on their own or in pairs and check their answers in G2.1 SB p121.

Check answers with the class.

> **a)** 1 what → that/who 2 who → that/which
> 3 at where → where/at which 4 her → whose
> 5 ~~his~~ 6 Jones, 7 that → which
> **b)** 1, 2

GRADABLE AND NON-GRADABLE ADJECTIVES; ADVERBS

 Students do the exercise on their own or in pairs and check their answers in V2.1 SB p120.

Check answers with the class.

> 1 interesting 2 terrified 3 surprised
> 4 difficult/impossible 5 tired

VERB+*ING* AND PAST PARTICIPLES

 Students do the exercise on their own or in pairs and check their answers in G2.3 SB p122.

Check answers with the class.

> 2 leaving 3 trying 4 spoiling 5 opening 6 built
> 7 written 8 bored

2 Remarkable!

Student's Book p16–p25

2A Exceptional people

QUICK REVIEW ●●●

This activity reviews common English sayings. Students do the activity in pairs. They take turns to say the first part of one of the sayings in lesson 1C and ask their partner to complete it and say what it means. Ask students to do four sayings each.

Vocabulary intensifying adverbs
Grammar relative clauses with prepositions
Review sayings

Reading and Grammar

1 a) Introduce the topic by asking students who they think 'the cleverest man on earth' is (or might have been).

Focus students on the title and introduction of the article and on the picture of Kim Peek. Students discuss what questions they want to ask in pairs. Elicit ideas from the class.

b) Students do the exercise on their own.

c) Students do the exercise on their own or in pairs. Check answers with the class.

> 1F Kim hasn't appeared in a well-known film but the film *Rain Man* was based on his life.
> 2T
> 3T
> 4F Doctors advised putting him in an institution, but his parents took him home instead.
> 5F Although Kim is charming and affectionate, he hasn't always been socially confident.
> 6T

d) Students do the exercise on their own or in pairs.

Check answers with the class. Point out that *gait* /geɪt/ is a formal word for describing a way of walking and is not very common in day-to-day English; for example, instead of saying *He has an abnormal gait*, we would probably say *He walks funnily*. However, *gait* is commonly used by medical professionals.

Also point out that in the context of walking, *shuffle* /ˈʃʌfəl/ means 'walk by pulling your feet slowly along the ground instead of lifting them'.

> 1 transformed 2 intimidating 3 simultaneously
> 4 keeps an eye on 5 shuffling gait 6 flits

e) Students discuss the questions in pairs. Elicit ideas from the class.

EXTRA IDEAS

- Younger students may not have heard of *Rain Man* or may not recognise the name of the film if it was translated into their own language when the film was released. Download and print a copy of the film poster from the Internet and ask any students who have seen the film to try and recount the plot.

- Write these words and phrases from the article on the board: *bellow of laughter, bespectacled, lightning speed, sought out, bear hug, marked*. Ask students to guess the meaning of the words and phrases from the context. Ask what helped them guess.

Help with Grammar Relative clauses with prepositions

Ask students to do **1** in Preview 2, SB p15 if necessary.

2 a)–e) Students do the exercises on their own or in pairs and check their answers in **G2.2** SB p121.

Check answers with the class.

- **a)** More formal, usually written English: *He is looked after by his father Fran, on whom he totally depends. It's Kim's life on which an Oscar-winning film was based.*
  Less formal, usually spoken English: *He is looked after by his father Fran, who he totally depends on. It's Kim's life that an Oscar-winning film was based on.*
- Point out that one sentence in each pair comes from the article they have just been reading. Also point out that the meaning of the two sentences in each pair is the same; it is the register that is different.
- **b)** In more formal, usually written English, *who* changes to **whom** after a preposition and *that* changes to **which**.
- Point out that in order to transform informal sentences of this type into more formal sentences, we: change *that* or *who* to *whom* if it refers to a person; change *that* to *which* if it refers to a thing; move the preposition from the end of the sentence to before the relative pronoun.
- Highlight that *whom* is rarely used in spoken English, where it would sound very old-fashioned.
- Remind students that *whom* should always be the object of the sentence, not the subject.

- **c)** the previous clause
- Point out that *both of them, all of them* and *none of them* sound much more natural in spoken English than *both of which, all of which,* etc.: *This is one of many theories – none of them have been proved yet.*
- **d)** 1 Kim also has a brother and a sister, **both of whom** are exceptionally clever.
  2 He had sought out encyclopaedias, atlases and telephone directories, **all of which** he memorised.
- Remind students that, as they still introduce non-defining relative clauses, phrases such as *both of whom, all of which,* etc. need to be preceded by a comma.
- Point out that in non-defining relative clauses, prepositional phrases such as *at which point* and *in which case* can be used to comment on the whole situation in the previous clause: *When Kim was a child, doctors advised putting him in an institution, **at which point** his parents took him home instead and introduced him to books.*
- Highlight that other determiners can also be combined with *of which/whom*, for example, *each, part, some, very little/few, a number*. Superlatives can also be combined with *of which/whom*: *There were many great films in 2008, **the best of which** I think were European.*
- Point out that certain nouns (e.g. *the level/degree/ stage*) can be combined with *at/to which*. In addition, *the effect* and *the anniversary* can be combined with *of which*: *… we must celebrate the discovery of DNA, **the anniversary of which** …*
- Also point out that in formal writing, we can use *whose* after a preposition in relative clauses: *I was inspired by the poet Dante, **from whose** work this quotation has been taken.*
- Finally, point out that in relative clauses, we can use *where* instead of *in/at which* to talk about location: *This is the house **where/in which** she was born.*

3 Focus students on the example answer. Remind students that each sentence should only have one preposition: *This is the name by which he was known ~~by~~.*
Students do the exercise on their own or in pairs.
Check answers with the class.

> 2 She should consult the students for whom she is responsible. 3 He embarked on a long journey, from which he never returned. 4 Mahler is the composer with whom he is always associated. 5 I'm impressed by the speed at which he runs. 6 The artist eventually finished the picture on which he'd been working.

4 Focus students on the example answer. Students do the exercise on their own or in pairs.
Check answers with the class.

> 2 She has two children, neither of whom look like her. 3 Tim interviewed several people, all of whom were unsuitable. 4 She gave me four tops, only one of which I wore. 5 There were only two flights that day, both of which were full. 6 I studied German at school, none of which I remember.

Listening

5 a) Introduce the topic by asking students to name their favourite artist and say why they like his/her work.
Focus students on the photo of Tommy McHugh. Ask students to discuss what they like or dislike about his work. Check answers with the class.

b) Tell students they are going to listen to a radio programme about Tommy McHugh. Be prepared with definitions, examples, etc. to pre-teach *sculpt* /skʌlpt/, *carve* /kɑːv/ and *brain haemorrhage* /ˈbreɪn ˌhemərɪdʒ/.
Point out that *carve* is also used in the context of cutting meat, especially larger cuts (e.g., a leg of lamb, a whole chicken or turkey).

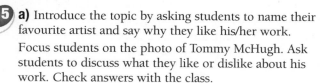 **R2.1** Play the recording (SB p149). Students listen and answer the question. They compare answers in pairs. Check the answer with the class.

Point out that in this context *cooking the tea* refers to cooking the evening meal, not to making a cup of tea. In the UK, the evening meal is sometimes referred to as *tea*, especially among working-class people. In the North of England, *tea* is often preceded by a possessive adjective: *What are you having for your tea?*

> As a way of letting out his frustration and anger after suffering a brain haemorrhage.

c) Play the recording again. Students listen and answer the questions.
Check answers with the class.

> 1 fifties 2 volcano 3 aftercare 4 artist 5 creativity 6 write 7 quality 8 adventure

--- **EXTRA IDEAS** ---

- Write these words and phrases from the recording on the board: *a bit of a rough past, took it out on me, an outlet, unnerved, hit home, nothing to write home about*. Ask students to look at R2.1, SB p149 and guess the meaning of the words and phrases from the context. Ask what helped them guess.
- Ask students to discuss whether they think artistic talent is something that people are born with or whether it can be 'learned'. Ask how they think people like Tommy McHugh fit into their argument.

35

Vocabulary Intensifying adverbs

Ask students to do **2** in Preview 2, SB p15 if necessary.

 a) Students do the exercise on their own or in pairs and check their answers in V2.2 SB p120.

Check answers with the class.

Point out that there are no rules about which adverbs intensify which verbs or adjectives; students will have to learn the adverb–verb/adjective combinations individually.

Point out that we can also say *I absolutely believe, I was incredibly disappointed, I totally agree.*

Point out that *quite* can be used in front of non-gradable adjectives or adverbs to mean 'truly' or 'completely': *He's* **quite remarkable**.

Point out that when *quite* is used in front of gradable adjectives or adverbs it means 'fairly': *It's* **quite expensive**.

Highlight that the stress and intonation are different with the different meanings of *quite*. Drill the sentences which contain *quite*, chorally and individually, highlighting how the stress and intonation change.

Highlight that we use *a bit/a little/slightly* in front of comparative adjectives or adverbs, not *quite*: *The city is a* **bit more peaceful** *than I expected it to be.* not ~~The city is quite more peaceful …~~

> **2** strongly **3** vividly **4** highly **5** perfectly **6** utterly
> **7** highly **8** perfectly

b) Model the activity by writing five true and false sentences about yourself on the board. Ask students to guess which are true. Students do the activity on their own.

c) Put students into pairs. Students take turns to tell each other their sentences and to guess which of their partner's sentences are false.

 Students work on their own.

Give students one minute to write down the name of a person who they think should win an award for being exceptional; it could be a famous person or a friend/family member.

Focus students on the example sentences and ask students to write down five reasons that he/she should win the award, using adverbs, relative clauses and prepositions where possible.

 a) Put students into groups.

Students take turns to tell each other about the person they have chosen for the award. Tell students to vote for the person they think is the most deserving. The majority vote wins.

b) Ask each group to tell the class about who they voted for.

> ── EXTRA IDEA ──
> * Ask students to write a profile of the person they have chosen, as if for a newspaper, for homework.

> ── EXTRA PRACTICE AND HOMEWORK ──
> **Ph** **Class Activity** 2A The great brain game p136 (Instructions p119)
> **2 Review** Exercises 1 and 2 SB p24
> **CD-ROM** Lesson 2A
> **Workbook** Lesson 2A p9
> **Preview 2** Exercise 3 SB p15

 2B # Memorable places

QUICK REVIEW ●●●

This activity reviews relative clauses with prepositions and intensifying adverbs. Focus students on the example. Students do the first part of the activity on their own. Set a time limit of one minute. Put students into pairs. Students take turns to describe their people and places, using relative clauses with prepositions and intensifying adverbs if possible. Their partner has to guess the person or place that they are describing.

Reading and Grammar

 Introduce the topic by asking students where they last went on holiday and why they chose that place or type of holiday.

> **Vocabulary** adjective word order
> **Grammar** participle clauses
> **Review** relative clauses with prepositions; intensifying adverbs

Focus students on the list of criteria for choosing a holiday. Students do the exercise in pairs.

a) Focus students on the article. Ask students what they understand by the title of the article. (*Lose your heart somewhere* means 'fall in love with' somewhere.)

Be prepared with definitions, examples, etc. to pre-teach *lush, canal, lagoon, monsoon, backwaters, canoe* /kə'nuː/ and *hammock*.

Point out that *backwater* can be used in a literal sense – to describe the part of a river where the water doesn't flow –

but also in a metaphorical sense to negatively describe a place which is not influenced by new ideas or events happening in other places: *I grew up in a rural backwater*.

Students read the article on their own and then discuss in pairs why the writer fell in love with Kerala.

> It's beautiful and hypnotic; it has lush vegetation, white beaches and vividly green countryside; it's unspoilt; it's less touristy than Goa.

b) Students do the exercise on their own or in pairs. Check answers with the class.

> **1** Because she wanted to avoid the monsoons. **2** That it was so unspoilt. **3** It will get much more popular, due to having been nominated one of *National Geographic*'s '50 must-see destinations of a lifetime'. **4** By canoe along the backwaters. **5** People catch fish using their teeth. **6** Because of Ayurveda – the natural Indian healthcare which is practised there.

— **EXTRA IDEA** —

- Write these words and phrases on the board: *only a matter of time before/until, stopover, cluster, tuck into, indulgent*. Ask students to guess the meaning of the words and phrases from the context. Ask what helped them guess.

c) Students discuss the questions in pairs. Ask each pair to share their ideas with the class.

Help with Grammar Participle clauses

Ask students to do **3** in Preview 2, SB p15 if necessary.

Go through the introductory bullet with the class and make sure that students understand what a participle clause is, using the examples in bold in the article.

Explain that we often use participle clauses in writing, but that they are much less common in spoken language.

3 **a)–d)** Students do the exercises on their own or in pairs and check their answers in G2.4 SB p122.
Check answers with the class.

- **a)** a) 1, 2 b) 3, 5 c) 4
- **b)** When we use participles instead of connecting words, we usually leave out the subject and sometimes the auxiliary. We also change the verb to the present, past or perfect forms of the participle.
- Point out that participle clauses are always separated from the main clause by (a) comma(s).
- Highlight that using participle clauses is quite formal, and that sentences can be made less formal-sounding by replacing the participle clause with a connecting word, as in these examples. The meaning remains the same.

- **c)** b) time c) cause d) time e) condition
- Point out that the subject of the participle clause and the subject of the main clause are usually the same: *Looking out of the window, Verity noticed the sun had almost set.*
- Point out that when we use *not* in a participle clause, it usually comes before the participle: *Not wanting to wait any longer, he left.* However, it can come after the participle when it refers to another verb in the sentence: *Pretending not to notice him, she walked straight past.*
- Explain that if the action in the main clause is the result of the events in the participle clause, we use a perfect participle not a present participle: *Having lost our credit cards, we had to get some money sent to us.*
- Finally, point out that prepositions such as *after, by, in,* etc. can be used with a present or perfect participle clause in order to make the meaning clearer: *By not eating between meals, she managed to reach her target weight.*

4 Do the first question with the class. Students do the exercise on their own or in pairs. Check answers with the class.

> **1** Because I didn't know my way around Kerala, I headed straight for the Tourist Information office.
> **2** The rain was very heavy at that time of year, so it caused flooding everywhere.
> **3** If it is visited out of season, Kerala is not full of tourists.
> **4** After she'd saved up/been saving up for ages, Lauren finally went out and booked her flight.
> **5** While I was surfing through the channels, I came across a really good programme on India.

5 Focus students on the example. Students do the exercise on their own or in pairs. Check answers with the class.

> **2** Having spoken to them, I feel much happier about the situation.
> **3** Not wanting to arrive late, I called a taxi.
> **4** Flicking through his address book, I noticed something strange.
> **5** Coming from Brazil, he's not used to such cold weather.
> **6** You'll annoy people, talking like that.

— **EXTRA IDEA** —

- Write on the board: *Even after I had … , I still couldn't …; Now that I have … , I feel …; I didn't want to … , so I …; As I … , I noticed … .* Students work on their own and write sentences about themselves using the prompts. In pairs, students take turns to say their sentences and rephrase their partner's sentences using participles.

Listening

6 **a)** Focus students on the pictures. Introduce the topic by asking how many students have been to either the Galápagos Islands or Ireland. Tell students they are going to listen to two people, Bruce and Melissa, talking about their holidays in the Galápagos Islands and Ireland.

Be prepared with definitions, examples, etc. to pre-teach *forbidding, lodge, gravel, dinghy* /dɪ'ŋgi/ and *choppy*.

R2.2 **R2.3** Play the recordings (SB p149). Students listen and answer the questions. They compare answers in pairs. Check answers with the class.

> Bruce enjoyed his holiday; Melissa did not.

— EXTRA IDEA —

- Before doing **6a)**, ask students if they can predict the answers to the questions, based on the words that you have pre-taught. Students then listen to check their predictions.

b) **R2.2** Play the recording again. Students listen, tick the correct sentences and correct the mistakes.

Check answers with the class.

> 1F The Galápagos Islands are about 600 miles off the coast of Ecuador.
> 2F Bruce says 'they organised this boat trip **for us** which lasted about a week'.
> 3F He remembers the greyness.
> 4F The sea was very cold.
> 5T

c) **R2.3** Play the recording again. Students listen and answer the questions.

Check answers with the class.

> 1 They wanted beautiful sandy beaches and lush green hills. Also, Melissa says that many Americans like to visit Ireland.
> 2 They were renting it from some friends of friends.
> 3 Eighteen hours.
> 4 It was raining very hard.
> 5 Instead of being a sandy beach, it was actually a strip of gravel; it was also a half-hour sail away across choppy water.

d) Students discuss the questions in pairs. Ask each pair to share their ideas with the class.

— EXTRA IDEA —

- ✍ Write these words from the recordings on the board: *flappy, lush, pounding, gear*. Ask students to look at R2.2 and R2.3, SB p149 and to guess the meaning of the words from the context. Ask what helped them guess.

Help with Vocabulary   Adjective word order

Go through the introductory bullet and the table with the class.

7 **a)–c)** Students do the exercises on their own or in pairs and check their answers in **V2.3** SB p120.

Check answers with the class.

- **a)** Check that students understand *breath-taking, marble* and *picture-book*.
  1 breath-taking – opinion; high – size; snow-capped – material 2 delicious – opinion; Thai – origin; fish and coconut – material 3 extravagant – opinion; white – colour; marble – material 4 picture-book – opinion; medieval – age; Italian – origin
- Drill the phrases chorally and individually, highlighting that the main stress in the phrase falls on the first adjective.
- Point out that *breath-taking, snow-capped* and *picture-book* are all compound adjectives. They are usually written with a hyphen, and when spoken the first word is stressed.
- Explain that commas are used to separate two or more adjectives that are of the same type: *a beautiful, delicious peach*. In this example, both adjectives are adjectives of opinion. However, in *an expensive Italian restaurant, expensive* and *Italian* are different types of adjective, and a comma is not used to separate them.
- Students may initially find it difficult to identify adjectives of opinion. They may not immediately grasp that an adjective such as *beautiful* is expressing an opinion rather than a fact. To try and help students to remember this, you may like to teach them the saying *Beauty is in the eye of the beholder*, which means that not all people have the same opinions about what is attractive.
- **b)** By adding phrases beginning with *and*, *with* or *in* or adding a relative clause.
- Point out that a compound noun cannot be separated by other words: *a leather address book* not *an address leather book*.
- Remind students that the more they listen to and read English, the easier it will be for them to use adjectives in the correct order without even thinking about it.

— EXTRA IDEA —

- ✍ Write the column headings from **V2.3** SB p120 on the board. Ask students to write a sentence describing an object in the classroom, containing at least three adjectives. Nominate students to come to the board and write their sentences, using the correct columns of the table.

Check that students understand *vibrant* and *sprawling*. Pay particular attention to the pronunciation of *sprawling* /ˈsprɔːlɪŋ/.

Do the first question with the class. Students do the exercise on their own or in pairs.

Check answers with the class. Drill the phrases chorally and individually.

> 2 an interesting old leather box
> 3 the vibrant, sprawling modern capital
> 4 that fine old French wine
> 5 a small 14ᵗʰ-century castle
> 6 that expensive black suede jacket
> 7 an energetic young Welsh sheepdog
> 8 an uncomfortable antique velvet armchair

 Pre-teach *Victorian*. Point out that adjectives formed from the names of English and British monarchs are sometimes used as an adjective to describe things from the periods of their reigns. The most common are *Victorian* (for Queen Victoria, 1837–1901), *Elizabethan* (for Queen Elizabeth I, 1558–1603), *Georgian* (for Kings George I, II and III, 1714–1811) and *Edwardian* (for King Edward, 1901–10). *Victorian, Georgian* and *Edwardian* are commonly used to describe architecture built in that period: *I live in a three-storey Georgian house in London.*

Focus students on the example. Students do the exercise on their own or in pairs.

Check answers with the class. Drill the phrases chorally and individually.

> 2 a spacious, modern flat, which is well-decorated and inexpensive 3 a classic, round-necked sweater, in blue cotton 4 a funny, well-written contemporary drama, which is original and superbly-acted 5 a scruffy young writer with dark hair and a beard 6 an Italian sports model in metallic grey with a sun-roof

---

Get ready … Get it right!

 Students work on their own. Give students two minutes to think of a place they have been to which they either love or hate. Ask students to write down as many adjectives as they can think of to describe it.

> **— EXTRA IDEA —**
> • Ask weaker students to copy the column headings from **V2.3** SB p120 and write their adjectives in the appropriate columns; it will help them to use the adjectives in the correct order during **11**.

 a) Put students into groups and focus them on the example.

Students take turns to describe their place to the rest of the group. Encourage students to ask follow-up questions if possible.

b) Ask each group to nominate one person to tell the rest of the class which place sounded the best or worst and why.

> **— EXTRA IDEA —**
> • Ask students to write a short travel article about their favourite holiday destination for homework. They should follow the same structure as the article on SB p19 with the headings 'Why?', 'What shouldn't I miss?' and 'A perfect day'.

> **— EXTRA PRACTICE AND HOMEWORK —**
> **Ph Class Activity** 2B Survival at sea p137 (Instructions p120)
> **Ph Help with Listening** 2 Taking part in a conversation p190 (Instructions p182)
> **2 Review** Exercises 3 and 4 SB p24
> **CD-ROM** Lesson 2B
> **Workbook** Lesson 2B p11

 # 2C Spoilt for choice

QUICK REVIEW ●●●
This activity reviews adjective word order. Students do the activity in groups. Focus students on the example. Ask one student to describe something using one adjective. The next student adds another adjective in the correct order. The game continues until someone in the group gives up or makes a mistake.

 Introduce the topic by asking how many students have visited England. Ask where they went and why.

Tell students to close their books and make a list of all the places in England they have heard of or been to.

Vocabulary adjectives: describing places
Skills Reading: a tourist board website; Listening: interview about tourism; Speaking: talking about your country; Writing: a guide to your country
Real World making recommendations
Review adjective word order

Check answers with the class and write them on the board.

Choose two or three places from the list and ask students to talk about what they know about those places.

Introduce the topic by asking students if they have ever used a tourist information website to find out about a place they planned to visit. Ask what other sources of information are available for travellers.

Focus students on the photos and website extracts. Be prepared with definitions, examples, etc. to pre-teach *a wealth* /welθ/ *of*, *stately home*, *sheer* /ʃɪə/ and *timelessness*.

Bristol, Bath, York, Birmingham and Stratford-upon-Avon are all cities.

Cornwall, Warwickshire /ˈwɒrɪkˌʃə/, Herefordshire /ˈherəfədˌʃə/ and Norfolk /ˈnɔːfək/ are all counties.

The Lake District is a popular holiday destination in the northwest of England, famous for its lakes and mountains.

The Norfolk Broads are a network of rivers and lakes in the county of Norfolk.

The Cotswolds are a range of hills in the west of England.

Students discuss the question in pairs. Ask each pair to share their ideas with the class.

--- EXTRA IDEA ---
- Ask students to visit www.enjoyengland.com, where they can find further information about the places on the map. Give each student a city or county to research and write a short report about.

 a) Focus students on the words in bold. Students do the exercise on their own or in pairs.

Check answers with the class.

Point out that *bustling* is often used in a positive context. To describe something that is busy in a bad way, we would say *crowded*.

Also point out that *vibrant* is also often used to describe very bright colours: *She painted her bedroom a vibrant shade of orange*.

Finally, point out that although *a host of* and *a wealth of* both mean 'a large amount of' or 'many', *a wealth of* can only be used to describe something good or positive; for example, *A wealth of attractions* not *A wealth of problems*.

> a) rural splendour b) a host of c) bustling d) vibrant

b)–c) Students do the exercise on their own or in pairs and check their answers in **V2.4** SB p120.

Model and drill the new words, paying particular attention to the pronunciation of *quaint* /kweɪnt/ and *medieval* /ˌmediˈiːvəl/.

Point out that *meandering* and the verb *meander* are often used with negative connotations: *She made a long meandering speech about the value of tourism*. However, it can also be used positively, suggesting a lack of time pressure: *We spent the day meandering around a pretty fishing village*.

Check that students understand the difference between *unique* and *only*: *The Leaning Tower of Pisa is unique* (not *The Leaning Tower of Pisa is only*) and *Lying on the beach is the only thing I like to do on holiday* (not *Lying on the beach is the unique thing I like to do on holiday*).

> East of England: unspoilt, meandering, ancient, unique
> Southwest England: diverse, cosmopolitan, beautiful, Roman, wild, rugged, coastal, quaint, golden, sandy, medieval

 a)–b) Tell students they are going to listen to an interview with Kate Johnson, who works in tourism. Be prepared with definitions, examples, etc. to pre-teach *breakdown* and *head to*.

R2.4 Play the recording (SB p150). Students listen and answer the questions. They then compare answers in pairs.

Check answers with the class. Encourage students to explain why any of the figures surprised them.

> That most of them only visit London. That they don't take advantage of what the rest of England has to offer.
> 27.4 million = the number of overseas visitors to England last year
> 3.5 million = the number of American visitors to England last year
> 2 million = the number of French visitors and German visitors to England last year
> 1.7 million = the number of Spanish visitors to England last year
> 1.2 million = the number of Italian visitors to England last year

 a) Tell students they are going to listen to more of the interview with Kate, in which she talks about the diversity England has to offer as a holiday destination. Be prepared with definitions, examples, etc. to pre-teach *rolling, the masses, picturesque thatched cottage* and *cobbled* /ˈkɒbəld/ *street*.

R2.5 Play the recording (SB p150). Students listen and make notes.

b) Students compare answers in pairs.

Play the recording again for students to check their answers.

Check answers with the class.

> **Possible answers**
> **Cornwall** – you can surf and do water sports; good for family holidays.
> **Norfolk Broads** – good for family holidays; you could hire a boat; 125 miles of waterways; peaceful countryside.
> **Lake District** – good for climbing and hiking; breath-taking scenery.
> **Northumberland/Cotswolds** – quaint villages and rolling countryside; you can escape the masses and see picturesque villages with thatched cottages and country pubs.
> **York** – dates back to pre-Roman times; walled city with cobbled streets; York Minster is Europe's second largest Gothic cathedral; on Sundays, bells ring out all over the city.

6 Tell students they are going to listen to the final part of the interview with Kate, in which she talks about cities and food. Introduce the topic by asking students what they think about English food. Does it have a good or a bad reputation? Ask them what they think the most popular food in England is (the answer is given in R2.6).

`R2.6` Play the recording (SB p150). Students listen and answer the question.

Check the answer with the class.

> Because the cities are so cosmopolitan.

7 Students do the activity in pairs. Ask each pair to share one or two of their ideas with the class.

8 a) Students do the activity on their own. Give students five minutes to make their notes.

b) Go through the bullets in the Real World box. Check students understand *be after* and *be into.*

Students do the activity in groups. If you have a multilingual class, group different nationalities together. Ask each group to share one or two of their ideas with the class.

Writing Extension

9 Tell students to read the website extracts again and underline any expressions that they can use in their own writing.

Encourage students to use some of the adjectives that they have learnt in this unit, remembering to use them in the correct order. This task can be set for homework.

 Ask students to turn to SB p106 and look at *Little Wonders.* This song was recorded by the American artist Rob Thomas in 2007 for the Disney film *Meet the Robinsons.*

1 a)–b) Introduce the song by explaining what a *wonder* is (something that causes a feeling of great surprise and admiration). For example, we refer to the seven wonders of the world, which include sights like the Taj Mahal and Stonehenge. Ask students what they think 'little wonders' might be.

Focus students on verbs 1–5. Point out that all of them describe movement and that they all appear in the song, metaphorically in some cases. Students do the exercise on their own and compare answers in pairs.

Check answers with the class.

Point out that *roll, twist, slide* and *wash away* can all be used transitively and intransitively.

> 1c) 2d) 3e) 4a) 5b)

2 a)–b) Students do the exercise on their own and compare answers in pairs.

c) `R2.7` Play the recording. Students listen and check their answers. Play the recording again if necessary.

Check answers with the class.

> 2 shoulder 3 remember 4 twists 5 turns
> 6 falls away 7 remain 8 slide 9 shine 10 turn
> 11 heart 12 wash away 13 feel

3 Students do the exercise on their own and compare answers in pairs. Check the answer with the class.

> 2

2 Review

See p32 for ideas on how to use this section.

1 2 with whom 3 both of whom 4 none of which
5 for which 6 after whom 7 on whose 8 all of which

2 2 vividly 3 bitterly 4 entirely 5 highly 6 firmly
7 deeply 8 completely

3a) 2 Eating 3 Having eaten 4 Having seen 5 Seeing
6 Seen 7 Having read 8 Read 9 Reading 10 Given
11 Having given 12 Giving

3b) Possible answers
2 Because Lucy eats in restaurants all week she prefers
to cook for herself at weekends.
3 Because I had eaten such a big lunch earlier that day,
I didn't feel like any dinner.
4 She had seen the film three times already, so she decided
to give it a miss.
5 Because she saw her ex-boyfriend approaching, she ran
and hid.
6 If you see her from a distance, she looks like a 20-year-old!
7 After I had read the instructions twice, I began to
assemble the desk.

8 If you read the poem out loud, it sounds much better.
9 Because I read the report so quickly I missed a lot of
mistakes.
10 If I was given the chance, I'd love to learn how to ski.
11 After she gave/had given Fred the job, she immediately
regretted her decision.
12 If I give myself an extra day, I should be able to finish
the job.

4 1 beautiful big old 2 attractive 16-year-old
3 extraordinary wide emerald-green 4 long dark shiny
5 round wooden 6 tall dark-haired Italian

5 1 unspoilt 2 diverse 3 quaint 4 vibrant 5 rugged
6 unique

Progress Portfolio

See p32 for ideas on how to use this section.

Accurate Writing

CONNECTING WORDS: time (1)
PUNCTUATION: apostrophes

1 Introduce the topic by asking students what the words
and phrases in the box have in common (they are all
connecting words and phrases used to talk about time).

Students do the exercise on their own or in pairs and
check their answers in **AW2.1** SB p123.

Check answers with the class.

Point out that using a form used for the future after *as
soon as* and *the moment* is a very common error. These two
phrases should always be followed by a present or past
verb form, never one for the future.

Also point out that *then* can often come before or after the
subject of the sentence (*Then he realised the mistake … /
He then realised the mistake …*).

Finally, highlight that although *as* and *while* are similar
in meaning to *meanwhile*, they are not interchangeable
(*I caught a glimpse of Steve ~~meanwhile~~ I was hurrying down
the street. I sat anxiously waiting for the call. ~~As/While~~, I
tried to get on with some work …*). *Meanwhile* is often used
at the beginning of a clause to talk about what is/was
happening at the same time as something else happening
in the previous clause.

> 1 As soon as/The moment 2 Ever since
> 3 originally/first 4 From then on/Ever since
> 5 as/while 6 Afterwards 7 Then 8 Meanwhile

2 Introduce the topic by asking students what we use
apostrophes for in English. Elicit ideas from the class.

Students do the exercise on their own or in pairs and
check their answers in **AW2.2** SB p123.

Check answers with the class.

Point out that even native English speakers sometimes
make mistakes with *its* and *it's*. Remind students that *it's*
can only ever mean *it is* or *it has*. In all other cases, *its* is
correct. Also point out that *its'* is always incorrect; that
form does not exist.

Point out that when a person's name ends in *s* (e.g. *James*),
it is common to just add an apostrophe to the end of the
word rather than an *'s* to show the possessive. Both
versions are possible (*James' car is red./James's car is red.*).
However, when using *'s* as the contracted form of *is*, only *'s*
is possible (*James's coming to dinner. ~~James' coming to
dinner.~~*)

> 1 There's a lot of mud on the car's wheels. 2 Are you
> absolutely sure it's not hers? 3 Britain's most popular
> pets are cats. 4 I really can't remember its name.
> 5 Where's the students' coffee bar? 6 I think it's
> written by Charles Dickens. 7 I'd listen carefully to
> the women's opinions if I were you.

3 **a)–b)** Focus students on the extract. Explain that in
addition to the incorrect underlined connecting words of
time, there are six mistakes in the use of apostrophes. Ask

students to concentrate on the connecting words first, then turn their attention to the apostrophes.

Students do the exercises on their own and check their answers in pairs.

Check answers with the class.

> I vividly remember the first time I saw Venice because it's so beautiful and **there's** nowhere else like it in the entire world. [1]**As soon as/The moment** you come out of the station you see all the **boats** going up and down the Grand Canal, which contributes to **its** fairytale atmosphere. I think it's one of **Europe's** most romantic cities. I [2]**first** went there with my parents when I was ten, and I've been going there [3]**ever since**, for the last 20 years. [4]**As/While** I'm going along in the river bus, I still can't stop looking at the fantastic **buildings** which line the canals. **Its** unique architecture makes Venice a real open-air museum! I [5]**then** love wandering around the narrow streets and going window-shopping.

> **EXTRA PRACTICE AND HOMEWORK**
>
> **Workbook** Accurate Writing Exercises 3 and 4 p84

Preview 3

SUBJECT AND VERB INVERSION

 1 Students do the exercise on their own or in pairs and check their answers in **G3.2** SB p125.

Check answers with the class.

> **a) 1** Correct **2** No, nor did I. **3** Look. Here comes the doctor. **4** Correct **5** Correct **6** Have you any idea where my glasses are? **7** Do you remember what they said about taking vitamin C? **8** Correct **9** I don't know what his problem is. **10** Correct **11** He asked me if I was taking any extra vitamins.

> **b) 2** Neither have I. **3** He asked me what I was planning to do this weekend. **4** I wonder if he still works with Megan. **5** So does Leo. **6** Look. Here comes the traffic warden. **7** Is this where you work? **8** I don't know where he lives. **9** He wanted to know when he could come. / He wants to know when he can come. **10** Have you any idea what Jill would like for her birthday?

3 Well-being

Student's Book p26–p35

3A Being confident

QUICK REVIEW ●●●
This activity reviews intensifying adverbs. Students do the first part of the activity on their own. Put students into pairs. Students take turns to say their sentences. Encourage students to ask follow-up questions if possible.

Vocabulary connotation: positive and negative character adjectives
Grammar introductory *it*
Review intensifying adverbs

Vocabulary Positive character adjectives

 a) Introduce the topic by asking students how many words they can think of to describe people positively.

Focus students on the words in the box. Model and drill the words, paying particular attention to the pronunciation of *courageous* /kə'reɪdʒəs/, *spontaneous* /spɒn'teɪniəs/ and *cautious* /'kɔːʃəs/.

Students do the exercise on their own and check their answers in V3.1 SB p124.

Check answers with the class.

Point out that *trusting* does not mean the same as *trustworthy*. If a person is *trusting*, it means that they trust other people; if a person is *trustworthy*, it means that you can trust them.

Highlight that although *careful* is very similar in meaning to *cautious*, they are not always interchangeable. For example, we always say *be careful* not *be cautious*.

b) Students do the exercise on their own.

c) Students do the exercise in pairs. Encourage students to ask follow-up questions if possible.

Reading and Grammar

 Students do the exercise in pairs. Ask each pair to share some of their ideas with the class.

 a) Focus students on the words in the box. Students check the meaning of the words. Be prepared with definitions, examples, etc. to give students if necessary. Model and drill the words, paying particular attention to the pronunciation of *triumph* /'traɪəmf/ and *accolade* /'ækəleɪd/.

b) Focus students on the article. Check students understand *spotlight* in heading a). Students do the exercise on their own or in pairs.

Check answers with the class.

> a) 4 b) 2 c) 1 d) 5 e) 3

> **EXTRA IDEA**
> • Before students read the article, ask them what kind of person might be described as a wolf or a sheep. Ask students to read the article and compare their ideas with those in the article.

 Students do the exercise on their own or in pairs. Encourage students to find direct quotes from the article to support the statements.
Check answers with the class.

> 1 The writer says 'So surely we all hate it when we lose!' 2 The article says that 'it surprised him to discover that while some people became stressed after losing out to a rival in a laboratory task, others became stressed after winning'. 3 The article says 'it's not an aspect of their personality that they are conscious of'. 4 The article says 'for low-power individuals public recognition is equally stressful and they would do anything to avoid it'. 5 The article quotes Dr Wirth as saying 'If you can figure which one you are [wolf or sheep], you can tailor your working environment to suit you'. She also says that knowing which category you fall into can bring benefits.

 Students discuss the questions in groups. Ask each group to share their ideas with the class.

> **EXTRA IDEA**
> • ✏️ Write on the board the following animals, which are all also used to describe people: *chicken, cow, fox, ox, pig, weasel*. In pairs, students discuss what kind of person these animals might describe. (In English they are: *chicken* = a coward; *cow* = an offensive term for a woman; *fox, weasel* = someone who can't be trusted; *ox* = someone very strong; *pig* = a rude, greedy or offensive person.)

Help with Grammar Introductory *it*

Go through the introductory bullets and identify the different phrases in the article.

 a)–c) Students do the exercises on their own or in pairs and check their answers in G3.1 SB p125.
Check answers with the class.

> • a) 2 It's not an aspect …
> 3 it's difficult to know
> 4 it follows that not winning is stressful
> 5 it surprised him to discover

- Highlight that in each of the examples for **a)** from the article, *it* is being used to avoid having a long and grammatically complex subject of the verb; for example: *… it's clear that one of these 'unquestionables' is that everyone wants to win* instead of *everyone wanting to win is clearly one of those 'unquestionables'*.

- Point out that *appear* and *transpire* can also be used to introduce a *that* clause. Remind students that the *that* clause cannot go at the beginning of these types of sentence. For example, we cannot say ~~That not winning is stressful it follows~~.

- Point out that in structures with *it* + verb + object + infinitive with *to* + *that*, the verb is often related to feelings, for example, *amaze, annoy, astonish, concern, frighten, hurt, scare, shock, upset, worry*.

- Explain that we can use *it* as the object of a verb where *it* refers to a clause later in the sentence.

- **b)** **1** we all hate it when we lose **2** find it difficult to cope with losing

- Point out that *can't bear, can't stand, dislike, enjoy, like, love, prefer, resent* and *understand* can also be used in the structure verb + *it* + *when*.

- Point out that *believe* and *consider* can also be used in the structure verb + *it* + adjective + infinitive with *to*.

- Point out that we don't use introductory *it* if the subject of the verb is a noun: *their fears were completely unfounded* not ~~it was completely unfounded their fears~~.

- Encourage students to make a note of the common expressions with introductory *it* and to make an effort to learn and use them: **It's no good** *getting all upset about it.* **It's no use** *asking her, she's busy.* **It's no wonder** *that we got ill.* **It's no coincidence** *that they arrived together.*

 7 Focus students on the example answer. Students do the exercise on their own or in pairs.

If students are having difficulty transforming the sentences, point out that in each case the only word missing is *it*. Once they have put *it* at the beginning of the sentence, they only need to rearrange the remaining words so that they make sense.

Check answers with the class.

> **2** It's strange that she refused a promotion.
> **3** It won't be easy to get this finished on time.
> **4** It means a lot to have a good working relationship with someone.
> **5** It is obvious that we need people with more experience.

 8 **a)** Focus students on the example answer. Model the exercise by writing some sentences about yourself on the board.

Students do the exercise on their own.

b) In pairs, students take turns to tell each other their sentences. Encourage students to ask follow-up questions.

Ask each pair to share one or two of their sentences with the class.

Listening and Vocabulary

 9 **a)** Tell students they are going to listen to a preview of a radio programme about 'impostor syndrome'. Check that students understand *impostor*.

Be prepared with definitions, examples, etc. to pre-teach *bluff your way through* and *find somebody out*.

R3.1 Play the recording (SB p150). Students listen and answer the question.

Check the answer with the class.

> Impostor syndrome is the feeling that although you seem successful and capable to other people, inside you feel like an impostor; that is, that you are just pretending to be successful and capable and that you will soon be found out.

b) Focus students on the pictures of Valerie, Richard and Miranda. Tell students they are going to listen to each of the three people talking about 'impostor syndrome'.

R3.2 Play the recording (SB p150). Students listen and fill in the gaps.

Check answers with the class. Point out that the phrase *good fortune*, as used by Miranda, doesn't necessarily have anything to do with having money, or having 'a fortune'. It is a general expression for saying 'good luck'.

> **1** Valerie **2** Richard **3** Richard **4** Valerie **5** Miranda

c) Play the recording again. Students listen and choose the correct answers.

Check answers with the class.

> **1** a) doesn't think b) experienced **2** a) makes b) aren't any **3** a) feels b) isn't

> ── EXTRA IDEA ──
> - Write these words and phrases from the recording on the board: *come late to something, rumble to the fact that, overcome, catch out, nagging, trick.* Ask students to look at R3.2, SB p150 and to guess the meaning of the words and phrases from the context. Ask what helped them guess.

10 Students discuss the questions in groups. Ask each group to share their ideas with the class.

Help with Vocabulary Connotation: positive and negative character adjectives

Go through the introductory bullet and check that students understand *connotation*.

11 **a)–d)** Students do the exercises on their own and compare their answers in pairs. They then check their answers in **V3.2** SB p124.

Check answers with the class.

- **a)** 1 Yes 2 arrogant 3 Positive: confident; negative: arrogant
- **b)** reckless – courageous; tight-fisted – thrifty; finicky – meticulous; extravagant – generous; gullible – trusting; obstinate – determined; impetuous – spontaneous; timid – cautious
- Model and drill the words, paying particular attention to the pronunciation of *impetuous* /ɪmpetʃuəs/.
- Point out that there is no such word as *reckful*. The opposite of *reckless* is *cautious* or *careful*.
- Tell students that it may help them to remember *tight-fisted* by picturing a person refusing to let go of a handful of coins by keeping their fist squeezed tightly shut. Also point out that *tight-fisted* is often shortened to *tight*: *I had dinner with my boss last night, but he was too tight to pay the bill.*
- In addition to describing people, *finicky* can also be used to describe tasks that are difficult because they require a large amount of attention to small detail: *Mending a watch is very finicky.*
- *Timid* and *shy* are very similar in meaning, but *timid* also has a sense of being easily frightened, while *shy* does not. For example, *I've got a very timid cat* (= my cat is easily frightened) and *I've got a very shy cat* (= my cat is nervous, especially around people).

12 **a)** Model the exercise by describing yourself, using the adjectives from **1a)** and **11b)**.

Students do the exercise on their own.

b) Students do the exercise in pairs. Ask each pair to share their ideas with the class.

Get ready ... Get it right!

13 Focus students on the sentences. Students do the exercise on their own. Give students 5–10 minutes to make notes for and against each sentence.

14 **a)** Students discuss the sentences in **13** in groups. Encourage students to use expressions such as *It's ridiculous to say ...* , *It's clear that ...* , *It follows that ...* ; etc.

b) Ask each group to tell the class which sentences they agreed with.

> **EXTRA IDEA**
> - Run the activity as a debate. Divide the class into two groups, A and B. Group A argue for each of the sentences, group B against. Give each group two minutes per sentence to make their case.

> **EXTRA PRACTICE AND HOMEWORK**
>
> **Ph** **Class Activity** 3A Connotation crossword p139 (Instructions p121)
> **Ph** **Help with Listening** 3 Leaving things out p191 (Instructions p183)
> **3 Review** Exercises 1, 2, 3 and 4 SB p34
> **CD-ROM** Lesson 3A
> **Workbook** Lesson 3A p14
> **Preview 3** Exercise 1 SB p25

3B A happy, healthy life

QUICK REVIEW ●●●

This activity reviews introductory *it*. Students do the first part of the activity on their own. Put students into pairs. Students take turns to say their sentences. Encourage students to ask follow-up questions.

Vocabulary Phrasal verbs: health

1 **a)** Introduce the topic by asking students how many phrasal verbs they can think of related to health. ✏ Elicit ideas from the class and write them on the board. Check students understand *bug* (here = an illness caused by a microorganism).

Vocabulary phrasal verbs: health
Grammar inversion
Review introductory *it*

Students do the exercise on their own or in pairs and check their answers in **V3.3** SB p124. Check answers with the class.

Point out that *get over sb/sth* is also used after a painful or unhappy experience such as the end of a relationship: *It's taken three months, but I think I'm finally getting over Simon* or losing someone close: *It can take years to get over the death of a spouse or close relative.*

Highlight that *bunged up* is a synonym for *blocked up*, especially when referring to your nose: *I've got a bunged/blocked up nose.*

Come down with can be used as a synonym for *go down with*: *I think I'm coming/going down with flu.*

Break out in can be used as a synonym for *come out in*: *I've broken/come out in a rash all over my chest.*

b) Model and drill the questions, paying particular attention to where the stress falls in each phrasal verb.

In pairs, students take turns to ask and answer the questions. Ask each pair to share one or two of their ideas with the class.

Reading and Grammar

2 Introduce the topic by asking students what they understand by *well-being* (feeling healthy and happy).

Put students into groups of four. Focus students on the photos, headline and introduction. Make sure students understand *treadmill* /ˈtredmɪl/ and what a *punishing diet* might be.

Students do the exercise in groups of four.

 Elicit ideas from the class and write them on the board.

3 **a)** Keep students in the same groups and give each student a letter (A, B, C and D). Student As turn to SB p109, student Bs turn to SB p112, student Cs to SB p115 and student Ds to SB p116.

Focus students on their three extracts. Be prepared with definitions, examples, etc. to pre-teach *moderation, cholesterol* /kəˈlestərɒl/, *giggles, eczema* /ˈeksɪmə /, *hay fever* /heɪ ˈfiːvə/, *decay* and *chronic* /ˈkrɒnɪk/.

Students do the exercise on their own. Encourage students to make detailed notes.

b) Students work in the same groups. Students take turns to tell each other the answers to their questions. Encourage students to ask follow-up questions if possible.

Ask students to tell the class the most interesting piece of information they learned from the article.

Student A

a) Eat more curry, get a hobby, drink more coffee.

b) Curries protect against Alzheimer's, stress and depression and can help you lose weight. Having a hobby can ease depression, lower stress, improve mood and immune systems and may reduce the risk of high blood pressure. Coffee can lower the risk of diabetes, relax muscles, improve speed of thought and lower the risk of heart attacks for women.

c) Meals containing chillies burn up more calories than other meals. Men who have hobbies are less likely to be sick and absent from work than men who don't. Women who drink coffee may reduce the risk of a heart attack by up to 30%; the research was carried out on 32,000 women over six years. Also, drinking six or more cups of coffee a day reduces the risk of diabetes by 54% for men and 30% for women.

Student B

a) Eat dark chocolate, brush your teeth, laugh a lot.

b) Eating dark chocolate can reduce blood pressure, bad cholesterol and the risk of dying from heart disease. Brushing your teeth saves visits to the dentist and may prevent strokes or heart attacks. Laughing reduces pain and diabetes symptoms, improves the immune system and burns up calories.

c) Flavonoids in dark chocolate reduce the risk of dying from heart disease by 20%. Research based on 700 people found that those with gum disease were more likely to suffer from narrowing of blood vessels that can lead to heart attacks. Laughter burns up calories at the rate of 2.31 a minute. An average day's laughter gets rid of all of the calories in a pepperoni pizza.

Student C

a) Drink tea, get a pet, chew gum.

b) Drinking tea helps prevent heart disease and flu, promotes hair growth and weight loss, can reduce the risk of heart attack and can improve mental performance. Laughter is linked to good health, and dog owners laugh most; pet dogs can lower heart rate and reduce stress; owning a cat reduces the risk of developing eczema and hay fever in children. Chewing gum is good for oral health, helps people eat fewer snacks and calories, is good for face muscles, high blood pressure and diabetes and may prevent tooth decay.

c) Three or more cups of tea a day reduce the risk of heart attack. Thirty-minute walks with a dog are 87% more effective for heart health than going for walks on your own. People who chew gum eat fewer snacks and 10% fewer calories.

Student D

a) Eat fish, take up singing, get married.

b) Eating fish protects you from or treats almost anything, from bad backs to asthma; it contributes to healthy brain cells and good eyesight and it may help women to have cleverer children. Choral singing increases immunity, reduces depression, improves cognitive function and mood and increases feelings of well-being. Getting married can extend your life, reduce the risk of heart disease and catching colds and lower blood pressure.

c) Women who eat plenty of sardines, tuna and salmon during pregnancy may have cleverer children. Singing helps people cope with chronic pain, lowers stress levels and boosts the immune system. Married men are 70% more likely to live longer than single men.

EXTRA IDEA

- Ask each student to write a list of facts based on what they have read – some true and some false – and ask their group if they can guess which are true and which are false. For example, *Did you know that curry can help cure colds? It contains a special enzyme which kills the virus.*

a) If you have a multilingual class, group different nationalities together. (Otherwise, students work in the same groups as in **3**.) Students discuss the questions in groups.

b) Focus students on the speech bubbles. Ask each group to share their ideas with the class.

> — EXTRA IDEA —
> • Ask students to share any other health tips or advice they have. What keeps them healthy or helps them get better when they have been ill? What 'alternative remedies' have they tried or would be interested to try?

Help with Grammar

Ask students to do **1** in Preview 3, SB p25 if necessary.

Go through the introductory bullet with the class and make sure students understand what limiting adverbials and negative adverbials are. An adverbial is any word or phrase which functions as an adverb. Point out that the subject and auxiliary verb are inverted when we begin a sentence with a limiting or a negative adverbial.

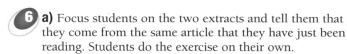 **a)–d)** Students do the exercises on their own or in pairs and check their answers in **G3.3** SB p125.

Check answers with the class.

- **a)** 2 does dental hygiene save 3 did he agree 4 do you hear 5 have experts come 6 should you exercise
- Model and drill the sentences. Point out that the main stress in sentence 2 is on *only*, in 3 on *last week* and in 6 on *no*.
- Point out that in sentences 1–6, *seldom, rarely* and *only recently* are examples of limiting adverbials; *not only, not until* and *under no circumstances* are examples of negative adverbials.
- Point out that the pairs of sentences in **G3.3** SB p125 all have the same meaning; the difference is that the inverted sentences are more emphatic.
- **b)** Past Simple – *did*; Present Simple – *do/does*
- Remind students that the subject agrees with the auxiliary, not the main verb: *Not only **does he** enjoy …*
- Highlight that the auxiliary verb we use in inversion depends on the verb form in the sentence that we are inverting. Students should recognise the pattern of using *did* for Past Simple, *do* for Present Simple, *have* for Present Perfect and *had* for Past Perfect.
- Remind students that we never use auxiliary verbs with modal verbs, and the same rule applies in inversion; when inverting modal verbs we simply invert the subject with the modal: *Under no circumstances **would I ask** him to do this.*
- **c)** 1 will things get better 2 did we start going for long walks

- Highlight that inversion can occur after another complete clause beginning with *not until, only when, only if, only after*: **Not until** ~~learns she~~ she learns to relax will things get any better; **Only when** ~~got we~~ we got the dog did we start going for long walks.
- Point out that we also use inversion after *neither* or *nor* when it introduces a negative clause that is related to one mentioned previously: *Unfortunately, Colin didn't listen to me, and **neither did he take** the doctor's advice.*
- Point out that although inversion is common in literary and formal texts, it is also used in less formal spoken and written English as a way of adding emphasis or dramatic effect: *No way **should people drive** to work if they can possibly walk.*
- Point out that we don't use inversion with *not … either*: *I don't like fish and I don't like curry either.* not ~~… either do I not like curry~~.
- Point out that we can find inversion in literature after adverbials of place: **Into the room** *walked Johan.*
- If you have any football fans in your class, you may like to share with them a famous inversion used by former England manager Graham Taylor. On seeing that England's opponents were moving into a position where they were likely to score, he was filmed saying *Do I not like that* under his breath. This quote became so well known that it was used as the title of his autobiography.

 a) Focus students on the two extracts and tell them that they come from the same article that they have just been reading. Students do the exercise on their own.

b) Students do the exercise in pairs.
Check answers with the class.

> 1 Only recently **have experts suggested** that there are many health benefits from being exposed to sunlight. Not only **does it help** reduce depression and pain, it also reduces high blood pressure.
> 2 Seldom **do we hear** anything positive about drinking wine. However, research suggests that not only **does drinking a moderate amount of red wine reduce** the risk of heart attacks, it can also help protect elderly people from mental decline. But of course, under no circumstances **should people drink** and drive.

7 Focus students on the example answer. Students do the exercise on their own or in pairs. Remind students that the new sentences must mean the same as the original ones. Check answers with the class.

> 2 Not for a minute did I think I'd enjoy having a dog, but it's great. 3 Not only was I stressed out, I was getting ill too. 4 Under no circumstances should you agree to do overtime for nothing. 5 Not until she spoke did I realise it was Jin.

Listening

 8 **a)** Tell students they are going to listen to six people talking about what they do to cheer themselves up. Ask students to predict what the people might say. Students do the exercise in pairs.

 Check answers with the class and write them on the board.

b) Be prepared with definitions, examples, etc. to pre-teach *feel down, perspective, pick-me-up, art deco* /ˌɑːt ˈdekəʊ/, *atomiser, zip around* and *cynicism* /ˈsɪnɪsɪzəm/.

R3.3 Play the recording (SB p150). Students listen and check if any of their predictions were correct.

> — **EXTRA IDEA** —
>
> • Write the following words and phrases on the board and pre-teach if necessary: *shoebox, sociable, top speed, kite, eyebrow*. Ask students to make their predictions about what the people on the recording will say based on these words and phrases.

c) Focus students on the quotes and questions.

Play the recording again. Students listen and answer the questions.

Check answers with the class.

> **CONVERSATION 1**
> **a)** A shoebox. **b)** Planning something sociable or fun to do.
>
> **CONVERSATION 2**
> **a)** Put on perfume. **b)** Her bike.
>
> **CONVERSATION 3**
> **a)** Kite flying. **b)** About anything that is threatening to get a little bit too serious or that is bothering him more than it should be.

 9 **a)** Introduce the topic by asking students what they understand by 'fillers' and if they can think of any examples in English. Elicit ideas from the class and write them on the board.

Ask students if fillers exist in their own language and why they think people use them (in order to give themselves time to think and plan what they are going to say next).

Tell students they are going to listen to the rest of conversation 3.

R3.4 Play the recording (SB p151). Students listen and underline examples of redundancy.

b)–c) Students compare answers in pairs. Check answers with the class.

Point out that although it is perfectly natural to use fillers such as *um* and *er* in speech to give yourself some thinking time, students should try not to overuse them. Specifically, they should try not to overuse the same filler (e.g. *um*), especially in short succession, as it can be hard to listen to. This problem is especially common in non-native speakers, although less so at Advanced level.

Also point out that the phrase *you know* is extremely common in English, but that it does not literally mean 'do you know?' It is simply used as a filler to give you time to think of what to say next; it is not a direct question.

Point out that in addition to hearing *you know* as a common filler, students may hear a variation: *you know what I mean*, often shortened to /nɑː ˈmiːn/. This phrase is very common but does not function as a filler. It is used when you think that the person listening understands and so you do not need to say any more: *I can't believe they fired him, you know what I mean?* Students should be careful not to confuse the two expressions.

> FRAN Well, generally if I, <u>um</u>, <u>if</u> I'm not feeling, <u>um</u>, too happy then, <u>um</u>, I need something to work towards, so, <u>um</u>, I try and make contact with friends that I don't really see very often and, <u>um</u>, <u>and</u> I find that if I'm, <u>I'm</u> with them then I <u>kind of</u> forget about what's going on at the time and just remember the things I, <u>you know</u>, used to do with them, and, <u>um</u>, they just <u>kind of</u>, <u>er</u>, accept my personality so I don't have to, <u>you know</u>, that, <u>that</u> trivial thing that's usually making me not very happy. Doesn't really mean very much to them so …

Get ready … Get it right!

10 Model the activity by writing a list of what you do to cheer yourself up on the board.

Students write their lists on their own. Remind students that they should write both the activity and the positive benefits associated with it.

11 **a)** Students do the activity in groups. Encourage students to use inversion to help them emphasise the advice that they are giving. Refer students to the speech bubble for an example.

b) Ask each group to describe their group's most unusual and popular ideas.

> — **EXTRA PRACTICE AND HOMEWORK** —
>
> **Ph** **Class Activity** 3B This is my life p140 (Instructions p121)
>
> **Ph** **Vocabulary Plus** 3 Health idioms p174 (Instructions p169)
>
> **3 Review** Exercises 5 and 6 SB p34
>
> **CD-ROM** Lesson 3B
>
> **Workbook** Lesson 3B p16

3C It's the way you say it

Vocabulary euphemisms
Real World being tactful
Review inversion

QUICK REVIEW ●●●
This activity reviews inversion. Students do the first part of the activity on their own. Put students into pairs. Students take turns to say their partner's sentences without inversion.

1 **a)** Introduce the topic by asking students what they think a euphemism is (a word or phrase used to avoid saying something that could be considered offensive). Ask students if they have an equivalent of euphemism in their own language and whether it is commonly used.

Focus students on the phrases in bold, explaining that these are examples of euphemisms. Do the first question with the whole class.

Students do the exercise on their own or in pairs and check their answers in **V3.4** SB p124.

Check answers with the class.

> 2 an old person 3 old-fashioned 4 is old and in bad condition 5 getting old; not able to hear well/a bit deaf
> 6 ill 7 difficult to look after; very difficult 8 cold

b) Students do the exercise in pairs.

> — **EXTRA IDEA** —
> ● ✎ Write other euphemisms on the board and see if students can guess the real meaning. For example: *between jobs* (unemployed), *pass away* (die), *put an animal to sleep* (painlessly kill an animal which is ill and in pain; a vet does this), *start a family* (have a first child), *affordable* (cheap), *low-income* (poor).

2 **a)** Focus students on the pictures and ask them to describe what is happening in each and what emotions each of the characters might be expressing.

Students do the exercise in pairs. Elicit ideas from the class.

> **Possible answers**
> A disagree B refuse an invitation C complain
> D give your opinion

b) Make sure students understand what being tactful means (being careful not to say or do anything that could upset someone).

Students do the exercise in pairs. Elicit ideas from the class.

Make sure students understand that you would probably be more tactful in situations A, B and D, where you have some kind of personal relationship with the person to whom you're speaking.

3 **a)** Tell students they are going to listen to four conversations in which people respond to situations A–D. Point out that for each situation they are going to hear the same person respond in two different ways. Be prepared with definitions, examples, etc. to pre-teach *hips* and *tough*.

R3.5 Play the recording (SB p151). Students listen and match each conversation to situations A–D in **2a)**.

Check answers with the class.

> 1B 2D 3A 4C

b) Play the recording again. Students listen and answer the question. They compare answers in pairs.

> 1a) 2b) 3b) 4a)

> — **EXTRA IDEA** —
> ● Ask students to discuss what it was that made those responses sound more tactful. Refer students to R3.5, SB p151 and ask them to find examples of tactful language.

Real World Being tactful

4 **a)–b)** Students do the exercise on their own or in pairs and check their answers in **RW3.1** SB p126.

Check answers with the class.

> ● **a)** 2 using modals
>   3 using vague language
>   4 not sounding negative
>   5 using adverbs of attitude
> ● Point out that some of the words/phrases presented in **RW3.1** SB p126 will be instantly recognisable to native speakers as expressions used to say something tactfully. For example, if you said to your boss *We must all get together some time*, he or she would probably recognise it as an excuse for not committing to a social engagement. Likewise, if you told your host that the steak they had just cooked for you was *on the tough side*, it would still be taken as a criticism of their cooking, even though it was delivered in a more tactful way than *it was tough*. Finally, if you told a friend who was appearing in a play that you'd *seen better performances*, he or she would still probably take it as a direct criticism.

- Point out that using past forms in this context is most common when making excuses for not accepting an invitation, as in this example. It is also common when explaining tactfully why you haven't done or didn't do something. Other verb forms which refer to the past (e.g. the Present Perfect) can also be used: *I've been meaning to call you, but I've been really busy* or *I was going to let you know about the party, but I didn't think you'd want to go.*

5 Tell students that tone of voice is important when being tactful.

 Play the recording (SB p151). Students listen and practise saying the sentences.

Point out how we use a slower, more hesitant rhythm when we are trying to say something tactfully.

Also point out that certain words are stressed in each sentence, either because they are content words or because the speaker wants to contrast one thing with another:
We were <u>planning</u> to <u>go</u> to the <u>cinema</u> <u>tomorrow</u>.
I'd <u>go</u> for <u>black</u> <u>instead</u>, if <u>I</u> were <u>you</u>.
We must <u>all</u> <u>get</u> <u>together</u> <u>some</u> <u>time</u>.
I <u>think</u> <u>darker</u> <u>colours</u> <u>suit</u> you <u>better</u>.
And quite <u>honestly</u>, I've <u>seen</u> <u>better</u> <u>performances</u>.

6 a) Students do the exercise on their own or in pairs. Check answers with the class.

> 1 B 2 C 3 A 4 D

b) Students do the exercise in pairs. Check answers with the class.

Possible answers
1 Unfortunately, we've got other plans. Let's do it soon, though. 2 Some dishes were fine, but others not so good. 3 I think the ending could have been better. 4 You might want to try a more appropriate colour for this occasion.

7 a) Focus students on conversations 1–4. Do the first question with the class. Students do the exercise in pairs. Check answers with the class.

Possible answers
1 Unfortunately, we can't next weekend. We were planning to go to Lisbon. 2 It was quite good. I thought the staff at the hotel were on the rude side, though. 3 Well, that style's definitely in fashion this season; but I wonder if longer hair suits you better. 4 The room could do with being a little bigger, to be honest.

b) Students work in groups of four. Tell one pair in each group to act out one of their conversations. The other pair suggests improvements to make the responses more tactful.

8 a) Put students into pairs. Students write a conversation for one of situations 1–3 and then role-play it.

b) Students swap papers with another pair. Encourage students to extend the conversation as far as possible.

— EXTRA IDEA —
- Ask one or two more confident pairs to act out their whole conversation in front of the class.

┌─ EXTRA PRACTICE AND HOMEWORK ─
│ Ph **Class Activity** 3C Tactful or tactless? p141 (Instructions p121)
│ Ph **Class Activity** 1–3 Review Board game p142 (Instructions p121)
│ **3 Review** Exercise 7 SB p34
│ **CD-ROM** Lesson 3C
│ **Workbook** Lesson 3C p18
│ **Workbook** Reading and Writing Portfolio 3 p60
│ **Preview 4** Exercises 1 and 2 SB p35

3 Review

See p32 for ideas on how to use this section.

1 2 trusting 3 cautious 4 meticulous 5 spontaneous 6 confident 7 thrifty 8 determined

2 2 Holly soon realised it was impossible to get a work permit. 3 It would be wonderful to have more free time. 4 I'd love it if you came round to visit more often. 5 I'd appreciate it if you could turn down the heating. 6 I find it difficult to concentrate when there's music on.

3 2 It's no secret that Pat's after the top job. 3 It can't be that difficult to get there by public transport. 4 It's obvious that everyone is completely exhausted. 5 It's no use asking him to help. 6 It isn't easy looking after young children all day.

4a) 1 reckless 2 arrogant 3 extravagant 4 finicky 5 gullible 6 obstinate 7 impetuous 8 timid 9 tight-fisted

5 1 down; on 2 up; around 3 up; out 4 up; over

6 2 did I hate 3 should anyone drive 4 did I understand 5 did we manage 6 do you find 7 did I realise 8 have we begun

7 1 challenging 2 bit of a handful 3 be economical with the truth 4 getting on a bit 5 senior citizens 6 a bit on the chilly side

Progress Portfolio

See p32 for ideas on how to use this section.

Accurate Writing

CONNECTING WORDS: contrast (1)
SPELLING: one word, two words or hyphenated

 a)–b) Students do the exercise on their own or in pairs and check their answers in **AW3.1** SB p126.

Check answers with the class.

Students may struggle with the difference between *whereas* and *although/even though*. Point out that while *whereas* and *although/even though* are used to contrast information in two clauses, *whereas* is always used to introduce an element of comparison into the contrast. If students are in doubt about which word to use, ask them to identify the two clauses in the sentence and decide if there is any element of comparison; if there is, they should use *whereas*. For example, Clause 1: *They fell asleep* Clause 2: *I was awake for hours* = comparing falling asleep and being awake. Clause 1: *I can't drive* Clause 2: *I've had lessons* = a contrast, but no comparison.

If students are confused about when to use *but* and when to use *however*, point out that if you want to contrast information between two clauses in the same sentence, you should use *but*. To contrast information in two separate sentences, *however* is better. This rule should help your students avoid mistakes.

Highlight that many native speakers use incorrect punctuation with *however*, especially when it links two main clauses: ~~Our flight was delayed, however we still arrived on time~~. *Our flight was delayed; however, we still arrived on time.*

> **a)** **2** They fell asleep, whereas I was awake for hours.
> **3** I can't drive, although I've had lessons. **4** Amy still plays tennis, whereas I stopped playing ages ago.
> **5** I got lost, although I'd been there before.
>
> **b)** **1** Although/Even though **2** although/even though/ but **3** Whereas **5** Although/Even though **5** Although/ Even though **6** However **7** whereas/but **8** However

 Students do the exercise on their own or in pairs and check their answers in **AW3.2** SB p126.

Check answers with the class.

Remind students that if they are in any doubt about whether something should be one word, two words or hyphenated, they should consult their dictionary. Encourage students to record multiple entries in their vocabulary books for words which have more than one form, showing when each form is used.

Point out that two-word adjectives are usually hyphenated (*a well-behaved child, a two-bedroomed house, a half-hearted attempt*).

> **1** everyday **2** Every one **3** hundred-year-old
> **4** anyone **5** any way **6** may be

 a)–b) Focus students on the extract. Point out that in addition to the four underlined mistakes, there are five spelling mistakes. Ask students to concentrate on the underlined mistakes first, and then correct the spelling mistakes.

Students do the exercises on their own or in pairs.

Check answers with the class.

> **Everyone** I know feels low at times, [1]**whereas** I honestly don't. [2]**Although/Even though** I do sometimes feel a bit low on energy, it's not something that happens **every day**. **Maybe** it's related to the weather.
>   **Anyway**, when I do feel a bit low on energy I have a quick shower and that usually works. [3]**However**, my brother is very different. If he's a bit low, he actually goes for a **ten-kilometre** run. [4]**Although/Even though** he's actually 39, he sometimes behaves like a 20-year-old fitness fanatic!

— EXTRA IDEA —

* For homework, ask students to write a short essay about what they do when they feel down. Ask them to contrast what they do with what a friend or family member does.

— EXTRA PRACTICE AND HOMEWORK —

Workbook Accurate Writing Exercises 5 and 6 p84–p85

Preview 4

FUTURE VERB FORMS

 1 Students do the exercise on their own or in pairs and check their answers in `G4.1` SB p127.

Check answers with the class.

Highlight the following contrasts, which may still be causing students problems at this level:

- Present Simple v. Present Continuous for timetabled events (e.g. *the train leaves at ten* v. *I'm getting an early flight tomorrow*);
- arrangement v. plan or intention (arrangements often being things that you would have written in your diary);
- *will* v. *be going to* for predictions (although there is often very little difference).

b)1 c)3 d)4 e)7 f)8 g)5 h)6

 2 Students do the exercise on their own or in pairs and check their answers in `G4.1` SB p127.

Check answers with the class.

1 have finished; I'll try 2 'm going to call; 'll be seeing him 3 going to get; won't start 4 start; 'll enjoy 5 'll be leaving; gets

4 Civilised

Student's Book p36–p45

4A Society and the media

Student's Book p36–p45

QUICK REVIEW ●●●

This activity reviews euphemisms. Students do the first part of the activity on their own. Set a time limit of two minutes. Put students into pairs. Students take turns to make sentences using the phrases from their partner's list. Encourage students to use any other euphemisms they may have encountered since lesson 3C.

Vocabulary News collocations

 a) Introduce the topic by pointing out that there are several common collocations in English related to the news and media.

Students do the exercise on their own and check their answers in **V4.1** SB p127. Check answers with the class.

Model and drill the collocations, paying particular attention to the pronunciation of *tabloid* /'tæblɔɪd/, *glossy* and *libel* /'laɪbəl/.

Remind students that verb–noun collocations are only one of the types of collocation that exist in English. Other types include adverb–adjective (e.g. *highly desirable*), adjective–noun (e.g. *tall building*), noun–noun (e.g. *customer service*), verb–preposition (e.g. *get on*) and verb–adverb (e.g. *see clearly*).

Point out that although *tabloid* refers to the size of the newspaper, the word is commonly used to refer to a type of newspaper – that is, a popular paper with lots of pictures and short, simple stories. The opposite of a *tabloid* is a *broadsheet*, originally named because it was printed in a larger format than a *tabloid*. However, in the UK many broadsheet papers are now printed in tabloid format (e.g. *The Times*); their content means that they are not referred to as tabloids, though. The differences between tabloid and broadsheet newspapers is discussed in more depth in lesson 4C.

Also point out that *libel* refers mainly to written statements; spoken statements of a similar nature are referred to as *slander*. The adjective from *libel* is *libellous*: *He's being sued for a libellous article he wrote last year.*

Finally, point out that *the headlines* refers to the main points of the news that are broadcast on television or radio (e.g. *This is the six o'clock news. The headlines today: …*), whereas *a headline* is the title of a story in a newspaper.

> read the tabloids/glossy magazines; seek publicity; hold a press conference; receive a lot of coverage; sue for libel; hit the headlines; make the front page; issue a press release; run a story

Vocabulary news collocations
Grammar phrases referring to the future
Review euphemisms

─ **EXTRA IDEAS** ─

• Students work in pairs and take turns to test each other on the collocations. One student says a word/phrase from column B in **1a)** (e.g. *the headlines*), and his/her partner says the whole collocation (e.g. *hit the headlines*).

• Ask students to find other examples of collocations in **V4.1** (*glossy magazines, press conference, front page* and *press release*).

b) Students do the exercise on their own. Check answers with the class.

> 1 glossy 2 seek 3 coverage 4 make 5 sued 6 run

c) Students do the exercise in pairs. Encourage students to ask follow-up questions. Ask each pair to share their ideas with the class.

Reading and Grammar

 a) Students do the exercise in pairs. Elicit ideas from the class.

b) Focus students on the words and phrases in the box. Students check the meaning of the words and phrases. Be prepared with definitions, examples, etc. to give students if necessary.

Model and drill the words, paying particular attention to the pronunciation of *axe* /æks/, *lawsuit* /'lɔːsuːt/ and *spouse* /spaʊs/. Point out that the word *suit*, as in *lawsuit*, is derived from the word *sue*, which students looked at in **1a)**.

c) Focus students on the four news items and the five headlines a)–e). You can set a time limit of two minutes to encourage students to read for gist. Students do the exercise on their own, and then compare answers in pairs. Check answers with the class.

> a) 1 b) 3 c) 4 d) Does not belong to any of the stories
> e) 2

d) Students do the exercise on their own. Encourage students to paraphrase information from the articles rather than reproduce it verbatim.

Check answers with the class.

Possible answers

1 a) … they want the aviation industry to pay for the impact it has on the environment. **b)** … they already have to pay more money to fly during the school holidays.

2 a) … they are being sued for $65 million for losing a pair of trousers that were later found. **b)** … two signs that were displayed on the dry cleaner's walls, which says made fraudulent claims.

3 a) … they want to reduce the number of accidents caused by young drivers. **b)** … a no-alcohol limit for newly qualified drivers for their first year, regardless of age.

4 a) … not guilty of 'invasion of privacy'. **b)** … homes.

EXTRA IDEA

- Write these words and phrases from the articles on the board: *the height of, premium, fraud, undergo, ruling.* Ask students to guess the meaning of the words and phrases from the context. Ask what helped them guess.

---

3 Students discuss the questions in groups. Ask each group to share their ideas with the class.

Help with Grammar Phrases referring to the future

Ask students to do **1** and **2** in Preview 4, SB p35 if necessary.

4 a)–d) Students do the exercises on their own or in pairs and check their answers in G4.2 SB p127.
Check answers with the class.

- **a)** **b)** **The** driving age **is** set to rise. **c)** **The** sale of bugging devices **is** about to go through **the** roof. **d)** **A/The** new TV boss **is** on the verge of axing reality TV shows. **e)** **A** dry cleaner's **is** to face **a** lawsuit over **a** pair of trousers.
- Point out that newspaper journalists often use the highlighted phrases in headlines a)–e) to refer to the future in headlines.
- Explain that to make a headline into a sentence we might need to add articles or missing auxiliary verbs.
- **b)** 1 the words/phrases in pink
  2 the words/phrases in blue
- Point out that of all the phrases used to talk about something that is ready to happen, probably in the near future, *about to* is used to refer to things that are most imminent: *Get the umbrella – it's about to rain.*
- **c)** We use a verb+*ing* (or noun) after *on the verge of.* We use an infinitive after the other phrases.
- Point out that *due to* is usually used to talk about a specific time: *Building work is due to start in March.*

- Point out that we sometimes use *not about to* to mean 'not willing to': *I'm not about to drop everything just to go and pick her up from the station.*
- Explain that we can also say *on the point/brink of* + verb+*ing* (or noun) to refer to things in the near future. Highlight that *on the brink of* usually refers to something bad, exciting or important and is more formal than *on the point of*: *A large bank is on the brink of collapse.*
- Point out that we can't refer to a specific time after *on the verge of/on the brink of*: *He's on the verge of/on the brink of resigning ~~next week~~.*

5 Students do the exercise on their own or in pairs. Check answers with the class.

2 is due to retire **3** are on the verge of turning back
4 is about to sign **5** is to settle for

EXTRA IDEA

- As a class, brainstorm five current news stories in which something is ready to happen and write them on the board. Ask students to write headlines for each story, using the phrases from G4.2 , SB p127.

---

6 a) Model the exercise by writing a few sentences of your own on the board. Students do the exercise on their own.

b) Students do the exercise in pairs. Encourage students to ask follow-up questions. Ask each pair to share one or two of their ideas with the class.

Listening

7 a) Students do the exercise on their own. Remind students that in the first instance they should list the most popular programmes in their country, not just the programmes that they like or watch.

b) Students compare lists in pairs. If students are working with a partner from a different country, who may not have heard of the programmes on his/her list, encourage students to describe them. Ask each pair to share their ideas with the class.

EXTRA IDEA

- Before doing **7a)**, brainstorm types of television programme and write them on the board.

---

8 a) Focus students on the news extract. Students do the exercise on their own or in pairs.
Check answers with the class.

Fact-based programmes – for example, documentaries and wildlife films – and drama and comedy.

b) Tell students they are going to listen to two people, Sue and Dan, discussing television programmes. Be prepared with definitions, examples, etc. to pre-teach *bankrupt* /ˈbæŋkrʌpt/, *indictment* /ɪnˈdaɪtmənt/, *template* /ˈtempleɪt/ and *costume drama* /ˈkɒstjʊm ˌdrɑːmə/.

Check students know what *Big Brother* is. (It is one of the original reality TV shows; in it, contestants live in a house for several weeks and have their entire existences filmed and broadcast to the outside world. Every week a contestant is voted off the show until one person, the winner, remains. The show has been a hit in over 70 countries.)

Point out that costume dramas are particularly popular in the UK, and the US to some extent. The genre is characterised by elaborate costumes and sets which are designed to be evocative of a certain time. Many costume dramas are based on historical figures or famous works of literature. Typical examples of TV costume dramas might include *John Adams*, *Great Expectations* and *Pride and Prejudice*.

Focus students on the three questions.

R4.1 Play the recording (SB p151). Students listen and answer the questions.

Check answers with the class.

> 1 Reality TV programmes; they help her to relax.
> 2 He thinks they're 'rubbish' and 'poke fun at people … at their misery'.
> 3 Sport and comedy.

c) Students do the exercise in pairs.

d) Play the recording again. Students listen and check their answers to **8c)**.

Check answers with the class.

> 1 Dan 2 Sue 3 Sue 4 Dan 5 Sue 6 Sue 7 Dan

 9 a) Focus students on the words and phrases in bold. Remind students that all of these words and phrases were used in R4.1.

Students do the exercise on their own or in pairs.

Check answers with the class.

> b) 2 c) 3 d) 5 e) 4

b) Students discuss the question in pairs or groups. Ask each pair or group to share their ideas with the class.

— EXTRA IDEA —
- Write these phrases from the recording on the board: *put your feet up*, *let it wash over you*, *more fool them*. Ask students to look at R4.1, SB p151 and to guess the meaning of the phrases from the context. Ask what helped them guess.

Get ready … Get it right!

10 a) Focus students on the six sentences. Students do the exercise on their own. Give students 5–10 minutes to make a list of reasons why they agree or disagree with the sentences.

b) Students discuss the statements in groups. Encourage students to justify their opinions and to try and persuade any members of the group who don't agree with them to change their minds.

c) Ask each group to share their conclusions with the class.

— EXTRA IDEA —
- Before doing **10a)**, ask students to list how forms of entertainment (e.g. films, television and music) have changed in the last 50 years. How did people use to watch or listen to them (e.g. at the cinema, on VHS tapes)? How do they watch or listen to them now?

— EXTRA PRACTICE AND HOMEWORK —

Ph **Class Activity** 4A No comment! p143 (Instructions p122)

Ph **Vocabulary Plus** 4 Words used in newspaper headlines p175 (Instructions p170)

Ph **Help with Listening** 4 Disagreeing p192 (Instructions p184)

4 Review Exercises 1, 2 and 3 SB p44

CD-ROM Lesson 4A

Workbook Lesson 4A p19

4B Cities and technology

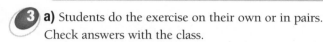
Vocabulary near synonyms
Grammar future in the past
Review phrases referring to the future

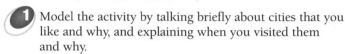

QUICK REVIEW ●●●

This activity reviews phrases referring to the future. Students do the activity in groups. Students discuss stories that are in the news at the moment. Encourage students to use the phrases referring to the future that were introduced in lesson 4A.

Reading and Vocabulary

1 Model the activity by talking briefly about cities that you like and why, and explaining when you visited them and why.

Students do the activity in pairs. Ask each pair to share any interesting experiences with the class.

2 **a)** Focus students on sentences 1–5.

Make sure students understand *trade* and that it can also be used as a verb. Point out that *commerce* is a synonym for *trade* but cannot be used as a verb (*commerce* appears in the article that students are going to read).

Point out that *country* and *countryside* are synonyms only when referring to land not in towns or cities; that is, *countryside* does not mean *country* in the sense of England, France, etc.

Students do the exercise on their own or in pairs.

Check answers with the class.

b) Focus students on the article. Be prepared with definitions, examples, etc. to pre-teach *urban* /ˈɜːbən/, *rural* /ˈrʊərəl/, *forerunner*, *grain*, *hub* and *leap* /liːp/.

Point out that the title of the article – 'The world goes to town' – is a play on words: *go to town* can mean 'travel to the centre of a town', but it can also mean 'do something in an intense, eager way'.

Also point out that a *town* is larger than a village but smaller than a *city*. In the UK, it used to be that all cities had to have cathedrals – that is, if it didn't have a cathedral, it was a town not a city. However, the use of the term *city* is now more commonly based on population size than the presence of a cathedral.

Students do the exercise on their own or in pairs.

Check answers with the class.

Point out that *homo urbanus* is a new term, coined to refer to the fact that most people now live in urban environments. It is a variation of *homo sapiens*.

Possible answers
1 … of the need to find food. **2** … began living together in cities. **3** … war, disease, misgovernment or economic failure. **4** … they were looking for work in the factories. **5** … developments in medicine.

— EXTRA IDEA —
- Before students read the article, ask them to predict from the title what it will be about.

3 **a)** Students do the exercise on their own or in pairs. Check answers with the class.

> **a)** Humans started building villages 11,000 years ago; by that time, man had been around for 120,000 years.
> **b)** In the 1800s, 3% of the world's population lived in cities; nowadays the figure is over 50%.
> **c)** In 1900, 13% of the world's population had become urban; that figure leaped to 50% in little over 100 years and is expected to grow to 75% by 2050.

— EXTRA IDEA —
- Write the numbers on the board. Ask students to close their books and in pairs try to remember what the link between the numbers was.

b) Students do the activity in groups. Ask each group to share their ideas with the class.

— EXTRA IDEA —
- For homework, ask students to turn their notes from **3b)** into a short essay with the title 'People are not designed to live in cities'.

4 Put students into two groups. Students in group A turn to SB p108 and students in group B turn to SB p111.

a) Put students into pairs with someone from the same group. Students do the exercise in pairs.

Check answers with each group individually. Point out that *Mumbai* was formerly known as *Bombay*.

b) Students do the exercise in pairs. Highlight that these figures show by how many people the populations of these cities grow *per hour* not *per day*.

Students will find out the answers in **4d)**.

c)–d) Reorganise the class so that a student from group A is working with a student from group B. Students take turns to give their answers.

— EXTRA IDEA —
- With weaker classes, write the following expressions on the board and encourage students to use them in **4c)–d)**: *We think/We're guessing that/We're pretty sure that/We know that the population of … is growing at a rate of … people per hour/is remaining constant. That's right/wrong.*

e) Ask each pair to share their reactions with the class.

> **EXTRA IDEA**
>
> - Ask students to discuss in pairs or groups why they think the population growth in São Paulo, Shanghai and Mumbai is so high while in Tokyo, Berlin and Warsaw the figures are so low. What factors might be contributing to the growth rates? Ask each pair or group to share their ideas with the class.

Help with Vocabulary Near synonyms

Introduce the topic by reminding students why we use synonyms (to avoid repeating the same words so that what we say or write sounds less repetitive and more interesting).

Focus students on the example sentences. Point out that *huge* and *large* and *immigrants* and *people* are what we call 'near' or 'partial' synonyms – words which are similar in meaning but which are not always interchangeable in all contexts.

 a)–b) Students do the exercises on their own or in pairs and check their answers in V4.2 SB p127.

Check answers with the class.

> - **a)** 2 a village a settlement
>   3 country folk rural inhabitants villagers
>   4 improvements developments
>   5 the land the countryside
>   6 disease pestilences
> - Highlight that not all near synonyms are interchangeable in all contexts. This can be because the words vary in their degree of **formality**. For example, *kid* is more informal than *child*. We could say either to a friend: *How are the children/kids?* However, in more formal, written English we would not find the word *kid*: *There are 14.8 million children in the UK.* It can also be because of **collocation**. We can say *a huge/large number*, but *large* does not collocate with *problem*: *a huge/~~large~~ problem*. Other near synonyms are not interchangeable because of the **grammatical agreement** involved. For example, we can say *I like/enjoy travelling*. We can also say *I like to travel*, but not *I enjoy to travel*. Finally, **connotation** can mean that near synonyms are not interchangeable. If we describe someone as *determined* or *obstinate*, each word has different connotations. *Determined* has positive connotations whereas *obstinate* has negative ones.
> - Advise students to check in an online thesaurus if they want to find synonyms (and antonyms), for example, http://thesaurus.reference.com. However, also point out that they should be wary of overusing the synonym function on their word processor, if they have one, for the very reasons outlined in the **TIP!** – that the words may not in fact be interchangeable. If in doubt, students should consult both words in their dictionary to check usage.

 Focus students on the words and phrases in the box. Students check the meaning of the words and phrases. Be prepared with definitions, examples, etc. to give students if necessary. Students do the exercise in pairs. Remind students that they will need to change the form of some of the words to fit the context.

Check answers with the class.

> 1 enjoy 2 urban 3 gazing at 4 passers-by 5 vehicles
> 6 standstill 7 are forced to 8 exasperating
> 9 suddenly 10 allow

 Focus students on the example. Students do the exercise on their own or in pairs.

Check answers with the class.

> 2 gazing at 3 enjoy 4 mate 5 furious 6 reckless

> **EXTRA IDEA**
>
> - Students work in pairs and take turns to test each other on the near synonyms. One student says a word in italics from **7**, for example, *big*, and his/her partner says the near synonym(s).

Listening and Grammar

 a) Focus students on photos 1–4. Remind students that *Star Trek* is a science-fiction television programme which aired from 1966 to 1969. Seventy-nine episodes were produced, and the show spawned numerous spin-offs. Set in the 23rd century, *Star Trek* follows the adventures of a spaceship called the *Starship Enterprise* and its crew. *Star Trek: The Next Generation* was a spin-off show which began in 1987 and ran until 1994. The events in the show take place 80 years after the original *Star Trek*.

Check that students understand *prop*.

Students discuss the question in pairs or groups.

Check suggestions with the class and write them on the board.

b) Tell students they are going to listen to extracts from a documentary about *Star Trek*. Be prepared with definitions, examples, etc. to pre-teach *rival* /ˈraɪvəl/, *probe*, *prototype* /ˈprəʊtəʊtaɪp/, *MRI* /eməˈrˈaɪ/ (see below), and *CT scan* /siːˈtiːˌskæn/ (see p59).

R4.2 Play the recording (SB p151). Students listen and check their answers to **8a)**.

Check answers with the class, comparing them to the suggestions which you wrote on the board in **8a)**.

Point out that *cell phone* is American English; in British English the term is *mobile (phone)*.

Also point out that *NASA* /ˈnæsə/ (The National Aeronautics and Space Administration) is an agency of the United States government, established in 1958, which is responsible for the country's public space programme.

Point out that *MRI* stands for *magnetic resonance imaging*; it is a system used to produce images of the organs inside a human body.

Finally, point out that *CT* stands for *computed tomography*; a *CT scan* takes detailed pictures of areas inside the body from different angles.

Possible answers
1 cell phones 2 space shuttles 3 medical scans, for example, MRI or CT scans 4 Digital music formats and players, for example, MP3s and iPods

— **EXTRA IDEA** —
- ✎ Write these words and phrases from the recording on the board: *bewilderment, interstellar, strive for, beam, pave the way for*. Ask students to look at R4.2, SB p151 and to guess the meaning of the words and phrases from the context. Ask what helped them guess.

9 Play the recording again. Students listen and choose the correct answer.

Check answers with the class.

1 someone working for another company 2 10
3 a scientist involved in the exploration of space
4 leave the solar system 5 wasn't 6 has produced
7 was working for 8 preceded

10 Tell students they are going to listen to some more extracts from the *Star Trek* documentary.

Focus students on speech bubbles A–D. Be prepared with definitions, examples, etc. to pre-teach *earthling* /ˈɜːθlɪŋ/ and *geek* /giːk/.

Point out that Silicon Valley is in California, the United States. The name was originally coined to refer to the large number of companies in the area who designed and manufactured silicon chips for computers, but it is now used to refer to the high-tech sector as a whole.

Also point out that Spock was one of the main characters on *Star Trek*; he is shown lying down in photo 3, SB p41.

R4.3 Play the recording (SB p41). Students listen and fill in gaps 1–4 in speech bubbles A–D.

Check answers with the class.

A into their reality B inventors C modern technology
D entertainment

Help with Grammar Future in the past

11 **a)–d)** Students do the exercises on their own or in pairs and check their answers in **G4.3** SB p128.

Check answers with the class.

- **a)** In the first sentence we know the result (our ideas were successful). In the second sentence we are predicting the result (our ideas are going to be successful).
- **b)** a) 2 b) 1

- **c)** *would* + infinitive
  was/were supposed to + infinitive
  was/were about to + infinitive
  was/were to + infinitive
- Point out that in order to talk about the future seen from the past, we use the past tenses of the verb forms that we would usually use to talk about the future.
- Point out that we often use these forms when we are reporting; for example, if we are recounting what somebody said they were going to do: *She said **she was going to** come early*.
- Remind students that we often need to change time expressions when we talk about the future seen from the past: *There is to be a meeting about it **tomorrow**. → There was to be a meeting about it **the following day***.

12 Students do the exercise on their own or in pairs. Remind students that some of the sentences are correct.

Check answers with the class.

1 Kelly **was** going to come, but her car broke down.
2 I had no idea that it **would** be this exhausting!
3 Correct 4 I **was** about to leave the house when I remembered you were coming. 5 I **was** supposed to call my sister before she left, but I forgot. 6 We **were** to stay in a hotel near the beach, but it closed down.
7 Correct

— **EXTRA IDEA** —
- With lower-level groups, before doing **12**, point out that two of the sentences are correct.

13 **a)** Model the exercise by completing some of the sentences with true and false information about yourself. Ask students to guess which sentences are true. Encourage students to ask follow-up questions.

Students do the exercise on their own. Remind students that at least two of their sentences should be true.

b) Students do the exercise in pairs. Encourage students to ask follow-up questions. Ask each pair to share any particularly interesting sentences that their partner came up with – true or false – with the rest of the class.

Get ready … Get it right!

14 Put students into three groups, group A, group B and group C. Students in group A turn to SB p109, students in group B turn to SB p112 and students in group C turn to p114.

a) Students work in pairs with someone from the same group. Focus students on the pictures. If necessary, pre-teach *umbrella, chopsticks, fishing reel* (p109), *stationery, toilet roll, dispenser* (p112), *commuter* and *headgear* (p114). Students discuss the questions in pairs.

b) Reorganise the class into groups of three, with one person from group A, one from group B and one from group C in each group. Make sure that each group has paper and pens. Students take turns to describe the inventions that they have looked at and explain what they were supposed to do. Focus students on the speech bubbles as an example. Tell students that they should try and draw what is being described to them.

c) Tell students to turn to the appropriate page and compare their drawings. Students discuss which they think is the best and weirdest invention. Ask each group to share their ideas with the class. Finally, ask each group to show the drawings which were closest or furthest from the actual invention.

┌─ EXTRA IDEA ─────────────────────────────
● In groups, students think of two inventions. Ask each group to present their inventions to the class.
└──

┌─ EXTRA PRACTICE AND HOMEWORK ────────────
 Class Activity 4B Guess the word p144 (Instructions p122)
4 Review Exercises 4, 5 and 6 SB p44
CD-ROM Lesson 4B
Workbook Lesson 4B p21
└──

 Making a splash

QUICK REVIEW ●●●
This activity reviews near synonyms. Students write a list of near synonyms on their own. Put students into pairs. Students take turns to tell each other their near synonyms. Check answers with the class.

┌──
Vocabulary newspaper language
Skills Reading: stories from tabloid and broadsheet newspapers; Listening: an interview with a sub-editor; Speaking: creating a front-page news story; Writing: a newspaper story
Real World persuading
Review near synonyms
└──

1 a) Introduce the topic by explaining that there are two types of British newspapers: the tabloids (e.g. the *Daily Mail*, the *Sun*, the *Daily Express*) and the broadsheets (e.g. *The Times*, the *Independent*, the *Daily Telegraph*). Focus students on the two front pages. Point out that the newspapers are from the same day.

Students do the exercise in pairs. Elicit answers from the class. Students will check their answers in **1b)**.

b) Tell students they are going to listen to an interview with Andrew Cook, a sub-editor on a national tabloid newspaper.

Point out that a newspaper sub-editor is responsible for ensuring that the tone, style and layout of the copy submitted by a journalist matches the 'house style' of the newspaper. Sub-editing involves making sure that all of the copy is accurate, makes sense and reads well. Sub-editors also lay out the story on the page and may be involved with overall page design. The activities of a sub-editor are called *subbing* (e.g. *We can't publish that story yet – it hasn't been subbed*).

Be prepared with definitions, examples, etc. to pre-teach *sober* /ˈsəʊbə/ and *downmarket*. Point out that *sober* is used to mean the opposite of *drunk*, but can also be used in the context of *serious*, as in the interview.

Explain that the sub-editor talks about *The Times*, which is a broadsheet, like the *Guardian* in **1a)**.

R4.4 Play the recording (SB p152). Students listen and check their answers to **1a)**.
Check answers with the class.

> 1 The *Daily Mirror* has large headlines and pictures while *The Times* uses smaller headlines and presents the news in a more sober way.
> 2 The *Daily Mirror* is a tabloid and the *Guardian* is a broadsheet.
> 3 Tabloids sell the most.
> 4 Broadsheets appeal to people who are interested in more serious stories; tabloids are more downmarket.

c)–d) Play the recording again. Students listen and complete the sentences. They compare answers in pairs.
Point out that sentences 1–9 are paraphrased – that is, they are not direct extracts from the interview.
Check answers with the class.

> 1 smaller 2 serious; sober 3 think; react 4 800
> 5 3 million 6 political 7 crime 8 the middle 9 families

e) Focus students on the words/phrases in bold. Students do the exercise on their own or in pairs.
Check answers with the class.

1 serious newspapers 2 deliver their message in a very direct and unsubtle way 3 a forceful, immediate attraction 4 with a red band along the top 5 the main story on the front page 6 the core, or main part, of our circulation

---

EXTRA IDEA

- Ask students to discuss which of the two papers they would most like to read, based on the front pages and what Andrew says.

---

 a) Introduce the topic by asking students how they think the writing style of broadsheet and tabloid newspapers might differ, based on what they learnt about them from **1a)–e)**.

Focus students on the two newspaper stories. Be prepared with definitions, examples, etc. to pre-teach *avert*, *catastrophe* /kæˈtæstrəfi/, *swoop in*, *short of*, *crush*, *undercarriage* /ˈʌndəˌkærɪdʒ/, *skid* and *slide*.

Students do the exercise on their own or in pairs. Check answers with the class.

b) Tell students they are going to listen to more of the interview with Andrew Cook. Give them time to read statements 1–3.

R4.5 Play the recording (SB p152). Students listen and decide if the statements are true or false. Then they find examples from story A.

Check answers with the class.

1F The first sentence in story A is 18 words long; the first sentence of story B, which contains more or less the same information, contains 27 words. 2T For example, *heroic*, *averted catastrophe* and *swooped in*. 3T Story A contains four separate paragraphs, whereas story B contains only two.

---

c) Students do the exercise on their own or in pairs. Check answers with the class.

Point out that *snappy* can also mean 'sharp and irritable': *Don't be snappy with me! I'm only trying to help*. It can also be used to describe someone who dresses fashionably and well: *He's a very snappy dresser*.

Also point out that *crisp* in the sense of 'very clear' can also be used to describe the weather, especially in winter: *A crisp winter's day*.

Finally, point out that *crash, bang, wallop* is used to describe something loud and usually painful: *I was standing at the top of the stairs and suddenly – crash, bang, wallop – I was at the bottom of the stairs! Wallop* means 'hit something hard'.

---

1 Shorter, more concise language that gets your attention or communicates an idea quickly. 2 Sentences which are very clear. 3 A very simple, direct style. 4 Showing that you understand the audience.

---

d) Students discuss the questions in pairs or groups. If you have a multinational class, group different nationalities together.

Ask each pair or group to share one or two of their ideas with the class.

 Tell students they are going to listen to one more extract from the interview with Andrew, in which he explains how a story gets chosen for the front page of a tabloid newspaper.

R4.6 Play the recording (SB p152). Students listen and answer the questions.

Check answers with the class. Point out that a news editor is different from a sub-editor. The news editor is responsible for the overall content and direction of a newspaper; many final decisions on which stories are run, and in which part of the newspaper, rest with the news editor.

---

1 The news editor.
2 In the most exciting and accessible way.
3 The editor.

 Put students into three groups, group A, group B and group C. Students in group A turn to SB p110, students in group B turn to SB p113 and students in group C turn to SB p114. Tell students that group A are news editors from a tabloid paper and that groups B and C are reporters. The reporters are going to have to convince the news editors that their stories deserve to be on the front page.

Students work in pairs with someone from the same group. Be prepared with definitions, examples, etc. to pre-teach *gale*, *pensioner* /ˈpenʃənə/, *hailed* and *trace*. Students write the first paragraph of their story.

Reorganise the class into groups of three, with one person from group A, one from group B and one from group C in each group. Focus students on the Real World box. Model and drill the sentences, paying particular attention to how the words are stressed in order to sound more persuasive.

Student Bs and student Cs present their stories to student As. Tell student As to give clear reasons for why they have chosen one story.

Ask each student A to share his/her reasons for choosing that story with the class.

EXTRA IDEA

- Ask students to rate each other: did they come across as persuasive and convincing? If so, what did they do well? If not, how could they improve?

Writing Extension

 This activity can be set for homework. Encourage students to use the information in **2a)–c)** to make sure their writing is in the correct style.

Ask students to turn to SB p106 and look at *Summer in the City*. This song was recorded by The Lovin' Spoonful and was a number one hit for the band in the summer of 1966.

 Students discuss the questions in groups. Ask each group to share their ideas with the class.

 a)–b) R4.7 Play the recording. Students listen and do the exercise on their own and compare answers in pairs.

Check answers with the class.

> 2 neck 3 Been 4 a shadow 5 half dead 6 Walking
> 7 world 8 a girl 9 dance 10 heat 11 pity 12 can't
> 13 Cool 14 pretty 15 cat 16 look 17 wheezing
> 18 meet

3 a) Students do the exercise on their own.

Check answers with the class.

> a) sidewalk b) cool c) wheezing

b) Students do the exercise in pairs.

Check answers with the class.

> **1 and 2 Pros:** summer nights are fun (*but at night it's a different world … despite the heat it'll be all right*); people dress nicely and look good in the summer evenings (*dressing so fine and looking so pretty*); there are lots of opportunities to meet girls (*go out and find a girl*)
> **Cons:** feeling dirty (*back of my neck getting dirty and gritty*); the intense heat (*walking on the sidewalk, hotter than a match head*); not being able to escape the heat (*Doesn't seem to be a shadow in the city*); people not looking their best (*all around, people looking half dead*)

— EXTRA PRACTICE AND HOMEWORK —

Ph **Class Activity** 4C The powers of persuasion p145 (Instructions p123)
CD-ROM Lesson 4C
Workbook Lesson 4C p23
Workbook Reading and Writing Portfolio 4 p63
Progress Test 4 p210
Preview 5 Exercise 1 SB p45

4 Review

See p32 for ideas on how to use this section.

> **1** 1 receive 2 hold 3 seek 4 read 5 run 6 hit 7 sue
>
> **2a)** 1 going to retire 2 is about to 3 is due to have 4 sure to/bound to 5 unlikely to/probably not going to 6 are set to fall 7 on the point of applying/about to apply
>
> **4a)** 2e) 3d) 4b) 5c) 6g) 7f)
>
> **5a)** 2 huge 3 friend 4 infuriates 5 like 6 made 7 allowed
>
> **5b)** 1 Yes 2 No (collocation) 3 No (formality) 4 Yes 5 No

> (grammatical agreement) 6 No (grammatical agreement) 7 No (grammatical agreement)
>
> **6a)** 2 was supposed to call 3 wouldn't stay 4 was about to leave 5 was going to be 6 would join 7 were going to demonstrate 8 was just going to call 9 would bump

Progress Portfolio

> See p32 for ideas on how to use this section.

Accurate Writing

CONNECTING WORDS: contrast (2)
PUNCTUATION: capital letters and full stops

 Students do the exercise on their own or in pairs and check their answers in AW4.1 SB p128.

Check answers with the class.

Point out that it is not generally acceptable in written language to use *however* after *but*. (*The government's latest measures are a step in the right direction, but, ~~however~~, they don't go far enough.*)

Highlight that we do not use *in spite of/despite* as conjunctions. We use *although/though*: *Although he was late, he stopped to buy some flowers*. not *~~In spite of/Despite he was late~~ …*

Point out that after *in spite of/despite* we usually use a noun or verb+*ing*: **In spite of/Despite** *the weather, we had a great time*. **In spite of/Despite** *being late, they allowed us into the theatre.*

> 1 but 2 Although 3 In spite of 4 Nevertheless/However 5 nevertheless 6 Despite 7 In spite of 8 Despite/In spite of 9 Nevertheless

 Students do the exercise on their own or in pairs and check their answers in AW4.2 SB p128.

Check answers with the class.

Point out that full stops are not normally used after abbreviations if the last letter of the abbreviation is the same as the last letter of the word when written in full (e.g. *Mister, Mr*). However, we put a full stop after an abbreviation if the last letter of the abbreviation is different from the last letter of the word when written in full (e.g. *Professor, Prof.*).

Also point out that it is becoming increasingly common for people to use fewer capital letters in text messages and also sometimes in informal emails. Although this is generally acceptable, it does depend strongly on the context of the message. A formal email should always be written using correct capitalisation.

> The circled full stops are optional.
> **Dear S**am,
> **I**'ll meet you on **T**ues. 11 **D**ec. at **W**aterloo **S**tation at 8⊙30 a⊙m. **I**'ve checked out films, music gigs, etc. There's loads on. **D**o you fancy a trip down the **R**iver **T**hames? **I**f you do, we could get a boat to the **T**ower of **L**ondon. **L**ook forward to showing you the sights.
> **A**ll the best,
> **P**ete
>
> **M**r **S**am **B**aker
> 25 **L**ime **S**t⊙
> **B**radford
> **BD**5 8**LM**
> **U**⊙**K**⊙

 a)–c) Focus students on the extract. Point out that in addition to the underlined mistakes, there are also mistakes with capital letters and full stops. Ask students to focus on the underlined mistakes first.

Students do the exercises on their own or in pairs.

Check answers with the class.

> Have you ever been to New York.[incorrect]? I went to New York, U.S.A. [matter of personal style] for the first time last **D**ecember. The trip was a birthday present from my **parents**. [1]**Despite/In spite of** only being there for a long weekend, **T**hursday to **S**unday, I had an amazing time. I visited all the main sights, **t**he Rockefeller Building, Central Park, etc. – they were great. In fact, [2]**although** it snowed, I went to the **park** every day. I stayed with my father's friends – Prof. [matter of personal style] Anais Boyer and Dr. [matter of personal style] Pierre Boyer, who both teach at New York University. Their apartment is quite far from the city centre, but [3]**nevertheless** I walked into town every day.

> ─ EXTRA PRACTICE AND HOMEWORK ─
> **Workbook** Accurate Writing Exercises 7 and 8 p85

Preview 5

REFLEXIVE PRONOUNS (1)

 Students do the exercise on their own or in pairs and check their answers in **G5.1** SB p130.

Check answers with the class.

Point out that some verbs that are reflexive in other languages aren't reflexive in English, for example, *meet, relax, feel*.

> **1** In sentence a), she is teaching someone else to swim. In sentence b), she's not teaching anybody else to swim – that is, she is the student and the teacher.
> **2** In sentence a) the children are allowed to read books individually. In sentence b) each child is allowed to read a story to another child or other children.
> **3** In sentence a) someone else is going to redecorate the house. In sentence b) the speaker is emphasising the fact that he/she is going to redecorate the house, not someone else.
> **4** In sentence a) Geoff went to the cinema alone. In sentence b) he simply went to the cinema.

VERB + INFINITIVE WITH *TO* OR VERB+*ING* (1)

 Students do the exercise on their own or in pairs and check their answers in **V5.2** SB p129.

Check answers with the class.

> **1** to cut down on **2** allow **3** to choose **4** to keep on **5** watching **6** to find **7** to break **8** sitting down **9** to see **10** (to) organise **11** thinking **12** to take up **13** to play

5 It's just a job!

Student's Book p46–p55

5A Behind the glamour

Student's Book p46–p55

Vocabulary word building (1): prefixes with multiple meanings
Grammar reflexive pronouns (2)
Review news collocations

QUICK REVIEW ●●●
This activity reviews news collocations. Students do the first part of the activity on their own. Set a time limit of two minutes. Put students into pairs. Students take turns to say the noun in the collocation; their partner says the verb. Encourage stronger students to practise noun–noun and adjective–noun collocations, too – for example, *press release* and *glossy magazine*.

Reading and Vocabulary

 Introduce the topic by asking students who the biggest celebrities are in their country and why they are famous. Ask students who they think the biggest celebrities in the English-speaking world are.

Focus students on the two questions. Students discuss the questions in pairs. Ask each pair to share their ideas with the class.

─ EXTRA IDEA ─
● As another way of introducing the topic, bring a selection of images of celebrities from the English-speaking world to class and ask students if they recognise them or can guess why they are famous.

 a) Introduce the topic by asking students what they think a personal assistant (PA) to a celebrity does.

Focus students on the words and phrases in the box. Students check the meaning of the words and phrases. Be prepared with definitions, examples, etc. to give to students if necessary.

Model and drill the words and phrases, highlighting the pronunciation of *drudgery* /ˈdrʌdʒəri/ and *limo* /ˈlɪməʊ/. Point out that *limo* is short for *limousine*.

Students do the exercise in pairs. Remind students that they are discussing the advantages and disadvantages of being a PA to a celebrity – not of being a celebrity. Ask each pair to share their ideas with the class.

b) Focus students on the photo and elicit that the PA is the woman on the right, and Sharon Stone is the woman on the left. Students do the exercise in pairs. Check answers with the class.

Point out that *Cinderella* is a popular fairy tale in which a young woman is forced to work hard for her family, with no reward.

Also point out that a *premiere* is the first opening night of a new film; it is often a celebrity-filled event, where the stars of the film arrive by limo and walk up a red carpet to the entrance of the cinema. *Roll out the red carpet* means 'give an important person a special welcome'.

Advantages
proximity to the stars; feeling powerful; dressing up in the celebrity's clothes and going to a premiere; feeling like 'superwoman'
Disadvantages
not paid particularly well; round-the-clock obligations; drudgery; the job an end in itself, not a stepping stone to fame; no real friendship or interaction with the celebrity

─ EXTRA IDEA ─
● ✍ Write these words and phrases from the article on the board: *break in, stand to reason, round-the-clock, the bulk of, stepping stone, humble, stupor*. Ask students to guess the meaning of the words and phrases from the context. Ask what helped them guess.

3 a) Students do the exercise on their own or in pairs. Encourage students to find examples in the article to support their answers. Do the first question with the class. Check answers with the class.

1 *have their own organisation* (… is also home to the Association of Celebrity Personal Assistants …)
2 *to be near famous people* (Proximity to the stars appears to be the only perk … the job is usually an end in itself, rather than a stepping stone to fame.)
3 *feel important* (We assistants are the gatekeepers, and that's a powerful position to be in.)
4 *sacrifice their own domestic life* (… it's probably better if you don't have a spouse, or kids, or pets or even plants.)
5 *selfless* (The most important thing is not to express or even think about your own needs.)
6 *challenges* (Another, more common joy came on the days when she worked so hard she was almost in a stupor. "If … you've done all the things they throw at you … you feel like superwoman.")
7 *having more time for herself* (… she was also serious about making more time for herself.)

b) Focus students on the two questions. Students discuss the questions in pairs.

Ask each pair to share their ideas with the class.

Help with Vocabulary Word building (1): prefixes with multiple meanings

Go through the introductory bullet with the class and check students understand what a prefix is (a letter or group of letters that is added to the beginning of a word to make a different word).

 4 **a)–c)** Students do the exercises on their own or in pairs and check their answers in **V5.1** SB p129.

Check answers with the class.

> - **a)** b) counter- c) super- d) over- e) semi-
>   f) under- g) pseudo-
> - **b)** 1b) 2c) 3f) 4a) 5d) 6e)
> - Point out that students shouldn't confuse *inter-* with *intra-*, which means 'within' as opposed to 'between' (e.g. *intra-EU trade* = trade within the EU).
> - Point out that although some prefixes are similar in meaning (e.g. *over-* and *super-*), they are rarely, if ever, interchangeable.
> - Highlight that *super-* can also mean 'over' or 'above'. For example, the *superstructure* is the part of a building that is above ground (i.e. not the foundations).
> - Point out that *pseudo-* is often used disapprovingly.
> - Finally, point out that words which begin with prefixes are sometimes hyphenated and sometimes not. Most prefixes are often (but not always) hyphenated when used adjectivally, but there are no firm rules. Advise students to check in their dictionaries.

 5 **a)** Students do the exercise on their own or in pairs.
Check answers with the class.

> 1 over 2 over/under 3 inter 4 counter 5 semi
> 6 super

b) Students ask and answer the questions in pairs. Encourage students to ask follow-up questions.

Ask each pair to share their ideas with the class.

Listening and Grammar

 6 **a)** Introduce the topic by asking students what an 'extra' is and what their job might involve. Focus students on the photo.

Students discuss the questions in pairs.

Ask each pair to share some of their ideas with the class.

b) Tell students they are going to listen to an interview with two extras.

Write the three headings from **6a)** on the board.

Be prepared with definitions, examples, etc. to pre-teach *amateur dramatics* /ˌæmətə drəˈmætɪks/, *hang around*, *fall into sth*, *bump into*, *standoffish*, *fray* (in the context of *nerves do get frayed*) and *dip in/out of*.

R5.1 Play the recording (SB p152). Students listen and make notes and then compare notes in pairs.

 Elicit answers from the class and write them on the board. Point out that the *principals* that Kate refers to are the main actors on the set.

> **Working hours** You never know when you're going to be needed; long; unpredictable
> **Pay** You get paid more if you have to react to what someone says; money not bad at all, for what you do; money reasonable
> **Kind of roles they get** Crowd scenes, as a wedding guest or person in street; sometimes postman or taxi driver

c) Tell students they are going to listen again to Daniel.
R5.2 Play the recording (SB p152). Students listen and answer the questions.
Check answers with the class.

> 1 He's always been keen on amateur dramatics and sees being an extra as keeping in contact with the acting world. 2 He's a writer, so he always takes his laptop with him and gets on with some work. 3 Half the time, he can't even spot himself unless he really concentrates. 4 It makes a change, and he gets paid more, but it's disappointing when he is edited out, which often happens. 5 He doesn't think there is any chance that it will happen.

7 **a)** Tell students they are going to listen again to Kate.
R5.3 Play the recording (SB p152). Students listen and answer the questions.
Check answers with the class.

> 1 She knew someone who had done it and thought it would be a good way of supplementing her income and enjoying herself at the same time. 2 All sorts of people: young drama students, solicitors, bored housewives. 3 The stars themselves are quite friendly on the whole. 4 Lots of standing around; there are times when you feel very tired; if there are delays, nerves get frayed; the hours are unpredictable. 5 It's good being able to dip in and out of different worlds. (Earlier in the recording she also says that the money is reasonable and that you can have a chat and a good laugh with the other extras.)

b) Students discuss the questions in pairs.
Ask each pair to share some of their ideas with the class.

Help with Grammar Reflexive pronouns (2)

Ask students to do **1** in Preview 5, SB p45 if necessary.

 8 **a)–c)** Students do the exercises on their own or in pairs and check their answers in **G5.2** SB p130.

Check answers with the class.

- **a)** a) 1 b) 3 c) 2
- **b)** 1 concentrate 2 meet 3 enjoying myself
  4 help themselves 5 feel
- Highlight the following verbs with reflexive pronouns: *enjoy yourself, help yourself, exert yourself, pride yourself on, occupy yourself with.*
- Also point out that some verbs – for example, *dress, shave* and *wash* – are only reflexive if we want to emphasise that someone does the action themselves.

 9 Students do the exercise on their own or in pairs.

Check answers with the class.

1 Concentrate ~~yourselves~~ on what I'm saying.
2 Correct 3 I'm feeling ~~myself~~ a bit tired today.
4 I've brought a friend with ~~myself~~ **me**.
5 Correct
6 Correct
7 They're going to meet ~~themselves~~ (**each other**) outside the cinema.
8 Correct

Get ready … Get it right!

 10 Put students into pairs, student A and student B. Student As turn to SB p110 and student Bs turn to SB p113.

a) Explain that student As are personal assistants and student Bs famous people. Focus students on the list of complaints.

Make sure Student A understands *on duty*. Students do the exercise on their own. Encourage students to make notes about what they are going to say.

b) Students do the exercise in pairs. Encourage students to use reflexive pronouns as necessary.

── EXTRA IDEAS ──

- ✏ Write the following phrases on the board for students to use as prompts: *do something myself/yourself; clean up after myself/yourself; have some time for myself; I like the job itself, but … ; I pride myself on … , but I can no longer … .*
- Ask each pair to report back on the compromise that they managed to reach. Are both parties happy?

── EXTRA PRACTICE AND HOMEWORK ──

Ph **Class Activity** 5A Prefix Pelmanism p146 (Instructions p123)
5 Review Exercises 1 and 2 SB p54
CD-ROM Lesson 5A
Workbook Lesson 5A p24
Preview 5 Exercise 2 SB p45

5B The young ones

QUICK REVIEW ●●●
This activity reviews prefixes with multiple meanings. Students do the first part of the activity on their own. Set a time limit of five minutes. Put students into pairs. Students take turns to say their sentences and ask follow-up questions.

Reading and Vocabulary

 1 **a)** Introduce the topic by asking students if they think age has anything to do with talent – that is, do you need to have reached a certain age to be truly successful at sport, music, etc.? Ask students to justify their answers.

Students discuss the questions in pairs. Ask each pair to share their ideas with the class.

Vocabulary verb + infinitive with *to* or verb+*ing* (2); verb–noun collocations
Review prefixes with multiple meanings

b) Focus students on the article. Point out that the title is a reference to a popular British TV comedy of the 1980s about a group of four students living together in a shared house and a 1961 film starring Cliff Richard about a young musician. Both were called *The Young Ones*. However, in the context of this article, it refers to the age of the people who have become very successful in their field.

Point out that the Mercury Music Prize is an annual music prize awarded for the best album from the United Kingdom or Ireland.

Tell students that *Dizzee Rascal* is pronounced /ˌdɪzi ˈrɑːskəl/.

Point out that *dressage* /ˈdrəsɑːʒ/ is the training of a horse to make specific controlled movements.

Explain that *cerebral palsy* is a type of brain damage which causes physical disability.

Finally, explain that Peace One Day is an organisation that works to raise awareness of Peace Day. This is held on September 21st and is a day of non-violence and ceasefire around the world.

Students discuss the question in pairs. Ask each pair to share their ideas with the class.

 a) Put students into four groups, group A, group B, group C and group D. Group A turns to SB p110, group B turns to SB p113, group C turns to SB p115 and group D turns to SB p116.

Be prepared with definitions, examples, etc. to pre-teach *kit* (Theo Walcott text), *press on*, *kicked out*, *tightrope*, *beats* (Dizzee Rascal text), *physiotherapy* /ˌfɪziəʊˈθerəpi/, *grace*, *mindset* (Sophie Christiansen text) and *screw up* (Iris Andrews text).

Students make notes on their own in answer to the questions.

b) Students discuss the questions in **2a)** in their groups.

 Reorganise the class into groups of four with a student from groups A, B, C and D in each group.

While students are discussing their ideas, monitor and help with language as necessary. Encourage students to ask follow-up questions.

Check answers with the class.

Tell students that Arsenal – who Theo Walcott plays for – is a London-based football team.

Point out that when Dizzee Rascal says *making beats*, he is referring to making the instrumental backing tracks over which hip-hop, or rap, lyrics are sung.

Explain that when Dizzee Rascal says *If I hadn't had music, I would have been on the streets* he means that he would have been unemployed and out of school, spending time with other people his age in public spaces in large cities, often getting into trouble with the police. *Be on the streets* can also mean 'be homeless', but in this context it does not.

> **Theo Walcott**
> 1 At the age of 10. He was spotted by a coach who came to his school.
> 2 Dedication, ability to work hard, wanting to be better every day and learn something new every day.
>
> **Dizzee Rascal**
> 1 When he was 14. His music teacher helped and encouraged him.
> 2 Ability to keep on working, self-motivation.
>
> **Sophie Christiansen**
> 1 At the age of six. In order to make physiotherapy fun (she has cerebral palsy).
> 2 Determination to succeed, strong will.

> **Iris Andrews**
> 1 When she was 15. She has always asked questions about the world.
> 2 Passion for what she does.

 a) Students do the exercise in groups. Encourage students to find evidence in the text to support their answers.

Check answers with the class.

> 1 Dizzee Rascal. He says 'If I hadn't had music, I would have been on the streets'.
> 2 Sophie Christiansen. She says 'It has been hard on my family. When I compete, I get really intense and argue with Mum'.
> 3 Iris Andrews. She says 'I often feel like I'm a complete fraud – that I'm going to get found out soon'.
> 4 Theo Walcott. He says 'I learned so much about how players cope with all the pressure'.
> 5 Iris Andrews. She says 'Doing this helps me to get a broader perspective on my own life'.
> 6 Theo Walcott. He says 'The hardest bit was living away from my mum'.
> 7 Dizzee Rascal. He says 'A lot of the time I feel separated from other people my age'.
> 8 Sophie Christiansen. She says 'But competing has turned my life around. I used to be quite shy and self-conscious'.

b) Students discuss the questions in pairs. Ask each pair to share their ideas with the class. Encourage students to justify their answers.

Help with Vocabulary Verb + infinitive with *to* or verb+*ing* (2)

Remind students that when we use two verbs together, the form of the second verb usually depends on the first verb. Point out that while some verbs take either the infinitive with *to* or verb+*ing*, some verbs have more than one verb pattern, sometimes with a difference in meaning, sometimes not.

Ask students to do **2** in Preview 5, SB p45 if necessary.

 a)–b) Students do the exercise on their own or in pairs and check their answers in **V5.3** SB p129.

Check answers with the class.

> ● **a)** 1 *forget* + **verb**+*ing* = looks back to memories of the past; *forget* + **infinitive with *to*** = refers to now or the future 2 *go on* + **verb**+*ing* = continue an action; *go on* + **infinitive with *to*** = begin a new action 3 *mean* + **verb**+*ing* = involve/necessitate; *mean* + **infinitive with *to*** = intend 4 *regret* + **verb**+*ing* = be sorry for what's already happened; *regret* + **infinitive with *to*** = be sorry for what you're about to say

- Point out that when *forget* is followed by verb+*ing*, it is usually preceded by *never*: **I'll never forget seeing** *the Pyramids of Egypt for the first time.*
- Point out that verbs of the senses (*see, notice,* etc.) can be followed by object + verb+*ing* when describing a repeated action or an action in progress: *He **noticed me playing**.* Or they can be followed by an object + infinitive when describing a single or a completed action: *I **saw him get** into the car.* Point out that other verbs of the senses that follow this pattern include *watch, hear, feel* and *smell*. Also point out that *look* and *listen* do not follow this pattern.
- You could remind students that the following verbs also have a different meaning depending on the verb pattern:
  try + verb+*ing* = do something as an experiment: *I **tried eating** only two meals a day, but I still didn't lose any weight.*
  try + infinitive with *to* = make an effort: *I **try to go** swimming at least twice a week.*
  like + infinitive with *to* = choose to do something because you think it is a good idea: *I **like to jog** before work.*
  like + verb+*ing* = enjoy something: *I **like jogging** before work – it helps me to relax.*
  stop + verb+*ing* = cease the activity that you were doing: *He **stopped eating** and looked up.*
  stop + infinitive with *to* = stop in order to do something: *He **stopped to eat** at a roadside restaurant.*

EXTRA IDEAS

- ✍ Before students do **5a)**, brainstorm with the class as many verbs as possible which take verb+*ing*, infinitive with *to*, object + infinitive, object + infinitive with *to*, or infinitive. A list is in **V5.2** SB p129.
- In pairs, students practise making sentences with the words in red in **V5.2** SB p129. Student A makes a sentence using the verb and one verb pattern; student B has to make a sentence using the other verb pattern. For example, **A** *I forgot to turn the oven off when I left home this morning.* **B** *I'll never forget getting on a plane for the first time.*

6 Students do the exercise on their own or in pairs. Check answers with the class.

> 1 to tell 2 leaving 3 meeting 4 to write 5 to lock
> 6 talking 7 to email 8 shouting

7 a) ✍ Model the exercise by writing some sentences about yourself on the board using the prompts.
Students do the exercise on their own.

b) Students do the activity in pairs. Encourage students to ask follow-up questions.

Ask each student to tell the rest of the class one interesting thing they learned about their partner. For example, *I learned that Alejandro will never forget visiting his aunt and uncle in … .*

Listening

Draw students' attention to the introductory bullet point and introduce the topic by asking students what the equivalents of GCSE and A level exams are in their countries.

GCSEs are the most common exams taken by schoolchildren in England, Wales and Northern Ireland (the equivalent in Scotland is the Standard Grade). The core GCSE subjects are English (with many schools also requiring students to take English Literature), Mathematics and Science. Welsh or Welsh Second Language is a core subject in schools in Wales and Religious Studies is compulsory in some Northern Irish schools. Some schools throughout England, Wales and Northern Ireland also require their pupils to take ICT (Information Communications Technology).

Most universities require students to have passed A levels in certain subjects before accepting them onto an undergraduate course.

A *sixth-form college* is a school in Britain for 16–18-year-olds.

Point out the meaning of the following terms, which all appear in R5.4:

Work experience is when a student temporarily works without payment for an employer to gain experience.

A *gap year* is when a student decides to postpone starting university for a year either to travel, work or save some money.

The Old Bailey is the central criminal court in England.

8 **a)** Focus students on the photos of Claire, Will and Charlie. Tell students they are going to listen to an interview with the three 18-year-olds, who have all taken their A levels. Give students time to read the three questions.

R5.4 Play the recording (SB p152). Students listen and answer the questions. Students compare answers in pairs. Check answers with the class.

> 1 Will 2 Claire 3 Charlie

EXTRA IDEA

- ✍ Write these words and phrases from the recording on the board: *a step up, out of my depth, click, daunting.* Ask students to look at R5.4, SB p152 and to guess the meaning of the words and expressions from the context. Ask what helped them guess.

b) Play the recording again. Students listen and tick the true sentences. Students compare answers in pairs. Check answers with the class.

> 1 b) 2 a) 3 b)

c) Students discuss the questions in pairs. Ask each pair to share their ideas with the class. Encourage students to justify their answers.

> — EXTRA IDEA —
> • Ask students to write a short essay about the ways in which life was easier or harder for their parents' or grandparents' generation compared with theirs.

Vocabulary Verb–noun collocations

9 **a)** Focus students on the words/phrases in the box. Point out that all of them are used to talk about finishing school and starting university.

Students do the exercise on their own or in pairs and check answers in V5.4 SB p129.

Check answers with the class.

Point out that *do work experience* refers to carrying out the work experience while *get work experience* can also refer to obtaining a work experience placement: *I'm doing work experience at my father's company. I got work experience at a law firm through a friend of the family.*

> **do** a degree, English, work experience, a course, an exam, research
> **get** a degree, good results, a good education, work experience, a place at university

b) Focus students on the verbs in the box. Students do the exercise on their own or in pairs and check answers in V5.4 SB p129.

Check answers with the class.

Point out that although *do a course* and *go on a course* are often interchangeable, when you are talking about a course that you are currently doing, only *do a course* or *be on a course* is possible: *I'm doing/on a Spanish course at the moment* not *I'm going on a Spanish course at the moment*. *Take a course* is also common in American English.

Also point out that although it is common to say *be awarded a prize*, we do not say *be awarded an award*; *receive* or *get an award* is more common.

> **carry out** research; **sit** an exam; **enrol on** a course; **take** a course/an exam; **gain** work experience; **obtain** a degree/a good education/a place at university/good results; **have** a degree/a good education/a place at university/an exam; **be awarded** a degree; **achieve** good results

c) Students do the exercise in pairs. Encourage students to ask follow-up questions.

Ask students to tell the class the most interesting thing they learned about their partner.

Get ready … Get it right!

10 Focus students on the seven ideas. Make sure students understand *curriculum*.

Students do the exercise on their own. Encourage them to write at least six suggestions.

> — EXTRA IDEA —
> • Before students write their suggestions, brainstorm with the class other areas to add to the seven already given; for example, the use of technology, the length of the school day/school holidays.

11 **a)** Students discuss their ideas in groups. Ask each group to agree on the best three suggestions.

b) Ask each group to share their ideas with the class. Then ask the class to vote for the most popular ideas.

> — EXTRA IDEA —
> • Hold a mini-election. Make half the class voters and the other half politicians. Divide the politicians into pairs or small groups. Each pair or small group of politicians has three minutes to present their proposals for changes to the educational system to the rest of the class in the most persuasive way possible. The voters then cast their votes. The politicians with the most votes win.

> — EXTRA PRACTICE AND HOMEWORK —
> Ph **Class Activity** 5B Picture story p147 (Instructions p124)
> Ph **Help with Listening** 5 Talking about problems and solutions p193 (Instructions p185)
> **5 Review** Exercises 3 and 4 SB p54
> **CD-ROM** Lesson 5B
> **Workbook** Lesson 5B p26

5C Priorities

QUICK REVIEW ●●●

This activity reviews verb + infinitive with *to* or verb+*ing*. Students do the first part of the activity on their own. Set a time limit of five minutes. Put students into pairs. Students say their pairs of sentences and discuss the difference in meaning.

1 a) Introduce the topic by asking students who currently work what they like and dislike about their job, and students who do not currently work what they think they will like and dislike most about the world of work.

Focus students on the phrases in bold, explaining that the phrases all refer to the world of work.

Students do the exercise on their own or in pairs and check the meanings of any words they don't know in SB p130.

Check answers with the class.

Point out that instead of saying *stuck in a rut*, we can just say *be in a rut*: *I've been in a rut at work for over a year now.*

Point out that a *dead end* is a road which does not lead anywhere. It can also be used metaphorically to refer to a situation that isn't going anywhere: *The negotiations reached a dead end after hours of discussion.*

Tell students that being *self-employed* is often referred to as being *freelance*, meaning that you do work for several different organisations rather than just being employed by one.

Finally, explain that we can say *she's paid a pittance* or *she works for a pittance*.

Model and drill the phrases, paying particular attention to the stress patterns.

b) Students do the exercise in pairs. Encourage students to ask follow-up questions. Ask pairs to share with the class the most interesting thing that they learned about each other.

2 a) Focus students on cartoons A–D and their captions. Check that students understand *redundant* and *crèche*. Students discuss the questions in pairs. Elicit answers from the class.

> A inequality of pay
> B the 'long hours culture'
> C the minimum wage
> D lack of childcare for working mothers

b) Students discuss the questions in groups of three. Ask each group to share their ideas and conclusions with the class.

EXTRA IDEA

- For homework, students choose one of the questions a)–d) and write a for-and-against essay.

---

3 Tell students they are going to listen to three extracts from a conversation between Josh, Tracey and Liz, in which they discuss jobs.

 Play the recording (SB p153). Students listen and match the extracts to three of the topics in **2b)**.

Check answers with the class.

Explain that *the City* is the financial district of London and is used to describe not only the geographical area but also the people and organisations that work in it. For example: *I work in the City. The City reacted angrily to news that the government wants to increase taxes.* The equivalent of *the City* in New York is *Wall Street*.

Point out that *saddo* is a derogatory slang term for a sad person, where sad means 'not fashionable/interesting' or 'having no friends'. *Saddo* would not be used to describe someone who was sad in the sense of 'upset'.

Explain that a *chicken and egg situation* is one where it is not clear which of two events came first or caused the other. It comes from the proverbial question *Which came first – the chicken or the egg?*

Finally, tell students that *whoopee* is a loud, excited shout, often of happiness: *Whoopee! It's time to go home!* However, it is often used sarcastically, as in this example.

> **a)** extract 1 **b)** extract 2 **d)** extract 3 They do not discuss topic c).

EXTRA IDEA

- ✍ Write these words and phrases from the recording on the board: *astronomical, means to an end, flash*. Ask students to look at R5.5, SB p153 and to guess the meaning of the words and phrases from the context. Ask what helped them guess.

---

4 a) Tell students they are going to listen to extract 1 again. **R5.6** Play the recording (SB p153). Students listen and answer the questions. Students can check answers in pairs. Check answers with the class.

> 1 That some people – for example, company directors and corporate lawyers – get paid too much money, and that there are some professions which are underpaid by comparison. 2 That historically people have been paid less because they have fewer qualifications.

b) Tell students they are going to listen to extract 2 again. **R5.7** Play the recording (SB p153). Students listen and identify the arguments that are **not** mentioned.

Check answers with the class.

> Illness, divorce and early retirement are not mentioned.

c) Tell students they are going to listen to extract 3 again. **R5.8** Play the recording (SB p153). Students listen and answer the questions.

Check answers with the class.

> **1** Giving them flexibility so that parents can drop the kids off at school or work at home if one of them is ill.
> **2** Men. They would work part-time in order to look after the kids.
> **3** People with no kids might resent it if working mothers or fathers have special treatment.

Real World Conversational strategies

5 **a)–c)** Students do the exercises on their own or in pairs and check their answers in **RW5.1** SB p131.

Check answers with the class.

- **a)** b)1 c)2 d)6 e)5 f)7 g)4 h)9 i)10 j)8
- Point out that the phrase *You look dubious, Liz* is just one example of how to include somebody in the conversation, in this case by directing a statement at them and using their name. Other examples might include *What do you think, Liz?, Any thoughts, Liz?* or *You look like you agree/ disagree, Liz.*
- **b)** 2c) 3e) 4d) 5h) 6f) 7g) 8j) 9i) 10b)
- Model and drill all of the phrases, paying particular attention to the stress patterns. Point out that we would probably give more stress to certain words in order to sound more emphatic, for example, *Not to mention*, *That's exactly what I was trying to get at* and *All I'm saying is … .*

> **EXTRA IDEA**
> - Play the recordings again. Ask students to listen and underline the phrases from **RW5.1** in R5.5, SB p153.

6 **a)** Focus students on the conversations and the words in bold. Remind students that they may need to change other parts of the sentence in order to make the phrases from **5a)** and **b)** fit. Also point out that there may be more than one possible answer. Do the first question with the class.

Students do the exercise on their own or in pairs.

Check answers with the class.

1 You've got me there **2** Oh, I don't know about that. **3** By 'a few friends' you mean two or twenty?/What do you mean when you say 'a few friends'? **4** Yes, well, but anyway, his foreign policy, …/Yes, well, but to get back to what I was saying about his foreign policy … **5** That's exactly what I was trying to get at./That's precisely what I mean.

b) Students do the activity in pairs.

> **EXTRA IDEA**
> - Ask stronger students to role-play their conversations in front of the class.

7 **a)** Focus students on R5.5, SB p153. Students do the activity in groups of three. Encourage students to write at least eight more lines and to try to bring the conversation to a conclusion.

b) Students do the activity first in groups and then in front of the class. With weaker groups, give them more time to rehearse. With stronger groups, ask them to try and act out their conversations without notes.

c) Ask the class to vote for the best ending for each extract. Ask some students to justify their decision.

8 Students do the activity in groups of three. If students cannot think of an issue that is in the news at the moment, give them a topic to discuss (unemployment, education reform, national health, crime, etc.). Encourage students to use as many of the strategies in **5** as possible.

> **EXTRA IDEA**
> - After completing **8**, ask students to rate each other: did they all have an opportunity to speak? Did they involve other people and encourage them to speak? Did they reach a conclusion?

> **EXTRA PRACTICE AND HOMEWORK**
> **Ph** **Class Activity** 5C Carry on talking p148 (Instructions p124)
> **Ph** **Vocabulary Plus** 5 Phrasal verbs with *out, back* and *down* p176 (Instructions p170)
> **5 Review** Exercise 5 SB p54
> **CD-ROM** Lesson 5C
> **Workbook** Lesson 5C p28
> **Workbook** Reading and Writing Portfolio 5 p66
> **Progress Test 5** p212
> **Preview 6** Exercise 1 SB p55

See p32 for ideas on how to use this section.

1a) 1 locked 2 action 3 foot 4 worked 5 famous
6 balance

2a) 1 It's really important to concentrate ~~yourself~~ when driving. 2 Correct 3 Shall we **meet/meet each other** ~~ourselves~~ outside the cinema? 4 Correct 5 Are you feeling ~~yourself~~ ill today? 6 Correct 7 I think I'd better take a jumper with ~~myself~~ **me**. 8 Correct

3 1 a) going b) to go 2 a) to tell b) telling 3 a) doing
b) to do 4 a) to study b) studying

4a) 1 doing/sitting 2 getting 3 gain/get 4 got 5 did
6 did/took 7 obtaining/getting 8 do

5a) 2b) 3a) 4e) 5f) 6c) 7g)

Progress Portfolio

See p32 for ideas on how to use this section.

Accurate Writing

CONNECTING WORDS: time (2)
SPELLING: *ie* or *ei*

 Students do the exercise on their own or in pairs and check their answers in **AW5.1** SB p131.

Check answers with the class.

> 1 instantly 2 Before 3 immediately 4 After 5 after
> 6 Eventually 7 Lately 8 Up until

 Students do the exercise on their own or in pairs and check their answers in **AW5.2** SB p131.

Check answers with the class.

Point out that when *i* and *e* appear together in words, they can be spelled *ie* or *ei*.

Highlight that if the sound of the two letters is /iː/, we write *ie* (with some exceptions such as *seize*). If the sound of the two letters is not /iː/, we usually write *ei*: *eight*, *their*, *neighbour*. The exceptions to this rule include *friend* and *patience*.

Also point out that many native English speakers have problems with *ie* and *ei*. The popular rhyme *i before e except after c* helps many people to remember the rule. However, it is also important to know the exceptions to the rule, as given in **AW5.2** SB p131.

> 1 receive 2 neighbour 3 patience 4 experience
> 5 fields 6 relieved 7 achieve 8 seized 9 conceited
> 10 deceiving

 a)–b) Students do the exercises on their own or in pairs. Point out that in addition to the underlined words/phrases that need correcting, there are also spelling mistakes in some of the words in bold.

Check answers with the class.

> **a)** 1 instantly 2 later 3 Finally/Eventually 4 Up until
> **b)** neighbourhood patient field achievement

┌─ **EXTRA PRACTICE AND HOMEWORK** ─────────
Workbook Accurate Writing Exercises 9,10 and 11
p85–p86

Preview 6

WAYS OF COMPARING

 a)–b) Students do the exercises on their own or in pairs and check their answers in **G6.1** SB p133.

Check answers with the class.

Go through the **TIPS!** in **G6.1** SB p133 with the class and check students understand them.

> **a)** 2 nowhere near as scary 3 twice as hard
> 4 slightly more willing 5 just as helpful 6 no longer
> 7 considerably better 8 almost as difficult

> **b)** A big difference: a great deal, nowhere near, twice, considerably
> A small difference: slightly, almost
> No difference: just, no

ADVERBS

 Students do the exercise on their own or in pairs and check their answers in **G6.3** SB p134.

Check answers with the class.

> 2 hard 3 high 4 late 5 unhappily 6 easily 7 well
> 8 surprisingly 9 fine

6A A curious science

Vocabulary words with different but related meanings
Grammar formal and informal ways of comparing
Review work expressions

QUICK REVIEW ●●●

This activity reviews work expressions. Students do the activity in pairs. Check that students understand the words and phrases in italics. Students take turns to ask and answer questions using the words and phrases. Encourage students to ask follow-up questions.

Reading and Vocabulary

 a) Focus students on the definition of *quirky*. Point out that *quirky* can be used to describe types of behaviour as well as things and people. For example, we can say *My dad's always been quirky*, we can refer to someone as having a *quirky sense of humour*, or we can talk about enjoying a *quirky film*.

Focus students on the picture. Ask students to describe what's happening in it, and to discuss what kind of behaviour is illustrated.

> **Possible answers**
> anti-social behaviour; women's behaviour; behaviour in supermarkets; disregard for rules in supermarkets

b) Focus students on extracts A–C. Be prepared with definitions, examples, etc. to pre-teach *go about your everyday life, anti-social behaviour* /ˌæntɪˈsəʊʃəl bɪˈheɪvjə/, *disaffected, mindset* and *hooligan* /ˈhuːlɪgən/.

Students do the exercise on their own or in pairs. Check answers with the class.

In extract A, point out that British supermarkets often have a '10 items or fewer' checkout, which can only be used if you have fewer than 10 items to pay for. The intention is that those checkouts move faster than the others.

In extract C, point out that *moo, woof* and *quack* are the sounds attributed in English to cows, dogs and ducks respectively.

> 1 C 2 A 3 B

> ── EXTRA IDEA ─────────────
> ● Put students into groups of three. Students read one extract each and take turns to explain it to the other members of their group.

c) Students do the exercise on their own and compare answers in pairs.

Check answers with the class.

> 1F The aim of Trinkhaus's research was to investigate the behaviour of ordinary people going about their everyday lives.
> 2T
> 3F Trinkhaus believes that women van drivers drive faster than men unconsciously.
> 4F Dutch psychologists discovered that people who imagined the mindset of university professors answered more general knowledge questions correctly than people who imagined the mindset of football hooligans.
> 5T
> 6F One of the jokes posted on the website was about animals.
> 7T

d) Students discuss the question in pairs or groups. Ask each pair or group to share their ideas with the class.

Help with Grammar Formal and informal ways of comparing

Ask students to do **1** in Preview 6, SB p55 if necessary.

 a)–c) Students do the exercises on their own or in pairs and check their answers in G6.2 SB p133.

Check answers with the class.

- **a)** a) the blue words/phrases: decidedly, a good deal, significantly, distinctly
  b) the pink words/phrases: somewhat, barely any, marginally
- Point out that *decidedly* and *distinctly* both mean 'very obviously'.
- Also point out that we can say *a great deal* instead of *a good deal* and *hardly* instead of *barely*.
- **b)** a) way, loads, miles b) a tiny bit
- Point out that we can also say *a bit* and *a little bit* instead of *a tiny bit* and *tons* instead of *way/loads/miles*.
- Point out that the following informal phrases with *not … as* can be used to show big differences: *not half/nearly/anywhere near as … .*
- Also point out the following informal phrases with *… the same as* can be used to show very small differences: *pretty much/more or less/much the same as … .*

3 a) Model the exercise by completing some of the sentences with your own ideas.

Students do the exercise on their own.

b) Students compare sentences in pairs. Encourage students to ask follow-up questions.

Ask each pair to share one or two of their ideas with the class.

 4 a) Do the first question with the class. Students do the exercise on their own or in pairs.

Check answers with the class.

> **Possible answers**
> **2** Eating at home is way/miles/loads less fun than eating in a restaurant. **3** Going to work is way/miles/loads more tiring than going to school. **4** Being married is loads/miles/a tiny bit better for your health than being single. **5** Having a bath is loads/a tiny bit more relaxing than having a shower.

b) Students say their sentences in groups. Encourage students to justify their answers.

Ask each group to share one or two of their ideas with the class. Did they all agree? Why?/Why not?

Listening and Vocabulary

 5 a) Focus students on the words and phrases in the box. Students check the meaning of the words and phrases. Be prepared with definitions, examples, etc. to give students if necessary.

Patrol should be taught as a verb in this instance. Pay particular attention to the pronunciation of *crawl* /krɔːl/ and *pebble* /ˈpebəl/.

Focus students on the picture. Ask students to describe what's happening in it.

b) Tell students they are going to listen to four friends talking about strange behaviour.

R6.1 Play the recording (SB p153). Students listen and answer the question.

Check the answer with the class.

Point out that Liverpool Street is one of the principal London train stations. King's Lynn is a town in Norfolk, a county in the east of England.

> The picture illustrates the story about the couple who take stuffed animals onto the train with them.

> ─ **EXTRA IDEA** ─
> • ✎ Write these words from the recording on the board: *hop* (used twice), *undercover, grubby, heap*. Ask students to look at R6.1, SB p153 and to guess the meaning of the words from the context. Ask what helped them guess.

c) Play the recording again. Students listen and complete the summaries.

Check answers with the class.

> **1 a)** books **b)** sweater
> **2 a)** back **b)** seat
> **3 a)** toys **b)** ignored
> **4 a)** pebbles; compare **b)** odd

d) Students discuss the question in pairs or groups. Encourage students to justify their answer.

Ask each pair or group to share their ideas with the class.

> ─ **EXTRA IDEA** ─
> • Ask students what they think Alex meant by *'cos we're British, nobody would say anything*. Ask students what they would have done in his situation. Would they have said anything?

Help with Vocabulary Words with different but related meanings

Go through the introductory bullets with the class.

 6 a)–d) Students do the exercises on their own or in pairs and check their answers in **V6.1** SB p132.

Check answers with the class.

> • **a)** 1b) 2a) 3d) 4c) 5e) 6f)
> • **b)** unusual or peculiar – odd
>   pleasant – sweet
> • **c) 1** a division or subdivision of something
>   **2** horizontally level without variation **3** interrupt (or interruption of) the regularity, uniformity or arrangement of something **4** without pattern or interesting features **5** a great amount or weight of something
> • Point out that *plain* can also mean 'obvious and easy to understand' (e.g. *plain English*).
> • With stronger groups, introduce the topic of heteronyms – words which are spelled identically but are different in meaning and pronunciation (e.g. *lead* – show someone the way; *lead* – the heavy metal). A comprehensive list can be found here: http://www-personal.umich.edu/~cellis/heteronym.html
> • Point out that if students go on to study English for specific purposes (e.g. legal English, medical English, business English, English for computing), they will encounter many examples of words which they may recognise from general English, but which have completely different meanings depending on the context. For example, in computing a *field* is the part of a database where you type information.

EXTRA IDEA

- Ask students to brainstorm other words which have different meanings (e.g. *mean, book, kind*). Are the different meanings of the words related or not?

 7 a) Students do the exercise on their own or in pairs. Check answers with the class.

> 1 heavy 2 flat 3 plain 4 break 5 branch 6 sweet

b) Students do the exercise in pairs. Ask each pair to share one or two of their ideas with the class.

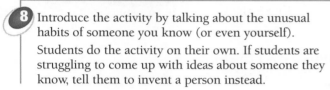 **Get ready … Get it right!**

8 Introduce the activity by talking about the unusual habits of someone you know (or even yourself).

Students do the activity on their own. If students are struggling to come up with ideas about someone they know, tell them to invent a person instead.

EXTRA IDEA

- Before doing **8**, brainstorm with the class other ideas for unusual habits and write them on the board.

9 a) Students do the activity in groups. Encourage students to ask follow-up questions.

b) Ask each group to talk about some of the unusual behaviour that they discussed. Encourage other groups to ask follow-up questions.

EXTRA PRACTICE AND HOMEWORK

[Ph] **Class Activity** 6A Anti-social behaviour p149 (Instructions p125)

[Ph] **Help with Listening** 6 Asides p194 (Instructions p185)

6 Review Exercises 1 and 2 SB p64

CD-ROM Lesson 6A

Workbook Lesson 6A p29

Preview 6 Exercise 2 SB p55

6B But is it ethical?

QUICK REVIEW ●●●
This activity reviews words with different but related meanings. Students do the first part of the activity on their own. Set a time limit of three minutes. Remind students that the meaning of the words should be different in each phrase. Put students into pairs. Students compare phrases. Ask each pair to share one or two of their phrases with the class.

Vocabulary word pairs
Grammar position of adverbials
Review words with different but related meanings

Vocabulary Word pairs

 1 a) Introduce the topic by telling students what a word pair is (an expression of two words or phrases which are joined by *and* or *or*).

Point out that word pairs are not the same thing as collocations.

Focus students on the phrases in bold. Also check that students understand *ad campaign*.

Students work on their own and tick the words they know. They check any new phrases in **V6.2** SB p132.

Point out that some word pairs are used for emphasis. For example, *Each and every student must register for the exam tomorrow* is more emphatic than *Every student must register for the exam tomorrow*.

Highlight that certain devices are commonly used in making word pairs. Recognising these devices may help students to remember them. The devices include:

- repetition (*take it or leave it, over and over again*);
- alliteration – the use of the same sounds at the beginning of words (*on and off, part and parcel of*);
- using words with opposite meanings (*take it or leave it, hit and miss, make or break*);
- using words with similar meanings (*pick and choose, each and every, in leaps and bounds, sick and tired of*).

EXTRA IDEA

- Before doing **1a)**, write one or two of the word pairs from **V6.2** SB p132 on the board. In pairs or groups, students brainstorm as many word pairs as they can. The pair or group who comes up with the longest list of word pairs is the winner.

b) Students do the exercise in pairs. Encourage students to justify their answers. Make sure that each student has the chance to ask and answer the questions.

Ask each pair to share one or two of their ideas with the class.

Listening

 a) Focus students on the two adverts. Students discuss the questions in pairs. Ask each pair to share their ideas with the class.

> Advert A is for Coca-Cola, the soft drink. Advert B is for the Apple iPod MP3 player.

b)–c) Tell students they are going to listen to two people who have a background in advertising, Graham and Lindsay, discussing the adverts.

Be prepared with definitions, examples, etc. to pre-teach *slogan* /ˈsləʊgən/, *strapline* and *silhouette* /ˌsɪluˈet/. Point out that *slogan* and *strapline* (R6.2) mean more or less the same thing. Technically, though, a *strapline* can only appear in written format, for example, in an advert or as part of a logo.

R6.2 R6.3 Play the recordings (SB p154). Students listen and answer the question. They compare answers in pairs. Check answers with the class.

> Graham is impressed with the Coca-Cola advert because of the slogan 'It's the real thing'. He likes the way the slogan makes Coca-Cola feel like a part of people's everyday lives. He's also impressed with how the slogan became completely linked to Coca-Cola – that is, if you said the slogan, people thought of the product.
>
> Lindsay likes the iPod advert because of the design elements – the use of the silhouettes, the bright colours – and also because of how the advert portrays a kind of lifestyle as opposed to saying anything about how the product works or what it does. She thinks the advert will have an effect on how people advertise in the future.

 a) Tell students they are going to listen to Graham again. R6.2 Play the recording again. Students listen and choose the correct answers.
Check answers with the class.

> 1 still works 2 the effectiveness of the slogan 3 didn't need to mention 4 well-being 5 is

b) Tell students they are going to listen to Lindsay again. Make sure students understand *trendy*.
R6.3 Play the recording again. Students listen and check the correct answers.
Check answers with the class.

> 1 visual effect 2 memorable 3 make people look trendy 4 has 5 will

c) Focus students on questions 1–3. Students discuss the questions in pairs.
Ask each pair to share some of their ideas with the class.

Point out the difference between *advertising* and *marketing*. *Marketing* is the word used to describe how a business identifies its customers, develops products or services that those customers want or need, lets the customer know about those products and services, and sells and distributes the products or services to them. *Advertising* is a branch of marketing; it involves promoting a product or service to customers, often through paid media (e.g. newspapers, television).

> ── EXTRA IDEAS ──
> * If any students work in advertising or marketing, ask them to talk about what they do. Encourage other students to ask questions.
> * For question 3, group students of different nationalities together. Ask them to compare their countries and then share their ideas with the class. Which are the most image-conscious countries?

Reading and Grammar

 a) Focus students on the two photos and the questions. Point out that the smaller photo is of a wristband.
Elicit answers from the class.

b) Focus students on the words and phrases in the box. Students check the meaning of the words and phrases. Be prepared with definitions, examples, etc. to give students if necessary.

Model and drill the words, paying particular attention to the pronunciation of *sneaky* /ˈsniːki/, *cynical* /ˈsɪnɪkəl/ and *innovative* /ˈɪnəˌveɪtɪv/.

c) Students do the exercise on their own and check answers in pairs.
Check answers with the class.
Point out that *stealth* means 'an action or movement that is hidden or unseen' and that *buzz* means 'a feeling of excitement or energy'.

> Stealth marketing involves using new and unexpected techniques to grab consumers' attention.
> Buzz marketing involves generating positive, unofficial information about a brand, often passed around by word-of-mouth.

> ── EXTRA IDEA ──
> * Before students read the article, focus them on the title. Ask them to predict what they think the article will be about.

d) Students do the exercise on their own or in pairs.
Check answers with the class.

> 1 Because they have seen too many and have become cynical.
> 2 Because a study a few years ago showed that only 18% of television campaigns in the US generated a positive return on investment.

3 Current campaigns are experimenting with new ways of communicating, not just billboards, newspaper ads or cinema ads.
4 Indirect advertising can be tolerated if it's entertainingly done.
5 It can have the opposite effect of what was intended if it is overused or done badly.
6 Nike has gained good publicity with its charitable fundraising.
7 Because ultimately we are the only ones who can decide what we want to believe, and what we want to buy.

5 a) Focus students on the nouns/verbs in blue in the article. Students do the exercise on their own or in pairs. Check answers with the class.

> 1 resistance 2 hype 3 renovation 4 crisis
> 5 accumulation 6 despises 7 respects 8 antagonises

b) Students discuss the questions in groups. Encourage students to justify their answers and to ask follow-up questions.
Ask each group to share their ideas with the class.

Help with Grammar Position of adverbials

Ask students to do **2** in Preview 6, SB p55 if necessary.

6 a)–c) Students do the exercises on their own or in pairs and check their answers in G6.4 SB p134.
Check answers with the class.

- **a)** 1 inside the bathrooms 2 These days 3 by force 4 sometimes 5 probably 6 Interestingly 7 every day
- Point out that adverbials of **place** describe where something happened; adverbials of **time** when something happened; adverbials of **manner** how something is done; adverbials of **indefinite frequency** and **definite frequency** how often something happens; adverbials of **level of certainty** how likely something is to happen; adverbials of **comment** express an opinion.
- Point out that adverbials can go in three different positions in a sentence: front position (before the subject), mid position (between the subject and verb or immediately after *be* or an auxiliary verb), and end position (immediately after the verb or at the end of the clause).
- Go through the **TIPS!** in the Position of adverbials section of G6.3 SB p134 with the class and check students understand them.
- **b)** 1 a) Jan and I worked on the Volkswagen advert but we didn't work on anything else. b) Jan and I, and nobody else, worked on the Volkswagen advert. 2 a) Joe's been to Tonga in addition to everywhere else he's been. b) You might not expect Joe to have been to Tonga, but he has.

- Point out that focusing adverbials come before the word/phrase that we want to stress.
- Also point out that the positioning of focusing adverbials can affect the meaning of the sentence: *only* and *even* usually go in mid position; however, if they only refer to the subject, they come before it in front position.

7 a) Students do the exercise on their own or in pairs. Check answers with the class.

> 1 People **sometimes** like the adverts on television better than the programmes. (*Sometimes* could also go in front position: *Sometimes people like …*) 2 **In the future**, adverts on billboards will die out./Adverts on billboards will die out **in the future**. 3 **Even** I am fascinated by car adverts, and I don't like cars!/I am fascinated by car adverts, and I don't **even** like cars! 4 Correct 5 **Every year**, the same brands have the most popular products./The same brands have the most popular products **every year**. 6 Correct 7 Correct (*Often* could also go in front position: *Often, children see products they want to have on TV.*)

b) Students compare answers in pairs and say if they agree with the sentences.
Ask each pair to share one or two of their ideas with the class.

8 Students do the exercise on their own. Point out that the places in the sentence where the adverbials should go are marked with a ⅄ symbol.
Check answers with the class.

> 1 **Obviously**, I **always** dislike having to do housework **at weekends**. 2 I will **probably** do the run **on Saturday** to raise money for charity. 3 **Only** one of my essays will **definitely** be finished **by then**. 4 **Annoyingly**, my car **often** breaks down **without any warning**. 5 That actress is **even** more popular than her brother **these days**.

Get ready … Get it right!

9 Model the activity by talking about an advertising campaign that you think is or was effective.
Focus students on the six topics. Make sure students understand *catchphrase* and *target market*. Students do the exercise on their own. Encourage students to make notes on all six of the topics if they can.

> EXTRA IDEA
> - Set **9** for homework, asking students to find images from the advertising campaign in magazines or from the Web.

a)–b) Students do the activity in groups of three. Make sure that each member of the group has the chance to speak. Ask each group to decide which campaign they think is or was the best.

Ask each group to share their ideas with the class.

EXTRA PRACTICE AND HOMEWORK

Ph **Class Activity** 6B Grab a word game p150 (Instructions p125)

Ph **Vocabulary Plus** 6 New words from the Internet p177 (Instructions p170)

6 Review Exercises 3 and 4 SB p64

CD-ROM Lesson 6B

Workbook Lesson 6B p31

 # 6C Short story radio

QUICK REVIEW ●●●

This activity reviews word pairs. Students do the activity in pairs. Students take turns to say the last part of the word pairs. Students can check answers in **V6.2** SB p132.

Vocabulary dramatic verbs

Skills Reading: a short story extract; Listening: someone talking about writing and reading short stories; a short story extract; Speaking and Writing: telling a story

Real World telling a story

Review word pairs

 a) Introduce the topic by brainstorming types of fiction (crime, sci-fi, etc.). Write them on the board. Students discuss the questions in groups. Ask each group to share their ideas with the class.

b) Focus students on the blog extract. Students do the exercise on their own or in pairs.

Elicit answers from the class.

 a) Tell students they are going to listen to an interview with John McRae, a professor of literature, an actor and a writer.

Focus students on the three questions. Be prepared with a definition, examples, etc. to pre-teach *hook in*.

R6.4 Play the recording (SB p154). Students listen and answer the questions.

Check answers with the class.

> 1 A beginning (the context or premise), a middle (development and/or complication) and an end (the resolution). 2 A joke, a narrative. 3 It needs to hook the listener in – that is, it has to grab their attention.

b) Play the recording again. Students listen and fill in the gaps.

Check answers with the class.

> 1 premise 2 development 3 complication 4 resolution

 a) Focus students on the story 'Confessions of a love-struck tourist'. Check that students understand *love-struck*.

Students do the exercise on their own. Elicit answers from the class.

Point out that *No. 1* refers to being the best-selling record in the UK pop music charts. *Tight Fit* were the band who were number one at that point in 1982.

Also point out that *yours truly* is a phrase used to refer to yourself when you are speaking. It is usually used to talk about something you have to do against your will: *All my colleagues called in sick, so yours truly had to work a double shift!* In the short story it is used in a more humorous way.

> It appears to be a love story.
> The story is organised along the same lines explained by John McRae. The premise is that the narrator and his friends are on holiday. The development is meeting Kirsti in the nightclub.

EXTRA IDEA

● Write these words and phrases from the story on the board: *cringe, somersault, have other fish to fry, gloat, pluck up, pout, burly*. Ask students to guess the meaning of the words and phrases from the context. Ask what helped them guess.

---

b) Students do the exercise on their own and then compare their summaries in pairs.

Elicit some answers from the class.

> **Possible answer**
> The narrator is on holiday with friends. One night, he meets a beautiful girl in a nightclub. He can't believe his luck. They arrange to meet for dinner the next day. The narrator arrives at the restaurant and sees someone looking at him.

c) Students discuss the question in pairs. Elicit answers from the class.

> The story is told in an informal style. Examples of informal language include *mates, out-of-this-world beautiful, lads, bite to eat, as if!*

4 Students do the exercise in groups. Elicit answers from the class.

 5 a) Tell students they are going to listen to the end of the story. Make sure students understand *time-share*. This is when you buy a share in a holiday house or apartment which is owned by several different people; each owner is entitled to use the property for a particular period of the year. Time-share selling has a reputation for being notoriously high pressured: anecdotal reports include potential customers being taken to faraway offices and left in uncomfortable situations (no water, no air conditioning, etc.) until they give in and buy a share. **R6.5** Play the recording (SB p154). Students listen and answer the questions. Elicit answers from the class.

> The man drove him to an expensive-looking building in the mountains. Kirsti was there and she made him go inside, into a large room with some other people. After ten minutes he realised he was in a time-share presentation, and walked out angrily. Kirsti tried to persuade him to stay but he refused, and walked home. The next day, he and his friends went to the same club and Kirsti walked over to him. She wanted £200 from him and threatened to tell his friends she wasn't his girlfriend if he didn't pay. He agreed to pay, but only if she kissed him. She did, and then dragged him away to go to the bank.

b) Students do the exercise in pairs.

Check answers with the class. Point out that when Mike says *Here comes your missus*, he does not mean that they are married. *Missus* is used in British English as an informal way of saying *wife*, but it can also refer to girlfriends. Some people think it is a slightly derogatory term, so it should be used with caution.

> 1T 2F He walked back. 3T 4F He made Kirsti kiss him in front of his friends. 5T 6F He thinks it was worth it to kiss the most beautiful girl he'd ever seen.

--- **EXTRA IDEA** ---
- ✏️ Write these words and phrases from the recording on the board: *shoo someone along, dash after someone, watch like a hawk, blurt out, snort*. Ask students to look at R6.5, SB p154 and to guess the meaning of the words from the context. Ask what helped them guess.

 6 a) Introduce the topic by telling students that the writer of the short story they have just listened to used certain language for dramatic effect.

Focus students on the words in the box. Model and drill the words, paying particular attention to the pronunciation of *cajole* /kəˈdʒəʊl/.

Students do the exercises on their own or in pairs and check their answers in **V6.3** SB p133.

Check answers with the class.

> 2 stormed out 3 leapt up 4 hissed 5 grabbed
> 6 dragged 7 nudged

b) Students do the exercise in pairs. Check answers with the class.

> **The correct order, with extra information**
> 2 He felt humiliated that he had been seen as the kind of person who went to a time-share presentation. 1 She pointed out that they were miles away from anywhere, and if he stayed they could go for a meal afterwards. 7 Kirsti was walking up to James in the club, but he hadn't noticed. 3 He didn't want Kirsti to meet his friends, or they would find out what had really happened the previous evening. 5 James wanted to impress his friends, so he agreed to give her the money if she kissed him. 4 James now had to fulfil his part of the deal by giving her the money. 6 It looked as if Kirsti was dragging him off for a different reason.

 7 a)–b) Introduce the topic by asking students if they found the short story easy to listen to – that is, if they felt involved in the story. Ask students to explain why/why not.

Tell students they are going to listen to John McRae's tips for involving a listener. Be prepared with definitions, examples, etc. to pre-teach *gripping, frivolous* /ˈfrɪvələs/ and *flow* /fləʊ/.

R6.6 Play the recording (SB p154). Students listen and fill in the gaps in the notes and answer the question.

Check answers with the class.

> **a)** • adverbs; verbs   • pace; stress   • tension   • tone
> **b)** A twist in the tail is an unexpected change or event towards the end of a story.

 8 a)–b) Tell students they are going to practise telling stories. Focus students on the list of ideas. Point out that students can use any one of these ideas or one of their own.

Students do the exercise on their own. Remind students that they should only make notes, not write the whole story.

c) Focus students on the Real World box. Go through the techniques with the class.

Put students into pairs. Students take turns to practise telling their stories. Encourage students to use the techniques from the table.

d) Students work in groups. Make sure that each student has the opportunity to tell their story. Encourage students to use John McRae's tips for encouraging the listener.

Ask each group to nominate their favourite story.

--- **EXTRA IDEA** ---
- Ask students to rate each other: did they use techniques from the table? Did they use any of John McRae's techniques for involving the listener? If so, which ones did they use particularly effectively? If not, what could they have done better?

Writing Extension

 a)–b) Students do the exercise on their own and then read each other's stories. This activity can be set for homework.

 Ask students to turn to SB p107 and look at *Chasing Cars*. This song was recorded by the British band Snow Patrol in 2006.

 Students discuss the questions in groups. Ask each group to share their ideas with the class.

 a)–b) Focus students on verses 1–8. Students do the exercise on their own and compare answers in pairs.

c) R6.7 Play the recording. Students listen and check their answers.

> 1 We'll do it all
>   Everything
>   On our own
> 2 We don't need
>   Anything
>   Or anyone
> 3 I don't quite know
>   How to say
>   How I feel
> 4 Those three words
>   Are said too much
>   They're not enough
> 5 Let's waste time
>   Chasing cars
>   Around our heads

> 6 I need your grace
>   To remind me
>   To find my own
> 7 All that I am
>   All that I ever was
>   Is here in your perfect eyes, they're all I can see
> 8 I don't know where
>   Confused about how as well
>   Just know these things will never change for
>   us at all

3 Students do the exercise in pairs. Check answers with the class.

Possible answers
1 They are probably lovers.
2 The singer doesn't feel like he needs other people.
3 A new beginning.
4 Doing something dangerous.

EXTRA PRACTICE AND HOMEWORK

Ph **Class Activity** 6C What a joke! p151 (Instructions p126)

Ph **Class Activity** 4–6 Review Cash quiz p152–p153 (Instructions p126)

6 Review Exercise 5 SB p64

CD-ROM Lesson 6C

Workbook Lesson 6C p33

Workbook Reading and Writing Portfolio 6 p69

Progress Test 6 p214

Preview 7 Exercise 1 SB p65

---

6 Review

See p32 for ideas on how to use this section.

1a) 1 Sentence a) indicates a bigger difference. 2 Sentence a) indicates a bigger difference. 3 Sentence a) indicates a smaller difference. 4 The sentences have the same meaning. 5 In sentence a), driving is more stressful; in sentence b), travelling by plane is more stressful. 6 The sentences have the same meaning.

2 2 a) flat b) flat 3 a) break b) broken 4 a) plain b) plain 5 a) branch b) branches

3 1 tired 2 choose 3 leave 4 parcel 5 break 6 bounds 7 off

4a)
B Sorry, I've been **at the Town Hall** [correct] to see Monica's show.
B I thought she performed **brilliantly** …
A **Unfortunately** [correct], that **often** happens.
A Yes, I'll **probably** go and see it **next Thursday** [correct], if I can get tickets.
B Yes, I think it's on **every day** until the end of March.

4b) place: at the Town Hall
time: next Thursday
definite frequency: every day
indefinite frequency: often
level of certainty: probably
comment: Unfortunately
manner: brilliantly

5 1 cajole 2 drag 3 hiss 4 grab 5 nudge 6 leap up
7 storm out

Progress Portfolio

See p32 for ideas on how to use this section.

Accurate Writing

CONNECTING WORDS: purpose
PUNCTUATION: colons and semi-colons

 Students do the exercise on their own or in pairs and check their answers in `AW6.1` SB p135.

Check answers with the class.

Point out that we can use *so as/in order* (for something) + infinitive with *to* to talk about the purpose of an action, and that these phrases come at the beginning of a clause.

Also point out that in spoken English and less formal written English, we can use an infinitive with *to* instead of *in order/so as.*

Highlight that when we simplify *in order/so as* + infinitive with *to* to just an infinitive with *to*, we never use *for*: *We have done research ~~for~~ to see which adverts are the most popular.*

Point out that we also use *in order that, so that* and *so* to talk about the purpose of an action, and that these words also come at the beginning of a clause.

Finally, point out that *so that* is less formal and more common than *in order that.*

Go through the **TIPS!** in `AW6.1` SB p135 with the class and check students understand them.

> 1 Correct 2 In order **for** the campaign … 3 Correct
> 4 I'd like to do a copywriting course so **that I can** go into advertising. 5 I'll send you some possible slogans **so that** you can decide. 6 Correct

 Students do the exercise on their own or in pairs and check their answers in `AW6.2` SB p135.

Check answers with the class.

Point out that we use colons to introduce lists or to indicate a subdivision of a topic. We also use them when the second clause of a sentence explains the first.

Point out that we use semi-colons instead of full stops or commas to separate two main clauses which are connected in meaning.

Finally point out that semi-colons are used in lists when items in the list contain commas. This use of semi-colons is not optional. For example, *Three things contributed to his breakdown: large debts; his divorce from his wife of thirty years, Anne; and the death of his father, an important figure in his life.*

> 1 There are three solutions: we could get an overdraft, sell the company or close it down. 2 I began to get a bit nervous; to calm myself down I made myself a drink. 3 The meeting will be held in the library: the Board Room is being decorated. 4 I used to live in France; I'm now based in Tokyo. 5 My father has gone into hospital: he's having a minor operation.

 a)–b) Students do the exercise on their own or in pairs. Check answers with the class.

> **a)** 1 in order to/to 2 to wander 3 so as/in order
> **b)** goods: ago; cities; fine:

> ┌─ EXTRA PRACTICE AND HOMEWORK ─
> **Workbook** Accurate Writing Exercises 12 and 13 p86

Preview 7

CONDITIONALS: BASIC FORMS

 a)–d) Students do the exercises on their own or in pairs and check their answers in `G7.1` SB p137.

Check answers with the class.

> **a)** 2d) 3c) 4a)
>
> **b)** 1 zero 2 first 3 second 4 third
> zero: *if* + subject + Present Simple, subject + Present Simple
> first: *if* + subject + Present Simple, subject + *will/won't* + infinitive
> second: *if* + subject + Past Simple, subject + *'d* (= *would)/wouldn't* + infinitive
> third: *if* + subject + Past Perfect, subject + *'d* (= *would)/wouldn't* + *have* + past participle
>
> **c)** a)4 b)1 c)3 d)2
>
> **d)** 2 will work 3 would you choose 4 hadn't seen 5 look after

PASSIVE FORMS

 Students do the exercise on their own or in pairs and check their answers in `G7.3` SB p138.

Check answers with the class.

Remind students that in passive sentences we can use *by* + 'the agent' to say who or what does the action. We only include the agent when it is important or unusual information.

> 2 He's being blamed for the current problems.
> 3 *Bleak House* was written by Charles Dickens.
> 4 I was always being encouraged to write (by my teacher).
> 5 My car has been stolen.
> 6 All the food had been left (by the kids).
> 7 The results are going to be announced soon.
> 8 My mother should be told.
> 9 Fred could have been invited.

7A Getting away with it

Vocabulary phrases with *get*
Grammar conditionals: non-basic forms
Review position of adverbials

QUICK REVIEW ●●●

This activity reviews the position of adverbials. Students do the first part of the activity on their own. Set a time limit of five minutes. Make sure students understand what type of adverbial each of the words in italics is. Put students into pairs. Students take turns to say their sentences. Encourage students to ask follow-up questions.

Reading and Vocabulary

1 a) Introduce the topic by asking students how they would describe a 'typical' prison.

Focus students on the photos. Ask students to describe what they can see.

Ask students what they think makes this an 'open' prison and how open prisons might differ from closed prisons. Tell students they will find out more about the difference between open and closed prisons when they read the article.

> ── EXTRA IDEA ───────────────
> • Begin the class by brainstorming types of crime. Ask students to classify them into more and less serious crimes.

b) Focus students on the words and phrases in the box. Students check the meaning of the words and phrases. Be prepared with definitions, examples, etc. to give students if necessary.

Model and drill the words and phrases.

Point out that *rehabilitation* can also refer to returning a person to health after an illness, especially when there has been some kind of serious physical damage (e.g. after a car crash).

Also point out that *crop* often collocates with *bumper* to mean 'a very good crop': *a bumper crop of potatoes*.

Finally, point out that although *citizen* means somebody who is a member of a specific country, it often implies somebody who abides by the rules and laws of the country they live in – that is, that they are a *good citizen* or a *law-abiding citizen*.

c) Students read the article and find the answer to the question.

Check the answer with the class.

Point out that the expression *It's a hard life*, used as the title of the article, is often used sarcastically to refer to things or activities which are in fact easy. For example, A *I had to work three hours today.* B *Three hours? It's a hard life, isn't it!*

Also point out that *drug smuggling* is importing or exporting illegal narcotics and that a *fraudster* is someone who has committed *fraud* – obtaining money by deceiving people.

> Because the emphasis is on rehabilitation through ecology – tending cattle, growing organic crops, etc. – as opposed to punishment. Inmates are encouraged to develop a sense of responsibility by taking care of the nature around them.

d) Students do the exercise on their own.

Check answers with the class.

> **1** Bastoey prison is situated on Bastoey island – an island in the middle of the Oslo fjord, covered with lush woodland.
> **2** Prisoners can play tennis, go horse riding in the forest, swimming in the sea and cross-country skiing.
> **3** Prisoners tend cattle, grow organic crops, cut trees into timber and restore the wooden houses on the island.
> **4** Prisoners live in comfortable houses with 3–5 other prisoners.
> **5** Family members can visit the prison at weekends; prisoners can leave the island to stay with relatives.
> **6** The prison is cheaper to run than a closed one, as lower security means fewer employees.

e) Focus students on the words in bold. Point out that there are eight pairs of near synonyms, for example, *inhabitants, residents*.

Students do the exercise on their own or in pairs.

Check answers with the class. Point out that many of the near synonyms in the text are used in the same paragraph, or at least very close together. This is because the writer is trying to avoid repeating the same words, in order to make her writing more interesting to read.

> prison, jail
> prisoners, convicts
> family members, relatives
> individuals, people
> criminals, offenders
> staff, employees
> campaigners, reformers

f) Focus students on the quotes. Students do the exercise in pairs or in groups. Encourage students to justify their answers.

Ask each pair or group to share some of their ideas with the class.

> **EXTRA IDEAS**
> - Students debate the four quotes in teams, one team arguing for and one team against.
> - Write these words from the article on the board: *tool, ecology, confront*. (Note that *tool* is used twice in the article, the second time metaphorically.) Ask students to guess the meaning of the words from the context. Ask what helped them guess.

Vocabulary Phrases with *get*

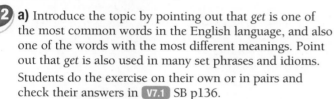

2 a) Introduce the topic by pointing out that *get* is one of the most common words in the English language, and also one of the words with the most different meanings. Point out that *get* is also used in many set phrases and idioms.

Students do the exercise on their own or in pairs and check their answers in **V7.1** SB p136.

Check answers with the class.

Point out that in the phrase *get your own back*, the possessive pronoun changes depending on the subject of the sentence: *I got my own back, you got your own back*, etc.

Also point out that *get away with* can also be used to mean 'escape with', especially in the context of a robbery: *Thieves got away with £3 million of jewellery after a daring armed robbery*.

Draw students' attention to the difference between *get round* and *get round to*; the use of *to* changes the meaning completely.

Finally, highlight that *get through to* can also be used to talk about reaching somebody by telephone: *I've been calling all morning, but I can't get through to Bill*.

> 1d) 2c) 3e) 4b) 5f) 6a) 7g)

b) Model the exercise by completing some of the sentences so that they are true for you.

Students do the exercise on their own.

c) Students do the exercise in pairs. Encourage students to ask follow-up questions.

Ask each pair to share one or two of their ideas with the class.

Listening and Grammar

3 a) Focus students on the words and phrases in the box. Students check the meaning of the words and phrases. Be prepared with definitions, examples, etc. to give students if necessary.

Model and drill the words and phrases, paying particular attention to the pronunciation of *saliva* /sə'laɪvə/, *sweat* /swet/ and *fibre* /'faɪbə/.

b) Focus students on the two questions. Students do the exercise in pairs. Encourage students to use the words from **3a)**.

Ask each pair to share some of their ideas with the class.

c) Tell students they are going to listen to a radio interview with a science journalist. Be prepared with definitions, examples, etc. to pre-teach *silk* and *woolly* /'wʊli/.

Focus students on the two questions.

R7.1 Play the recording (SB p155). Students listen and answer the questions.

Check answers with the class.

> She talks about kidnapping and burglary.
> Forensic evidence usually leads to the criminals being arrested.

d) Give students time to read 1–5. Play the recording again. Remind students that they are going to complete some notes. The sentences are not taken verbatim from the interview.

Students listen and complete the notes. Check answers with the class.

> 1 glass 2 paint 3 gloves/socks 4 gloves/socks
> 5 wool 6 smooth 7 silk 8 quietly 9 sell

> **EXTRA IDEA**
> - Write these words from the recording on the board: *outwit, barefoot, stagger out*. Ask students to look at R7.1, SB p155 and to guess the meaning of the words from the context. Ask what helped them guess.

4 a) Tell students they are going to listen to the rest of the interview with Zoë. Focus students on the words in the box. Students check the meaning of the words. Be prepared with definitions, examples, etc. to give students if necessary.

Model and drill the words, paying particular attention to the pronunciation of *alibi* /'ælɪbaɪ/ and *icicle* /'aɪsɪkəl/.

Elicit ideas from the class about what crime Zoë is going to talk about.

b) Be prepared with definitions, examples, etc. to pre-teach *get rid of* and *trace back to*.

R7.2 Play the recording (SB p155). Students listen and check their answer to **4a)**.

Check the answer with the class.

> She is talking about murder.

c) Play the recording again. Students listen and answer the questions. They can check the answers in pairs.

Check answers with the class.

1 They are cool and detached and very good actors.
2 The age of the maggots in a body can give you an idea of when the person died. 3 The kind of place you're in will attract different kinds of flies, which can help you tell if a murder was committed in the countryside or in an urban area. 4 It's easy to find out where it was obtained and to trace it back to the suspect. 5 Destroy it or get rid of any distinguishing marks. 6 An icicle, because it would melt and therefore vanish completely.

EXTRA IDEA

- Write these words and phrases from the recording on the board: *would-be murderer, water-tight alibi, creepy crawlies, the likelihood of something.* Ask students to look at R7.2, SB p155 and to guess the meaning of the words and phrases from the context. Ask what helped them guess.

---

d) Students discuss the question in pairs or groups. Ask each pair or group to share some of their ideas with the class.

Help with Grammar Conditionals: non-basic forms

Ask students to do **1** in Preview 7, SB p65 if necessary. Go through the introductory bullet. Explain that we can use a variety of verb forms in conditional sentences.

5 **a)–c)** Students do the exercises on their own or in pairs and check their answers in **G7.2** SB p137. Check answers with the class.

- **a)** 2 third conditional 3 second conditional 4 zero conditional
- Point out that the future with *be going to* is used instead of the present to show future intention; a continuous form is used instead of a simple form to emphasise an action in progress; and a modal is used instead of a present form, to give advice, for example.
- Point out that although these non-basic forms use different verb forms, the meaning of the conditional is still the same. For example, sentence 1 is talking about a possible event or situation in the future; sentence 2 is talking about an imaginary situation in the past; sentence 3 is talking about an imaginary situation in the future; and sentence 4 is talking about something that is always true. The difference is in what we want to show or emphasise: in sentence 1, a future intention; in sentences 2 and 3, an action in progress; and in sentence 4, that the sentence is a piece of advice.
- Go through the **TIP!** in **G7.2** SB p137 with the class and check students understand it.
- **b)** i) imaginary situations
  ii) The clauses are referring to past and present times as follows: *If the kidnapper hadn't licked that envelope*

(past), *he wouldn't be in prison now* (present); *If the kidnapper hadn't licked that envelope* (past), *he wouldn't have gone to prison* (past); *If they weren't such good actors* (present), *most of them would have been found out much earlier* (past); *If they hadn't been such good actors* (past), *most of them would have been found out much earlier* (past).
  iii) Sentences 1a) and 2a). They are called mixed conditionals because they are a combination of two different conditionals: in this case second and third conditionals.
  iv) *If the kidnapper hadn't licked that envelope, he wouldn't be in prison now.* = He licked the envelope, and he's still in prison now.
  If the kidnapper hadn't licked that envelope, he wouldn't have gone to prison. = He licked the envelope and went to prison; we don't know if he is still in prison.
  If they weren't such good actors, most of them would have been found out much earlier. = They are good actors, but they were eventually found out anyway.
  If they hadn't been such good actors, most of them would have been found out much earlier. = They were good actors, but they were eventually found out anyway; we do not know if they are still good actors.
- Point out that in mixed conditionals, the main clause and the *if* clause can sometimes refer to different time periods. The most common combinations are second and third conditionals.
- Go through the **TIP!** in the **Mixed conditionals** section in **G7.2** SB p138 with the class and check students understand it.
- Go through the **Formal conditionals** section in **G7.2** SB p138 with the class or ask them to read it for homework.

6 Students do the exercise on their own or in pairs. Remind students that sometimes both verb forms are possible. Check answers with the class.

1 dropped 2 were hoping 3 Both are possible.
4 're making 5 Both are possible. 6 Both are possible.

7 **a)** Do the first question with the class. Students do the exercise on their own or in pairs. Check answers with the class.

2 If we hadn't missed a lesson, we'd understand what the teacher's saying. 3 I wouldn't have agreed to go to the club if Fred didn't work there. 4 If I hadn't twisted my ankle, Tim wouldn't be playing in the tennis tournament today instead of me. 5 If my brother didn't love working with young people, he wouldn't have become a teacher. 6 If Jess wasn't/weren't so lazy, she would have finished her coursework. 7 If you had taken my advice, we wouldn't be so late now!

- ✎ With weaker groups, write the following prompts on the board to help students decide which type of mixed conditional to use:

  2 *third, second*   5 *second, third*
  3 *second, third*   6 *second, third*
  4 *third, second*   7 *third, second*

- With stronger groups, ask students to identify which clauses refer to the past and which clauses refer to the present.

b) Focus students on the three questions. Students discuss the questions in pairs. Encourage students to ask follow-up questions.

Ask each pair to share some of their ideas with the class.

Get ready … Get it right!

8 Focus students on the two statements about prisons. Students do the activity in pairs. Encourage students to come up with several advantages and disadvantages for open and closed prisons.

9 Ask students to say if they are in favour of open or closed prisons.

If you have roughly equal numbers, put all of those in favour of closed prisons into group A and those in favour of open prisons into group B. If you do not have equal numbers, nominate students from the larger of the two groups to work in the smaller group.

a) Put students into pairs within each group. Students do the activity in pairs.

b) Tell students that they are going to role-play a meeting about how best to deal with crime. Put students into groups of four: one pair from group A and one pair from group B. Students take turns to give their points of view. Make sure that each student has the chance to speak. Encourage students to use at least one mixed conditional and one non-basic conditional. Ask each group to try and come to a consensus on how best to deal with the issue of crime.

c) Ask each group to decide which is the best way to deal with crime – open or closed prisons. Each group must decide one way or the other.

d) Ask each group to share their ideas with the class.

EXTRA IDEA
- For homework, ask students to write a for-and-against essay on the topic of open prisons.

EXTRA PRACTICE AND HOMEWORK
Ph **Class Activity** 7A You said it! p154 (Instructions p127)
7 Review Exercises 1, 2 and 3 SB p74
CD-ROM Lesson 7A
Workbook Lesson 7A p34
Preview 7 Exercise 2 SB p65

7B Every step you take

Vocabulary phrasal nouns
Grammar impersonal report structures
Review mixed conditionals

QUICK REVIEW ●●●
This activity reviews mixed conditionals. Students do the first part of the activity on their own. Set a time limit of five minutes. Encourage students to use at least one mixed conditional and one non-basic conditional. Put students into pairs. Students take turns to say their sentences. Encourage students to ask follow-up questions.

Listening and Vocabulary

1 a) Focus students on the four newspaper headlines. Be prepared with definitions, examples, etc. to pre-teach the vocabulary in the headlines or bring in a set of dictionaries for students to check the meanings themselves.

Tell students they will be focusing on the words in red later.

Ask students to share information about whether these topics are issues in their countries.

Point out that a *tax exemption* is permission not to pay some or all of your taxes. The reasons for tax exemptions vary from country to country (or state to state in the US), but may include being married, having children, having served in the armed forces, etc.

The question of whether or not people should be charged to have their rubbish picked up has been controversial in the UK. The idea has been put forward as a way of encouraging people to throw away less and recycle more.

In order to be considered clinically *obese*, a person must be 20–30% over the ideal weight for their age and height.

EXTRA IDEA
- Ask students to discuss what they think the four headlines have in common. (They all relate in some way to how much the state intervenes in our day-to-day lives.)

b) Tell students they are going to listen to three people discussing how much the state should intervene in people's lives. Be prepared with definitions, examples, etc. to pre-teach *enclosed*, *landfill*, *bias* /'baɪəs/ and *forsake* /fə'seɪk/.

R7.3 Play the recording (SB p155). Students listen and answer the question.

Check the answer with the class.

> The onset of obesity in childhood is not discussed.

c) Play the recording again (SB p155). Students listen and answer the questions.

Check answers with the class.

> **Banning smoking** Stefano feels that state intervention is justified in this area to a degree; that is, he thinks that it's OK for the state to ban smoking in enclosed public places, but to do so in unenclosed public spaces – for example, parks – would be too much.
> **Plans to charge for rubbish** Hiltrud feels that state intervention is justified here because landfills are filling up quickly, meaning that we are running out of space to put our rubbish. She also thinks that it's fairer that the more people throw away the more they should have to pay.
> **Tax exemptions for married people** Justyna doesn't think that state intervention is justified in this area, as it promotes marriage over other types of partnership; she doesn't think that the state should be able to intervene in people's lifestyle choices.

2 Focus students on the four topics. Students discuss them in pairs. Ask each pair to share some of their ideas with the class.

> ─ EXTRA IDEA ─
> - Divide the class into two and debate the four topics. Group A should argue in favour of more state intervention, group B against.

Help with Vocabulary Phrasal nouns

3 **a)–d)** Introduce the topic by asking students if they can guess what phrasal nouns are. If necessary, draw their attention to the examples in red in the newspaper headlines.

Students do the exercises on their own or in pairs and check their answers in **V7.2** SB p136.

Check answers with the class.

- **a)** A break (verb), up (particle)
  B cry (verb), out (particle)
  C set (verb), back (particle)
  D set (verb), on (particle)
- Point out that when phrasal nouns begin with a particle (e.g. *outlook* or *downpour*) they are written without a hyphen.

- Also point out that when phrasal nouns begin with a verb (e.g. *kick-off* or *breakdown*) they sometimes have a hyphen and sometimes not. Point out that there are no rules about when a phrasal noun which begins with a verb will be hyphenated or not. Encourage students to use their dictionaries.
- Finally, point out that some phrasal nouns are made up of the same words as phrasal verbs, but have different meanings. Encourage students to double-check the meaning of phrasal nouns in their dictionaries.
- **b)** *Outcry* and *onset* reverse the order of the verb and particle. *Outcry* and *onset* cannot be made into phrasal verbs with the same meaning.
- **c)** *Break-up*, *outcry* and *setback* are all countable.
- Point out that not all phrasal nouns can be made into phrasal verbs, for example, *update*, *overkill*.
- Highlight that although it is not always possible to turn a phrasal verb into a phrasal noun students may be able to guess the meaning of unknown words by identifying the phrasal verbs that they are formed from.

4 Focus students on the phrasal nouns in bold in sentences 1–7. Point out that each of the words can be replaced by a word or phrase from the box which means the same thing.

Students do the exercise on their own or in pairs.

Check answers with the class.

> 1 beginning of the football match 2 delay caused by a problem 3 forecast 4 contribution 5 heavy rain 6 informal gathering 7 number of people who are accepted

> ─ EXTRA IDEA ─
> - With stronger groups, ask students to identify which phrasal nouns from 1–7 have a different meaning from the phrasal verbs from which they are formed. (*Look out* = be careful, try to notice; *take in* = understand.)

Reading and Grammar

5 **a)** Introduce the topic by asking students what they understand by the name *Big Brother*. Although many students may recognise it as the name of a popular reality TV show, *Big Brother* is actually a fictional character from George Orwell's novel *1984*. He is the dictator of Oceania, a totalitarian state where everyone is under complete surveillance all of the time. Nowadays, the term *Big Brother* is often used to describe the increasing number of ways in which people are watched by the state, for example, through the use of CCTV cameras, ID cards and databases which hold information about us.

Focus students on the words and phrases in the box. Students check the meaning of the words and phrases. Be prepared with definitions, examples, etc. to give students if necessary.

Model and drill the words, paying particular attention to the pronunciation of *iris* /ˈaɪrɪs/.

b) Focus students on the pictures. Students discuss the questions in pairs or groups.

 Elicit ideas from the class and write them on the board.

> **Possible answers**
> **Places**: car parks, streets in town centres, roads, hospitals, shops, airports, cashpoints, schools.
> **Reasons could be**: to catch people stealing, being violent or committing a driving offence.

c) Students read the article. As a class, compare the ideas on the board with those in the article.

Explain that an internet *service provider* is a company that supplies access to the Internet, usually for a monthly fee.

Highlight that *RFID* is pronounced /ˈɑːfɪd/.

Explain that the *congestion zone* is an area of London where motorists have to pay to enter with their vehicles. Cameras record the registration numbers of all vehicles entering the zone, and if you do not pay the congestion charge within a stipulated amount of time, you receive a fine.

Check answers with the class.

> CCTV cameras operate in both public and private buildings.

d) Students read the article again and do the exercise on their own or in pairs.

Check answers with the class.

> 1F Opinion appears to be divided on identity cards.
> 2F Anyone who can read the cookies on a computer knows which websites the person has visited. 3T
> 4F RFID tags can also be used on people. 5T 6T
> 7F Any organisation can listen to your mobile phone conversations with the co-operation of the phone company. 8T

e) Focus students on the three questions. Students discuss the questions in groups. Ask each group to share their ideas with the class.

> **Help with Grammar** Impersonal report structures

Ask students to do **2** in Preview 7, SB p65 if necessary. Go through the introductory bullet with the class.

6 **a)–c)** Students do the exercises on their own or in pairs and check their answers in G7.4 SB p138.

Check answers with the class.

- **a)** To make impersonal report structures we can use:
  – *it* + passive + **that** + clause
  – subject (*CCTV cameras*) + passive + **infinitive with *to***
  – *there* + passive + **infinitive with *to***
- Point out that in structures with *there* + passive + infinitive with *to*, the verb which follows the passive is almost always *be*: **There are rumoured to be** *nearly 100 people dead* not ~~There is rumoured to have died nearly 100 people~~.
- Explain that we can use a variety of infinitive forms with impersonal report structures: *She is known **to have spent** five years in India. He is rumoured **to be resigning** next month.*
- **b)** are not
- Explain that *seem* and *appear* can also be used to distance yourself from what you are reporting.
- We can use a *that*-clause after *seems/appears*, **but** only when the subject is *it*. In all other cases, the verbs must be followed by infinitive with *to*. Also point out that *that* is optional in clauses with *seem* and *appear*, so if in doubt students should just leave it out.
- Point out that *seem* and *appear* can be followed by a variety of infinitive forms, in the same way as in sentences using the passive: *She appears **to have been lying** this whole time.*
- We can use *would* with *seem/appear* to make a statement more tentative: *It **would** appear that the cameras are not working.*

7 Do the first question with the class.

Point out that a *store card* (question 3) is a credit card issued by a particular shop for use only in that shop.

Students do the exercise on their own. Check answers with the class.

> 2 Most people in this country appear to be against the introduction of ID cards.
> 3 75% of people are estimated to have at least one store card.
> 4 The government is rumoured to be introducing RFID tags in passports next year.
> 5 Big stores are alleged to be keeping detailed personal records of their customers.
> 6 Secret monitoring of children seems to have become acceptable in some schools.

— **EXTRA IDEA** —
- With stronger groups, write the sentences on the board without reproducing the bold. Ask students to rewrite the sentences with no change in meaning.

Do the first question with the class. Students do the exercise on their own or in pairs.

Check answers with the class.

> **2** It is known that the rebels have withdrawn. The rebels are known to have withdrawn. **3** It is said that London is one of the most expensive cities in the world to live in. London is said to be one of the most expensive cities in the world to live in. **4** It is rumoured that the senior manager has resigned. The senior manager is rumoured to have resigned. **5** It is feared that more than 3,000 people have lost their lives in a devastating earthquake. More than 3,000 people are feared to have lost their lives in a devastating earthquake. **6** It is believed that the airport strike is affecting thousands of holiday flights. The airport strike is believed to be affecting thousands of holiday flights.

Get ready … Get it right!

 Put students into two groups, group A and group B. Students in group A turn to page 110 and students in group B turn to page 113.

a) Put students into pairs within their groups. Focus students on the three headlines. Check students in group A understand *outlaw*.

Students do the activity in pairs. Encourage students to add as much extra information as possible.

b) Put students into different pairs so that a student from group A is sitting with a student from group B. Students take turns to tell their stories. Encourage students to use impersonal report structures when telling their stories.

c) Students do the activity in the same pairs. Ask each pair to share one or two of their ideas with the class.

┌─ **EXTRA PRACTICE AND HOMEWORK** ─
Ph **Class Activity** 7B Fact or fiction? p155 (Instructions p127)
Ph **Vocabulary Plus** 7 Law and crime p178 (Instructions p170)
7 Review Exercises 4 and 5 SB p74
CD-ROM Lesson 7B
Workbook Lesson 7B p36

 ## 7C Not guilty!

QUICK REVIEW ●●●
This activity reviews phrasal nouns. Students do the first part of the activity on their own. Set a time limit of five minutes. Put students into pairs. Students take turns to say their sentences.

Vocabulary metaphors
Real World functions and intonation of questions
Review phrasal nouns

 a) Introduce the topic by asking students to explain what a metaphor is (a word or phrase which describes a thing, action, quality or person by referring to something else).

Focus students on the pairs of sentences. Point out that in each pair of sentences, the word in bold has a literal (i.e. basic) meaning in one sentence and a non-literal (i.e. metaphorical) meaning in the other.

Students do the exercise on their own or in pairs and check their answers in **V7.3** SB p136.

Check answers with the class. Point out that *warm* collocates with *welcome*, and it can also be used to describe people: *He's a very warm person*.

Also point out that units of time are not used with *fly*: *Time flies* not *Hours/minutes fly*. However, they **are** used with *fly by* (= go past quickly): *The hours/days/months flew by and soon it was time to go home.*

> **2 a)** NL – friendly and affectionate **b)** L
> **3 a)** L **b)** NL – attacked
> **4 a)** NL – filled with large numbers or amounts **b)** L
> **5 a)** L **b)** NL – clever and quick to learn
> **6 a)** L **b)** NL – the inspector understood
> **7 a)** NL – stopped moving and became completely still
> **b)** L
> **8 a)** L **b)** NL – passed very quickly
> **9 a)** NL – become very stressed because of work pressure, etc. **b)** L

b) Model the activity by saying a few sentences about yourself using the metaphors from **1a)**.

Students do the exercise on their own.

c) Students do the exercise in pairs. Encourage students to ask follow-up questions.

Ask each pair to share one or two of their sentences with the class.

- Encourage students to record the literal and non-literal meanings of words side by side in their vocabulary books, along with an example sentence showing both meanings.
- Ask students if metaphors exist in their own language and how they are used.

 a) Focus students on the picture and ask them to describe what is happening.

> A young man is being questioned by the police.

b) Tell students they are going to listen to an extract from a play.

R7.4 Play the recording (SB p155). Students listen and answer the questions. Check answers with the class.

Explain that *End of* is a colloquial British English term, used to mean 'End of story'. Also point out that *you tell me* is a common sarcastic response, used when someone is trying to avoid answering a question themselves. Finally, explain that *old bag* is a derogatory term for an elderly lady.

> Mike is a suspect because his alibi is suspicious, he knew that George (the victim of the burglary) would be out and that he'd just been paid £2,000, he was seen by a neighbour going back to his flat that evening, and has an expensive phone even though he is unemployed. Mike is alleged to have stolen money from his flatmate.

c) Play the recording again. Students listen and fill in the gaps. Check answers with the class.

> 1 ex-girlfriend 2 alibi 3 half; seven 4 two thousand
> 5 builder 6 stairs 7 pizza 8 neighbour 9 soap opera
> 10 unemployed

EXTRA IDEA

- Ask students to fill in the gaps in pairs *before* listening for a second time, to see how much they have remembered. Students then listen again to check their answers.

d) Students discuss the questions in pairs. Ask each pair to share their ideas with the class.

EXTRA IDEA

- Write these words and phrases from the recording on the board: *swarm, stash, nip out* and *give or take*. Ask students to look at R7.4, SB p155 and to guess the meaning of the words and phrases from the context. Ask what helped them guess.

 Focus students on the phrases in bold. Encourage students to look at R7.4, SB p155 to help them guess the meaning of the phrases from the context. Students do the exercise on their own or in pairs.
Check answers with the class.

> 1 it all seems very odd to me 2 living very close to you
> 3 we're not together all of the time 4 we are not naive
> 5 I no longer knew what was happening 6 must have hurt you/been very difficult for you, losing your job

EXTRA IDEA

- Ask students to explain each example of metaphorical language from **3**. For example, if something *strikes* you as odd, it 'suddenly hits you'. If someone lives *on your doorstep*, they don't literally live in front of your door, but still very close.

Real World Functions and intonation of questions

Introduce the topic by checking that students understand the difference between *pronunciation* (making the sounds of words or letters) and *intonation* (the rise and fall of the voice when you speak). Point out that intonation can often be varied in order to change meaning.

4 a)–b) **R7.5** Play the recording (SB p156). Students listen and do the exercises on their own or in pairs. They can check their answers in **RW7.1** SB p139.
Check answers with the class.

- **a)** 1 N 2 C 3 C 4 C 5 N
- Model and drill the sentences, paying particular attention to the falling and rising intonation.
- **b)** 1 falling 2 rising 3 falling
- Go through the **TIP!** with the class.

c)–d) **R7.6** Play the recording (SB p156). Students listen and do the exercise. They can check their answers in **RW7.1** SB p139.
Check answers with the class.

- **c)** 1 a) 2 c) 3 d) 4 b)
- Model and drill the sentences, paying particular attention to the falling and rising intonation.
- Also point out how tone of voice is important in conveying meaning in questions 1–4. Model and drill the aggressive/defensive tone of voice from question 2 and the sarcastic tone of voice from question 3.
- Go through the **TIPS!** in **RW7.1** SB p139 with the class or ask students to read them for homework.

5 a) Focus students on the questions and tell them they are going to hear them, too.

`R7.7` Play the recording (SB p156). Students listen and identify which question is requesting new information. They can check answers in pairs.

Check the answer with the class.

> Question 4 is asking for new information.

b) Ask students to turn to R7.7, SB p156. Play the recording again. Students listen and notice the sentence stress and intonation.

c) Put students into pairs. Play the recording again. Students listen and read the exchanges, copying the sentence stress and intonation.

 6 a) Put students into pairs, student A and student B. Student A reads the instructions on SB p73, student B turns to SB p115.

Remind students that Emma is Mike's ex-girlfriend and his alibi for the night of the burglary. Explain that student A is playing a police officer and student B is playing Emma.

`R7.4` Play the recording again if necessary, to remind students of Mike's story.

Focus student As on the list of things to find out. Encourage students to write out their questions, using their own ideas and those in the list. Encourage students to use a variety of question types and to make a note of which intonation pattern they should use with each question.

Focus student Bs on the information. Encourage students to add their own ideas, answering the questions in brackets.

b) Put students into pairs. Encourage student As to make notes, especially on anything that contradicts Mike's story.

c) Put students into groups of four, two student As and two student Bs. Students discuss the evidence. Ask each group to share their ideas with the class.

─── EXTRA IDEAS ───

- After completing **6**, ask students to rate each other: did they all have an opportunity to speak? Did they involve other people and encourage them to speak? Did they reach a conclusion? If yes, what were they good at? If not, how could they improve?

- As an extended speaking activity, organise a trial for Mike, with students playing Mike, Emma, the policeman and policewoman, the judge, the prosecutor and the defence lawyer. The rest of the class play the jury and decide if Mike is innocent or guilty.

─── EXTRA PRACTICE AND HOMEWORK ───

Ph **Class Activity** 7C Crime circle p156 (Instructions p128)

Ph **Help with Listening** 7 Opinions p195 (Instructions p186)

7 Review Exercise 6 SB p74

CD-ROM Lesson 7C

Workbook Lesson 7C p38

Workbook Reading and Writing Portfolio 7 p72

Progress Test 7 p216

Preview 8 Exercise 1 SB p75

7 Review

See p32 for ideas on how to use this section.

1a) 1 round 2 round 3 away 4 at 5 my own back
6 through 7 into

2a) 1 is going 2 been taking 3 phoned/would phone
4 use/should use 5 told 6 want to catch/'m going to catch

3a) 1 'd be sitting 2 'd give 3 owned 4 would've finished
5 wouldn't feel/wouldn't be feeling 6 spoke 7 hadn't changed

4 1 down 2 off 3 on 4 out 5 back 6 in

5 1 are reported to be increasing/to have increased
2 is feared 3 is expected to be 4 are rumoured to be
seeking/to have sought/to have been seeking
5 appear to be/to have been 6 seems to be/to have been

Progress Portfolio

See p32 for ideas on how to use this section.

Accurate Writing

CONNECTING WORDS: condition
PUNCTUATION: commas

1 Students do the exercise on their own or in pairs and check their answers in **AW7.1** SB p139.

Check answers with the class.

Point out that we can use *unless* in conditionals to mean *if not* in order to say that something can only happen in particular circumstances.

We can use *in case* to talk about something we do in order to be ready for possible future situations.

We can use *otherwise* to talk about an undesirable situation which would happen if something else didn't happen.

We often use *provided/providing, as long as* and *assuming,* instead of *if* in conditionals. Also point out that *provided/providing* and *as long as* mean 'only if (this happens)'.

We can use *whether* instead of *if* when we mention two alternatives. We put it in front of the first alternative.

Imagine and *suppose/supposing* both mean 'form a picture in your mind about what something could be like'.

Finally, point out that we can use *imagine* and *suppose/supposing* as an alternative for *if* in questions.

> **1** Unless **2** otherwise **3** as long as **4** providing
> **5** Whether **6** Supposing

2 Students do the exercise on their own or in pairs and check their answers in **AW7.2** SB p139.

Check answers with the class.

Point out that we use commas in the following situations:

– after introductory clauses beginning with *after, although, as, because, if, since, when* and *while*;
– to separate three or more words, phrases or clauses written in a series, although not usually before the final *and*;
– after introductory words such as *surprisingly* and *however*;

– either side of clauses, phrases and words which are not essential to the meaning of the sentence, for example, non-defining relative clauses;
– after the verb and before the opening quotation marks in direct speech;
– before the closing quotation marks in direct speech when the quotation is followed by the speaker;
– to separate two or more adjectives that are of the same type in describing a noun;
– in geographical names;
– in dates;
– in addresses.

Commas are also used before the person you are addressing: *Hello, Anna; Goodbye, Nick; Sorry, everybody.*

For information on when to use semi-colons instead of commas, see **AW6.2** SB p135 and p81 of this book.

> **1** If you have intruders in the house, it's better not to challenge them. **2** Avoid keeping expensive computers, handbags and wallets on view. **3** However, you should also be well insured. **4** Door chains and spy holes, which your landlord will probably fit, help to reduce crime. **5** The police officer said, "You should set up a Neighbourhood Watch scheme." **6** You should install a burglar alarm, otherwise you'll regret it.

3 **a)–b)** Students do the exercise on their own or in pairs.
Check answers with the class.

> **a)** 1 in case 2 otherwise 3 unless 4 as long as/providing
> **b)** Commas (in order of appearance):
> after an introductory clause, a non-defining relative clause, after an introductory word, to separate words written in a series, after an introductory clause, after an introductory word, after an introductory clause, to introduce direct speech.

┌─ **EXTRA PRACTICE AND HOMEWORK** ─────────
│ **Workbook** Accurate Writing Exercises 14 and 15
│ p86–p87
└───────────────────────────────────────

Preview 8

WISH, IF ONLY ...

1 **a)–c)** Students do the exercises on their own or in pairs and check their answers in **G8.1** SB p141.

Check answers with the class.

> **a)** 1 Correct 2 knew 3 was/were 4 wasn't/weren't
> 5 had known 6 Correct 7 could 8 Correct 9 would get
> **b)** 2 but I don't. (present) 3 but he's not/he isn't.
> (present) 4 but it is. (present) 5 but I didn't. (past)

> 6 but we weren't. (past) 7 but I can't. (present) 8 but
> they won't. (future) 9 but she won't. (future)
> The auxiliary verb is in the form of the situation now.
> **c)** 1b) would tell
> 2a) had b) had had
> 3a) could see/could have seen b) could have seen
> 4a) hadn't had to b) didn't have to
> 5a) would stop b) had stopped

8 What's stopping you?

8A   Finding time

QUICK REVIEW ●●●
This activity reviews literal and metaphorical meanings. Students do the first part of the activity on their own. Set a time limit of five minutes. Put students into pairs. Students compare sentences.

> **Vocabulary** phrases with *time*
> **Grammar** past verb forms with present or future meaning
> **Review** metaphors

Vocabulary Phrases with *time*

 a) Focus students on the phrases in bold. Students do the exercise on their own and check the new phrases in **V8.1** SB p140.

Model and drill the phrases, paying particular attention to whether or not *time* is stressed (see **V8.1** SB p140).

Point out the following:

We sometimes say *I've got loads/tons of time to kill.*

In plenty of time can often be replaced with *with time to spare*: *If I take the motorway, we'll arrive with time to spare.* However, *have time to spare* cannot be replaced by *in plenty of time.*

Take your time can be used sarcastically when someone is very late or has taken a long time to do something: *You took your time! I've been waiting hours!*

For the time being can be used at the beginning or end of a clause: *For the time being, I'm going to stay in London. I'm going to stay in London for the time being.* Notice that when used at the end of a clause, it is not preceded by a comma.

We can say *it's only a question of time* to mean the same as *it's only a matter of time.*

We cannot say ~~there's no time like the past/future~~.

We can use *give sb a tough time* to mean the same as *give sb a hard time.*

> ── **EXTRA IDEA** ──
> * ✎ Before doing the exercise, write the word *time* in the centre of the board. Divide the class into groups and give them five minutes to think of as many phrases with *time* as they can. Invite one person from each group to come up and write a phrase on the board. Continue until each group runs out of phrases. The group which writes the last phrase is the winner. This activity would also work at the beginning of the next lesson to review the phrases that students have learned.

b) Students do the exercise on their own.

c) Put students into pairs. Students take turns to say their sentences. Encourage students to ask follow-up questions. Ask each student to share something they learned about their partner with the class.

Reading and Grammar

 a) Students do the exercise on their own.

b) Put students into pairs. Students compare lists and choose two people who have had 'the greatest effect' – either good or bad.

c) Ask each pair to share their choices with the class and to justify them.

d) Focus students on the article. Be prepared with definitions, examples, etc. to pre-teach *eruption*, CO_2 *emissions* /sɪːəʊˈtuː ɪˌmɪʃənz/, *hurricane* /ˈhʌrɪkən/ and *green* (in the sense of 'protecting the environment').

Students do the exercise on their own. You can set a time limit of two minutes to encourage students to read quickly for gist.

Check answers with the class.

> 1c) 2b) 3a)

> ── **EXTRA IDEA** ──
> * Before students read the article, ask them to discuss what the title of the article means and what they think the article will be about.

3 Students do the exercise on their own. Check answers with the class.

Explain that Yellowstone is a national park in the state of Wyoming and is home to an active volcano.

A *direct debit* is a regular automatic payment made from your bank account. For example, many people pay their bills each month by direct debit to avoid having to make payments by cheque or in cash.

> **1** To work on a documentary about the fictional eruption of a volcano in Yellowstone National Park. **2** Because he (the head of NCAR) is convinced that global warming does exist and thought that everyone else was also convinced. **3** Because it meant Eddy returned home convinced that global warming was real and that it was a very serious problem. **4** He employed someone to do an 'eco-audit' on his house; he went to a meeting of his local Green Party; he became a Green Party candidate and election organiser. **5** He uses them as examples of how one person can change and how this can set off change in others.

- Write these words and phrases from the article on the board: *wreck, I'd sooner, set off, grand*. Ask students to guess the meaning of the words and phrases from the context. Ask what helped them guess.

4 Students discuss the questions in pairs. Ask each pair to share some of their ideas with the class.

Possible answers
1 The saying means that people need to take responsibility for things and act now, rather than hoping that someone else will do it or that it can wait.
2 An eco-audit would involve assessing how much energy you use to run your house. It would probably examine lighting, heating and water consumption, etc. Recommendations might include using energy-efficient light bulbs, improving insulation and using less water.
4 Travel less by car or plane, recycle more, eat locally grown or sourced food to cut down on food miles, etc.

EXTRA IDEA

- For homework, students use the Web to research ways of making their home greener. Students then present their ideas to the class.

Help with Grammar Past verb forms with present or future meaning

Ask students to do **1** in Preview 8, SB p75 if necessary. Focus students on the introductory bullet point.

5 **a)–d)** Students do the exercises on their own or in pairs and check their answers in **G8.2** SB p141. Check answers with the class.

- **a)** i) No ii) Yes
- **b)** Pink: infinitive with or without *to*
  Blue: Past Simple or Past Continuous
- When *it's time* and *would prefer* are followed by a verb, we use an infinitive with *to*. When *would sooner* and *would rather* are followed by a verb, we use an infinitive.
- **c)** a past verb form
- We can say *It's about time …* or *It's high time* + subject + past verb form to suggest that something is urgent.
- When we talk about past situations with *would sooner/would rather* + subject + verb, we use the Past Perfect or Past Perfect Continuous.
- When the preference is also in the past, we can use *would have preferred it if*: We **would have preferred it if** you **had warned** us at the time.

6 Students do the exercise on their own or in pairs. Check answers with the class.

1 I'd prefer it if we met/were meeting at the cinema.
2 I'd sooner David did/was doing/had done the clearing up. 3 It's time to have a break. 4 We'd prefer to go on Tuesday. 5 I'd rather you didn't smoke/hadn't smoked in here. 6 It's about time Pete admitted he was wrong.

EXTRA IDEA

- If some students finish faster than others, ask them to rewrite sentences 1–6 by removing or adding the subject of the second clause. For example, *I'd prefer it if we met at the cinema – I'd prefer to meet at the cinema.*

7 **a)–b)** Students do the exercise on their own and then compare answers in pairs.
Check answers with the class.

1 I'd rather people **didn't** drop litter in the streets.
2 Correct 3 I'd prefer **it if** more people were environmentally conscious. 4 It's high time people **stopped** using cars in cities. 5 I'd rather my family **spent/had spent/were spending** more time together.
6 I'd prefer it if people **didn't** use their mobiles on public transport. 7 Correct 8 I'd prefer **it if I lived/to live** nearer to the coast.

c) Students do the activity in pairs. Encourage students to ask follow-up questions. Ask each student to share one thing they learned about their partner with the class.

Listening and Speaking

8 **a)** Focus students on the words in the box. Students check the meaning of the words. Be prepared with definitions, examples, etc. to give students if necessary.
Model and drill the words, paying particular attention to the pronunciation of *soot* /sʊt/, *incinerator* /ɪnˈsɪnəreɪtə/ and *federal* /ˈfedərəl/.

Point out that in a federation, the word *federal* is used to describe anything related to the government of the whole country, as opposed to government at state or local level: *federal law, federal crime, federal taxes, federal government, the federal reserve,* etc.

b) Tell students they are going to listen to Eddy Canfor-Dumas talking about a woman called Hazel Henderson. Focus students on the three questions.
R8.1 Play the recording (SB p156). Students listen and choose the correct answers. They can check answers in pairs.
Check answers with the class.

1 dirty 2 levels of air pollution made public
3 governments all round the world

c) Put students into groups of three, student A, student B and student C. Focus each student on their prompts. Students tick those in their list that they could talk about at this stage.

Remind students that Bristol is a city in the southwest of England.

> **EXTRA IDEA**
> * Ask students to make as many notes as they can under the prompts in **c)** *before* listening to the recording again.

d) Play the recording again. Students listen and make notes on their section of the story.

e) Give students a few minutes to organise their notes and prepare how they are going to summarise their part of the story.

> **EXTRA IDEA**
> * Allow weaker students to check information in R8.1, SB p156 if necessary.

f) Students work in the same groups and take turns to read out their summaries. Encourage students to point out any information that their partner missed.

> **EXTRA IDEAS**
> * Write these phrases from the recording on the board: *media outlet, take sth on*. Ask students to look at R8.1, SB p156 and to guess the meaning of the phrases from the context. Ask what helped them guess.
> * Ask students to use the Web to research Hazel Henderson and give a short presentation about who she is and why she is famous.

Get ready … Get it right!

9 **a)** Model the activity by talking to the class about the three famous people that you would spend the evening with.

Students do the activity on their own. Remind students that they should pick three people that they think have made a difference to the world – positive or negative – not just three famous people they would like to meet.

b) Students work on their own and write one question for each of their guests.

10 **a)** Students work in pairs and take turns to talk about who they would choose and what questions they would ask. Encourage students to try and imagine what the conversation would be about.

b) Each pair agrees on the three most interesting guests.

c) Ask each pair to tell the class who their guests are and what they would probably talk about.

d) Write the dinner party guests on the board in groups and ask the class to vote for which dinner party they would most like to go to. Encourage students to justify their answers.

> **EXTRA PRACTICE AND HOMEWORK**
>
> **Ph** **Class Activity** 8A The council meeting p157–p158 (Instructions p128)
> **Ph** **Help with Listening** 8 Small words p196 (Instructions p187)
> **8 Review** Exercises 1 and 2 SB p84
> **CD-ROM** Lesson 8A
> **Workbook** Lesson 8A p39

8B Fear!

QUICK REVIEW ●●●

This activity reviews past verb forms with present or future meaning. Students do the first part of the activity on their own. Set a time limit of five minutes. Remind students that at least one of their sentences should be false. Put students into pairs. Students take turns to say their sentences. Encourage students to ask follow-up questions. Students guess if their partner's sentences are true or false.

Listening and Vocabulary

1 **a)** Focus students on the four questions. Check students understand *ancestors*. Students discuss the questions in pairs. Ask each pair to share some of their ideas with the class.

Vocabulary *wherever, whoever, whatever*, etc.; word building (2): suffixes
Review past verb forms with present or future meaning

> **EXTRA IDEA**
> * Before **1a)**, ask students to work in pairs and brainstorm as many different emotions as they can think of. Students then compare their list with the words in question 1. (Students would then skip question 4 in **1b)**.)

b) Tell students they are going to listen to a radio programme about emotions. Be prepared with definitions, examples, etc. to pre-teach *guilt* /gɪlt/, *embarrassment*, *shame, pride, sympathy* /ˈsɪmpəθi/ and *spill*. Point out that *sympathy* has nothing to do with being 'nice'; this is a common false friend.

R8.2 Play the recording (SB p156). Students listen and check their answers to questions 2–4 in **1a)**.
Check answers with the class.

> 2 Yes, they do. 3 Whenever they came across something that frightened them, they would run away; whenever they came across something that disgusted them, they wouldn't eat it; whatever gave them pleasure, they would do more of it, etc. 4 There are the higher emotions of: guilt, embarrassment, shame, pride and sympathy.

c) Give students time to read quotes 1–5. Play the recording again. Students listen and answer the questions.
Check answers with the class.

> 1 That men don't experience the same emotions as women. 2 Using photographs of facial expressions to see if people could identify the basic emotions. 3 The basic emotions. 4 Spill coffee on yourself. 5 Basic emotions are caused by an act itself; higher emotions are caused by what others might think of you.

d) Focus students on the statement in italics. Make sure students understand *trigger*. Students discuss the statement in groups.
Ask each group to share their ideas with the class.

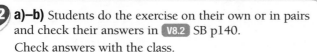
Help with Vocabulary *wherever, whoever, whatever, etc.*

2 a)–b) Students do the exercise on their own or in pairs and check their answers in **V8.2** SB p140.
Check answers with the class.

- **a)** 1b) 2a) 3a) 4a)
- Point out that *whenever* can mean 'every time'.
- Explain that *whoever*, *whichever* and *whatever* can be the subject and object of the verb.
- Point out that *whichever* is often followed by *of*.
- Also point out that we can use *wherever, whoever, however, whatever, whenever* and *whichever* to show surprise or to emphasise something.
- We can use these same words in informal conversation to answer a question when we want to say that we really don't mind. However, highlight that the use of *whatever* in this context also suggests that the speaker doesn't care, and can seem rude.

3 Students do the exercise on their own or in pairs. Check answers with the class.

> 1 whatever 2 However 3 whichever 4 whichever/whatever 5 Whenever 6 Whoever 7 Whatever 8 Wherever/Whenever

4 a)–b) Students do the exercise on their own and compare answers in pairs. Students say which of the sentences are true for them. Encourage students to ask follow-up questions.
Check answers with the class.
Ask each student to share one thing they learned about their partner with the rest of the class.

> 1 whatever 2 However 3 However 4 Whenever/Wherever 5 Whatever 6 Wherever 7 Whoever 8 Whatever/Whichever

Reading and Vocabulary

5 a) Focus students on the three questions. Students discuss the questions in pairs. Encourage students to ask follow-up questions.
Ask each pair to share their ideas with the class.

b) Focus students on the words in the box. Students check the meaning of the words. Be prepared with definitions, examples, etc. to give students if necessary.
Model and drill the words, paying particular attention to the pronunciation of *chisel* /ˈtʃɪzəl/ and *mediocre* /ˌmiːdiˈəʊkə/.

c) Be prepared with a definition, examples, etc. to pre-teach *thrill*. Students do the exercise on their own or in pairs.
Check answers with the class.

> 1 The writer heard somebody breaking into her house. She sent her husband downstairs to investigate. 2 A fear-avoider.

6 a)–b) Students do the exercise on their own and compare answers in pairs. Remind students that they are not just looking for which sentences are true and which are false; some aren't mentioned at all.
Check answers with the class.

> 1T ('I stood at the top of the stairs with my heart trying to escape my body.')
> 2 Not mentioned
> 3F ('I wouldn't wish it on anyone')
> 4T ('Are these the drivers I see overtaking other cars on the wrong side of the road and jumping red lights?')
> 5 Not mentioned
> 6F ('I so courageously sent my husband downstairs to investigate.')
> 7 Not mentioned

Help with Vocabulary Word building (2): suffixes

7 **a)–c)** Introduce the topic by reminding students what a suffix is (a letter or letters added to the end of a word to make a new word). Point out that suffixes can be used to create nouns, verbs, adjectives and adverbs.

Students do the exercises on their own or in pairs and check their answers in **V8.3** SB p140.

Check answers with the class.

- **a)** **1** change, a change; challenge, a challenge **2** disturbance (-ance), recovery (-y), rider(s) (-r), division (-sion), survival (-al), excitement (-ment), failure (-ure) **3** happiness (-ness), possibility (-ity)
- **b)** **1** adjectives **2** adverbs **3** adjectives **4** verbs
- Point out that unfortunately there are no rules about which suffixes should be added to which words in order to make new words; students will need to learn the words individually and double-check in a dictionary if they are not sure. However, recognising which suffixes are typical with nouns, verbs, adjectives and adverbs may help students to guess the meaning of unknown words.
- Highlight that just because a word ends in *-ly*, it isn't necessarily an adverb. Also point out that some adverbs do not end in *-ly* (e.g. *hard*, *well*).
- Point out that replacing the final *e* in a word with a suffix isn't a hard and fast rule. For example, *surviveal* and *cultureal* are incorrect, but *excitement* and *courageous* are correct. However, changing a *y* to an *i* is a hard and fast rule: *happyness*.
- Go through the **TIPS!** in **V8.3** SB p140 with the class or ask students to read them for homework. Point out that *-ize* spellings are becoming more common in British English. If students are taking Cambridge ESOL exams, they should be aware of the need to be consistent in the choice of *-ise* and *-ize* endings.

8 **a)–b)** Students do the exercise on their own and then compare answers in pairs. Encourage students to use their dictionaries if necessary.

Check answers with the class. Point out that *lovable* means 'easy to love' whereas *lovely* means 'very nice' or 'very pleasant'. Both would be possible in sentence 1.

2 teller **3** pleasure **4** imaginations **5** entertainment **6** liven **7** scary **8** clearly **9** traditional **10** thankfully

Get ready … Get it right!

9 **a)** Model the activity by writing on the board a list of things that frightened you as a child or frighten you now. Ask students if they were or are frightened by the things on your list.

Focus students on the list of ideas. Students do the activity on their own. Encourage students to use their own ideas as well as those in the list.

 b) Model the activity by writing a list of things that you enjoy but which might frighten some people. Ask students what they think of your list.

Students do the activity on their own.

10 **a)** Students do the activity in groups. Encourage students to identify other students who had or have similar fears to theirs. Ask each student to share one thing they have learned about another student with the rest of the class.

b) Ask each student how they would describe themselves – as a thrill-seeker or fear-avoider.

— EXTRA IDEA —
- Divide the class into two groups, thrill-seekers and fear-avoiders. Put students into pairs – one from each group – and ask them to discuss what makes them a thrill-seeker or fear-avoider. Can the thrill-seekers convince the fear-avoiders to take more risks? Can the fear-avoiders convince the thrill-seekers to be less reckless?

— EXTRA PRACTICE AND HOMEWORK —

Ph **Class Activity** 8B The thrill-seekers p159 (Instructions p129)

Ph **Vocabulary Plus** 8 Stress patterns in long words p179 (Instructions p171)

8 Review Exercises 3 and 4 SB p84

CD-ROM Lesson 8B

Workbook Lesson 8B p41

8C The pros and cons

Vocabulary idiomatic phrases
Skills Reading: a modern poem; Listening: people
discussing whether it's better to be a man or a woman;
Speaking: class survey about gender; Writing: summarising
a class survey
Real World explaining choices
Review *wherever, whoever, whatever*, etc.

 a) Put students into groups of the same sex if possible.
Focus students on the ideas. Students do the exercise in
groups. Encourage students to use their own ideas as well
as those on the page.

Be aware that discussing gender issues can lead to heated
debate. Be prepared to defuse any tension that arises and
to monitor the discussions in this lesson to make sure that
everybody has the chance to express their views.

b)–c) Ask each group to share their conclusions with the
class. Encourage each group to justify their answers.

 Write any points that the class agrees on in a corner
of the board and leave them there throughout the lesson.

a) Introduce the topic by asking students if they ever read
poetry, either in English or in their own language. Ask
students what might be difficult about reading poems in
a different language (e.g. the use of metaphorical and
symbolic language, an unfamiliar format, the use of
cultural or historical references).

Tell students they are going to listen to and read a poem
by Sophie Hannah, a contemporary British poet.

R8.3 Focus students on the poem and play the recording.
Students listen and read at the same time.

Focus students on the questions. Students do the exercise
on their own or in pairs.

Check answers with the class.

> 1 Whether or not to phone a man she has been seeing.
> 2 Because she weighs up the pros (advantages) and cons
> (disadvantages) of phoning him.
> **3 Pros of phoning** He'll be pleased if I phone to ask
> him how he is; it will make me look considerate and he
> likes considerate people; he'll be reassured to see that I
> haven't lost interest; if I phone him right now I'll get to
> speak to him sooner than I will if I sit around waiting
> for him to phone me; he might not want to phone me
> from work in case someone hears him.
> **Cons of phoning** Someone might hear and begin (or
> continue) to suspect that there's something between us;
> there's always the chance he'll back off if I come on too
> strong; if I make it too easy for him, he'll assume I'm
> too easy.
> **Pros of not phoning** The less keen I appear, the more
> keen he's likely to be; if I make no effort, that leaves
> him with more of a challenge; if I don't phone I can
> always say, later, that I went off him first.

EXTRA IDEA
● Before reading the poem, students listen to it. Ask
students if they can summarise what the poem is
about.

b)–c) Students do the exercises on their own or in pairs.
Check answers with the class.

> b)6 c)1 d)2 e)3 f)5 g)4 h)10 i)8 j)9

 a) Focus students on the phrases in the box. Students do
the exercise on their own or in pairs.
Check answers with the class.

> b) go off
> c) back off
> d) make the first move
> e) come on strong

b) Students discuss the questions in pairs. Point out that
the cultural issue that the poem raises is whether or not
women can or should take the initiative in beginning a
relationship.

Ask each pair to share their ideas with the class.

 a) Introduce the topic by asking students if they've ever
taken part in a survey. What were they asked about?

Focus students on the two questions. Students discuss
how they think most people would answer them.

b) Tell students they are going to listen to six people
answering the questions in **4a)**.

R8.4 Play the recording (SB p157). Students listen and
answer the questions.

Check answers with the class.

> Two people said 'yes' to question 1.
> Four people would choose to be the same gender.

 a) Put students into two groups, A and B. Play the
recording again. Students listen and make notes.

b) Put students into pairs so they are working with
someone from the other group. They compare notes.

Check answers with the class.

Do you think that being a man or a woman has ever stopped you from doing something you wanted to do?
Em No. Has worked as a labourer. **Bob** No. Hasn't really thought about it. Never had any problems with sport or work. **Mick** Thinks about how he can't give birth. **Kay** Wanted to play football as a child but couldn't. **Joey** No, but being a woman makes life harder and more complicated. Having a job and a family can be difficult. **Dan** No. Doors have been opened.

If you could live your life again as a man or a woman, which would you choose and why?
Em As a woman because she's enjoyed her life so far. **Bob** As a man because he enjoys it, but as a woman for a day or two to gain empathy. **Mick** As a man. (He doesn't give any reasons.) **Kay** As a man. She wouldn't have to queue up in the toilets; men only have to think of one thing at a time. **Joey** As a woman. Women are better communicators and have richer lives with their friends; they can have it all if they work at it. **Dan** As a man **or** a woman. It would be wonderful to come back.

 6 a) Elicit answers from the class.

b) Focus students on the Real World box. Model and drill the sentences, paying particular attention to the intonation pattern in sentences which begin with *whereas* or *while*.

Students interview as many people as they can in five minutes and make notes. Encourage students to ask follow-up questions and to take detailed notes.

c) Put students into pairs, preferably of different genders. Students compare notes and discuss the questions. Ask each pair to share their most interesting findings with the class.

--- EXTRA IDEAS ---

- Focus students on the answers to **1** which you wrote on the board at the beginning of the lesson. Ask students if they still agree with these points, or if anything they have discussed in the lesson has changed their minds.

- Ask students to rate each other: did they put their opinions across persuasively and convincingly? Did they justify their opinions? If so, how did they do this well? If not, how could they improve?

Writing Extension

 7 Students write the report on their own. This activity can be set for homework.

--- EXTRA IDEA ---

- As a class, brainstorm some language that could be used in each stage of the report: *This survey examined people's responses to … ; Responses were taken from … ; The results were as follows: … ; In conclusion, the data shows that … .*

 Ask students to turn to SB p107 and look at *You Gotta Be*. This song was recorded by the British singer Des'Ree in 1994.

 a) Students do the exercise in pairs. Encourage students to say the words out loud to make sure they rhyme.
Check answers with the class.

> you–to tears–fears said–read you–view pace–face
> unfolds–holds

b) Students do the exercise on their own or in pairs. Tell students they will have the opportunity to listen to the song to check their answers.

c) R8.5 Play the recording. Students listen and check their answers.

> **2** holds **3** fears **4** tears **5** said **6** read **7** you
> **8** view **9** you **10** pace **11** to **12** face

 2 Students discuss the question in pairs. Check answers with the class.

> *Try and keep your head up to the sky* = try and be positive
> *Stand up and be counted* = make yourself known
> *love will save the day* = love is the most important thing; we can rely on love
> *The world keeps on spinning* = everything continues, no matter what
> *Can't stop it, if you try to* = you shouldn't fight against things that you can't stop or change

 3 Students discuss the question in pairs. Ask them to share their ideas with the class.

--- EXTRA PRACTICE AND HOMEWORK ---

Ph **Class Activity** 8C What a dilemma! p160 (Instructions p129)
CD-ROM Lesson 8C
Workbook Lesson 8C p43
Workbook Reading and Writing Portfolio 8 p75
Progress Test 8 p218

8 Review

See p32 for ideas on how to use this section.

1 1c) 2e) 3f) 4b) 5d) 6g) 7h) 8a)

2a) 1 B came 2 A to do B see 3 A apologised B made
4 A had B to finish 5 A went B gave 6 A to move B stayed

3 2 Whatever needs doing, you can rely on me. 3 However many times I wash my hair, it always looks greasy.
4 Whatever you do, don't tell my mum I've lost her camera.
5 Whichever road you take to get to the station, it'll take the same amount of time. 6 Whoever wrote this certainly can't spell. 7 Whenever I ring Mick, he's always out.

4a) 1 courageous, moody, cultural, talented, sympathetic, friendly 2 confidently, finally, recently 3 nationalise, widen, clarify 4 creative, dependent, remarkable 5 disturbance, recovery, division, excitement, failure, plan, change

4b) 2 finally 3 widen 4 possibility 5 creative

Progress Portfolio

See p32 for ideas on how to use this section.

Accurate Writing

CONNECTING WORDS: comment adverbials
SPELLING: commonly misspelled words

 a)–b) Students do the exercises on their own or in pairs and check their answers in **AW8.1** SB p141.

Check answers with the class.

Point out that comment adverbials usually appear in front position, but that they can also appear in final position: *Amazingly, I wasn't late./I wasn't late, amazingly.*

a) 1 obviously; fortunately 2 Quite honestly; In fact
3 Unfortunately; To be honest 4 Amazingly

b) 1 Frankly 2 Apparently 3 According to
4 Personally 5 actually

 Students do the exercise on their own or in pairs and check their answers in **AW8.2** SB p141.

Check answers with the class.

1 necessary 2 acquaint 3 receipt 4 government
5 succeed 6 address 7 business 8 accommodate
9 medicine 10 exaggerate 11 admitted 12 colleague

 a)–b) Students do the exercise on their own or in pairs.

Check answers with the class.

a) 1 Unfortunately 2 in fact 3 frankly 4 To be honest
5 surprisingly 6 Clearly 7 quite honestly

b) Spelling mistakes (in order of appearance): address, business, colleague, accommodation, exaggeration, admitted, necessary.

EXTRA PRACTICE AND HOMEWORK

Workbook Accurate Writing Exercises 16 and 17 p87

Preview 9

SIMPLE V CONTINUOUS

 a)–b) Students do the exercises on their own or in pairs and check their answers in **G9.1** SB p143.

Check answers with the class. Point out that sentence 3 could be correct if somebody had been dying for a long period of time and we wanted to refer to what they were doing on that date. However, it is unlikely. Sentence 5 could be correct in a conversation such as the following: A *I can't believe you made so many friends when you were in Barcelona!* B *I was living there for six years, remember.* However, it would be more common to use the Past Simple.

Sentence 8 could be correct if you wanted to emphasise the fact that you and Jim crossed paths on leaving/entering. However, the Past Simple with *turn up* would probably be more common here.

a) 1I 2U 3U 4C 5U 6C 7C 8U 9C

b) State verbs: prefer, understand, know, recognise, want, suppose, agree, mean, seem, contain, consist, belong, own
Activity verbs: plan, play, do, walk, listen, study, talk, take, give

A/AN, THE OR NO ARTICLE (–)

Students do the exercise on their own or in pairs and check their answers in **G9.3** SB p144.

Check answers with the class.

1 the 2 a 3 a 4 an 5 the 6 a 7 The 8 – 9 –

9 Cash

Student's Book p86–p95

9A Where does it all go?

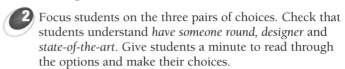

Vocabulary *price* and *cost*
Grammar simple v continuous: verbs with different meanings
Review suffixes

QUICK REVIEW ●●●

This activity reviews suffixes. Students do the first part of the activity on their own. Set a time limit of five minutes. Encourage students to work from dictionaries if necessary. Put students into pairs. Students take turns to say their words and check if they are the same. Check answers with the class.

Vocabulary *price* and *cost*

1 a) Introduce the exercise by asking students if they can explain the difference between *price* and *cost*. Tell students that *price* means 'the amount of money for which something is sold'; *cost* means 'the amount of money needed to buy, do or make something'. Write the example sentences from the introduction to **V9.1** SB p142 on the board if necessary.

Students do the exercise on their own or in pairs and check their answers in **V9.1** SB p142.

Check answers with the class.

Point out that although *price* and *cost* are very similar in meaning, they are rarely interchangeable. Encourage students to learn which phrase takes each word individually.

Also point out the following:

The *cost of living* would include things like the price of food, petrol, utilities, rent/mortgage, etc.

Although we say *half-price* and *full-price*, we don't say *quarter-price*, etc.

Priceless does not mean 'very cheap'; in fact, it means the exact opposite: so expensive it does not have a price.

We often say *cost an absolute fortune* to say that something was extremely expensive.

We can say *underpriced* as well as *overpriced*.

The adjectives *pricey* and *costly* both mean 'expensive' but can be used in different ways. *Pricey* is informal: *I wanted to buy a new suit but it was a bit pricey costly*. *Costly* is rather formal. *Costly* can be used to mean something that has cost a great deal of money or anything else valuable (e.g. time, success): *The council has decided not to proceed with the plans for the bypass because it would be too costly. Fearns's missed penalty proved costly as Telford went on to lose 2–1.*

> 1 cost 2 priced 3 cost 4 price 5 cost 6 price 7 cost
> 8 price 9 priced

b) Students do the exercise in pairs. Ask each pair to share one or two of their ideas with the class.

Reading and Grammar

 Focus students on the three pairs of choices. Check that students understand *have someone round, designer* and *state-of-the-art*. Give students a minute to read through the options and make their choices.

Elicit answers from the class. Ask students to justify their choices.

3 a) Focus students on the article. Be prepared with definitions, examples, etc. to pre-teach *cast-off* /ˈkɑːst ɒf/, *flash, prize, folk* /fəʊk/ and *fulfilment*.

Students do the exercise on their own or in pairs. Check answers with the class.

A *season ticket* is a ticket which allows the holder to watch a certain number of football matches within a period of time (usually all of the home matches for one team in one season) for a lower price than buying tickets one-by-one.

> Experiences are becoming more popular. Material goods are becoming less popular.

> ─ **EXTRA IDEA** ─
> ● Before students read the article, ask them to look at the photos and the title of the article. Ask students if they can predict what the article will be about.

b)–c) Students do the exercises on their own or in pairs. Check answers with the class.

> 1T 2F The Porsche's brakes cost as much as a flying lesson or a no-expense-spared – i.e. very expensive – weekend in Rome. 3F The super-rich want their favourite band to play at their party as a birthday present rather than a Maserati. 4F People go to cafés because they want to enjoy the experience of eating or drinking in a social setting. 5F Once societies reach a certain point of affluence they move away from materialism.
>
> *a fat bank account* = a bank account with a lot of money in it
> *tick all the boxes* = fulfil all of the requirements for something

- Write these words and phrases from the article, which all relate to the topic of money, on the board: *no-expense-spared, disposable income, materialism, affluence.* Ask students to guess the meaning of the words and phrases from the context. Ask what helped them guess.

d) Group students of different nationalities together if possible. Students discuss the questions in groups. Ask each group to share their ideas with the class.

Help with Grammar Simple v continuous: verbs with different meanings

Ask students to do **1** in Preview 9, SB p85 if necessary.

Go through the introductory bullet with the class and check that students understand what 'states' and 'activities' mean when referring to verbs.

4 **a)–c)** Students do the exercises on their own or in pairs and check their answers in `G9.2` SB p143.

Check answers with the class.

- **a)** b) fitting c) expect d) expecting e) see f) seeing g) think h) thinking
- **b)** 1a) possesses b) is experiencing
  2a) seems b) is performing
  3a) seems b) going to see
  4a) (the texture) is b) is experiencing something physical
  5a) originates b) is travelling
  6a) shows a permanent state b) is showing a temporary state
  7a) believe something is probably true b) are thinking something exists although in fact it is not real or true
  8a) has a heaviness of a certain amount b) are measuring the heaviness of an object
- Point out that many of the verbs which have different meanings when used in the simple or continuous are verbs of perception: *see, look, feel,* etc.
- Also point out that the same difference in meaning applies when the verbs are used in the past: *I now saw why* (= I now understood why). *I was seeing my friend Joe that night* (= I was meeting my friend Joe that night).
- Finally, point out that we can use both the simple or continuous form of the verb *feel* to mean 'experience something physical/emotional': *She feels/'s feeling happier.*

5 **a)–b)** Students do the exercise on their own and compare and explain their answers in pairs.

Check answers with the class.

1 My new trainers **don't fit** me properly. 2 I **see** what you're trying to say. 3 It **looks** easy, but it's not.
4 I **think** Kay's having lunch now. 5 Correct 6 Correct
7 I **expect** she'll want to eat before she leaves. 8 Correct
9 I **weigh** 60 kilos. 10 This material **feels** really soft.

6 **a)–b)** Students do the exercise on their own and compare answers in pairs.

Check answers with the class.

1 looks; feels 2 have 3 is appearing 4 expect
5 'm thinking 6 'm not feeling/don't feel; 'm having
7 's expecting

- With stronger groups, ask students to explain their answers to **6a)**. Why is one form correct and the other incorrect?

Listening and Speaking

- Write 'Money can't buy happiness.' on the board. Ask students whether they agree with the statement and make a note of how many students agree with it. When students do **8c)**, find out how many have changed their minds based on listening to R9.1.

7 Focus students on the picture of Maureen, Peter and Cate. Tell students they are going to listen to the three of them discussing whether money can buy you happiness.

`R9.1` Play the recording (SB p157). Students listen and choose the best sentence.

Check the answer with the class.

The City is the financial district of London. People who work in the City typically work very long hours for large sums of money. The *money markets* are the global markets where money is borrowed and lent on a short-term basis.

Bill Gates founded Microsoft and is one of the richest individuals in the world. Since retiring from full-time work at Microsoft, he has dedicated much of his time to philanthropy.

In the last sentence of the recording, Cate says *Hear, hear!* This expression is used to show that you agree strongly with what another person has just said.

2

- Ask students to look at R9.1, SB p157 and find phrases for the following functions: clarifying what you mean(t), checking what someone else means/meant, signalling that you are about to disagree with what someone has said.

8 a) Students do the exercise in pairs. They will check their answers in **8b)**.

> 1F Only Maureen believes money can bring you happiness. 2T 3T 4F She does think money can buy you health. She gives as an example the very low life expectancy of people in a poor country. 5F She says, "I don't know about that!"

b) Play the recording again. Students do the exercise on their own and then check answers to **a)** and **b)** in pairs. Remind students that each gap in **b)** can have up to three words.

Check answers with the class. Point out that *wealthy* is a synonym for *rich*.

Also point out that *it's no joke* means 'it's very difficult'.

> 1 agree with 2 a) possessions b) time to do
> 3 a) make you happy b) wealthy 4 make you miserable
> 5 no joke 6 not true either 7 don't know

c) Students discuss the questions in groups. Encourage students to justify their answers.

d) Ask each group to share their ideas with the class. See if the class can come to a consensus.

— EXTRA IDEA —
• For homework, ask students to write a short essay entitled 'Can money buy you happiness?'.

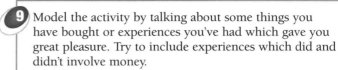
Get ready … Get it right!

 9 Model the activity by talking about some things you have bought or experiences you've had which gave you great pleasure. Try to include experiences which did and didn't involve money.

Students do the activity on their own. Encourage students to list things which did and didn't involve money.

10 a) Students do the activity in groups. Encourage students to ask follow-up questions.

b) Ask each group to share with the class the most interesting things or experiences their group discussed.

— **EXTRA PRACTICE AND HOMEWORK** —

Ph **Class Activity** 9A Verb dominoes p161 (Instructions p129)

Ph **Vocabulary Plus** 9 Formal and informal money expressions p180 (Instructions p171)

Ph **Help with Listening** 9 Different uses of *that* p197 (Instructions p187)

9 Review Exercises 1 and 2 SB p94

CD-ROM Lesson 9A

Workbook Lesson 9A p44

9B Cash-free

QUICK REVIEW ●●●
This activity reviews *price* and *cost*. Students do the first part of the activity on their own. Set a time limit of five minutes. Put students into pairs. Students compare lists. Ask each pair to share one or two of their ideas with the class.

Listening and Vocabulary

1 a) Introduce the topic by asking students how much money they think they would need to take with them in order to spend a week's holiday in the following places: London, New York, Barcelona, Tokyo, Bangkok, Buenos Aires. Then ask students if they think it would be possible to spend time in any of those cities if they had literally no money. What do they think would happen?

Focus students on the question. ✎ Elicit answers from the class and write them on the board.

b) Focus students on the photo. Ask if anyone has heard of Satish Kumar. If so, ask students to share what they know about him with the rest of the class.

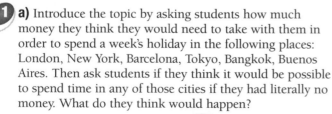
Vocabulary word building (3): productive suffixes
Grammar *a/an* v *one*; *few, a few, quite a few*
Review *price* and *cost*

Tell students they are going to listen to the first of three extracts from a radio programme about Satish Kumar. Be prepared with a definition, examples, etc. to pre-teach *means*. Give students time to read the questions.

R9.2 Play the recording (SB p158). Students listen and answer the questions.

Check answers with the class.

> 1 To walk round the world for peace, visiting the heads of state in various countries. 2 The teacher said that if they had money, they would end each day of walking by finding a restaurant and a bed and breakfast place; in doing so, they wouldn't meet anyone and wouldn't be able to pass their message on. However, if they didn't have money they'd be forced to rely on strangers, who were bound to ask them why they were walking round the world. 3 No.

c)–d) Tell students they are going to listen to the second extract. Focus students on a)–f). Be prepared with definitions, examples, etc. to pre-teach *a nuclear power* (as opposed to *nuclear power*) and *grave*.

R9.3 Play the recording (SB p158). Students listen and make notes. They compare answers in pairs.

Check answers with the class.

> **a)** The number of miles they walked. **b)** They met two women who worked in a tea factory. **c)** The two women gave them four packets of tea – one for each of the leaders of the four nuclear powers. The tea was accompanied by a message: "When you think you need to press the nuclear button, stop for a minute and have a fresh cup of tea." **d)** *No Destination* is the name of the book that Satish wrote about their journey. **e)** Their journey started at one grave – Gandhi's in India – and ended at another – John F Kennedy's in the US. **f)** They walked the entire way, apart from when they took boats to cross the English Channel and the Atlantic.

2 **a)** Tell students they are going to listen to the third extract. Focus students on the gapped text. Point out that there is one word missing per gap.

R9.4 Play the recording (SB p158). Students listen and fill in the gaps.

Check answers with the class.

> **1** flag **2** Russian **3** flags **4** socialist **5** brown **6** white **7** black **8** human being **9** human beings
> The point Satish is making is that people should try to forget what makes them different – what separates them – and concentrate more on what unites them. By doing so, we can learn to live in peace.

b) Tell students they are going to listen to all three extracts together. Focus students on sentences 1–4.

R9.2 R9.3 R9.4 Play the recordings again (SB p158). Students listen and decide if the statements are true, false or not mentioned.

Check answers with the class.

> **1** T **2** Not mentioned **3** F Nothing put them off. **4** Not mentioned

c) Check students understand *idealistic*. Students discuss the questions in groups. Ask each group to share some of their ideas with the class.

> **Help with Vocabulary** Word building (3): productive suffixes

Go through the introductory bullet with the class.

3 **a)–d)** Students do the exercises on their own or in pairs and check their answers in V9.2 SB p142.
Check answers with the class.

- **a)** 1 led 2 minded 3 free 4 worthy
- **b)** *-led* means 'controlled by'; *-minded* is used to describe people with a particular character or interest; *-free* means 'without an undesirable quality'; *-worthy* is used to say that something is suitable or deserving to receive a particular thing.
- **c)** 1 'can be' 2 'resistant to' 3 'to some degree or partly' 4 'thinking about or very concerned about something'
- Go through the **TIPS!** in V9.2 SB p142 with the class or ask students to read them for homework.
- Point out that productive suffixes can be used to create a vast array of different words. Some students may not want to try to learn all of the individual examples in V9.2 SB p142. They could concentrate on the meaning of the productive suffixes so that they can work out the meaning of new words which use those suffixes.
- Here are some other common words formed using these productive suffixes: *fat-free, hassle-free, trustworthy, creditworthy, absent-minded, fair-minded, breakable, movable, bullet-proof, frost-proof, class-conscious, price-conscious.*
- A hyphen is almost always used in words formed from productive suffixes except with *-ish, -able* and *-worthy*, which never take a hyphen. There are no hard and fast rules, though. For example, there is *waterproof* but also *bullet-proof* and *frost-proof*. If in doubt, students should check in a dictionary.

4 Students do the exercise on their own or in pairs. Check answers with the class.

> **1** resistant to the heat of the oven **2** quite red **3** without pollution **4** interesting enough to be included in the news **5** not able to be forgotten **6** controlled or run by the government **7** interested in politics **8** very concerned with fashion

5 **a)** Focus students on questions 1–7. Check students understand all of the words formed with productive suffixes.

Students do the exercise on their own.

b) Students take turns to ask and answer the questions in **5a)** in pairs. Encourage students to ask follow-up questions. Ask each pair to share one or two of their ideas with the class.

Reading and Grammar

6 **a)** Focus students on questions 1–4. Point out that we pay for things *by* cheque and card but *in* cash. Also point out that we talk about having cash *on* us when we are carrying it in a pocket or a bag. Check students understand *smart card* (a plastic card used to make financial transactions and to store personal information which can be read by a computer).

Students discuss the questions in pairs. Ask each pair to share some of their ideas with the class.

> 4 *e-cash* stands for 'electronic cash'.

b) Focus students on the title of the article. Introduce the topic by asking if anyone has paid for goods or services using their mobile phone. If so, was it easy? Would they recommend it to other people?

Students do the exercise on their own. Check the answer with the class.

> The writer is not sure whether we will become a cash-free society.

c) Check that students understand *disprove*. Students do the exercise on their own.

d) Students compare answers to **6c)** in pairs. Check answers with the class.

Students then discuss the question in pairs. Ask each pair to share their ideas with the class.

> 1 Smart cards and mobile phones are becoming an increasingly popular way to make all sorts of payments.
> 2 Compared to cheques or credit cards, it offers the speed of cash, but more so. It takes just one tenth of a second to complete most transactions ...
> 3 ... as no change is required, errors in counting are eliminated. Fraud and theft are also reduced and for the retailer it reduces the cost of handling money.
> 4 But the new system could prove to be a 'disruptive technology' as far as the banks are concerned.
> 5 ... Internet banking did not result in the closure of their high-street branches as was predicted.

--- EXTRA IDEA ---
- Write these phrases from the article on the board: *a thing of the past, (their) grip on, disruptive technology*. Ask students to guess the meaning of the phrases from the context. Ask what helped them guess.

e) Students discuss the questions in groups of three. Encourage students to justify their answer to question 2. Ask each group to share their ideas with the class.

> **Help with Grammar** *a/an v one*; *few, a few, quite a few*

Ask students to do **2** in Preview 9, SB p85 if necessary.
Go through the introductory bullets with the class and check students understand these uses of *one*.

7 **a)–d)** Students do the exercises on their own or in pairs and check their answers in [G9.4] SB p144.
Check answers with the class.

- **a)** 1 a 2 one
- Point out that when speaking, *one* is usually stressed whereas *a/an* is unstressed. Model and drill the examples.
- **b)** In the first response, the speaker is saying that a ten-pound note is the only note he/she has. In the second response, the speaker is saying that he/she has got one five-pound note, not three or four.
- Point out that we use *a* with singular countable nouns in exclamations: *What a big mistake! What a lovely day!*
- **c)** 1 quite a few 2 a few 3 few
- Point out that *few* is often used in more formal situations: *She has **few** friends.*
- Point out that *little/a little* is used with uncountable nouns in the same way as *few/a few* is used with countable nouns: *He spends **little** time with his children.* (not enough) *He spends **a little** time with his children.* (a small amount)
- Point out that we can make comparatives with *fewer (than)*. We use *fewer* with countable nouns: *There are **fewer reasons** these days to carry cash than ever before.* We use *less* with uncountable nouns: *People carry **less cash** than they did in the past.*
- Point out that *few, a few* and *quite a few* can be used as the subject or object of a verb, provided it is clear what they are referring to: *Over 1,000 people were evacuated from their homes; few ever returned. Many employees have been anxiously awaiting news of the company's bankruptcy; we'll be speaking to a few later today.*
- Highlight that sometimes we use a determiner and/or an adjective before *few*: *I've been very busy **these past few** weeks. They quickly gathered **their few** belongings and left.*
- Finally, point out that we can use *a good few* to mean 'a large number': *Lots of my colleagues are in their forties and fifties, but there are a good few who aren't.*

8 **a)–b)** Students do the exercise on their own and compare answers in pairs.

Model and drill the correct sentences, paying particular attention to the stress pattern in sentences with *a/an* or *one*.

Students tell their partner which sentences are true for them. Encourage students to ask follow-up questions.

Check answers with the class. Ask each student to share one interesting thing they learned about their partner with the class.

> 1 few (not many) 2 a/one (*One friend* would imply that the rest of your friends really do care about money.)
> 3 one (Only *one* is possible when talking about a particular day.) 4 one (This emphasises the number of

days you have free.) **5** little (not much) **6** one (Only *one* is possible with *the next*.) **7** a/one (*A snack* is much more likely.) **8** a few (*Quite* is always followed by *a few* not *few*.)

9 **a)–b)** Students do the exercise on their own and compare answers in pairs.

Check answers with the class.

A(n) should be replaced by *one* in the following instances: 2, 3, 5, 9 and 10.

— EXTRA IDEA —
* With stronger groups, ask students to explain their answers to **9a)**.

Get ready … Get it right!

Introduce the activity by reminding students about Satish Kumar and his companion.

Point out that the pair may often have found themselves in remote areas with no money and no contact with the outside world. Ask students how they think they coped.

10 **a)–b)** Students do the activities in pairs. If students are from different countries, ask them to imagine the experiment is taking place in the country where they are currently learning English. If students are having trouble coming up with a list of problems, give them some ideas: food, water, shelter, warmth, communication, etc.

11 **a)** Put the pairs into groups. Students discuss the questions. Ask students to identify the key skills that are missing from their group.

b) Groups tell the class how well and how long they would survive. Ask the class to decide which group would have the best chance of survival.

— EXTRA IDEA —
* Tell each group that they need to 'lose' one member of their group. Students take turns to justify why they should remain. The group then votes for who should leave.

— EXTRA PRACTICE AND HOMEWORK —
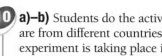 **Class Activity** 9B My partner p162 (Instructions p130)
9 Review Exercises 3 and 4 SB p94
CD-ROM Lesson 9B
Workbook Lesson 9B p46

9C A gloomy science?

QUICK REVIEW ●●●
This activity reviews productive suffixes. Students do the first part of the activity on their own. Set a time limit of three minutes. Put students into pairs. Students then swap lists of words and make sentences using their partner's words.

Vocabulary news and economics
Real World presenting information
Review productive suffixes

1 **a)** Focus students on the words/phrases in bold. Ask students what topic they think all of the words/phrases have in common. (They are all related to news and economics.)

Students do the exercise on their own or in pairs and check the meaning of any new words/phrases in **V9.3** SB p143. Model and drill the phrases, paying particular attention to which words are stressed.

Point out the following:

We can say *foreign aid* as well as *overseas aid*.

We can say *property market* as well as *housing market*. *Housing market* is the more common term, though.

Gender discrimination is often also called *sex discrimination*. *Race discrimination* is another common collocation.

b) Students do the exercise on their own.

c) If possible, put students from different countries into pairs. Students compare answers. Ask each pair to share one or two of their ideas with the class.

2 **a)** Students do the exercise in pairs. Make sure students understand *dry* and *dull*. Point out that the words are synonyms, but that *dry* is not generally used to refer to people; it is often used to refer to books, films, etc.

— EXTRA IDEA —
* Before **2a)**, brainstorm a list of school and university subjects and write them on the board. Make sure that *economics* is included in the list.

b) Ask each pair to share their ideas with the class. Ask students if they agree with each other's lists. Find out how many – if any – students thought that economics was an interesting subject. Encourage students to justify their answer.

3 Introduce the topic by reminding students that once schoolchildren in England and Wales have passed their GCSE exams, aged 16, they have the option of going on to study A levels. Most students take three subjects at A level, but some take as many as five or six.

Tell students they are going to listen to an economics teacher talking to a group of students about the value of doing economics at A level.

Give students time to read questions 1 and 2.

R9.5 Play the recording (SB p158). Students listen and answer the questions.

Check answers with the class.

> **1** Because they are considering studying economics next year. **2** How economics is related to real life; the intellectual challenge; future careers.

┌─ **EXTRA IDEA** ─────────────────────────────
• Write these words and phrases from R9.5 on the board: *settle down, a show of hands, gloomy*. Ask students to look at R9.5, SB p158 and to guess the meaning of the words and phrases from the context. Ask what helped them guess.
└──

4 **a)** Tell students they are going to listen to the next part of the lecture. Give students time to read sentences 1–4. Be prepared with a definition, examples, etc. to pre-teach *famine* /ˈfæmɪn/.

R9.6 Play the recording (SB p158). Students listen and tick the true sentence and correct the false ones.

Check answers with the class.

> **1F** It won't provide easy answers to world problems. **2T** **3F** You need a good understanding of mathematics and you have to be able to communicate clearly in writing. **4F** The study of economics provides a good grounding for many other careers.

b)–c) Give students time to read questions 1–6. Play the recording again. Students listen and answer the questions. They compare answers in pairs.

Check answers with the class.

> **1** The rise in current world food prices is likely to lead to a serious outbreak of famine in less-developed countries which rely on rice or wheat.
> **2** It isn't just the cost of producing it, but the cost of disposing of it when we throw it away.
> **3** People who are logical thinkers and who enjoy serious debate.
> **4** Yes. He says, "I'm not saying it's easy."
> **5** Because these careers also need an understanding of economics.
> **6** lively; exciting; challenging; satisfying

┌─ **EXTRA IDEA** ─────────────────────────────
• Write these words from the recording on the board: *outbreak, exploit, grounding, interdisciplinary*. Ask students to look at R9.6, SB p158 and to guess the meaning of the words from the context. Ask what helped them guess.
└──

5 Students discuss the questions in pairs. Encourage students to justify their answers to questions 1 and 3. Ask each pair to share some of their ideas with the class.

┌─ **EXTRA IDEA** ─────────────────────────────
• Ask students what they thought of the teacher's presentation style. Was the presentation clear and easy to follow? Why?/Why not?
└──

Real World Presenting information

Introduce the topic by asking students if they have ever had to give a presentation, either in English or in their own language. What did they find most challenging about it? Do they have any tips for what makes a good presentation?

6 **a)–d)** Students do the exercises on their own or in pairs and check their answers in **RW9.1** SB p145.

Check answers with the class.

> • **a)** In order to tell the audience what he will be speaking about and to give them an idea of the structure of the talk.
> • **b)** a) 8 b) 6, 9, 12 c) 3, 4, 11 d) 5, 10 e) 1, 7, 13
> • **c)** The talk has an introduction, three paragraphs about economics and a conclusion.

┌─ **EXTRA IDEAS** ────────────────────────────
• Play **R9.6** again. Students listen and tick the phrases from **RW9.1** SB p145 they hear.
• Write headings a)–e) on the board. Brainstorm with the class additional phrases for each of the headings.
└──

7 **a)** Students do the exercise on their own or in pairs. If students ask what an *apprenticeship scheme* is, ask them to try to guess from the context. They will find out the answer in **7b)**.

Check answers with the class. Point out that in a) *by* is correct because it is followed by verb+ing. We use *start with* + noun.

> **a)** of; by **b)** for; on to **c)** about **d)** before
> **e)** back to **f)** up **g)** In

b) Students do the exercise in pairs. Ask each pair to share some of their ideas with the class.

1 The talk is about *apprenticeship schemes* – organised plans for young people to work with older, more experienced people in order to learn a skill or trade.

8 **a)** Tell students that they are going to work in pairs to prepare a two-minute talk on the same topic. Each student will then give his/her talk to a different student.

Focus students on the list of topics. Check students understand *junk mail*. Remind students that they can also invent a topic if they prefer.

Focus students on instructions 1–3. Students do the activity in pairs.

b) Students make notes for their talk on their own.

Encourage students not to write out their talk word-for-word; it will help them to deliver it more naturally. However, weaker or more nervous students may prefer to write out a fuller version.

--- EXTRA IDEA ---

- As a class, discuss what constitutes good body language when giving a talk. For example, making eye contact with the audience, standing up straight, not putting your hands in your pockets. What other things are important? For example, tone of voice, good pronunciation, using the correct intonation all help to make a talk interesting to listen to.

c) Put students back with their partners from **8a)**. Students take turns to practise giving their talks. Encourage students to use the phrases from RW9.1 SB p145 and to give each other suggestions on how to improve.

Note that many students will have a tendency to give their talks in a monotone. Point out that varying intonation is vital in order to keep your audience interested in what you are saying. To illustrate the point, read some of R9.6, SB p158 in a monotone and ask students how it affected their ability to pay attention.

9 Put students into new pairs. Students take turns to give their talks. Encourage students to give feedback on their partner's content and delivery.

Ask some students to share their feedback with the rest of the class.

--- EXTRA IDEAS ---

- Ask one or two students to volunteer to give their talk to the whole class.
- Ask students to rate each other: did they put their arguments across persuasively and convincingly? Did they justify their arguments? If so, what were they good at? If not, how could they improve?

--- EXTRA PRACTICE AND HOMEWORK ---

Ph **Class Activity** 9C Entrepreneur enterprises p163 (Instructions p130)

Ph **Class Activity** Review 7–9 Across the board p164–p165 (Instructions p130)

CD-ROM Lesson 9C

Workbook Lesson 9C p48

Workbook Reading and Writing Portfolio 9 p78

Progress Test 9 p220

9 Review

See p32 for ideas on how to use this section.

1) 2 reasonably 3 half 4 tag 5 effective 6 over

2a) 1 hardly weighs 2 weigh/be weighing 3 have 4 expect 5 Are you expecting 6 feels/'s feeling 7 feels 8 think; see 9 doesn't fit 10 's appearing 11 appears

3a) 2 ish 3 able 4 conscious 5 related 6 proof 7 free 8 minded

4a) That you never know when something will turn out to be a blessing or a curse.

4b) 2 a 3 – 4 one 5 one 6 the 7 a 8 The 9 a/the 10 a 11 a/the 12 – 13 the 14 a 15 The 16 One/A 17 the 18 the 19 a 20 The 21 The 22 the 23 a 24 a 25 The 26 a 27 the 28 a/the 29 the 30 the 31 the 32 the 33 a 34 The 35 the 36 a

Progress Portfolio

See p32 for ideas on how to use this section.

Accurate Writing

CONNECTING WORDS: reason and result
SPELLING: -ible or -able

 Students do the exercise on their own or in pairs and check their answers in **AW9.1** SB p145.

Check answers with the class. Point out that we use *'cos* /kəz/ in informal speech to mean 'because'. However, this is not appropriate in formal written discourse.

Also point out that if we put a verb after phrases like *as a result of, due to* or *because of*, we use a verb+*ing* after the subject: *Because of the visibility being poor, there were several road accidents.* This is more common in formal contexts.

> **2** Mary's racket was broken, so I lent her mine. I lent Mary my racket because hers was broken./Because Mary's racket was broken, I lent her mine. **3** My Spanish is really bad. As a result, he didn't understand me. Because my Spanish is really bad, he didn't understand me. **4** Because of poor visibility, there were several road accidents. Visibility was poor. Consequently, there were several road accidents. **5** Since you don't want to help, I'll do it myself./I'll do it myself, since you don't want to help. As you don't want to help, I'll do it myself./I'll do it myself, as you don't want to help. **6** There were terrible floods. Therefore they lost all their crops. They lost all their crops because of terrible floods./Because of terrible floods, they lost all their crops. **7** Owing to the bad weather yesterday, I didn't go climbing. Because the weather was bad yesterday, I didn't go climbing.

 Students do the exercise on their own or in pairs and check their answers in **AW9.2** SB p145.

Check answers with the class. Point out that we use *-ible* if the root is not a complete word and *-able* if the root is a complete word.

Tell students that there are unfortunately many exceptions to the rules governing the use of *-ible* and *-able* endings, as given in **AW9.2** SB p145. Encourage students to use their dictionaries if they are in any doubt about which endings to use.

Point out that if a root ends in *-e*, we usually replace the *-e* with the suffix: *believe → believable*. However, there are some exceptions to this rule. For example, *replace → replaceable*, *notice → noticeable*, *change → changeable*.

> **1** edible **2** understandable **3** sensible **4** visible **5** doable **6** noticeable **7** believable **8** destructible **9** incredible

 a)–b) Focus students on the letter. Point out that in addition to the underlined mistakes, there are four spelling mistakes.

Students do the exercises on their own or in pairs. Check answers with the class.

> **a)** 1 consequently/therefore/as a result **2** due to/owing to/because of **3** As/Since **4** due to/because of **5** Consequently/Therefore/As a result
>
> **b)** Spelling mistakes (in order of appearance): responsible, noticeable, reliable, unacceptable.

EXTRA PRACTICE AND HOMEWORK
Workbook Accurate Writing Exercises 18 and 19 p87

Preview 10

MODAL VERBS (1): FUNCTIONS

1 **a)–b)** Students do the exercises on their own or in pairs and check their answers in **G10.2** SB p146.

Check answers with the class.

Point out that in the context of permission, *may* is more polite than *can*. *Could* is slightly more polite than *can* but less polite than *may*.

Point out that *must* and *have to* are often interchangeable in the positive. *Must* often has a sense of an internal obligation: *I really must get my suit dry-cleaned this weekend* (I'm not happy that my suit is dirty, and I want it to be clean). *Have to* often has a sense of external obligation: *I'm going to a wedding next week, so I have to get my suit dry-cleaned this weekend.*

Point out, however, that in the negative, *must* and *have to* have different meanings: *You mustn't see him* (= you are forbidden to see him); *You don't have to see him* (= it is not compulsory for you to see him, especially if you don't want to).

We often use *really* before *should* and *ought to* to give more emphasis: *He really ought to change his accountant.* This is common both when giving advice and criticising past behaviour.

In sentence 1 in **b)**, *could* is possible because it is being used to talk about a general situation. In sentences 2, 3 and 5, however, *could* is not possible because the sentences refer to specific situations. In sentence 4, both are possible because *couldn't* can be used to talk about specific situations in the past.

> **a)** 1a) 2e) 3c) 4d) 5h) 6b) 7g) 8f)
>
> **b)** 1 could/were allowed to **2** were allowed to **3** managed to **4** couldn't/didn't manage to **5** was able to **6** could **7** didn't need to

10A   Be creative!

Grammar subject/verb agreement
Review simple v continuous: verbs with different meanings

QUICK REVIEW ●●●

This activity reviews verbs with different meanings when they are used in the simple or continuous form. Students do the first part of the activity on their own. Remind students that they should write one sentence in a simple form and one sentence in a continuous form for each verb. Set a time limit of five to ten minutes. Put students into pairs. Students tell each other their sentences. Encourage students to ask follow-up questions.

Reading and Grammar

1 **a)** Focus students on the picture. Ask students to describe what they can see in the picture. (It shows a soldier removing a note from a carrier pigeon or adding one to it.)

Students discuss the topic in pairs. Ask each pair to share their ideas with the class.

— EXTRA IDEA —

- Before starting the activity, write the following categories on the board: *birds, reptiles, mammals, insects*. Students work in pairs and write as many animals as they can think of for each category in two minutes. Find out which pair has the most words.

b) Focus students on the words in the box. Students check the meaning of the words. Be prepared with definitions, examples, etc. to give students if necessary.

Model and drill the words, paying particular attention to the pronunciation of *siege* /siːdʒ/, *ingenious* /ɪnˈdʒiːniəs/ and *epitomise* /ɪˈpɪtəmaɪz/.

c) Students do the exercise on their own. Check answers with the class.

Point out the following:

The Sumerians founded one of the earliest known civilisations in the world, lasting from the late 6th millennium BC through to the 4th millennium BC. Sumer was located in Lower Mesopotamia, between Babylon and the Persian Gulf.

The Franco-Prussian War began in July 1870. In September the French emperor, Napoleon III, was captured and in October the commander of the French army surrendered. The Prussians then began a siege of Paris, which lasted until January 1871, when the city surrendered.

The information superhighway is a popular term used to mean the network along which information travels in a digital form.

A *gold rush* is when large numbers of migrant workers move to an area because gold has been found there. The California Gold Rush is one of the most famous.

The *transcontinental telegraph* was a system for sending and receiving messages by electrical or radio signals across the US.

> Pigeons were used to carry messages and letters, from as far back as 776 BC all the way through to the beginning of the 21st century.
> Horses were used, as part of the Pony Express, to take letters across the US in the 19th century.
> Dog teams were used to deliver mail in Alaska and Canada.
> Cats were used in British post offices to kill the rats and mice that were eating money orders.

— EXTRA IDEA —

- Ask students what they think *pushing the envelope* means and why it has been chosen as the title of the article. (*Push the envelope* means 'innovate or try to break through existing boundaries, often by making a large effort or by being inventive'.)

2 Focus students on sentences a)–f) but don't check any unknown vocabulary until after students have attempted the exercise.

Check answers with the class.

> 1d)   2e)   3c)   4f)   5a)   6b)

3 **a)** Focus students on the words/phrases in pink. Point out that all of them refer back to something earlier in the text. Point out that writers often use words/phrases in this way in order to make the text more cohesive and to avoid unnecessary repetition.

Do the first question with the class. Students then do the exercise on their own or in pairs.

Check answers with the class.

> *so* – that postal workers have been human
> *this ingenious method* – using pigeons that had been smuggled out of the city in balloons to deliver letters
> *these prized flocks* – the pigeons used by the British Army
> *these winged heroes* – the pigeons used by the British Army
> *even so* – although the public were fascinated by the Pony Express
> *a couple* – cats

b) Focus students on the words/phrases in bold. Students do the exercise on their own or in pairs.

Check answers with the class.

> 1 smuggled out 2 recruited 3 far-flung 4 vital link
> 5 ebb away 6 pensioned off

c) Students discuss the question in pairs. Ask each pair to share their ideas with the class.

— EXTRA IDEAS —

- Ask students to discuss whether they think it's fair for humans to use animals like this for work. Can students think of any jobs that animals do which they shouldn't? What would be the alternatives?

- Write these words from the article on the board: *timely, equine, wiry*. Ask students to guess the meaning of the words from the context. Ask what helped them guess.

Help with Grammar Subject/verb agreement

4 **a)–e)** Students do the exercises on their own or in pairs and check their answers in `G10.1` SB p146.

Check answers with the class.

- **a)** 1 have 2 was
- Point out that although *mail* refers to 'letters or parcels' – that is, multiple items – it is an uncountable noun, and can therefore only exist in the singular; it consequently takes a singular verb.
- **b)** 1 is 2 comes 3 is 4 was 5 were 6 were
- **c)** In group A, we use a singular verb. In group B, we use a plural verb.
- Tell students that *economics* is another example of a noun which ends in *-s* but is considered singular.
- Highlight that the following countries take singular verbs, despite ending in *-s: the Netherlands, the Bahamas, the United States, the Philippines, the United Arab Emirates.*
- Give students these other examples of nouns which are considered plural but don't end in an *-s: cattle, clergy, offspring, people, poultry* and *vermin.*
- Point out that *a pair of* takes a singular verb, even if what it is referring to is in the plural: *A good pair of scissors is essential if you want to cut clean lines.*
- **d)** 1 singular 2 plural
- Give students these examples of collective nouns, people and countries which can take either a singular or plural form depending on the focus: *bank, choir, class, club, committee, crowd, family, firm, fleet, flock, government, herd, jury, ministry, mob, nation,* (political) *party, school, staff, union.*
- Point out that when the subject consists of two or more nouns linked by *and/or*, we use a plural form: *A letter **and** a parcel **were forwarded** to our new address.*

- Point out that in clauses with *what* as subject, the verb is either plural (in more formal contexts) or singular (in more informal contexts): *What surprised me **was/were the sheer numbers** of pigeons used in the war.*
- Also point out that in complex sentences, the verb agrees with the main noun: *During the four-month siege, **more than a million letters were delivered** to the citizens of Paris.*
- Finally, point out that we use a singular verb with **the** number of but a plural form with **a** number of: **The** *number of applicants always **exceeds** the number of places.* **A** *number of people **have** complained to us.*

5 Students do the exercise on their own or in pairs. Check answers with the class.

> 1 prefer 2 says; is 3 is 4 is 5 recruits 6 seem

6 **a)** Students do the exercise on their own. Point out that both answers may be possible.

Check answers with the class.

> 1 is 2 is 3 is 4 is/are 5 talks 6 like

b) Students compare their answers in pairs. Encourage students to ask follow-up questions.

Ask each student to share one thing they learned about their partner with the rest of the class.

Listening

7 **a)** Focus students on the quiz. Students do the exercise in pairs. Don't check answers yet.

b) Tell students they are going to listen to part of a radio programme in order to check their answers.

`R10.1` Play the recording (SB p158). Students check their answers.

Check answers with the class.

> 1B 2B 3A 4A 5B

8 **a)** Focus students on sentences 1–7. Students check the meaning of the noun collocations. Be prepared with definitions, examples, etc. to give students if necessary. Point out that all of the noun collocations are used in R10.1.

— EXTRA IDEA —

- Students work in pairs and take turns to test each other on the collocations. One student says the first part of the collocation, for example, *a matter*, and his/her partner says the whole collocation, for example, *a matter of course.*

b)–c) Play the recording again. Students listen and answer the questions. They compare their answers in pairs.

Check answers with the class.

> 1 They have some interesting, not to say very strange, origins. **2** He travelled to the Far East. **3** Nobody really knows. **4** They are just a matter of opinion. **5** The first skyscraper. **6** Higher buildings led to larger numbers of people living and working in the same areas. **7** Merging the two designs for escalators.

d) Students discuss the questions in pairs or groups. Ask each pair or group to share their ideas with the class.

> ── EXTRA IDEA ──
> * For homework, students research the origins of a type of food or an everyday item (e.g. chocolate, chewing gum, lifts and CDs) using the Web, and give a short presentation to the class.

Get ready … Get it right!

9 Focus students on the photos. Check students know the words for all of the pictures. Students do the activity on their own. Encourage students to think about why they couldn't live without the items.

10 a) Students do the activity in pairs. Students compare lists and choose the five most useful items.

b) Put each pair with another pair. Students take turns to say which items they chose and why. Encourage students to justify their choices and to agree on the five most useful inventions.

c) Ask each group to share their list with the class. Write the lists on the board. Ask the whole class to choose the three most useful items. If students don't agree, ask them to justify their choices and try to convince the other members of the class.

> ── EXTRA IDEA ──
> * Tell students to imagine that they are being sent to live on a desert island for a year. Each group is allowed to take five non-food items with them. Ask each group to decide what they will take and why. Encourage students to justify their answers.

> ── EXTRA PRACTICE AND HOMEWORK ──
> **Ph** **Class Activity** 10A Secret auction p166 (Instructions p131)
> **10 Review** Exercise 1 SB p104
> **CD-ROM** Lesson 10A
> **Workbook** Lesson 10A p49
> **Preview 10** Exercise 1 SB p95

10B Stick with it!

QUICK REVIEW ●●●
This activity reviews subject/verb agreement. Students do the first part of the activity on their own. Tell students to use information about themselves and their own opinions. Set a time limit of five to ten minutes. Put students into pairs. Students take turns to say their sentences. Encourage students to ask follow-up questions.

Listening and Grammar

1 a) Model the exercise by talking to the class about someone you know who has been successful in what they do. Talk about whether their success was due to luck, talent or dedication. Students then do the exercise on their own.

b) Students do the exercise in pairs. Encourage students to ask follow-up questions. Ask a few students to share what they have discussed with the class.

2 a) Tell students they are going to listen to two people – Adela and Louie – talking about the people in the photos. Point out that Adela and Louie aren't the people in the photos. Be prepared with definitions, examples, etc. to pre-teach *stick with it*, *animation* /ˌænɪˈmeɪʃən/, *gifted* and *soloist* /ˈsəʊləʊɪst/.

> **Vocabulary** antonyms
> **Grammar** modal verbs (2): levels of certainty about the past, the present and future
> **Review** subject/verb agreement

R10.2 Play the recording (SB p159). Students listen and answer the question.
Check the answers with the class.

> The person in photo A is Tang Yun. The person in photo B is Adela's brother Martin.

> ── EXTRA IDEA ──
> * Before doing **2a)**, ask students to describe what they can see in the photos and to guess how the photos might tie in with what they've just been discussing.

b)–d) Put students into two groups, A and B. Give them time to read the prompts for their group.

Play the recording again. Students listen and make notes. They compare answers in pairs, working with a partner from their own group.

Put students into new pairs so that one student from group

A is working with one from group B. Students summarise to each other what the person they listened to said.

Check answers with the class.

> **Group A Latin:** Martin studied Latin and Greek at Oxford University.
> **Martin's talent:** He's naturally talented.
> **Saturday night:** It's Saturday night, and he'll probably be working.
> **His girlfriend:** She feels sorry for his girlfriend, as it can't be easy having Martin as a partner.
> **Being positive:** He's always so positive. Being positive is important.
> **Group B Luck:** He quotes Tiger Woods, who said that he noticed that the harder he practised the luckier he became.
> **Tang Yun's childhood:** He must have devoted most of his childhood to practising.
> **Louie's school:** He went to a school for gifted kids.
> **Gifted children:** The 'gift' seems to be that they don't mind spending hours practising.
> **Being a soloist:** He didn't stick with it enough to earn a living as a soloist.

e) Focus students on the modal verbs in the boxes. Students do the exercise on their own or in pairs. They will check their answers in **f)**.

f) Play the recording again. Students listen and check their answers to **e)**.

Check answers with the class. Point out that the answer to question 7 could also have been *can't*, with little or no change of meaning.

> **2** might **3** must **4** can't **5** shouldn't **6** 'll **8** must **9** may
> **10** can't; wouldn't

EXTRA IDEA

- With weaker groups, students do sentences 1–6 and then listen to the first part of R10.2 to check. Students then do sentences 7–10 and listen to the second part of the recording to check.

Help with Grammar Modal verbs (2): levels of certainty about the past, present and future

Ask students to do **1** in Preview 10, SB p95 if necessary. Go through the introductory bullet with the class, and remind students of modal verbs that express obligation, advice, permission, prohibition and levels of certainty.

 a)–d) Students do the exercises on their own or in pairs and check their answers in **G10.3** SB p147.
Check answers with the class.

- **a)** We use *will, won't, can't, must, would(n't)* when we think something is **definite**.
  We use *should* to express when we think something is **probable**.

We use *may, might, could* when we think something is **possible**.

- Point out that an important distinction here is between the meaning of *probable* and *possible*. Point out that if something is *probable* it is likely to happen; if something is *possible* it may or may not happen. *Probable* is therefore more likely than *possible*.

- **b)** a) present b) future c) past
- Highlight that *will* can be used to talk about levels of certainty in the present (sentence 1) and the future (sentence 6). It is often preceded by an adjective such as *sure* or *certain*, as in the examples in **2e)**.
- Highlight that *should* cannot be used to talk about something being probable in the past. For example, *he **shouldn't have told** her* means 'it wasn't a good idea that he told her'. *May, might* and *could* are used to talk about possibility in the past: *He **might not have told** her*.
- Point out that *ought to/ought not to* has the same meaning as *should/shouldn't*, but it sounds more formal.
- Point out that we use *may, might, could* – not *can* – to talk about levels of certainty.
- Also point out that we use *couldn't have* or *can't have* + past participle to mean certainty about the past: *It couldn't/can't have been easy*.
- Finally, point out that we use *can't, could, might, may* or *must* when we speculate – not *can* or *mustn't*: *He can't have known about it.* not ~~He mustn't have known about it.~~
- **c)** the present: modal verb + the infinitive without *to* and modal verb + *be* + verb+*ing*; the future: modal verb + the infinitive without *to*; the past: the modal + *have* + the past participle

---

4 Do the first question with the class. Students do the exercise on their own or in pairs.
Check answers with the class.

> **2** He can't have practised enough. **3** The parcel should arrive tomorrow. **4** Jan may be having lunch now.
> **5** They can't be enjoying the holiday, as they're coming home early. **6** Don't call him now, as (I'm pretty certain) he'll be sleeping. **7** They got there late, so they won't have had time to visit the exhibition. **8** She should have no problems finding the place.

EXTRA IDEA

- With stronger groups, write sentences 1–8 on the board without the words in brackets. Ask students to rewrite the sentences using their knowledge of modal verbs and **G10.3** SB p147 to help them.

---

5 a) Model the exercise by completing the sentences for yourself. Students do the exercise on their own.

b) Students do the activity in pairs. Encourage students to ask follow-up questions. Ask each pair to share something they've learned about their partner with the class.

Reading and Vocabulary

 6 a) Focus students on the quote and on the photo in the article. Check students know who David Beckham is. Elicit answers from the class.

> The quote means that in order to truly excel at something, you need to go beyond simply being able to do something; you need to master it perfectly.

b) Read the introduction to the article with the whole class in order to set the context. Check that students understand *mentor* and *protégé*.

Put students into pairs. Focus student A on the part of the article about Henrietta Brockway (SB p100). Focus student B on the part of the article about David Beckham (SB p101).

Students do the exercise in pairs. Check answers with the class.

> 1 They met at David Beckham's academy.
> 2 Henrietta says that she had to persuade her father to let her become a golfer. David says that he had total support from his father but that he used to make him practise controlling the ball for hours on end.

 7 a)–c) Students do the exercises on their own and compare answers in pairs.

Check answers with the class. Point out the following:

A *handicap* is a term used in golf to talk about the disadvantage given to a person taking part in the match in order to reduce their chances of winning. The lower your handicap, the better a golfer you are.

A *hole in one* is when a golfer manages to get the ball into the hole with only one shot. Holes in one are extremely rare, even for the world's best players.

Like in the context of *He was cooking and was, like, 'Sure you do.'* is a very common colloquial way of introducing what someone said. It is more commonly used by young people than older ones.

A *Barbie doll* is a popular children's toy.

A *driving range* is a place where people can go and practise their golf swings.

Shoot at goal means 'kick the ball at goal in order to try and score'.

> **b)** David Beckham says this about Henrietta. (*bright*)
> **c)** Henrietta says this about David Beckham. (*sweet*)
> **d)** Henrietta says this about David Beckham. (*down-to-earth*)

> **e)** David Beckham says this about Henrietta. (*has got a wise head on her shoulders*)
> **f)** Henrietta says this about David Beckham. (*determined*)

--- **EXTRA IDEA** ---
- Write these phrases from the article on the board: *handle yourself, professional circuit*. Ask students to guess the meaning of the phrases from the context. Ask what helped them guess.

Help with Vocabulary Antonyms

Introduce the topic by reminding students that using the correct adjective–noun collocations is important in order to sound natural and fluent in English.

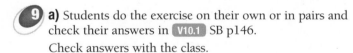 **8 a)–c)** Students do the exercises on their own or in pairs and check their answers in **V10.1** SB p146.

Check answers with the class.

> - **a)–b)** clear idea – rough idea
>   easy decision – hard decision
>   sweet guy – nasty guy
> - Point out that we can also say *tough decision*.
> - Also point out that adjectives must collocate with the nouns they are describing.
> - Other antonyms using the words in **V10.1** SB p146 include:
>   clear instructions – confusing instructions
>   a clear conscience – a guilty conscience
>   gentle exercise – hard exercise
>   a gentle slope/gradient – a steep slope/gradient
>   an old friend – a new friend
>   a dry topic – an interesting topic
>   plain paper – lined paper
>   a plain child – a pretty child
>   a strong smell – a faint smell

9 a) Students do the exercise on their own or in pairs and check their answers in **V10.1** SB p146.

Check answers with the class.

> 2 **a)** a dark colour **b)** a heavy meal
> 3 **a)** a strong wind **b)** an aggressive person
> 4 **a)** a young person **b)** a modern building
> 5 **a)** a low building **b)** a short person
> 6 **a)** a sweet wine **b)** a wet day
> 7 **a)** rich food **b)** a patterned shirt
> 8 **a)** a weak coffee **b)** a faint possibility

b) Students do the exercise in pairs.

Get ready ... Get it right!

10 a) Model the activity by making a list of things which you have done or tried to do and write them on the board. Students then do the exercise on their own.

b) Model the activity by answering the three questions in relation to your own list. Students then do the exercise on their own. Encourage students to make notes.

11 a) Students do the activity in groups of three. Encourage students to ask follow-up questions and to take notes on what the other people in their group say.

b) Put students into different groups of three. Students discuss the other two members of their original group, using their notes to help them. Ask each group to decide who is the most determined.

c) Ask each group to share their ideas with the class. Encourage students to justify their choice.

EXTRA IDEAS

- ✍ Write the names of the students that each team chooses as the most determined on the board. Then ask the class to vote for who they think is the most determined in the whole class.

- Ask students to find other examples of mentors and protégés (on the Web, if they have access to it), and to prepare and give a two-minute presentation about who the people are, how they met, and how they've influenced each other's life and work.

EXTRA PRACTICE AND HOMEWORK

Ph **Class Activity** 10B Give me the sentence p167 (Instructions p132)

Ph **Vocabulary Plus** 10 Idioms about success and failure p181 (Instructions p171)

10 Review Exercises 2 and 3 SB p104

CD-ROM Lesson 10B

Workbook Lesson 10B p51

10C Go for it!

QUICK REVIEW ●●●

This activity reviews modal verbs. Students do the first part of the activity on their own. Set a time limit of five to ten minutes. Put students into pairs. Students take turns to say their sentences. Encourage students to ask follow-up questions.

1 a) Introduce the topic by pointing out to students that by getting to the end of an advanced-level coursebook they have made considerable progress in their language learning.

Ask students to think back to when they first started learning English. Then ask students to imagine they are giving advice to someone in that same position.

Students do the activity on their own. Encourage students to make detailed notes.

b)–c) Students do the activity in groups.

Ask each group to share their ideas with the class. See if there is any advice that the whole class can agree on.

2 a) Introduce the topic by asking students how much of a language they think it would be possible to learn in just eight weeks.

Focus students on the photo. Elicit ideas from the class.

b) Focus students on the review. Read the subtitle of the article with the class so that students can check their answer to **2a)**. Make sure students understand *absorption* and *association*.

Vocabulary colloquial language
Skills Reading: a book review; Listening and Speaking: language-learning strategies; Writing: an action plan
Real World Giving advice
Review modal verbs

Be prepared with definitions, examples, etc. to pre-teach *guru* /ˈguːruː/ and *intuitive* /ɪnˈtjuːɪtɪv/.

Students do the exercise on their own or in pairs. Check the answer with the class.

This method of learning is a 'revolution' in the sense that it approaches language learning as a baby would – learning by association.

EXTRA IDEA

- ✍ Write these words and phrases from the review on the board: *permeates, tunes in with, knack*. Ask students to guess the meaning of the words and phrases from the context. Ask what helped them guess.

3 a) Students do the exercise on their own or in pairs. Check students understand *linguistic*.

Check answers with the class.

1 connecting ideas 2 children 3 unclear
4 making links 5 what he believes is self-evident

EXTRA IDEA

- With stronger groups, write sentences 1–5 on the board with gaps instead of choices in italics. Ask students to complete the sentences.

b) Students discuss the questions in groups. Ask each group to share their ideas with the class.

EXTRA IDEA

- Ask any students who use mind maps to show examples to the rest of the class and explain how they use them.

4 **a)** Students discuss the questions in pairs. Ask each pair to share their ideas with the class.

b) Tell students they are going to listen to Maria Pia, an advanced learner of English from Italy, talking about this same question.

`R10.3` Play the recording (SB p159). Students listen and see if Maria Pia agreed with what they had discussed in **4a)**. Students then answer questions 1–7.

Check answers with the class. Point out that *the classics* refers to the most famous works of literature in a language.

Also point out that Maria Pia uses the phrase *an awful lot*, which simply means 'very much'. The use of *awful* as an intensifier like this has nothing to do with its meaning of 'bad'. Maria Pia also uses *terribly* in a similar way: *… you run the risk of using words which are terribly out-of-date … .* Again, *terribly* is being used here as an intensifier, not in the sense of 'unpleasant'.

> 1 She memorised lots of vocabulary.
> 2 You can learn new words and keep up with what's going on in the country where the language you are learning is spoken.
> 3 You risk using words which are out-of-date.
> 4 Magazines and the Internet.
> 5 Watching television and listening to the radio.
> 6 Try to use them in conversation; write them down in a notebook.
> 7 Practise speaking as much as you can.

c) Tell students they are going to listen to another language learner, Bruce, talking about his experience of learning languages. Give students time to read statements 1–5.

Be prepared with definitions, examples, etc. to pre-teach *trashy* and *sponge* /spʌndʒ/.

`R10.4` Play the recording (SB p159). Students listen and check if the statements are true or false.

Check answers with the class.

> 1F He's had different levels of success. 2F He likes learning languages in a classroom at the beginning.
> 3T 4F He thinks people underestimate the amount of time it takes to learn a language. 5T

EXTRA IDEA

- Ask students to find evidence in R10.4, SB p159 for why sentences 1–5 are true or false.

5 **a)** Play the recording again. Students listen and answer the questions.

Check answers with the class.

> 1 Anything from trashy magazines to crime novels and love stories. He also reads things in translation and newspapers.
> 2 He thinks reading helps because it allows you to acquire new vocabulary, consolidate your knowledge of grammar and get a feel for the right word in the right place.
> 3 CDs and things that he downloads onto his iPod.
> 4 He feels he ought to do more grammar exercises because his grammar is a bit woolly.
> 5 If he looks up a word in a dictionary, he puts a tick next to it so that if he has to look it up again he sees the tick and knows that it's a high-frequency word.

b) Focus students on the words/phrases in bold. Point out that sentences 1 and 2 come from R10.3 and sentences 3–5 come from R10.4.

Students do the exercise on their own or in pairs. Encourage students to look at R10.3 and R10.4, SB p159 to help them guess the meaning of the words from the context.

Check answers with the class.

> 1 write it down 2 liking being with people
> 3 of low quality 4 unclear 5 changed

c) Students discuss the questions in groups. Ask each group to share some of their ideas with the class.

6 **a)** Students do the activity on their own.

Remind students that their list should be in the order of importance to them, not the order in which they assume the areas are most important from a linguistic point of view.

b) Focus students on the phrases in the Real World box. Check students understand all of them.

Students do the activity in groups. Encourage students to give advice using the phrases in the Real World box.

EXTRA IDEA

- Ask each student to share one piece of advice with the class.

Writing Extension

 7 a)–b) Students do the activity on their own.

Encourage students to break their action plan down into skills: *listening, reading, speaking* and *writing* as well as *vocabulary* and *grammar*.

Encourage students to think of things that will allow them to improve as many areas of their English as possible at once. For example, joining an English conversation club would allow students to practise their listening and speaking, learn new vocabulary and consolidate their knowledge of grammar.

Students compare plans in pairs.

This activity can be set for homework and then followed up in the next lesson.

EXTRA PRACTICE AND HOMEWORK

Ph **Class Activity** 10C A problem shared p168 (Instructions p132)

Ph **Help with Listening** 10 Presenting information p198 (Instructions p188)

CD-ROM Lesson 10C

Workbook Lesson 10C p53

Workbook Reading and Writing Portfolio 10 p81

Progress Test 10 p222

---

10 Review

See p32 for ideas on how to use this section.

1a) 1 Eating fish **is** good for you. 2 **Has** the mail arrived yet? 3 Correct 4 Only a few people **have** arrived. 5 The news today **is** very bad. 6 Correct 7 Anything **is** better than school! 8 Correct

2 2 a) He definitely hasn't paid yet. b) It's possible that he hasn't paid yet. 3 a) We didn't buy her that violin, but it was bad that we didn't. b) She will probably be back soon. 4 a) John is definitely still sleeping now. b) They will definitely have eaten by now. 5 a) It's not possible that they left already. b) I wasn't able to swim until I was six. 6 a) It is not possible that Lucy would forget to phone. b) He didn't often talk about his experiences in the war. 7 a) It is possible you will see me later, if I can make it. b) You have permission to start now.

3a) **Student A**
1 a strong wind 2 rich food 3 sweet wine
4 a smooth surface 5 a vague/rough idea 6 a weak coffee
7 a dark colour
Student B
1 an aggressive person 2 a patterned carpet 3 a wet towel
4 a calm sea 5 a cloudy sky 6 a faint possibility
7 a heavy meal

Progress Portfolio

See p32 for ideas on how to use this section.

End of Course Review

- The aim of this activity is to review language that students have learned throughout the course in a fun, student-centred way. The activity takes about 30–45 minutes. Check students understand *a counter, throw a dice, land on a square, move forward/back* and *have a rest*.

Give students time to read the rules on SB p104 and answer any questions they may have.

Ask students what happens when a student lands on a *Grammar* or *Vocabulary* square for the first time (they answer question 1 only).

Ask what happens when a second student lands on the same square (they answer question 2).

Also check what happens when a third or fourth student lands on the square (they can stay there without answering the question).

Put students into groups of four and give a dice and counters to each group (or students can make their own counters).

Ask a student with a watch in each group to be the time-keeper for the group. He/She should time students when they land on a *Keep Talking* square and have to talk about a topic for 45 seconds.

Students take turns to throw the dice and move around the board.

If a student thinks another student's answer to a question on a *Grammar* or *Vocabulary* square is wrong, he/she can check in the Language Summaries in the Student's Book or ask you to adjudicate.

While students are working, monitor and help with any problems.

The first student to get to the *Finish* square is the winner. Students can continue playing until all three students have finished. If one group finishes early, ask them to look at all the squares they didn't land on and answer the questions.

1 1 Yes. **2** No. Only *Having eaten* is correct.

2 1 **on** average, **out of** necessity, **in/out of** touch
2 in common, **in/out of** control, **on** purpose

4 1 We'll deal with that problem when it happens.
2 If you don't take the risk, you won't get the benefit.

6 1 The person (who/that) I spoke to suggested I phone.
2 I rarely have time to relax.

7 1 a huge old leather suitcase **2** a lovely white marble statue

10 1 thoroughly/really enjoy **2** highly/extremely unlikely

12 1 *determined* (positive) – wanting to do something very much and not letting anyone or any difficulties stop you; *obstinate* – unreasonably determined to act in a certain way despite persuasion **2** *courageous* (positive) – having the ability to control your fear in a dangerous or difficult situation; *reckless* – doing dangerous things and not caring about the risks and the possible results

13 1 I wish you **would go** away now. I'm busy! **2** Not only **does he go** to the gym every day, he runs too.

17 1 He's getting old. **2** This chair's old and has been in better condition.

19 1 Did you enjoy **yourself** at the party? **2** You really must concentrate.

21 1 In the first sentence, *appears* means 'seems'; in the second sentence, *'s appearing* means 'is performing'. **2** In the first sentence, *fits* means 'is the correct size'; in the second sentence, *'s fitting* means 'is putting in place'.

22 1 moody, widen, exciting **2** cultural, sympathetic, clarify

24 See **G6.2** SB p133.

26 See **V9.2** SB p142.

27 1 leave it; tired **2** off; over

30 1 Pete is the only one who eats fish; fish is the only food that Pete eats. **2** Jo has met the Queen in addition to all of the other people she has met; you might not expect Jo to have met the Queen, but she has.

31 1 half; partly **2** from above/on top/across; too much

34 1 See **V5.5** SB p130. **2** See **V4.1** SB p127.

36 1 Only *met* is correct. **2** Only *is alleged* is correct.

38 1 After he finished something else, he began to do law. He continued to do law. **2** It necessitated doing it fast. I intended to do it fast.

Photocopiable Materials

Class Activities

Instructions

There are 33 Class Activities worksheets (p133–p168). These worksheets give extra communicative speaking practice of the key language taught in the Student's Book. Each activity matches a lesson in the Student's Book. For example, *1A Getting to know you* matches lesson 1A. There is one activity for each lesson and also an additional review activity at the end of units 3, 6 and 9 that practises language from the preceding three units.

The Class Activities can be used as extra practice when you have finished each lesson or as review activities in the next class or later in the course.

Many of the activities involve students working in pairs or groups. When you have an odd number of students, you can:

- ask two lower-level students to share a role card;
- give two role cards to a stronger student;
- vary the size of the groups.

1A Getting to know you p133

Language

Time expressions with Past Simple and Present Perfect

Activity type, when to use and time

'Find someone who' activity. Use any time after lesson 1A. 15–25 minutes.

Preparation

Photocopy one worksheet for each student.

Procedure

- Give a copy of the worksheet to each student. Students work on their own and choose the correct verb form for each sentence in the first column. Check answers with the class.

- Explain to students that they are going to try and find someone in the class who matches each sentence in the first column. Elicit the questions that students will need to ask for each sentence. For example, *Have you read a good book in the past few weeks?*

- Point out the column for follow-up questions on the worksheet and elicit some possible questions from the class. For example, *What did you think of the book?* Also tell students that they will need to decide which verb form to use in each question they produce. Students write a follow-up question for each of questions 1–10. With a lower-level class, you can give students time in pairs to think of follow-up questions.

- Students move around the room and ask questions 1–10. If students aren't able to leave their seats, they should

ask as many students as they can who are sitting near them. Encourage students to talk to as many people as possible. Point out that they only need to find one person who answers 'yes' to each question. When they find a person who answers 'yes' to a question, they should write his/her name in the second column on the worksheet. Then they should ask him/her one or two follow-up questions and make notes about the answer(s) in the third column.

- Finally, ask students to tell the class interesting things they have found out about their classmates.

> **1** has read **2** has grumbled **3** worked **4** studied **5** chatted (if the student considers the week has finished); has been chatting (if the student considers the week has not finished) **6** started **7** has come **8** went (if the student considers the year has finished); has been (if the student considers the year has not finished) **9** has finished **10** has taken; has been studying

1B Student survey p134

Language

Cleft sentences

Activity type, when to use and time

Class survey. Use any time after lesson 1B. 25–30 minutes.

Preparation

Photocopy one worksheet for each group of three students. Cut into three separate worksheets.

Procedure

- ✍ On the board, write *When it's a hot weekend, most people in the class … .* Invite the class to predict what comes next. Elicit the question you'd need to ask in order to survey the class. For example, *When it's a hot weekend, what do you do?* Use this question to do a quick survey of the class to find out if their prediction was correct. Now write *What happens …* on the board and elicit the rest of the sentence from the class. For example, *What happens when it's a hot weekend is most people go to the beach.*

- Divide the class into three groups, A, B and C. Give a copy of the appropriate worksheet to each student and ask them, in their groups, to read through statements 1–4 in bold and predict the answers.

- Rearrange the class so that students are sitting in groups of three, with one student from group A, one from group B and one from group C in each group.

- Ask students to interview the members of their group in order to find out if their predictions are correct. Remind them to keep a note of the results of their survey.

- When the students have finished interviewing each other, ask them to return to their original groups and share the results of their interviews. Make sure they include themselves in the results.

- Ask the groups to work together to rewrite each sentence using the prompts to reflect the results of their survey. Monitor and help with accurate sentences where necessary.

- Invite each group to share their finished statements with the whole class and any information that surprised them.

> **Student A** 1 What happens when it's a rainy weekend is that most people in the class … 2 It's … that most people enjoy doing on a Saturday morning. 3 It wasn't until they were … that most people were allowed to stay up after 9 p.m. 4 What most people in the class do when they get stressed is …
> **Student B** 1 It'd be … that most people in the class would eat … if they wanted something special. 2 It's by … that most people in the class go to school/work. 3 It's not until … that most people in the class get up at the weekend. 4 What happens during summer evenings is that most people in the class …
> **Student C** 1 What most people have for breakfast is … 2 The reason why most people in the class chose this school is that … 3 It's … that most people in the class enjoy doing in their English lessons. 4 It's by … that most people in the class keep in touch with their friends.

1C In other words, … p135

Language
Explaining and paraphrasing

Activity type, when to use and time
Role play. Use any time after lesson 1C. 15–25 minutes.

Preparation
Photocopy one worksheet for each pair of students.

Procedure
- Put students into pairs.

- Tell students that they're going to imagine they are two colleagues who are sitting next to each other on the train on their way home from work. Students are going to write a conversation between them.

- ✎ On the board, write A *So, what do you think about …………… ?* B *Mmm, that's an interesting one. Well, …………… . In other words, …………… .* Elicit possible ideas from the class on how to complete the conversation.

- Give each pair a copy of the worksheet.

- In pairs, students complete the conversation using their own ideas.

- Students role-play the conversation in pairs. Encourage them to pay attention to the notes in italics and consider their intonation to bring the conversation to life. Ask more confident pairs to act out their conversation without the script.

- Rearrange the class so that each pair is sitting with another pair. If there is an extra pair, create a group with three pairs. Ask each pair to role-play their conversation.

- Elicit from the class the similarities and differences between the conversations they heard.

- Invite one group to role-play their conversation in front of the whole class.

2A The great brain game p136

Language
Relative clauses with prepositions

Activity type, when to use and time
Pairwork quiz. Use any time after lesson 2A. 20–25 minutes.

Preparation
Photocopy one quiz worksheet for each pair of students. Cut into two separate worksheets.

Procedure
- ✎ On the board, write *In his lifetime, Van Gogh wrote more than 800 letters. Many of them were sent to his brother Theo. (many of which)* Ask the class to help you rewrite the two sentences so that they're joined by *many of which.* For example, *In his lifetime, Van Gogh wrote more than 800 letters, many of which were sent to his brother Theo.* Ask the students if they think the information in this statement is true or false. (Answer: true.)

- Pre-teach *non-threatening, pathologist, pi, autistic* and *child prodigy.*

- Divide the class into two groups, A and B. Give each student a copy of the appropriate worksheet. Students are not allowed to show their quizzes to a student in the other group.

- Ask students to work in pairs with someone from the same group and join the two sentences in each bubble with the words in brackets.

- Check answers with the class.

- Pair a student from group A with a student from group B. Each student reads out a sentence. The other student says if it is true or false. If he/she is correct, he/she gets two points. Before students begin, point out that the answers to the quiz and some additional information are at the bottom of each worksheet.

- At the end of both quizzes, each student adds up his/her points. The student with the most points in each pair wins.

- Ask the class which facts they found most interesting and why.

- For follow-up, students with access to the Internet can research further information about each person.

Student A 1 Vincent Van Gogh's artistic career lasted for a ten-year period, during which he painted almost 900 pictures. 2 James Wannerton suffers from synaesthesia, a non-threatening neurological condition with which words that he hears activate his sense of smell. 3 There are more than 5,000 world languages, of which Harold Williams, the world's greatest linguist, spoke 58. 4 Aged seven, Akrit Jaswal from India proudly dressed up as a doctor, at which point he carried out his first operation. 5 Derek Paravicini can listen to a piece of music just once, after which he plays it back perfectly from memory.

Student B 1 In 1995 pathologist Thomas Harvey met up with a Princeton University neuroscientist to whom he gave Albert Einstein's diary. 2 In 2001, autistic artist Stephen Wiltshire took a helicopter ride across London, after which he created an amazingly detailed drawing from memory in just three hours. 3 In his mind, child prodigy Jay Greenberg can see a photograph of a new mathematical equation, to which he rarely has to make changes after he writes it down. 4 Akira Haraguchi has an amazing brain with which he can remember pi to 140,000 digits. 5 In 1994 Tony Cicoria was hit by lightning and became obsessed with playing the piano and classical music, neither of which he was interested in beforehand.

2B Survival at sea p137

Language
Participle clauses

Activity type, when to use and time
Information gap. Use any time after lesson 2B. 15–20 minutes.

Preparation
Photocopy one worksheet for each pair of students. Cut into two separate worksheets.

Procedure
- Tell students that they are going to read a true story about a sailing trip from Cornwall in the UK to the Caribbean. Ask the students to predict what someone on such a trip might experience.
- Pre-teach *raft*, *spring a leak*, *drift* and *spear*.
- Divide the class into two groups, A and B. Give each student a copy of the appropriate worksheet.
- Put students into pairs so that a student from group A is working with a student from group B. Students are not allowed to look at each other's worksheets.
- Tell students that extract A is the first part of the story and extract N is the final part, but the other extracts of the story are mixed up. Student A starts by reading the first extract (extract A). Student B should find and read the second extract, student A should find the third and so on until the story is complete.

- Check answers with the class and ask students to discuss whether they think they could have coped in similar circumstances.

  K2 E3 I4 B5 M6 F7 J8 D9 H10 C11 L12 G13

2C Tourism role play p138

Language
Making recommendations

Activity type, when to use and time
Discussion and presentation. Use any time after lesson 2C. 25–35 minutes.

Preparation
Photocopy one worksheet for each student.

Procedure
- Divide the class into four groups, A, B, C and D. Put students into groups of four, with one student from groups A, B, C and D in each group.
- Ask students to brainstorm the advantages and disadvantages of tourism in their groups.
- Ask the groups to share their ideas with the class. Introduce the idea of *sustainable tourism*.
- Give each student a worksheet. Ask students to read the article about Calamango to decide if it is a place they would like to visit and why. Elicit some responses from the class.
- Ask students to read the instructions.
- Tell the class that you are the Minister of Tourism in Calamango and you would like to hear their recommendations for the Calamangan tourist industry. Give the groups a time limit (e.g. 15 minutes) to brainstorm recommendations. Remind students to consider the items on the bullet points on the role card.
- Give students another time limit (e.g. five minutes) to review their list of recommendations in groups and agree on the top three. Ensure that each student in each group has these three recommendations written down.
- Rearrange the class into groups of three or four so that student As are sitting together, student Bs are sitting together, etc.
- Tell the class that each student must present their recommendations to the others in their group. The group must then choose the best three recommendations and present these to the class.
- Ask each group to present their best three recommendations to the class.
- Ask the class to vote on the best three recommendations. If there is a tie, make the casting decision in your role as Minister of Tourism.

3A Connotation crossword p139

Language

Positive and negative character adjectives

Activity type, when to use and time

Paired crossword. Use any time after lesson 3A. 15–20 minutes.

Preparation

Photocopy one worksheet for each pair of students. Cut into two separate worksheets.

Procedure

- Divide the class into two groups, A and B. Give each student a copy of the appropriate worksheet. Point out that all the words in the crossword are from lesson 3A.
- Students work in pairs with a student from the same group and check they know the meanings of all the words in their crossword.
- Put students into new pairs so that a student from group A is working with a student from group B. Students are not allowed to look at each other's worksheets.
- Students then take turns to give clues for the words in their crossword. For example, *Five across is a negative adjective which means that you pay a lot of attention to small details.*
- Finally, students check their completed crossword and their spelling with their partner.

3B This is my life p140

Language

Inversion

Activity type, when to use and time

Writing activity. Use any time after lesson 3B. 15–25 minutes.

Preparation

Photocopy one worksheet for each student. Write a number in the box on the worksheet for each student in your class. For example, if you have 16 students, write 1–16 on the worksheets. Shuffle the worksheets so they are not in numerical order.

Procedure

- Give each student a copy of the worksheet.
- Students work on their own and complete the worksheet about themselves. Remind them that the text focuses on the use of inversion. Monitor and help with any student errors.
- Collect the completed worksheets and shuffle them. Put the worksheets up around the room.
- Put students into pairs. Each pair moves around the room and guesses who wrote each worksheet. Students should make a note of the number of each worksheet and the name of the student they think wrote it.

- Students continue until they have read all the worksheets. While they are doing this, read the worksheets yourself and make a note of any consistent errors that you were not able to pick up when monitoring previously.
- Check answers with the class and find out which pair had the most correct guesses. You can also ask students to say what they thought the most surprising or interesting thing they read was.
- Alternatively, shuffle the collected worksheets and redistribute them in random order. Students read the new worksheet and decide who wrote it. Students check answers with the class by reading out the worksheet and saying who they think wrote it.
- Finally, deal with any consistent errors that you noticed when reading the texts around the room.

3C Tactful or tactless? p141

Language

Being tactful

Activity type, when to use and time

Mingle. Use any time after lesson 3C. 15–20 minutes.

Preparation

Photocopy one worksheet for each group of 12 students. Cut the question cards into sets and shuffle each set. Cut out the *tactless* and *tactful* cards.

Procedure

- Give each student a question card and ask them to memorise it. Give each student a *tactful* or *tactless* card. Students are not allowed to look at each other's cards.
- Tell students that they are going to move around the class and ask their questions. Each student should answer the questions. If they have a *tactless* card, they can reply tactlessly. However, if they have a *tactful* card, they must reply as tactfully as possible. The aim is to guess which students are tactful and which are tactless.
- The students move around the room and ask and answer their questions. Encourage students to extend the conversations each time before moving on to another student. For example, A *Do you think I should change my hairstyle?* B *Well, it could be a bit more up-to-date.* A *Really? How?* B *Well, why don't you try that new salon in town? They might have some ideas that would really suit you.* A *OK, great! I'll give it a try.*
- After the mingle, ask the students to work in pairs and discuss which students they thought were tactless, in what way and how they could have been more tactful.

1–3 Review Board game p142

Language

Review of lessons 1A–3C

Activity type, when to use and time

Board game. Use any time after lesson 3C. 15–20 minutes.

Preparation

Photocopy one worksheet for each group of three or four students. You also need a dice for each group and a counter for each student.

Procedure

- Put students into groups of three or four. Give each group a copy of the board, a dice and counters (or students can use their own counters). Ask one student with a watch in each group to be the timekeeper. Students all start on the *Start* square.

- Students take turns to throw the dice and move around the board. When a student lands on a *Talk for one minute about* square, he/she must talk about the topic for one minute without hesitating. If he/she stops talking before the minute is up, he/she must move back to his/her previous square.

- When a student lands on one of the other squares, he/she must answer the question correctly in order to stay on the square. If a student can't answer the question correctly, he/she must move back to his/her previous square.

- If a student thinks another student's answer is wrong, he/she can check in the Language Summary in the Student's Book or ask you to adjudicate. If the answer is wrong, the student must move back to his/her previous square.

- If a student lands on a square which has already been answered, he/she must answer the question again (to check that he/she has been listening!).

- The game ends when one student reaches the *Finish* square.

- If one group finishes early, they can go through the squares they didn't land on in numerical order and discuss the answers.

> 1 spontaneous 2 picked 4 hard of hearing 7 Staying
> 9 louder than words 11 come out in 12 broadly
> speaking/in the main/on the whole/as a rule
> 13 He always butts in … 14 gullible 15 another man's
> poison 16 've been 18 unique 22 gorgeous Chinese silk
> 23 terms 24 finished 27 wonder 28 bitterly 29 Its
> condition is worse than in the past. 31 e.g. I think
> softer/more muted colours suit you better. 32 What I do
> if I'm tired **is** have a nap. 33 of which

4A No comment! p143

Language

Phrases referring to the future

Activity type, when to use and time

Information gap. Use any time after lesson 4A. 15–20 minutes.

Preparation

Photocopy one worksheet for each pair of students. Cut into three separate cards – one table and information card, one student A card and one student B card.

Procedure

- Tell the students that five media celebrities have recently issued press releases about their future plans. The students are journalists working for a national gossip magazine. They've discovered some additional information about the celebrities which will make great news stories. They have to pass on the stories to their editor but their notes have got mixed up and they can't remember which news story goes with which celebrity. They have to work with a partner to put them back together.

- Pre-teach *executive* and *plagiarise*.

- Divide the class into two groups, A and B. Give each student a copy of the appropriate card.

- Put students into pairs, so that a student A is working with a student B. Students are not allowed to look at each other's cards. Give each pair a copy of the table and information card which they can both look at.

- Each student takes it in turns to say a clue from his/her worksheet. The students work together to complete the table from the clues.

- ✍ While students are working, copy the table onto the board ready for checking.

- ✍ Elicit answers from the class and write them in the table on the board.

- Ask students if newspaper editors in their country would consider the information in this activity to be newsworthy or not. If so, have any celebrities in their country been caught out in this way?

> **John** newsreader, announcing retirement, was sacked for rudeness
> **Jim** film director, releasing a documentary about the environment, uses a private plane
> **Jack** ex-model, promoting a TV Internet service, downloaded music illegally
> **Jennifer** TV executive, being made head of a TV station, doesn't own a TV
> **Julie** soap star, publishing a book, copied someone's work

4B Guess the word p144

Language
Near synonyms

Activity type, when to use and time
Guess the word game. Use any time after lesson 4B. 20–25 minutes.

Preparation
Photocopy one worksheet for each group of four students. Cut into four separate cards.

Procedure
- Divide the class into four groups, A, B, C and D. Give each student a copy of the appropriate card.
- Students work in pairs with a student from the same group and check they know the meanings of all the words/phrases on their card. Students then write one or two near synonyms for the words/phrases on their card. Monitor and check that the words are suitable.
- Write *courageous* on a piece of paper and fold it over so it is not visible. Tell the class that there is a word on the paper that you want them to guess but there are two near synonyms that you are not allowed to say in your definition. Define the word *courageous* to the class without saying *brave* or *reckless*. For example, *This is an adjective which describes a person who can control his/her fear when there is danger*. When a student guesses the word, give him/her one point. Then invite the class to tell you which near synonyms you were not allowed to say (*brave* and *reckless*). Give one point to the students who guess each word first.
- Put students into groups of four, with one student from groups A, B, C and D in each group. Students are not allowed to look at each other's cards.
- Each student takes it in turns to give a definition of one of the words/phrases on his/her card and the other students try to guess it. However, the student giving the definition must **not** use any part of the word/phrase, or any near synonyms in their definition.
- The first student to guess the word/phrase gets one point. Students then have a chance to say what they think the forbidden near synonym was. The student who guesses each word/phrase first gets one point.
- When all words/phrases have been guessed, the student in the group with the most points wins.

> **Possible answers**
> **Student A** huge – large; settlement – village; humans – man/people; improvement – development
> **Student B** determined – obstinate; be forced to – have to; infuriating – exasperating; unexpectedly – suddenly
> **Student C** let – allow; angry – furious/cross; watch – gaze at; a standstill – a stop
> **Student D** urban – city; child – kid; country folk – rural inhabitants/villagers; friend – mate

4C The powers of persuasion p145

Language
Persuading

Activity type, when to use and time
Role play. Use any time after lesson 4C. 20–30 minutes.

Preparation
Photocopy one worksheet for each group of three students. Cut into three separate role cards.

Procedure
- Ask students if they are familiar with the paparazzi and if these photographers exist in their country. If necessary, explain that in many countries, such as the US and the UK, celebrities are often chased by the paparazzi and photographed when they are not working but are in a public place. These photographs are then sold for a high price to newspapers and magazines.
- Pre-teach *paparazzi*, *Member of Parliament* and *celebrity*.
- Divide the class into three groups: Members of Parliament, celebrities and magazine editors. Arrange the class so that each group is sitting together.
- Give each student an appropriate role card. Students work in their groups and prepare for the task on their cards.
- Rearrange the class so that students are sitting in groups of three, with one Member of Parliament, one celebrity and one magazine editor in each group.
- Ask each Member of Parliament to start the meeting and listen to the views of the celebrity and the editor. Encourage the Member of Parliament to ask questions, and express his/her own views. You can set a time limit of 15 minutes.
- Finally, ask each Member of Parliament to vote for or against the law and say why they were persuaded to make their decision.

5A Prefix Pelmanism p146

Language
Word building

Activity type, when to use and time
Pelmanism. Use any time after lesson 5A. 15–20 minutes.

Preparation
Photocopy one worksheet for each group of three students. Cut into sets. Shuffle each set.

Procedure
- Put the class into groups of three. Give each group a set of cards. Ask them to spread the cards out face down on the table in front of them, with the small cards (the prefixes) on the left and the large cards on the right.

- Students take turns to turn over one small card and one large card. If a student thinks the two cards match, he/she gives a definition of the word.
- If the cards match and the definition is correct, the student keeps the pair of cards and has another turn. If a student thinks that another student's cards don't match or the definition is wrong, he/she can challenge him/her. If students can't agree, they can ask you to adjudicate. If the cards don't match or the definition is wrong, the student puts the cards back face down **in exactly the same place** and the turn passes to the next student.
- The activity continues until all the cards are matched up. The student who collects the most cards wins.
- If a group finishes early, students can take turns in testing each other by saying the prefixes on the small cards.

5B Picture story p147

Language
Verb patterns

Activity type, when to use and time
Paired picture story. Use any time after lesson 5B. 20–30 minutes.

Preparation
Photocopy one worksheet for each pair of students.

Procedure
- Put students into pairs. Give each pair a worksheet.
- Ask students to reorder the pictures and make a story. Students can start with any picture, and create any order they like. They should include the phrases under each picture (using the names or pronouns as necessary) and make sure they use infinitive + *to* or verb+*ing* correctly. Encourage students to add extra information and make the stories as interesting as possible.
- Ask students to work with a different partner. Each student tells his/her story. Ask the pairs to see how similar or different their stories are.
- Ask a confident pair to tell their story to the class.

> **Possible answer**
> Tom was a young musician who wanted to go to music school. **He took a job** with a band, **which meant** visiting a different town each day.
>
> One day, he went into a café for a coffee. **He** immediately **noticed** the young waitress standing near him. She was beautiful and he couldn't take his eyes off her. **He watched her** serve some of the customers until she saw him and he politely looked away. After a few minutes, he took out his guitar and started to play. **She walked over to him, forgetting** to take a plate of eggs to a customer. She stood next to him for a few seconds and then started to sing with him. Tom was very surprised but very pleased. When they finished singing, they talked for a while, and she told him her name was Jeanette.

> Eventually Tom had to leave. **He meant** to ask her for her address, but he didn't have the courage. He left the café with a simple goodbye.
>
> A few months later Tom found himself in the town again. **He deeply regretted** not keeping in touch with Jeanette and wanted to see her again. He wanted to tell her that he had a place at music school, but when he went to the café, she wasn't there. He asked the manager for her address and wrote her a heartfelt letter, telling her that **he had never forgotten** meeting her and wanted to see her again.
>
> Several weeks later, Tom received a letter from Jeanette's mother. She said, "**I regret** to tell you that Jeanette has got married and moved away." Tom was devastated, but two weeks later he went to college. He began to write music and he wrote several songs about Jeanette. **He went on** to become a famous singer-songwriter. He always wondered if Jeanette heard his songs and realised some were about her.

5C Carry on talking p148

Language
Conversational strategies

Activity type, when to use and time
Discussion game. Use any time after lesson 5C. 15–20 minutes.

Preparation
Photocopy one worksheet for each group of three students. Cut into one set of phrase cards and one set of topic cards.

Procedure
- Divide the class into groups of three and give each group a set of phrase cards. Ask a member of each group to shuffle the phrase cards and then deal them out equally to each student in the group.
- Give each group a set of topic cards, face down in a pile in front of them. Tell students that the discussion topics review previous lessons.
- The dealer takes the first topic card, reads it out and starts the conversation. In turn, each student contributes to the conversation. They can agree or disagree with the topic on the card. While each student is speaking, he/she tries to use a phrase on one of his/her phrase cards in a natural way. When he/she has used a phrase, he/she puts the card down on the table face up.
- The aim of the game is for each student to use his/her six phrases within the conversation before the others. However, it must be done in a natural way. If the phrase is not used appropriately, the other students can object and the speaker is not allowed to put it down.
- If discussion on a topic stops, a player can pick up the next topic card and continue with that topic.
- If a group finishes early, they can deal the phrase cards again and play again using a different topic card.

6A Anti-social behaviour p149

Language
Formal and informal ways of comparing

Activity type, when to use and time
Ranking and discussion. Use any time after lesson 6A. 20–35 minutes.

Preparation
Photocopy one worksheet for each student.

Procedure
- Tell the class about a social habit that you find annoying (e.g. a neighbour playing very loud music) and elicit the concept of anti-social behaviour.
- Tell students that they are going to read a list of habits which some people might find anti-social and irritating and others might find acceptable. Check students understand *litter, swear words* and *jumping the queue*.
- Ask each student to read the list of habits and decide which ten are the most anti-social and harmful to society. Ask students to rank these from 1 to 10 (1 = the most anti-social).
- Put students into pairs. Ask each pair to compare answers and agree on the top five anti-social habits, then rank them from 1 to 5 (1 = the most anti-social). Encourage students to use informal ways of comparing when speaking. For example, *For me, someone eating in public isn't anywhere near as bad as someone eating with his/her mouth open because this is considered to be very bad manners in my country.* Students must convince each other that their choices are the worst by giving good arguments for and against each habit. Give students a time limit of ten minutes to reach an agreement.
- Ask pairs to work together in groups of four to compare answers and agree on the top five anti-social habits. Then students rank the habits from 1 to 5 (1 = the most anti-social). Encourage students to persuade the others that their list is the best one.
- Elicit the top five from each group and discuss how they came to an agreement.
- Ask each group to work together and write a short summary explaining their top five anti-social habits. Encourage students to use formal ways of comparing. For example, *We decided that someone driving over the speed limit is significantly more anti-social than any of the other habits because it is dangerous and shows a lack of respect for other drivers and pedestrians who could be seriously hurt.* Put the statements around the classroom and ask students to walk around and read the conclusions of each group.
- Finally, elicit any comments about the conclusions on the worst anti-social habits from the class and deal with any errors made when speaking and in the summaries.

6B Grab a word game p150

Language
Position of adverbials

Activity type, when to use and time
Sentence completion and board game. Use any time after lesson 6B. 15–25 minutes.

Preparation
Photocopy one worksheet for each student. Cut each worksheet into the board and the sentence card. You also need a dice for each group and a counter for each student.

Procedure
- ✎ On the board, write *I _____ drink coffee _____.* and *_____ I can _____ do my homework _____.* Elicit possible adverbials to fill each gap. For example, *I usually drink coffee at home. Unfortunately, I can never do my homework quickly.* Use these sentences to review the position of the different types of adverbial from **G6.4** SB p134.
- Put students into groups of three. Give each student a sentence card. Give each group a copy of the board, a dice and three counters (or students can make their own counters). Students all start on the *Start* square.
- Students take turns to throw the dice and move around the board. When a student lands on a square, he/she can choose one of the words/phrases and write it in one of the gaps in his/her sentences. He/She must cross this word off on the board so it is no longer available.
- Students can go around the board as many times as necessary to complete the game. If students land on a square where all of the words are crossed out, they are unable to use a word and must wait until their next turn.
- Monitor and help where necessary. Check that students are making correct choices.
- Students continue until one of them is able to complete all of his/her sentences. He/She must then show the sentence card to the other students. If the other students are happy that the sentences are correct, the student is the winner. You can adjudicate if the students are unsure.
- Ask students to discuss the winning student's completed sentences and make them true for themselves. For example, *I'm definitely going to get up early tomorrow because I have to be at work at 8.00.* Encourage students to ask follow-up questions.

Possible answers
1 I'll probably go to the cinema tomorrow. 2 Fortunately, I don't have to work in the morning. 3 I'm almost certainly going to get up early. 4 Luckily, I pick up languages quickly. 5 I usually go shopping at weekends. 6 Surprisingly, I occasionally like running at night. 7 Naturally, I've always had to do housework. 8 I often meet up with friends in the evenings. 9 I rarely work well when I'm under pressure.

6C What a joke! p151

Language
Telling a joke

Activity type, when to use and time
Speaking activity. Use any time after lesson 6C. 20–25 minutes.

Preparation
Photocopy one worksheet for each group of three students. Cut into three separate worksheets.

Procedure
- ✏️ Write on the board: *Man / walk / pet shop / say / "I'd like / puppy / for my son." / Shop assistant / reply / "Sorry / sir / we / not / do / part-exchange."*

- Tell the class that these are prompts to a joke. Elicit the joke in full and write the possible answer on the board under the prompts. *A man walks into a pet shop and says, "I'd like a puppy for my son." The shop assistant replies, "I'm sorry, sir. We don't do part-exchange."* Note that jokes are often told in the present tense to make the joke seem more immediate.

- Tell students that they are each going to tell a joke.

- Pre-teach *whine, shrug* and *bonnet*.

- Divide the class into three groups, A, B and C. Give each student a copy of the appropriate worksheet.

- Students work with another student in their group and write their joke from the prompts on the worksheet. Encourage students to think of ways to adapt the language in the joke to make it as funny as possible. Monitor and check students' ideas.

- Ask students to discuss techniques they can use to tell the joke in as interesting a way as possible. Encourage them to practise telling the joke to their partner.

- Rearrange the class so that students are sitting in groups of three, with one student from group A, one from group B and one from group C in each group.

- Each student tells his/her joke to the group.

- After each student has told his/her joke, each group decides which joke was the funniest.

- As a follow-up activity, ask students to tell a joke that they know to their group.

> **Possible answers**
> **Student A** The detective Sherlock Holmes and his assistant, Dr Watson, decide to go on a camping trip. They set off at 6 a.m. and head towards the mountains. Eventually they arrive at their destination and find a good place to put up their tent. They spend the next few days fishing. Every evening, they go for a walk, cook dinner and then go to sleep in their tent. In the middle of the last night, Holmes wakes up Watson. Holmes says, "Look up, Watson. What are you able to tell me?" Watson replies, "Well, I can see millions of stars and a planet. This suggests that humans are not the only life form. There must be life outside Earth." To which Holmes replies, "No, Watson! Somebody has stolen our tent!"

> **Student B** A dog sees a job ad. It says "Help wanted. You must be able to type, be good with a computer and be bilingual." The dog goes for an interview. The receptionist sees the dog and calls the office manager. When the manager arrives, the dog starts to whine. The manager laughs and says, "Sorry, but I can't hire you. You must be able to type." The dog immediately walks over to the typewriter and starts to type a perfect letter. The manager is surprised, to say the least, but he continues: "Sorry, I still can't hire you because you must be good with computers." The dog runs over to the nearest computer and starts to use the computer program. The manager is shocked and impressed, but says, "Sorry, I really can't hire you. The ad says that you must be bilingual." The dog walks calmly over to the manager, looks at him and says, "Meow!"

> **Student C** A man is driving a car down a country road. Suddenly, the car comes to a stop. It won't start again. The man gets out, opens the bonnet and looks inside. He doesn't know what to do. Suddenly, a voice says, "The oil filter is blocked. It needs cleaning." The man turns round but there's no one there, so he shrugs and continues looking. He hears the voice again: "The oil filter is blocked. It needs cleaning." The man turns and sees a black horse. The man can't believe it but follows the instructions anyway. He cleans the oil filter and gets back into the car. Amazingly, the car starts and so he continues on his journey. He stops at the next village and goes into a pub. The man tells the barman about the horse and his car. The barman asks, "Was it a black horse?" The man nods and asks, "How did you know?" The barman says, "Well, the white horse knows nothing about cars."

4–6 Review Cash quiz p152–p153

Language
Review of lessons 4A–6C

Activity type, when to use and time
Quiz. Use any time after lesson 6C. 20–25 minutes.

Preparation
Photocopy one team A worksheet for half the number of students in your class and one team B worksheet for the other half. Cut each worksheet into the score board and the question sheet.

Procedure
- Put the class into groups of four or six.

- Divide each group into two teams of two or three students, team A and team B. Give each student in each team a copy of the appropriate score board and question sheet. Students are not allowed to look at the other team's question sheet.

- Focus students on the score board. Tell students that there are eight categories of question. For each category there is a question worth £500 and a question worth £250. The £500 questions are more challenging than the

£250 questions. The aim is to be the first team to win £5,000 or more.

- Students toss a coin to decide which team starts. The starting team chooses a category and a question (e.g. Adverbials £500). The other team reads that question from the relevant section on their question sheet. If the team answers the question correctly, they can add the money (e.g. £500) to their score board. If the team answers the question incorrectly, they get no money and their total remains the same. In both cases, the question is crossed off the question sheet and cannot be answered again. Point out that the answers to the questions are in brackets on the question sheets.

- Students take it in turns to choose a category and answer the questions until a team reaches £5,000.

- Groups that finish early can ask each other the unanswered questions on their question sheets.

7A You said it! p154

Language
Conditionals

Activity type, when to use and time
Sentence completion and mingle. Use any time after lesson 7A. 15–25 minutes.

Preparation
Photocopy one worksheet for each group of four students. Cut into separate cards. Shuffle the cards in each set.

Procedure

- Give four cards from a single set to each student. Ask students to complete the conditional sentences with true information about themselves. If students cannot think of a way to complete a particular sentence, they can ask you for a different one. Students are not allowed to look at each other's cards.

- When students have completed their sentences, collect all the cards, put them in a bag and mix them up. Ask students to pick out one card each from the bag. (If students pick one of their own cards, they should put it back and pick another one.)

- Tell students that they are going to try and find the person who wrote the sentence on the card they have picked. Students prepare questions to find out who wrote the sentence on the card they picked.

- Students move around the class asking their questions. Point out that students may find someone who answers *yes* to the information on their card, but who didn't write that sentence. Students should therefore check they have found the correct person by asking *Is this your card?*

- When students have found the person who wrote their card, they keep the card and pick another from the bag. The activity continues until the bag is empty. The student with the most cards wins.

Possible answers

If I hadn't come to class today, I'd be watching TV at home now.

If the sun is shining, I often walk to work.

If I'm not going to have time to eat lunch, I usually have some chocolate.

If I could fly anywhere, I'd fly to Barbados.

If I hadn't been working/studying last week, I'd have gone to the beach.

If I'd had time to do my washing yesterday, I'd be wearing my jeans now.

If I get up early at the weekend, I usually go for a run.

If I weren't so busy, I'd have had a weekend away last month.

If I'm really enjoying a book, I stay up all night to finish it.

If I hadn't started learning English, I wouldn't have been able to pass my university exam.

If I have some free time tomorrow, I might go to the cinema.

If I weren't living with my flatmate, I'd probably be living with my parents.

If I'm going to be late home, I usually call my flatmate and tell her.

If it hadn't been raining last weekend, I'd have invited my friends round for a barbecue.

If I need to relax, I turn off my mobile phone.

If I meet up with friends this week, we'll probably go for a meal.

7B Fact or fiction? p155

Language
Impersonal report structures

Activity type, when to use and time
Sentence transformation and information gap. Use any time after lesson 7B. 20–25 minutes.

Preparation
Photocopy one worksheet for each pair of students. Cut into separate worksheets.

Procedure

- On the board, write *It _____ that a duck's quack doesn't echo but is this claim correct? (claim)* Elicit the correct form of the verb in brackets and write it in the gap (*is claimed*). Ask the students to answer the question. Tell them that the claim is a common myth or misconception and that in fact a duck's quack does echo, although quite softly.

- If necessary, pre-teach *chameleon*.

- Put students into two groups, A and B. Give each student a copy of the appropriate worksheet. Tell students not to look at the answers at the bottom of their worksheets and not to show their worksheets to a student in the other group.

- Students work in pairs with someone from the same group to complete the gaps with the correct form of the words in brackets. Check the sentences with the class without giving away the answers to the questions.
- Each pair now answers each question before checking their answers at the bottom of their worksheets.
- Rearrange the class so that a student from group A is sitting with a student from group B. Students take it in turns to read out a question on their worksheet. If a student answers a question correctly, he/she gets one point.
- Each student adds up their points. The student with the most points wins.
- Finally, ask the class which misconceptions they found most surprising and why.

> **Student A** 1 is often claimed to be 2 is generally assumed 3 is widely believed 4 is often thought to be 5 is sometimes said 6 was reported
> **Student B** 1 is widely believed 2 was reported 3 are said to exist 4 is often claimed 5 is sometimes feared 6 are thought to change

7C Crime circle p156

Language
Intonation of questions

Activity type, when to use and time
Discussion circle. Use any time after lesson 7C. 30–40 minutes.

Preparation
Photocopy one worksheet for each group of six students. Cut into separate discussion cards and keep in sets.

Procedure
- On the board, write 'Crime is increasing in my country.' Do you agree or disagree with this statement? Ask a student for their opinion and elicit some follow-up questions to find out more information about his/her opinion. For example, Why is it increasing? It's increasing just among some sections of society, isn't it? Elicit the correct intonation of the questions.
- Tell students they are going to discuss other crime issues. Pre-teach trial, televised, zero tolerance, death penalty, cyber-crime and rehabilitate.
- Divide the class into groups of six students. Divide each group in half, with three student As and three student Bs. Pair each student A with a student B.
- Give two discussion cards from each set to each student within each group.
- Student A reads out a statement and invites student B to give their opinion. Student A asks follow-up questions, using appropriate intonation. Student B then reads out a statement and invites student A to give their opinion. Student B asks follow-up questions, using appropriate intonation.

- At the end of the time limit (e.g. five minutes), both students make a note of their partner's opinions for later in the activity.
- Ask each student B to work with a different student A in their group. Repeat the previous two steps.
- Students continue to move around the group and discuss their statements until all the questions have been discussed.
- Rearrange the class so that in each group all the student As are sitting together and all the student Bs are together.
- Students discuss their questions in groups, and take turns to repeat the responses they received.
- Finally, elicit any surprising responses from the class.

8A The council meeting p157–p158

Language
Past verb forms with present or future meaning

Activity type, when to use and time
Debate. Use any time after lesson 8A. 30–45 minutes.

Preparation
Photocopy one agenda for each student and one set of role cards for each group of five students. Cut into agendas and separate role cards.

Procedure
- Explain that in cities and towns across the UK, local volunteers are elected to a council by the inhabitants of that city or town. The members of the council (councillors) make decisions about what should be done in the city/town and how government money should be spent. Ask students if they have elected councils and councillors in their city or town.
- Divide the class into five groups, A–E. Give each student in group A a copy of the student A role card and the agenda; each student in group B a copy of the student B role card and the agenda, etc. Try to choose confident students to be the Chair (student A).
- Give students time to read the information on the agenda and their role cards. Check they understand the situation. Students then work in their groups and follow the instructions on their role cards.
- While students are working, write useful language from **G8.2** SB p141 on the board: It's high time, I'd sooner, etc.
- Rearrange the class so that students are sitting in groups of five, with one student from group A, one student from group B, etc. in each group. Focus students on the language on the board and remind them to use this during the discussion.
- Ask the Chairs to start the meetings. Allow about 15–20 minutes for students to discuss all their options and arrive at a final spending plan.
- Finally, ask each Chair to share his/her group's conclusions with the class and describe how the decisions were made.

8B The thrill-seekers p159

Language
Word building (2): suffixes

Activity type, when to use and time
Gap-fill and information gap. Use any time after lesson 8B. 20–25 minutes.

Preparation
Photocopy one worksheet for each pair of students. Cut into two separate worksheets.

Procedure
- Ask the class if they know any thrill-seekers, personally or in the news.
- Divide the class into two groups, A and B.
- Pre-teach *phenomena* and *parachute jump*.
- Give each student a copy of the appropriate worksheet. Ask students to fill in the gaps with the correct form of the words in brackets. Students can use a dictionary if necessary.
- Check answers with the class.
- Students work in pairs with a student from the same group and write down 10 key words from the text that will help them to summarise it to a student from the other group.
- Put students into new pairs so that a student from group A is working with a student from group B. Ask students to cover their texts and use their 10 words to summarise the information about the thrill-seekers for their new partner.
- ✍ On the board, write *Why do you think these men do what they do? How do you think their families feel about it?* Ask the students to discuss these questions.
- Invite feedback from the class about their opinions of the men in the texts.

> **Student A** 1 adventurous 2 natural 3 annually
> 4 potentially 5 darken 6 investment 7 eagerness
> 8 active 9 diversified 10 memorable
> **Student B** 1 continuously 2 achievement 3 visibility
> 4 definitely 5 intensify 6 strengthen 7 acceleration
> 8 remarkable 9 determination 10 incidentally

8C What a dilemma! p160

Language
Explaining choices

Activity type, when to use and time
Discussion. Use any time after lesson 8C. 20–30 minutes.

Preparation
Photocopy a worksheet for each student.

Procedure
- Introduce the concept of a dilemma by reading out this example: *Imagine you want to give a friend an expensive watch but don't have much money. You could buy a cheap one and put it in an expensive box. Would you do this?* Elicit responses from the class. If the students do not use the Real World language (SB p83), demonstrate the task by answering the question yourself with some of the phrases. For example, *There's no way I'd do that because my friend would be sure to find out and I'd feel really embarrassed.*
- Give each student a copy of the worksheet. Ask students to read through dilemmas 1–10 and think about their choices. Give them time to think about their reasons for making those choices.
- Put students into pairs or groups of three and ask them to give and explain their choices.
- Elicit feedback from the pairs/groups about any surprising or contrasting ideas.

9A Verb dominoes p161

Language
Verbs with different meanings

Activity type, when to use and time
Dominoes. Use any time after lesson 9A. 15–25 minutes.

Preparation
Photocopy one set of dominoes for each pair of students. Cut into sets and shuffle each set.

Procedure
- Put students into pairs. Give one set of dominoes to each pair. The students share out the dominoes equally. Students are not allowed to look at their partner's dominoes.
- One student puts a domino on the table. His/Her partner puts another domino at either end of the first domino so that the two dominoes make a sentence. Encourage students to pay attention to the verb forms in bold when trying to match the dominoes. Once a student has matched two dominoes, he/she must explain the meaning of the verb form in bold in its context.
- Students continue taking turns to put dominoes at either end of the chain. If a student thinks the dominoes do not make a sentence, he/she can challenge his/her partner. If the sentence is incorrect, the student takes back the domino and the turn passes to his/her partner. If students can't agree, they can ask you to adjudicate.
- When a student can't put down a domino, the turn automatically passes to his/her partner.
- The game continues until one student has put down all of his/her dominoes, or until neither student can make a correct match. The student who finishes first, or who has fewer dominoes remaining at the end of the game, is the winner.

9B My partner p162

Language

Word building (3): productive suffixes

Activity type, when to use and time

Personalised information gap. Use any time after lesson 9B. 15–20 minutes.

Preparation

Photocopy one worksheet for each pair of students. Cut into two separate worksheets.

Procedure

- Divide the class into two groups, A and B. Give each student a copy of the appropriate worksheet.

- ✎ On the board, write the suffixes -able,- led, -worthy, -minded, -free, -proof, -ish and -conscious. Ask students to work in pairs with someone from their group and complete the statements using one of the suffixes on the board. While one suffix may fit more than one word, for the purpose of this activity each suffix can only be used once to complete all of the sentences correctly.

- Check answers with the class, with students calling out the suffixes only. Note that the suffixes are the same for both worksheets, even though the words are different.

- Put a student from group A with a student from group B. If possible, put students with someone they don't know very well. Students are not allowed to look at each other's worksheets.

- Students work on their own and write a *T* in the second column on the worksheet if they think the sentence is true about their partner or an *F* if they think it is false. Students are not allowed to speak to their partner during this stage of the activity.

- Students work with their partners and take turns to ask and answer questions about the sentences on their worksheets. For example, *Do you always drink sugar-free drinks?*

- For each prediction a student gets right, he/she gets a point. Encourage students to ask follow-up questions where possible. The student with the most points wins.

- Finally, students tell the class two things they found out about their partner.

> 1 free 2 ish 3 conscious 4 minded 5 able 6 proof
> 7 led 8 worthy

9C Entrepreneur enterprises p163

Language

Presenting information

Activity type, when to use and time

Presentation. Use any time after lesson 9C. 30–60 minutes, depending on the size of the class.

Preparation

Photocopy one worksheet for each student.

Procedure

- Divide the class into groups of three or four students, depending on the size of your class. For small classes, you may prefer pairs.

- Pre-teach *budding entrepreneur, struggling* and *flop*.

- Give each student a copy of the worksheet. Ask the students to read the advert and tell you if they have this kind of TV programme in their own country.

- Focus students on the instructions and products. Tell students that they can choose a type of product from those illustrated or use an idea of their own if they have one. It is acceptable for more than one group to choose the same kind of product. Elicit any questions the students have about the activity. If necessary, give a time limit (e.g. 5–10 minutes) for the presentations.

- Give each group time to prepare their presentation, 30 minutes, for example. Monitor and help with ideas where necessary. Encourage students to prepare their talks thoroughly using the language in RW9.1 SB p145 and to organise their ideas effectively. If possible, ensure the groups practise their presentations before giving them to the class.

- In turn, each group presents their product to the class. The class listen as the show's experts. After each presentation, invite the 'experts' to ask questions about the products. Encourage students to ask difficult questions.

- After all the presentations have been given, ask each 'expert' to write down the name of the best business idea presented on a piece of paper. They must **not** vote for their own idea. Count all the votes of the class. The product with the most votes is the winner.

7–9 Review Across the board p164–p165

Language

Review of lessons 7A–9C

Activity type, when to use and time

Board game. Use any time after lesson 9C. 20–35 minutes.

Preparation

Photocopy one board 1/team A question sheet for half the number of students in the class and one board 2/team B question sheet for the other half. Cut into separate boards and question sheets.

Procedure

- Put students into groups of four or six. Give each group a copy of board 1.

- Divide each group into two teams, A and B. Give each student in each team a copy of the appropriate question sheet. Students are not allowed to look at the other team's question sheet.

- Focus students on board 1. Tell students that G = grammar, V = vocabulary and M = mystery question. Explain that the first team to make a line from the left-hand side of the board to the right-hand side wins the game.

- Students toss a coin to decide who starts. The teams then take turns to choose a hexagon on the board. When a team chooses a hexagon, the other team reads a question from the relevant section on their question sheets. If a team answers correctly, they win the hexagon and mark it in a suitable way, for example, by colouring it in the team's colour. If the answer is incorrect, the hexagon remains available (the other team doesn't get it). Explain that the students must read out the questions in numerical order and the answers are in brackets on the question sheet.

- When a group has finished playing, you can give them a copy of board 2 and ask them to play again. If students have run out of questions in a particular category, they can ask questions from another category instead.

- Groups that finish early can ask each other the unanswered questions on their question sheets.

10A Secret auction p166

Language
Subject/verb agreement

Activity type, when to use and time
Auction game. Use any time after lesson 10A. 20–30 minutes.

Preparation
Photocopy one worksheet for each pair of students.

Procedure

- Tell students that they're going to have a secret auction. Check students understand how this works.

- Put the students into pairs. For larger classes, you may prefer to use groups of three or four students. Give each pair/group a copy of the worksheet.

- Tell the students that some sentences are correct and some are incorrect. Point out that the incorrect sentences can have one or two mistakes.

- Students work in their pairs/groups and decide if the subjects agree with the verbs in each sentence. If they think the sentence is wrong, they must decide how to correct it. Tell students not to share their ideas with other pairs/groups, as they will be competing against each other later.

- Tell students that they can now bid for these sentences at a secret auction and that they should try to buy as many sentences as possible. Explain that each pair has £5,000 to spend and that they can only bid in multiples of £100 (£100, £200, etc.).

- Start by auctioning sentence 1. Give students two minutes to discuss how much of their £5,000 they're willing to spend on buying this sentence. Make sure they write the amount next to the sentence on their worksheet.

- Elicit the bid each pair/group has written next to sentence 1. They must read the amount on their worksheets and cannot change it at this stage. The pair/group with the highest bid has the chance to buy the sentence. When a pair/group buys a sentence, they must say whether they think the sentence is correct, or tell you the correct version of the sentence, before they are allowed to own it. If this pair/group gets the sentence wrong, they lose the money they have bid, but **don't** get the sentence. You can then auction the sentence to the next highest bidder. If two or more pairs/groups bid the same amount, give them the chance to bid secretly again to see who bids more.

- When a pair/group buys a sentence, they deduct the price from the £5,000 on their worksheet. If they tried to buy a sentence but didn't get the sentence correct, they must still deduct the money they spent from their total. Students can only spend £5,000 during the whole auction.

- After sentence 1 has been sold, give the pairs/groups two minutes to discuss how much they want to spend on sentence 2. Elicit the bids from the pairs/groups and invite the winning pair/group to say if the sentence is correct or to give the correct version. Continue like this with each sentence.

- The pair/group that has bought the most sentences at the end of the game wins. If two pairs/groups have the same number of sentences, the one with the most money remaining wins.

1 The council **was** given more money by the Prime Minister. 2 ✓ 3 I think our luggage **weighs** much more than the airline **allows** us. 4 Painting pictures **is** a wonderful way to relax after a stressful day at work. 5 Five kilometres **is** quite a long way – not all of us **want** to walk that far. 6 Being an only child is difficult for children who **want** many brothers and sisters. 7 ✓ 8 The sports equipment **was** not put back in the cupboard after the game. 9 The number of traffic accidents **has** been declining for many years due to lower speed limits on many roads. 10 ✓ 11 One of my friends **loves** going to the cinema by herself which most people think is strange. 12 The company **is** moving to another city later this year so some staff are being made redundant. 13 ✓ 14 ✓ 15 Working from home is a popular option for a number of staff who **have** a long journey to work.

10B Give me the sentence p167

Language
Modal verbs of certainty

Activity type, when to use and time
Information gap activity. Use any time after lesson 10B. 15–20 minutes.

Preparation
Photocopy one worksheet for each pair of students. Cut into sentence cards.

Procedure
- Divide the class into pairs.
- On a piece of paper, write *He <u>must</u> have <u>gone</u> to <u>work</u>*. Tell the class that you have a sentence on your piece of paper that you want the class to say. You can give clues but you cannot say the three underlined words in the sentence. (You **can** say the other words.) Tell them that the sentence has a modal verb expressing certainty.
- Elicit the sentence from the students. For example, *It's 7 a.m. He was here but now he isn't. He left the house. He was wearing a shirt and tie and carrying his laptop.* When one of the students has said the correct sentence, show them the sentence on your piece of paper.
- Give each pair a set of sentence cards, placed face down in a pile in front of them.
- Each student takes it in turns to pick up a card and elicit the sentence from his/her partner. Tell students that they cannot use the words which are underlined in their sentence when explaining the sentence to their partner. Remind students that each sentence has a modal verb expressing certainty.
- The pairs start the game at the same time. The first pair in the class to complete all of the sentences wins.

10C A problem shared p168

Language
Giving advice

Activity type, when to use and time
Mingle. Use any time after lesson 10C. 20–25 minutes.

Preparation
Photocopy one worksheet for each group of eight students. Cut into separate cards.

Procedure
- Divide the class into groups of eight students.
- Tell students that they are going to have an end-of-course party with their classmates. However, they're not really in the party mood because they all have a problem that they're worried about. They're all hoping to get some advice from their classmates during the party. They must also listen to their classmates and give them advice. After the mingle, the class will decide which person is best at giving advice.
- Give a different card to each student in each group and ask them to read and memorise their problem.
- Ask students to mingle and discuss the problems with the other students in their group. If possible, put some music on to start the party. Give students a time limit (e.g. 15 minutes) to discuss their problems. Stop the music when the time limit is reached.
- Elicit some of the advice that the students received. Ask students to say which advice was the best and decide who was the best giver of advice in the class.

1A Getting to know you time expressions with Past Simple and Present Perfect

Find someone who …	Name	Follow-up questions
1 … *read/has read* a good book in the past few weeks.		
2 … *grumbled/has grumbled* about something since he/she woke up this morning.		
3 … *worked/has been working* in another city last month.		
4 … *studied/has studied* a foreign language, other than English, when he/she was younger.		
5 … *chatted/has been chatting* on the phone a lot this week.		
6 … *started/has started* work as soon as he/she left secondary school.		
7 … *came/has come* into contact with a lot of people during the last few days.		
8 … *went/has been* abroad more than once this year.		
9 … is going to meet a friend once this lesson *finished/has finished*.		
10 … *took/has taken* an English exam since he/she *studied/has been studying* English.		

© Cambridge University Press 2009   face2face Advanced Photocopiable

1B Student survey *cleft sentences*

Student A Student Survey

1 **When it's a rainy weekend, most people in the class … (*what?*).**

What happens when _____

2 **Most people in the class enjoy … (*what?*) on a Saturday morning.**

It's _____

3 **Most people in the class weren't allowed to stay up after 9 p.m. until they were … (*how old?*).**

It wasn't until _____

4 **When they get stressed, most people in the class … (*what?*).**

What _____

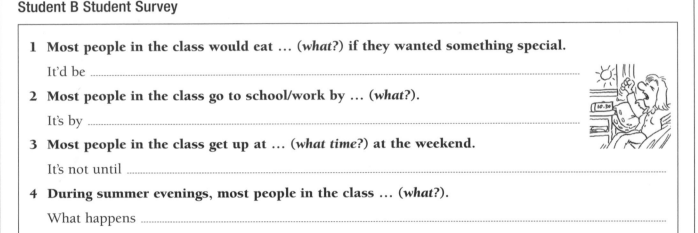

Student B Student Survey

1 **Most people in the class would eat … (*what?*) if they wanted something special.**

It'd be _____

2 **Most people in the class go to school/work by … (*what?*).**

It's by _____

3 **Most people in the class get up at … (*what time?*) at the weekend.**

It's not until _____

4 **During summer evenings, most people in the class … (*what?*).**

What happens _____

Student C Student Survey

1 **Most people in the class have … (*what?*) for breakfast.**

What _____

2 **Most people in the class chose this school because … (*what?*).**

The reason why _____

3 **Most people in the class enjoy doing … (*what?*) in their English lessons.**

It's _____

4 **Most people in the class keep in touch with their friends by … (*what?*).**

It's by _____

Instructions p118

Two colleagues are sitting next to each other on a train on the way home from work.

A So, what do you think about _____

_____ ?

B Mmm, that's an interesting one. Well, _____

_____

_____ . In other words, _____

_____ .

A So, what you're saying is that _____

_____ ?

B Well, in a way, but also _____

_____ . Don't you agree?

A Absolutely not! (*getting a little angry*) _____ . What I mean

by that is _____ .

B (*becoming annoyed*) I'm sorry, I'm still not sure what you're getting at.

A (*feeling more and more frustrated*) What I'm trying to say is that _____

_____ .

B (*showing disgust*) Really? That's absolutely ridiculous! _____

_____ which simply means that _____ .

A (*feeling angry now*) What rubbish! _____

_____ . Or to put it another way, _____ .

B (*raising his/her voice*) Well, I think you've lost your head! What about _____ ?

Which isn't to say that _____ , but _____

_____ .

A Right. My station's here. I love a good argument! Same time tomorrow?

2A The great brain game relative clauses with prepositions

Student A

1 Vincent Van Gogh's artistic career lasted for a ten-year period. During this time, he painted almost 900 pictures. (*during which*)

2 James Wannerton suffers from synaesthesia, a non-threatening neurological condition. With this condition, words that he hears activate his sense of smell. (*with which*)

3 There are more than 5,000 world languages. Harold Williams, the world's greatest linguist, spoke 58 of them. (*of which*)

4 Aged seven, Akrit Jaswal from India proudly dressed up as a doctor. Then he carried out his first operation. (*at which point*)

5 Derek Paravicini can listen to a piece of music just once. He then plays it back perfectly from memory. (*after which*)

Answers 1 True. He also drew over 1,000 pictures. **2** False. Words activate his sense of taste, therefore words can remind him of different foods. **3** True. It took him just two days to pick up Serbian. **4** True. He's now trying to find a cure for cancer. **5** True. He's also memorised hundreds of different pieces of written music.

Student B

1 In 1995 pathologist Thomas Harvey met up with a Princeton University neuroscientist. He gave Albert Einstein's diary to her. (*to whom*)

2 In 2001, autistic artist Stephen Wiltshire took a helicopter ride across London. After this he created an amazingly detailed drawing from memory in just three hours. (*after which*)

3 In his mind, child prodigy Jay Greenberg can see a photograph of a new mathematical equation. He rarely has to make changes to it after he writes it down. (*to which*)

4 Akira Haraguchi has an amazing brain. He can remember pi to 140,000 digits with it. (*with which*)

5 In 1994 Tony Cicoria was hit by lightning and became obsessed with playing the piano and classical music. He wasn't interested in these beforehand. (*neither of which*)

Answers 1 False. He gave her Einstein's brain which he'd kept after his death. **2** True. He's also done the same with several other world cities. **3** False. He can see a photograph of a complete written piece of music that he composes in his mind. **4** False. He can only do it to 100,000 digits! **5** True. Before the accident, he'd never played the piano.

face2face Advanced Photocopiable   © Cambridge University Press 2009

Instructions p119

Student A

Survival at sea

A

1 Steven Callahan set sail from the lovely countryside of Cornwall in the UK as part of a solo sailing race to the Caribbean. Having …

B

…… … correctly, they were able to turn sea water into drinkable liquid. Along with rainwater, he managed to survive with just enough water. Using …

C

…… … in the middle of the ocean and it wasn't long before it was out of sight. Could things get much worse? Yes, they could. Springing …

D

…… … ways to measure time and distance. Day after day, he drifted along with no sign of rescue. Then one day, sailing …

E

…… … Steven stranded on a raft with just a little water and food. Having been …

F

…… … just far enough away from the raft that it became more difficult to catch them. Determined …

G

…… … Steven's raft, local fishermen picked him up and took him to dry land. Having …

Student B

Survival at sea

H

…… … not far away from him, was a boat. He was overjoyed but soon realised it had no chance of seeing such a small raft floating …

I

…… … interested in survival techniques before the trip began, Steven had fortunately managed to grab two solar stills before his boat went down. Used …

J

…… … to stay alive, Callahan found ways to keep his mind occupied, thinking of …

K

…… … sailed for just six days of his journey, his ship hit something and sank, leaving …

L

…… … a leak, Steven's raft nearly sank and he had to keep it afloat for 33 days until, finally, he came upon an island near Guadeloupe. Having spotted …

M

…… … a spear that he managed to put together, he was able to catch some of the fish that were following his raft. However, they soon got clever, swimming …

N

14 … survived for 76 days at sea alone, travelled almost 3,000 kilometres, fought off sharks and passed nine boats which didn't see him, you'd think he would never want to sail again. However, despite his ordeal, he remains a keen sailor today.

A slice of heaven off the beaten track ...

Calamango may not be as well known as the Maldives or Seychelles but it's just as beautiful. Made up of ten islands in the Indian Ocean, this small country provides everything you could possibly want from a holiday – sandy beaches, lazy towns, historical ruins, a rainforest and friendly people.

The flora and fauna are glorious, with the Calamangan parakeet and several unique plant species being native to this country. The sea holds the key to this country's survival, providing a successful fishing industry for its inhabitants. Three of the islands are surrounded by coral reefs which have long attracted adventurous divers.

In the past, flights to Calamango have been limited but tourist facilities are starting to open up, so you might want to check it out before it becomes a busy tourist hotspot.

You work for the Ministry of Tourism in Calamango, a small developing country in the Indian Ocean. In the past, few flights have serviced the islands and so the economy has relied on the fishing industry.

The Calamangan President and the Minister of Tourism are looking to increase the number of tourists that visit the island in order to boost the economy, and are willing to invest in the top three best ideas presented to them. However, they are also concerned about the negative effects that increased tourism may bring and would like the industry to be as sustainable as possible.

The Minister of Tourism has invited all members of the Ministry to a brainstorming day where small groups will work together to come up with ideas for increasing sustainable tourism within Calamango. With the other members of your group, think of as many ideas as you can. Consider:

*   the kind of tourists you'd like to attract;
*   ways to attract them;
*   ways to reduce the negative impact of tourism on the environment;
*   ways to maximise the benefit of tourism to local people.

When you have finished, go through your list of ideas again and decide on the top three best recommendations.

Instructions p120

3A Connotation crossword positive and negative character adjectives

Student A

Student B

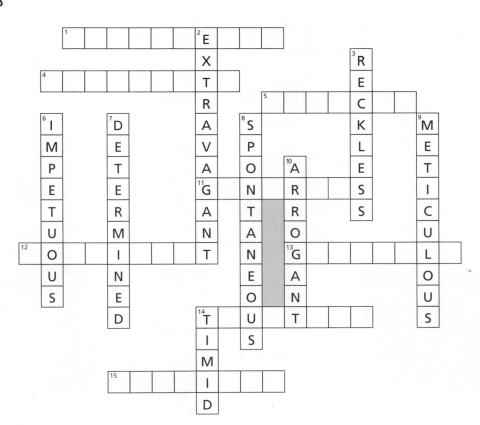

Instructions p121   © Cambridge University Press 2009   face2face Advanced Photocopiable

This is my life

When I was a child, my lifestyle was a little different from what it is now. Not only _____ and _____ ,
I also _____ because _____ .
However, never _____ and only once or
twice _____ because _____
_____ . In fact, not until _____

_____ .

These days not only _____ , I also
_____ because _____
_____ . Very rarely _____
_____ and under no circumstances _____
_____ because _____ .

Isn't life a funny thing? When I was a child, not for a minute _____
_____ !

Who am I?

Student number ☐

Could you lend me £10,000? I need a better car.	Can you look after my pets when I go on holiday? I have eight large dogs, one snake and 75 rats.
Do you think I should change my hairstyle?	I love the way this room is decorated. Do you?
Could you drive me to the airport tomorrow morning at 4 a.m.?	Would you like to watch my 50-hour collection of horror DVDs with me at the weekend?
Would you like to come bungee jumping with me at the weekend?	Can you come to my house tonight and clean it? I haven't time, and I don't really enjoy cleaning.
Could you run to the shops and buy me a sandwich? I'm hungry.	I'm going to a concert tonight. Could you do my homework for me, please?
Would you like to come round tonight and see my holiday photos? It's only a few thousand pictures.	I'm running a marathon on Sunday. Would you like to join me?

TACTFUL	**TACTFUL**	**TACTFUL**
TACTFUL	**TACTFUL**	**TACTFUL**
TACTFUL	**TACTFUL**	**TACTLESS**
TACTLESS	**TACTLESS**	**TACTLESS**

face2face Advanced Photocopiable

CLASS ACTIVITIES: PHOTOCOPIABLE

30
MOVE BACK TWO SQUARES

31
Tell your friend in a tactful way that his/her shirt is too bright.

32
Correct this sentence.
What I do if I'm tired have a nap.

33
Complete this sentence with a relative clause.
I wrote six short stories, all .... were rejected.

FINISH

29
Explain the meaning of this euphemism.
That bus has seen better days.

28
Choose the correct adverb.
He was *entirely/ bitterly/perfectly* disappointed with the result.

27
Complete this sentence.
It's no .... that he sings well.

26
MOVE FORWARD TWO SQUARES

25
Talk for one minute about a place you'd love to visit.

20
Complete this sentence about yourself.
Seldom do I ...

21
MOVE BACK TWO SQUARES

22
Put these adjectives in order.
Chinese / gorgeous / silk

23
Complete this sentence.
I'm on good .... with my boss.

24
Choose the correct verb form.
As soon as I *finished/ have finished*, I drove home.

19
Talk for one minute about a dish you'd recommend to tourists in your country .

18
Complete this sentence.
If there's only one of something, it's ....

17
THROW AGAIN

16
Choose the correct verb form.
I *went/'ve been* on holiday since I last saw you.

15
Complete this saying.
One man's meat is ...

10
Complete this sentence about yourself.
Only recently have I ...

11
Complete this sentence.
If I eat fish, I .... a rash.

12
Say two phrases which mean:
by and large

13
Correct this sentence.
He always butts out when I'm talking.

14
Which negative adjective has a similar meaning to:
trusting?

9
Complete this saying.
Actions speak ...

8
MOVE FORWARD TWO SQUARES

7
Choose the correct verb form.
Staying/Having stayed in a hotel, you have access to many facilities.

6
Talk for one minute about something you've done since your last lesson.

5
Complete this sentence about yourself.
It shocks me when ...

START

1
Which positive adjective has a similar meaning to:
impetuous?

2
Fill in the gap.
I think I've p............... up a cold from a classmate.

3
THROW AGAIN

4
What's a polite way of saying someone is a bit deaf?

Instructions p122

4A No comment! phrases referring to the future

Name		Job	Press release	News story
John				
Jim				
Jack				
Jennifer				
Julie				

Jobs
soap star
ex-model
film director
newsreader
TV executive

Press release
releasing a documentary about the environment
announcing retirement
being made head of a TV station
promoting a TV Internet service
publishing a book

News story
uses a private plane
copied someone's work
downloaded music illegally
was sacked for rudeness
doesn't own a TV

Student A

1 Julie's been in the Channel 6 soap *Riverside* for ten years and is to try her luck with writing a book at the same time.
2 Years at the top of his industry are likely to be the cause of the newsreader's impatience and impoliteness.
3 The person who's on the verge of being made boss of Channel 6 doesn't own a TV.

4 Jim is due to start directing a new film early next year.
5 The person who is to promote Channel 6's new TV Internet service has been downloading music from the Internet illegally.
6 The man whose retirement is set to be announced, was actually fired. It wasn't Jack.

Student B

1 The ex-model is to turn to advertising a web service for his new career.
2 Some parts of the book due to be released next week use text plagiarised from an unpublished novel written 20 years ago.
3 The person about to release the documentary on global warming hasn't been very environmentally friendly recently.

4 The newsreader isn't a woman.
5 John has never appeared, and is unlikely to ever appear, on a catwalk.
6 Ironically, it's the executive on the verge of great things who doesn't have a single TV in her house.

4B Guess the word near synonyms

Student A

huge	settlement	humans	improvement

✂

Student B

determined	be forced to	infuriating	unexpectedly

✂

Student C

let	angry	watch	a standstill

✂

Student D

urban	child	country folk	friend

Instructions p123

4C The powers of persuasion persuading

Member of Parliament

The government is considering the introduction of a new law preventing the paparazzi from photographing celebrities except at authorised events. You are a Member of Parliament who will have to vote for or against this law. To help you decide how to vote, you've invited two people knowledgeable about the subject: a celebrity and a magazine editor.

Write some questions to ask them to help you to make a decision. Consider:

- celebrities and their families;
- newspapers/magazines and their readers;
- the impact on society;
- health and safety issues.

After the meeting, you will be asked to vote for or against the law.

Celebrity

The government is considering the introduction of a new law preventing the paparazzi from photographing celebrities except at authorised events. You are a famous celebrity. You and your family are regularly followed by photographers but you think they are not entitled to do this. A Member of Parliament has invited you to a meeting to discuss your views on this law. You want to persuade him/her to vote **for** it.

Think about some persuasive arguments to support your point of view. Think about some opposing arguments that may be made and how you can respond to them. Consider:

- celebrities and their families;
- newspapers/magazines and their readers;
- the impact on society;
- health and safety issues.

Magazine editor

The government is considering the introduction of a new law preventing the paparazzi from photographing celebrities except at authorised events. You are the editor of the popular gossip magazine *Hi!* You regularly publish celebrity photos. You think that celebrities would not be celebrities without magazines like yours. A Member of Parliament has invited you to a meeting to discuss your views on the law. You want to persuade him/her to vote **against** it.

Think about some persuasive arguments to support your point of view. Think about some opposing arguments that may be made and how you can respond to them. Consider:

- celebrities and their families;
- newspapers/magazines and their readers;
- the impact on society;
- health and safety issues.

over	**cautious**	over	**hang**
under	**line**	under	**appreciated**
super	**fine**	super	**computer**
semi	**-detached**	semi	**-conscious**
counter	**attack**	counter	**argument**
inter	**continental**	inter	**change**
pseudo	**-intellectual**	pseudo	**-science**

Instructions p123

"I regret …"

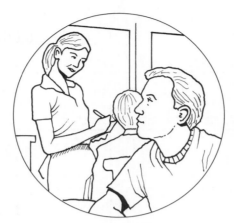

Tom/He noticed …

Tom/He had never forgotten …

Jeanette/She walked over
to him, forgetting …

Tom/He took a job …
which meant …

Tom/He meant …

Tom/He deeply regretted …

Tom/He went on …

Tom/He watched her …

face2face Advanced Photocopiable

Not to mention …	That's exactly what I was trying to get at.
You look dubious …	I'm with … on that.
All I'm saying is …	Carry on. You were saying?
Anyway, …	By that you mean …?
You've got me there!	Oh, I don't know about that.
That's precisely what I mean.	What I'm trying to say is …
What were you going to say?	Well, I can't disagree with that.
To get back to what I was saying …	I'd go along with that.
What do you mean when you say …?	Actually, I'm not sure you can say …

TOPIC CARD Friends are the new family.	**TOPIC CARD** Exceptional people are born exceptional.
TOPIC CARD This city/town is a great place for tourists to visit.	**TOPIC CARD** Everyone should keep up-to-date with the news.
TOPIC CARD Life is easier for young people than it used to be.	**TOPIC CARD** Celebrities have the best lifestyle.

Instructions p124

6A Anti-social behaviour formal and informal ways of comparing

Which of these social habits do you find the most anti-social? Choose your top 10 and then rank them in order from 1 (= the most anti-social) to 10.

	Rank
• someone with 15 items using the '10 items or fewer' checkout at the supermarket • someone ignoring a 'no smoking' sign • someone dropping litter • someone not stopping his/her car at a pedestrian crossing • someone on a train talking loudly on a mobile phone • someone not saying 'thank you' after you have held a door open for him/her • someone using swear words in public • someone using mobile phone 'text language' in an email • someone driving over the speed limit • someone blowing his/her nose in public • someone eating with his/her mouth open • someone jumping the queue at a bus stop or in a shop • dog owners letting their dogs run free • someone phoning a friend after 11 p.m. • someone making a lot of noise in the street at night • someone painting graffiti on a wall • someone eating in public • someone listening to an MP3 player and singing to the music in public • parents letting their children run around freely in a public area, such as a restaurant or a coffee shop • someone ignoring your phone calls	

Now discuss your answers with a partner. Compare your answers and agree on the top five most anti-social habits. Rank them in order from 1 (= the most anti-social) to 5.

6B Grab a word game position of adverbials

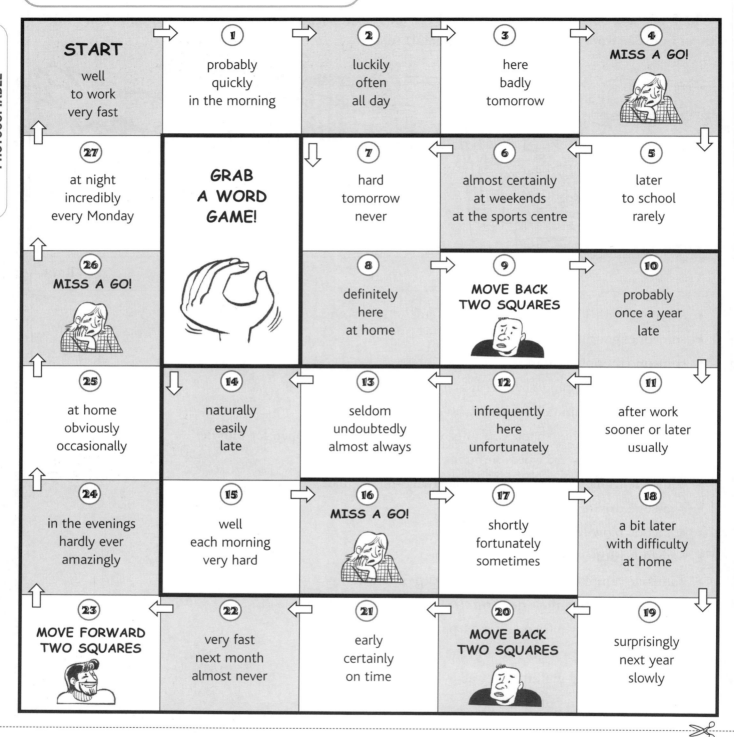

START well to work very fast	① probably quickly in the morning	② luckily often all day	③ here badly tomorrow	④ **MISS A GO!**
㉗ at night incredibly every Monday	**GRAB A WORD GAME!**	⑦ hard tomorrow never	⑥ almost certainly at weekends at the sports centre	⑤ later to school rarely
㉖ **MISS A GO!**		⑧ definitely here at home	⑨ **MOVE BACK TWO SQUARES**	⑩ probably once a year late
㉕ at home obviously occasionally	⑭ naturally easily late	⑬ seldom undoubtedly almost always	⑫ infrequently here unfortunately	⑪ after work sooner or later usually
㉔ in the evenings hardly ever amazingly	⑮ well each morning very hard	⑯ **MISS A GO!**	⑰ shortly fortunately sometimes	⑱ a bit later with difficulty at home
㉓ **MOVE FORWARD TWO SQUARES**	㉒ very fast next month almost never	㉑ early certainly on time	⑳ **MOVE BACK TWO SQUARES**	⑲ surprisingly next year slowly

1 I'll _____ go to the cinema _____ .

2 _____ , I don't have to work _____ .

3 I'm _____ going to get up _____ .

4 _____ , I pick up languages _____ .

5 I _____ go shopping _____ .

6 _____ , I _____ like running _____ .

7 _____ , I've _____ had to do housework.

8 I _____ meet up with friends _____ .

9 I _____ work _____ when I'm under pressure.

Instructions p125

6C What a joke! telling a joke

Student A

detective Sherlock Holmes / assistant Dr Watson / decide / go / camping trip. They / set off / 6 a.m. / head towards / mountains. Eventually / arrive / destination / find / good place / put up / tent. They / spend / few days / fishing. Every evening, they / go for a walk / cook dinner / sleep / tent. Middle / last night / Holmes / wake up / Watson. Holmes / "Look up. What / able / tell me?" Watson / "Can see / millions / stars / planet. Humans / not only / life form. Must / life / outside / Earth." Holmes / "No / Watson. Somebody / steal / tent!"

Student B

Dog / sees / job ad. It / say / "Help / want. Must / able / type / good with computer / bilingual." Dog / go / interview. / Receptionist / see / dog / call / office manager. When / manager / arrive / dog / start / whine. Manager / laugh / say / "Sorry / can't / hire you. You must / type." Dog / walk / over / typewriter / start type / perfect letter. Manager / surprised / continue / "Sorry / can't / hire you. You must / good / computers." Dog / run / computer / start / use computer program. Manager / shocked / impressed / but / say / "Sorry / can't / hire you. Ad / say / you must / bilingual." Dog / walk / calmly / manager / look / him / say / "Meow!"

Student C

Man / drive / car / country road. Suddenly / car / stop. Not / start again. Man / get out / open / bonnet / look / inside. Not know / what / do. Suddenly / voice / say / "Oil filter / block. Need / clean." Man / turn / no one / shrug / continue / look. Voice / again / "Oil filter / block. Need / clean." Man / turn / see / black horse. Man / not / believe / but / follow / instructions. Clean / oil filter. Car / start / he / continue / journey. Stop / next village / pub. Man / tell barman / horse / car. Barman / "Black horse?" Man / nod / ask / "How / know?" Barman / say / "Well / the white horse / know / nothing / cars."

face2face Advanced Photocopiable

Team A score board

Collocations	£500	£250
Prefixes	£500	£250
The future	£500	£250
Reflexive pronouns	£500	£250
Verb patterns	£500	£250
Ways of comparing	£500	£250
Adverbials	£500	£250
Mystery vocabulary	£500	£250

£5,000

£0

Team A question sheet

Collocations		Prefixes	
£500	**Complete the sentence.** I'm going to .... on a new Spanish course. (*enrol*)	**£500**	**Which prefix means *in opposition to*?** (counter)
£250	**Choose the correct verb.** The footballer *held/made* a press conference. (*held*)	**£250**	**Choose the correct prefix.** He's a *semi-/super-*professional footballer. (*semi-*)
The future		**Reflexive pronouns**	
£500	**Choose the correct verb form.** We *were supposed/supposed* to go to the party but our car broke down on the way. (*were supposed*)	**£500**	**Change one of the words in this sentence to make it more polite.** People such as you are great to have as friends. (*you > yourself*)
£250	**Is this sentence correct? If not, correct it.** He's on the verge of proposing to his girlfriend. (*correct*)	**£250**	**Complete this sentence with a reflexive pronoun.** I .... prefer tea to coffee. (*myself*)
Verb patterns		**Ways of comparing**	
£500	**Choose the correct verb form.** I saw the lorry *hit/hitting* the car. Then both drivers got out and started shouting at each other. (*hit*)	**£500**	**Complete this sentence.** We are paid pretty .... the same. (*much*)
£250	**Is this sentence correct? If not, correct it.** I'll never forget seeing you for the first time. (*correct*)	**£250**	**Does this sentence talk about a small or large difference?** He earns loads more money than he used to. (*large*)
Adverbials		**Mystery vocabulary**	
£500	**Put the word *hard* in the correct place in the sentence.** They don't work at school. (... *work hard* ...)	**£500**	**Complete the sentence.** The newspaper printed a story about him that was untrue so he sued them for .... (*libel*)
£250	**Is this sentence correct? If not, correct it.** He often leaves work early on Fridays. (*correct*)	**£250**	**Which word is not a synonym or near synonym of *angry*?** 1 furious 2 infuriating 3 annoyed (*infuriating*)

Instructions p126

Team B score board

Collocations	£500	£250
Prefixes	£500	£250
The future	£500	£250
Reflexive pronouns	£500	£250
Verb patterns	£500	£250
Ways of comparing	£500	£250
Adverbials	£500	£250
Mystery vocabulary	£500	£250

£5,000 ... £0

Team B question sheet

Collocations	Prefixes
£500 Complete this sentence. She .... a press release yesterday. (*issued*)	**£500 Which prefix means *not real*?** 1 semi- 2 pseudo- 3 counter- (*pseudo-*)
£250 Which verb is incorrect? *get/take/achieve* good results (*take*)	**£250 Which prefix is correct?** That weightlifter has *over/super*human strength! (*super*)
The future	**Reflexive pronouns**
£500 Complete the sentence with the correct form of *remember*. We knew we .... that day. (*would remember*)	**£500 Add a reflexive pronoun to emphasise the noun.** I like the house .... but not the location. (*itself*)
£250 Is this sentence correct? If not, correct it. School children are to facing new school tests. (*incorrect – are to face*)	**£250 Add the correct reflexive pronoun.** She loves singing to .... (*herself*)
Verb patterns	**Ways of comparing**
£500 Choose the correct verb form. Thank you for your letter, but I regret *to say/saying* that we do not have any job vacancies. (*to say*)	**£500 Complete this sentence.** We're more or .... the same age. (*less*)
£250 Is this sentence correct? If not, correct it. I heard you playing the guitar last night. (*correct*)	**£250 Does this sentence talk about a small or large difference?** My job's a tiny bit easier than it used to be. (*small*)
Adverbials	**Mystery vocabulary**
£500 Choose the correct word. I haven't travelled much. I've *even/only* been to London. (*only*)	**£500 What type of newspaper gives popular, sensationalist stories?** (*tabloid*)
£250 Is this sentence correct? If not, correct it. I go every so often there. (*I go there every so often.*)	**£250 What is an informal word for *child*?** (*kid*)

face2face Advanced Photocopiable

153

CLASS ACTIVITIES: PHOTOCOPIABLE

If I hadn't come to class today, I'd .... now.

If the sun is shining, I often ....

If I'm not going to have time to .... , I usually ....

If I could fly anywhere, I'd fly to ....

If I hadn't been working/studying last week, I ....

If I'd had time to .... yesterday, I'd .... now.

If I get up early at the weekend, I usually ....

If I weren't so .... , I .... last month.

If I'm really enjoying a book, I ....

If I hadn't started learning English, I wouldn't ....

If I have some free time tomorrow, I might ....

If I weren't living .... , I ....

If I'm going to be late home, I usually ....

If it hadn't been raining last .... , I'd ....

If I need to relax, I ....

If I meet up with friends this week, we'll probably ....

7B Fact or fiction? impersonal report structures

Student A

Fact or fiction?

1 The Great Wall of China .... the only man-made object which can be seen from the moon, but is this correct? (often/claim/be)

2 It .... that pasta originated in Italy, but is this true? (generally/assume)

3 It .... that chocolate is poisonous to dogs, but is this true? (widely/believe)

4 Blood .... red when it meets oxygen and blue when inside the body, but is this true? (often/think/be)

5 It .... that humans use just 10% of their brains, but is this statistic correct? (sometimes/say)

6 In a recent newspaper, it .... that men are four times more likely to be hit by lightning than women, but is this correct? (report)

Answers
1 No, it's not.
2 It's false. Archaeologists have proven that pasta existed in China 4,000 years ago.
3 Yes, it is.
4 It's false. It's dark red. Blood in your veins appears blue because of light reflection.
5 It's not. We use all of our brains.
6 It's true.

✂

Student B

Fact or fiction?

1 It .... that the Sahara is the world's largest desert, but is this correct? (widely/believe)

2 In a recent magazine, ... that humans share around 60% of their DNA with a banana, but is this correct? (report)

3 More overweight people than underfed people .... in the world, but is this statistic correct? (say/exist)

4 It .... by parents that eating carrots will help children to see in the dark, but is this true? (often/claim)

5 It .... that if you pull out one grey hair, two will grow in its place, but does this actually happen? (sometimes/fear)

6 Chameleons .... their colour in order to match their background, but is this really true? (think/change)

Answers
1 It's false. It's the world's largest hot desert. Antarctica is actually the largest desert.
2 It's true.
3 It's true.
4 It's false, but they are good for your health.
5 It's false.
6 It's false. They change their colour to suit their mood.

Instructions p127 · © Cambridge University Press 2009 · face2face Advanced Photocopiable

'People should not be allowed to own guns.' What is your opinion?

'People should be allowed to defend their property however they wish.' What is your opinion?

'Trials should not be televised.' What is your opinion?

'When a child commits a crime, it is the parents' fault.' What is your opinion?

'A zero tolerance policy is the best way to reduce crime.' What is your opinion?

'People who mistreat animals should go to prison.' What is your opinion?

'The death penalty should be used for serious crimes.' What is your opinion?

'Cyber-crime will be the biggest threat to our future security.' What is your opinion?

'The police should not carry guns.' What is your opinion?

'Violent crime is caused by watching violence on TV and in films.' What is your opinion?

'Prisons are not effective in reducing crime.' What is your opinion?

'Community service is a useful way to rehabilitate criminals and help society at the same time.' What is your opinion?

Instructions p128

8A The council meeting past verb forms with present or future meaning

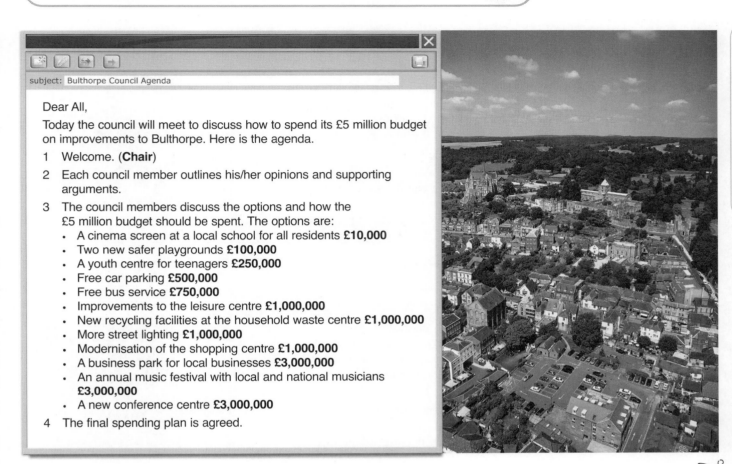

subject: Bulthorpe Council Agenda

Dear All,

Today the council will meet to discuss how to spend its £5 million budget on improvements to Bulthorpe. Here is the agenda.

1   Welcome. (**Chair**)

2   Each council member outlines his/her opinions and supporting arguments.

3   The council members discuss the options and how the £5 million budget should be spent. The options are:
- A cinema screen at a local school for all residents **£10,000**
- Two new safer playgrounds **£100,000**
- A youth centre for teenagers **£250,000**
- Free car parking **£500,000**
- Free bus service **£750,000**
- Improvements to the leisure centre **£1,000,000**
- New recycling facilities at the household waste centre **£1,000,000**
- More street lighting **£1,000,000**
- Modernisation of the shopping centre **£1,000,000**
- A business park for local businesses **£3,000,000**
- An annual music festival with local and national musicians **£3,000,000**
- A new conference centre **£3,000,000**

4   The final spending plan is agreed.

Student A: Councillor and chair

You're a businessperson who wants to develop Bulthorpe's commercial side. You want to attract people to Bulthorpe to improve the local economy and boost income for local businesses. You care also about the health of the community.

How would you spend the £5 million?
- Think about how to welcome the councillors at the meeting.
- Think about your preferences and supporting arguments for part two of the meeting.
- Think about how to persuade the other councillors during part three.

Student B: Councillor

You stay at home looking after your three children. You want to improve facilities in Bulthorpe, especially for children. You also think a good public transport system for the area is essential, and you realise the importance of safety on the streets. You play in an orchestra in your free time and know that many residents enjoy going to concerts held by local musicians.

How would you spend the £5 million?
- Think about your preferences and supporting arguments for part two of the meeting.
- Think about how to persuade the other councillors during part three.

© Cambridge University Press 2009 **face2face** Advanced Photocopiable

Student C: Councillor

You work at the local hospital and know that many patients are dependent on the bus services there. You feel that leisure and shopping facilities in Bulthorpe are limited and you're also concerned about the young people of Bulthorpe. You also want to see an increase in the amount of rubbish that is recycled.

How would you spend the £5 million?
- Think about your preferences and supporting arguments for part two of the meeting.
- Think about how to persuade the other councillors during part three.

Student D: Councillor

You're a hotel owner who wants to increase visitors to Bulthorpe to improve profits for local businesses. You don't have children and feel that young people in the area have had lots of money spent on them recently. Car parking is very expensive for you and your hotel guests.

How would you spend the £5 million?
- Think about your preferences and supporting arguments for part two of the meeting.
- Think about how to persuade the other councillors during part three.

Student E: Councillor

You're a librarian who feels that Bulthorpe must spend more on being environmentally responsible. You enjoy the arts in your free time and would like more facilities for people like you. You don't have time for sport yourself, but you feel it's important for the people of Bulthorpe to be healthy.

How would you spend the £5 million?
- Think about your preferences and supporting arguments for part two of the meeting.
- Think about how to persuade the other councillors during part three.

face2face Advanced Photocopiable © Cambridge University Press 2009

Instructions p128

Student A

The Storm Chaser

You're incredibly ¹................................... (adventure) but there are few unexplored places left in the world. What do you do? Well, if you're Canadian George Kourounis, you go to places when they are undergoing extreme conditions. He's the only man
in the world to have been in the middle of the three most dangerous ²........................... (nature) phenomena on earth: tornadoes, volcanoes and hurricanes.

Since his first tornado experience in 1998, George ³................................... (annual) visits Tornado Alley in the US. It's a ⁴........................... (potential) life-threatening activity involving hours of planning, but storm chasers long for the day when clouds
⁵................................... (dark) the sky. For many, storm chasing is an expensive hobby, requiring a lot of
⁶............................... (invest) in expensive equipment. But George has managed to turn it into a career, filming TV documentaries with an ⁷........................... (eager) that makes him a captivating presenter.

In 2005, George was lowered 60 feet into an
⁸................................... (act) volcano in Ethiopia where he filmed for 30 minutes. In the same year, George experienced four major hurricanes, the worst of which was Hurricane Katrina. While New Orleans was disappearing around him, George filmed the event from the third floor of a steel-enforced garage.

Not content with weather, George has
⁹................................... (diverse) into other areas for a new TV series, filming gorillas in Rwanda, sharks near Mexico and forest fires in Canada. And while many of us desire a wedding to remember, George's is more
¹⁰............................... (memory) than most. He recently got married on the edge of a volcano in the South Pacific.

Student B

Jumping Jay

What makes a man want to jump ¹................................... (continuous) from an airplane for 24 hours? American Willard 'Jay' Stokes could tell you.

A former member of the Special Forces, Jay set his first world record in 1995 when he made 331 parachute jumps in 24 hours. It was an amazing ²................................... (achieve) but he later did even better. In 1997 he completed 384 jumps and in 1999, 476.

After someone broke his record and reached the 500 mark in 2001, Jay didn't give up. Despite breaking his foot four weeks before, he managed to beat 10 hours
of freezing rain and poor ³................................... (visible) to reach 534 jumps in 2003. He also raised $20,000 for charity. Then Jay declared he'd had enough. He was sure someone could break the 600-jump barrier but it would
⁴............................... (definite) not be him.

However, three years later Jay announced he was going to give it a try. Knowing he had to ⁵...............................
(intense) his efforts, he and his team came up with a plan that would require the help of about 130 volunteers and the best equipment there was. Jay trained for several

hours a day to
⁶...............................
(strength) his body. For 24 hours Jay would jump from a plane at 2,100 feet, land, run to the waiting plane while stripping off his chute, put on a new chute and board the plane. The ⁷...............................
(accelerate) of the aeroplane into the air would be his only chance to rest.

After all the preparations, the day arrived and became a truly
⁸............................... (remark) one. Despite injuring his thigh, ⁹........................... (determine) pushed Jay on until he'd completed 640 jumps; one every 2 minutes and 15 seconds. All of this happening, quite
¹⁰............................... (incidental), on his 50th birthday.

1 If you saw an old man in a shabby coat stealing a bar of chocolate in a supermarket, would you report him?

2 If you were working with the boss's son and knew that he spent half his day on the Internet when you were working hard, what would you do?

3 Imagine that an old friend who hadn't answered your emails or phone calls for three years suddenly came to you asking for help. What would you do?

4 Suppose you were shopping and you found some really cheap and fashionable trainers, but you knew that the company employed children to make them. Would you buy the trainers?

5 If a friend told you he/she had a copy of the questions in the important exam you were taking the next day, and were worried about, would you look at it?

6 Imagine you were worried about a friend of yours because she was very unhappy but you didn't know why. While at her house, you saw her diary on the table. Would you read it?

7 If a colleague told your boss an idea that you had told her, and pretended it was hers, what would you do?

8 Imagine your favourite band had released a new album online. People could decide how much to pay to download it. How much would you pay?

9 Suppose you were walking down the street when someone (who looks very well-dressed) dropped a £50 note without noticing. Would you tell him/her?

10 Imagine you received an email from your boss, sent to you by mistake. In the email were horrible comments about you and your colleagues, although normally your boss was pleasant to you. What would you do?

Instructions p129

so tired today.	I **see** what	you mean.	Joe**'s expecting** a
phone call from his office.	Marilyn **looks** really	well, doesn't she?	Georgina **appears** to
be happy.	They**'re fitting**	our new kitchen later.	Our new baby son **weighs**
just over three kilos.	We're **having** a	great time, aren't we?	David **comes**
from the south of England.	Alex **is seeing** the	doctor at 10 a.m.	They **think**
it's too hot to work.	My son**'s been imagining** that a	monster lives in his cupboard.	Tom**'s being**
really naughty at the moment.	Tracey**'s appearing**	in a new musical.	This sofa **feels**
really soft and comfortable.	Anna **is** always	very funny, isn't she?	We**'re thinking**
of moving somewhere quieter.	Chris can't **fit**	into these trousers any more.	Terry**'s looking** at a
new painting he's bought.	She**'s weighing** the	rice.	Pat **has** a
birthday party every year.	Leigh**'s coming**	round later.	I **imagine** she
will easily pass her driving test.	I **expect** it'll	rain at the barbecue.	I**'m feeling** ever

Student A

	T or F?
1 He/She always drinks sugar-........................... drinks.	
2 He/She gets up at six-........................... .	
3 He/She is very price-........................... when shopping.	
4 He/She is strong-........................... .	
5 He/She always tries to be fashion........................... .	
6 He/She is always prepared for rain and carries around a water........................... jacket.	
7 He/She prefers teacher-........................... activities in the classroom.	
8 He/She considers him/herself to be very trust........................... .	

✂

Student B

	T or F?
1 He/She often eats fat-........................... food.	
2 He/She goes to bed at 11-........................... .	
3 He/She is very health-........................... .	
4 He/She is often absent-........................... .	
5 He/She can be change........................... .	
6 He/She has a child........................... medicine cupboard because he/she has young children.	
7 He/She prefers student-........................... activities in the classroom.	
8 He/She has never met an untrust........................... person.	

Instructions p130

Calling all budding entrepreneurs!

If you have a fantastic product but are struggling to get your business up and running, we may be able to help.

We're looking for innovative people to feature on our new TV show *Fortune or Flop*. You'll present your product to business experts who'll decide if you are worthy of the £100,000 investment prize.

You and your team have developed a new product (see the ideas below), but business is slow. You've decided to apply to *Fortune or Flop* to try to win £100,000. With your partners, prepare to present your product to the show's experts. Make your presentation as professional as possible. Include the following information:

1 the product – what it is, its name and what makes it different from similar products;
2 the market – what kind of person the product is aimed at (e.g. teenagers) and why;
3 marketing – how you will advertise the product;
4 why the experts should invest in your business and not anyone else's;
5 any other information you think will help win the prize.

After the presentation, the experts will ask you some questions. Prepare for any difficult questions you think they may ask.

Products

Choose one of these types of product or one of your own.

CLASS ACTIVITIES: PHOTOCOPIABLE

7–9 Review Across the board Review of lessons 7A–9C

Board 1

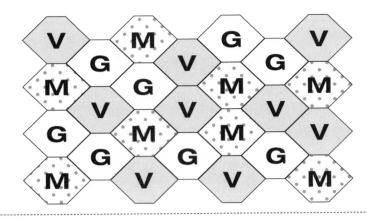

Team A question sheet

G Grammar

1 Make a sentence using these prompts: **It / think / that / house prices will drop this year.** (*It is thought that …*)
2 Choose the correct word: **Most of them disagreed but *a/one* person agreed with me.** (*one*)
3 Correct this sentence: **Pluto no longer believes to be a planet.** (*Pluto is no longer believed to …*)
4 Choose the correct verb form: ***I see/I'm seeing* what you mean.** (*I see*)
5 Make a sentence using these prompts: **I wish / I / go / doctor's / yesterday** (*I wish I'd gone to the doctor's yesterday.*)
6 Say the correct verb form: **I'd prefer it if she (stop) visiting me.** (*stopped*)
7 Say the correct verb form: **If I (not/work) now, I'd be sitting in my garden.** (*wasn't working*)
8 Choose the correct word: **There's *a/very* little sugar left, so we should have enough.** (*a*)
9 Make a sentence using these prompts: **I / sooner / you / do / your / homework** (*I'd sooner you did your homework.*)
10 Say the correct verb form: **She (expect) a baby in March.** (*'s/is expecting*)

V Vocabulary

1 Complete this sentence: **I was going to wash my car but just never got .... to it.** (*round*)
2 Complete this sentence with a suffix. **We think he's honest and trust........ .** (*worthy*)
3 Correct this sentence: **His mother cooked him about where he'd been that night.** (*grilled*, not *cooked*)
4 Complete this sentence: **They enjoyed themselves w........ they went.** (*wherever*)
5 Complete this saying: **There's no time like the ....** (*present*)
6 Complete this sentence with a phrasal noun: **There was a terrible d........ at our picnic. We were soaked!** (*downpour*)
7 Complete this sentence: **Temperatures have hit r........ levels this year.** (*record*)
8 Complete this sentence: **When I have time to k........ , I read a good book.** (*kill*)
9 Choose the correct word: **Sharing a car to work is very *price/cost*-effective.** (*cost*)
10 Complete the sentence with the correct form of the word: **I think her father is .... (remark)** (*remarkable*)

M Mystery

1 Name two methods used by scientists to catch criminals. (*e.g. DNA, fingerprints, saliva, fibres*)
2 In which country did workers take legal action against a hotel after they found a camera spying on them? (*US*)
3 In the radio play, what did Mike tell the police he'd gone to get when he left Emma's at 7.30 p.m.? (*a pizza*)
4 What did weather forecasters have to start doing in the US because of Hazel Henderson? (*giving a pollution index*)
5 Name three of Dr Ekman's six basic emotions. (*anger, disgust, fear, joy, sadness, surprise*)
6 What was one of the happiest, and free, sporting moments in Peter's life? (*winning a cup in a football tournament*)
7 Which popular device is likely to be used more and more in buying goods? (*mobile phone*)
8 How many students at the school were considering studying economics? (*two*)

Instructions p130

Board 2

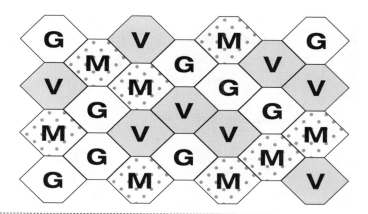

✂

Team B question sheet

 Grammar

1 Say the correct form of the verb: **If I hadn't missed the plane, I (be) in Spain now.** (*would be*)
2 Correct this sentence: **It estimates that most inhabitants support the proposal.** (*It is estimated that …*)
3 Choose the correct form of the verb: **That top *fits/is fitting* you nicely.** (*fits*)
4 Make a sentence using these prompts: **It / report / recently / that they are married.** (*It has been reported recently …*)
5 Say the correct form of the verb: **If they (not sleep), they would've seen him arrive.** (*hadn't been sleeping*)
6 Correct this sentence: **It's time we all stop work and go home.** (*stopped; went*)
7 Choose the correct word: **There are *a/very* few cups left. We need some more.** (*very*)
8 Say the correct form of the verb: **She (appear) quite sad at times.** (*appears*)
9 Choose the correct word: **I heard from *a/one* friend that you've got a new job.** (*a*)
10 Make a sentence using these prompts: **I / rather / you / come / home / early.** (*I'd rather you came home early.*)

V Vocabulary

1 Say the correct form of the word: **My teacher told me I had to make an (improve).** (*improvement*)
2 Complete this sentence with a phrasal noun: **I had a lovely g........-t........ with friends for my birthday.** (*get-together*)
3 Choose the correct word: **She screamed and shouted and then *flooded/stormed* out of the room.** (*stormed*)
4 Correct this sentence: **He got in music at an early age.** (*got into music*)
5 Choose the correct word: **The *price/cost* of living has increased recently.** (*cost*)
6 Complete this sentence with a phrasal verb: **They treated us badly and I won't let them get .... with it.** (*away*)
7 Complete this sentence with an appropriate suffix: **I bought some duty-........ perfume from the airport.** (*free*)
8 Complete this sentence: **I'm living with my parents for the time ....** (*being*)
9 Is this sentence correct? If not, correct it. **I donate money to help people in developing countries.** (*correct*)
10 Complete this sentence: **W........ he cooks tastes fantastic.** (*whatever*)

M Mystery

1 In which country is Bastoey prison? (*Norway*)
2 Name two types of information that are kept on ID cards. (*e.g. race, religion, medical history, biometric data*)
3 What relationship was Emma to Mike in the radio play? (*ex-girlfriend*)
4 Name one of the disasters that Eddy Canfor-Dumas wrote about. (*supervolcano or superstorm*)
5 What is the opposite of a thrill-seeker? (*fear-avoider*)
6 In Sophie Hannah's poem, what is she trying to decide? (*whether or not to call a man*)
7 What kind of car does Ben Maynard's friend Joe drive, but is thinking of selling? (*Porsche*)
8 How many miles did Satish and his companion walk around the world? (*8,000*)

10A Secret auction subject/verb agreement

1
The council were given more money by the Prime Minister.
£

2
Plenty of us help to clean up after the Christmas party each year.
£

3
I think our luggage weigh much more than the airline allow us.
£

4
Painting pictures are a wonderful way to relax after a stressful day at work.
£

5
Five kilometres are quite a long way and not all of us wants to walk that far.
£

6
Being an only child is difficult for children who wants many brothers and sisters.
£

7
Everyone was extremely helpful and kind when I had my broken leg.
£

8
The sports equipment were not put back in the cupboard after the game.
£

9
The number of traffic accidents have been declining for many years due to lower speed limits on many roads.
£

10
The research is progressing very well and a number of discoveries have been made.
£

11
One of my friends love going to the cinema by herself, which most people think is strange.
£

12
The company are moving to another city later this year so some staff are being made redundant.
£

13
The information was very useful for everyone who lives in the area.
£

14
Two hours is a really long time to be stuck in traffic which isn't moving.
£

15
Working from home is a popular option for a number of staff who has a long journey to work.
£

£5,000

Instructions p131

He <u>must</u> be at <u>work</u>.	He <u>can't</u> be <u>playing</u> <u>tennis</u>.
She <u>must</u> have <u>missed</u> the <u>bus</u>.	He <u>must</u> have <u>done</u> his <u>homework</u>.
They <u>may</u> have <u>been</u> on <u>holiday</u>.	She<u>'ll</u> be <u>watching</u> <u>TV</u>.
I <u>won't</u> have <u>finished</u>.	He <u>must</u> be at the <u>doctor</u>'s.
They <u>should</u> be <u>arriving</u> <u>soon</u>.	I'<u>ll</u> have <u>finished</u> by 10 p.m.
They <u>may</u> <u>eat</u> <u>out</u>.	They <u>might</u> have <u>gone</u> <u>home</u>.
She <u>might</u> be <u>sleeping</u>.	They <u>can't</u> have <u>bought</u> a <u>new</u> <u>car</u>.
They <u>wouldn't</u> be <u>doing</u> the <u>housework</u>.	He <u>won't</u> <u>arrive</u> before 6 p.m.
He <u>could</u> have <u>gone</u> to the <u>cinema</u>.	He <u>might</u> be at the <u>gym</u>.
I'<u>d</u> have <u>picked</u> you <u>up</u> from the <u>airport</u>.	They <u>could</u> be <u>having</u> <u>dinner</u> at 8 p.m.

   face2face Advanced Photocopiable

A

You've been working very hard lately. You've done lots of unpaid overtime and you feel that you deserve a pay rise. Your boss is a tough manager and recently refused to increase a colleague's salary. You don't know how to go about talking to your boss. Ask your classmates for some advice about what to do.

B

Your 14-year-old daughter wants to go to a rock concert with her friends. It finishes at midnight on a school night. You feel that this is very late and are worried about her safety. She's usually a good student but she didn't do very well in her recent tests. Ask your classmates for some advice about what to do.

C

You share a flat with an old school friend. This friend is great fun and you enjoy living together very much. However, your friend is also very untidy and leaves dirty plates everywhere. It's time you did something about it but you don't want the two of you to fall out. Ask your classmates for some advice about what to do.

D

Your teenage son has asked for a new pair of trainers because all of his friends have them. He works really hard and always helps out at home. The problem is that the trainers are very expensive and you can't afford them at the moment. Ask your classmates for some advice about what to do.

E

Your next-door neighbour often plays loud music after 7 p.m. It stops before you go to bed but it still drives you mad because you can't hear your TV. Your neighbour has recently helped you with some DIY so you don't want to upset him. Ask your classmates for some advice about what to do.

F

You've been in the same job for years. You really want to try something different but you worry that you might get a new job and hate it and you don't want to regret your decision. As well as that, you're not sure what kind of job you could do. Ask your classmates for some advice.

G

One of your friends often comes to your house unexpectedly and stays for ages. You're usually very busy and would prefer her to arrange a time before she visits. She's very sensitive and you don't know how to discuss it with her. Ask your classmates for some advice about what to do.

H

It's your friend's birthday next week and you have to buy him a present. Unfortunately he's very successful and has everything he needs. For your last birthday he spent a lot of money on you. You have no idea what to buy him. Ask your classmates for some advice.

Instructions p132

Vocabulary Plus

Instructions

There are 10 Vocabulary Plus worksheets (p172–p181). These worksheets introduce additional vocabulary that is not presented in the Student's Book and aim to help students become better and more independent learners. The topic of each Vocabulary Plus worksheet is linked to the topic of the corresponding unit in the Student's Book. There is an answer key at the bottom of each worksheet, which can be cut off if necessary. You will need to photocopy one Vocabulary Plus worksheet for each student.

- Use the worksheets as extra vocabulary input in class. We suggest you cut off the answer keys and check the answers after each exercise.

- Give them for homework for students to use on their own. You can either leave the answer keys on the worksheets so students can check the answers themselves or cut them off and check the answers at the beginning of the next class.

- When you have a mixed-level class, give them to students who finish longer speaking activities early. They can begin the worksheets in class and finish them for homework if necessary. You can then give the worksheets for homework to the other students at the end of the class.

- For further practice, ask students to look out for more examples of the type of language in the worksheet. They can look in articles, films, TV programmes and advertisements. Then they can bring examples to class for discussion or to display in the classroom.

1 Vague language p172

Language
stuff, (50)-odd, (40) or so, ages, tons, loads, masses, or anything, the early hours, (12)-ish, in the region of (25), (11) or thereabouts

When to use and time
Use any time after lesson 1B. 25–30 minutes.

Procedure

1 Students read the messages and answer the questions. They discuss their answers in pairs.

2 Focus students on the words and phrases in bold in the messages. Point out that these are examples of vague language. In the email, Julia uses it as a way of being relaxed and friendly. In the note, she wants to be deliberately vague because she thinks her neighbours will not like the truth. Students do the exercise on their own before checking in pairs. Check answers with the class.

3 Students do the exercise on their own or in pairs. Check answers with the class. Point out that *in the region of* and *or thereabouts* are more formal than the other expressions.

4 Students do the exercise on their own. When they have finished, put students in groups. Students take turns to ask each other the questions. Encourage students to ask follow-up questions.

2 Guessing the meaning of unknown words p173

Language
This worksheet does not introduce additional vocabulary. Instead, it shows students how to guess the meaning of unknown words by using contextual clues such as knowledge of the world, synonyms, the purpose, result or function of something, connecting words, pronouns and descriptions.

When to use and time
Use any time after lesson 2C. 20–25 minutes.

Procedure

1 Focus students on pictures A and B and ask them to describe what is happening. Students read the article and answer the question. Check answers with the class.

2 Students do the exercise on their own before checking in pairs. Check answers with the class. Point out that the purpose of this worksheet is not to teach these words, but to present ways of guessing the meaning of unknown words. Students do not need to learn these words.

3 a) Students do the exercise on their own before discussing answers in pairs. Point out that they should use the examples given to help them answer. Check answers with the class.

b) Put students into pairs or small groups to discuss their answers.

3 Health idioms p174

Language
run-down, pins and needles, under the weather, full of beans, black out, full-blown, like death warmed up, be over the worst, be back on your feet, throw a sickie, get the runs

When to use and time
Use any time after lesson 3B. 25–30 minutes.

Procedure

1 Pre-teach *hypochondriac* /ˌhaɪpəˈkɒndriæk/. Students do the questionnaire on their own. Students then compare results in pairs or small groups.

2 Students do the exercise on their own before checking in pairs. Check answers with the class. Model and drill each idiom. Highlight the pronunciation of *pins and needles* /ˌpɪnz ə ˈniːdəlz/, *full of beans* /ˌfʊl ə(v) ˈbiːnz/ and *get the runs* /ˌgeʔ ðə ˈrʌnz/. Point out that *full-blown* is not only used when talking about human health.

Students do the exercise on their own before discussing the sentences that are true for them in pairs or small groups. Encourage students to ask follow-up questions if possible.

4 Words used in newspaper headlines
p175

Language

boom, slash, cop, quiz, haul, plunge, bid, dash, brawl, hike, boost

When to use and time

Use at any time after lesson 4A. 25–30 minutes.

Procedure

 Focus students on the headlines. Students do the exercise on their own or in pairs. Discuss ideas with the class, but do not give answers.

 Students do the exercise on their own before checking in pairs. Check answers with the class.

 Students do the exercise on their own before checking in pairs. Check answers with the class. Point out that headlines often use short dramatic words that people do not use in everyday speech.

 Students do the exercise on their own. Students compare sentences in small groups.

5 Phrasal verbs with *out, back* and *down* p176

Language

sell out, narrow down, bounce back, buy out, knock down, wear out, play down, date back, dress down, claw back

When to use and time

Use at any time after lesson 5C. 25–30 minutes.

Procedure

 Students do the exercise on their own before checking in pairs. Check answers with the class.

 Students do the exercise on their own before checking in pairs. Check answers with the class. Model and drill the words, pointing out the stress on the particle.

 Students do the exercise on their own before checking in pairs. Check answers with the class. Point out that most particles have several different meanings and only one meaning of each particle is given here.

 a) Students do the exercise on their own before checking in pairs. Check answers with the class.

b) Put students into small groups to discuss the sentences. Encourage students to ask follow-up questions if possible.

> — EXTRA IDEA —
> * For homework, ask students to find phrasal verbs they have recorded in their vocabulary notebooks. Students try to identify some more meanings of particles using a dictionary if necessary.

6 New words from the Internet p177

Language

cyberactive, emarketing, surfer, SEO, google, page ranking, banner ad, viral advertising, advertainment, webinar, URL, action

When to use and time

Use any time after lesson 6B. 20–25 minutes.

Procedure

 Focus students on the advertisement. Students do the exercise on their own before checking in pairs. Check answers with the class.

 Students do the exercise on their own or in pairs. Check answers with the class. Point out that some of these words may not be in a dictionary as they are relatively new or have a new usage. Model and drill *cyberactive* /ˌsaɪbəˈræktɪv/, *emarketing* /ˈiːmɑːkətɪŋ/, *SEO* /ˌesiːˈjəʊ/, *banner ad* /ˈbænər æd/, *viral* /ˈvaɪrəl/, *advertainment* /ˌædvəˈteɪnmənt/, *webinar* /ˈwebɪnɑː/, *URL* /ˌjuwɑːrˈel/.

 Students do the exercise on their own or in pairs. Check answers with the class. Elicit any other new words that students can think of and discuss how the word was formed.

7 Law and crime p178

Language

crime figures, zero tolerance, violent crime, crack down, fare dodging, serious offences, flout the law, petty theft, enforce the law, community policing, video surveillance

When to use and time

Use any time after lesson 7B. 25–30 minutes.

Procedure

 a) Focus students on the chart. Students do the exercise in pairs. Ask one or two pairs for their opinion.

b) Students do the exercise on their own before checking in pairs.

 Students do the exercise on their own before checking in pairs. Check answers with the class. Model and drill the pronunciation of *flout* /flaʊt/, *petty theft* /ˌpeti ˈθeft/ and *surveillance* /sɜːˈveɪləns/.

3 **a)** Students do the exercise on their own before checking in pairs. Check answers with the class.

b) Put students into small groups to discuss the sentences. Encourage students to ask follow-up questions if possible.

> ── EXTRA IDEA ──
> * For homework, ask students to read some newspaper articles related to crime. They identify more collocations for the words *crime*, *law*, *offence* and *police*.

8 Stress patterns in long words p179

Language
The focus here is stress patterns in words ending with *-tion*, *-ity*, *-ical*, *-ic*, *-ify*, *-cial*, *-ible*, *-able*, *-ous* and *-ive*.

When to use and time
Use any time after lesson 8B. 25–30 minutes.

Procedure

1 **a)** Students work in pairs to discuss the question and make a list.

b) Students read the blog on their own, and then check their answers in pairs.

2 Students do the exercise on their own before checking in pairs. Check answers with the class.

3 Students do the exercise on their own before checking in pairs. Check answers with the class. Model and drill all the words in the table, highlighting the changes in word stress.

4 Point out that some suffixes affect the position of word stress in multi-syllable words. Students do the exercise on their own before checking in pairs. Check answers with the class.

5 Students do the exercise in pairs. Check answers with the class. Model and drill the words.

6 Put students into pairs or groups. Students take turns to ask each other the questions. Encourage students to use words from **2** and **5**. Monitor their discussions for correct stress placement.

9 Formal and informal money expressions p180

Language
stingy, tenner, experience cash-flow problems, outstanding debts, outgoings, purchases, skint, paid peanuts, quid, splash out

When to use and time
Use any time after lesson 9A. 15–20 minutes.

Procedure

1 Point out that voxpops are interviews in which members of the public are asked for their opinions on an issue. Students do the exercise on their own before checking with a partner. Check answers with the class.

2 Students do the exercise on their own before checking in pairs. Check answers with the class. Point out that the plural of *quid* is *quid* and that a five-pound note is called a *fiver* and a ten-pound note is called a *tenner*, but there is no special word for a 20-pound note. Model and drill the pronunciation of *stingy* /ˈstɪndʒi/, *debt* /det/ and *purchases* /ˈpɜːtʃəsəz/.

3 **a)** Students do the exercise on their own before checking in pairs. Check answers with the class.

b) Put students into small groups to discuss the sentences. Encourage students to ask follow-up questions if possible.

10 Idioms about success and failure p181

Language
go back to square one, sail through, get by, scrape through, get off to a flying start, fall behind, let something slip through your fingers, be a natural, go from strength to strength

When to use and time
Use at any time after lesson 10B. 20–25 minutes.

Procedure

1 Ask students about their experience of receiving school reports. Students do the exercise on their own before checking in pairs. Check answers with the class.

2 Students do the exercise on their own before checking in pairs. Check answers with the class. Model and drill the words and phrases, pointing out the missing sounds in *get by* /geʔ ˈbaɪ/ and *natural* /ˈnætʃrəl/, and the weak forms in *go from strength to strength* /gəʊ frəm ˌstreŋθ tə ˈstreŋθ/ and *go back to square one* /gəʊ bæk tə ˌskweə ˈwʌn/.

3 **a)** Students do the exercise on their own. Check answers with the class.

b) Put students into small groups. Students take turns to ask each other the questions in **3a)**. Encourage students to ask follow-up questions if possible.

1 Vague language

1 Read both messages from Julia. Who do you think she is writing to? What problems can you predict?

A

subject: Party

Hey!

Sorry I haven't replied before. I've been really busy with party **stuff**. I invited **50-odd** people and **40 or so** have said they'll come, so that's not bad. Even a couple of old school friends I haven't seen for **ages**! How weird will that be! So now all I've got to do is get it all sorted!! I'm just going to do **tons** of bread and cheese and salad. **Loads** of my friends are vegetarians so I won't have to do **masses** of meat **or anything**, which means it'll be cheaper ☺. Shame you have to catch the 11 o'clock train 'cos the party will probably go on till **the early hours**. I hope I can stay awake – I usually go to bed at **12-ish**. I wonder if anyone would notice?!

Anyway, great that you can come. See you on the 18th.

J

B

Dear Mr and Mrs Chenery,

I am writing to let you know that I am having a party here on Saturday 18th May. There will only be **in the region of** 25 people and we are planning to finish the party at **11 or thereabouts**, so I do hope we will not disturb you this time.

Best wishes,

Julia (no. 43)

2 Julia uses a lot of vague language, where she doesn't want to or can't be precise. Complete the table with words/phrases in **bold** from 1.

meaning 'approximately'	for imprecise nouns	exaggeration
	stuff	

3 Match the words/phrases in **bold** from 1 to precise words/numbers 1–12 that Julia did not use.

1 53   _50-odd_
2 41   _____
3 11.55   _____
4 24   _____
5 11.10   _____
6 preparations _____
7 or fish   _____
8 4 a.m.   _____
9 10 years   _____
10 15 loaves   _____
11 70%   _____
12 20 kilos   _____

4 Answer these questions for yourself. Be vague or precise.

1 How many cousins have you got?
2 How old is your oldest relative?
3 What time do you usually go to bed?
4 How many kilometres do you travel in an average week?
5 What's the population of your home town?
6 What are you going to do this weekend?
7 What kind of music don't you like?
8 Do you know what time of day you were born?
9 When did you last see your favourite primary school teacher?

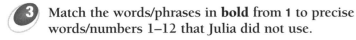

1 The email is to a friend and the note is to her neighbours. The neighbours may be angry if the party continues after 11 and there are more than 25 people. **2** **meaning 'approximately'** 50-odd; 40 or so; 12-ish; in the region of 25; 11 or thereabouts **for imprecise nouns** stuff; ages; tons; loads; **exaggeration** ages; tons; loads; masses **3** 2 40 or so 3 12-ish 4 in the region of 25 5 11 or thereabouts 6 stuff 7 or anything 8 the early hours 9 ages 10 tons 11 loads 12 masses

2 Guessing the meaning of unknown words

 1 Read the article about a little-known English tradition. Do not use a dictionary. Which picture matches the tradition?

(A)

(B)

An ancient tradition

Perhaps every country has its little-known local traditions and rural England is certainly no exception. Even most British people will be **baffled** if you ask them what **dwile flonking** is. But for the inhabitants of some villages in Eastern England, dwile flonking is a part of their tradition, one that some say dates back 400 years. So how do you play?

There are two teams and a '**jobanowl**' to look out for cheating and keep the score. The 'jobanowl' tosses a sugar **beet** from a nearby field to decide which team 'flonks' first. One member of this team, the first 'flonker', stands holding a '**driveller**' which has a beer-soaked 'dwile' on the end of it. The opposing team join hands in a circle around him and start '**girting**' in a clockwise direction. The man in the middle spins anti-clockwise and 'flonks' his 'dwile' at them. The higher on the body the rag hits somebody, the more points the 'flonker' scores; for example, a '**Wonton**' earns the flonker's team three points, a '**Morther**' two and a '**Ripper**' only one. And if he is new to the game or just a poor shot, he may find himself drinking a lot of beer. If he is unfortunate enough to get two '**Swadgers**' – this gives zero points – in a row he has to drink a pot of beer before the opposing team can pass the 'dwile' hand-to-hand around the circle. Presumably the score of the losing team rapidly deteriorates from then on!

 2 Choose the most likely definition for these words.

1 **baffled**
   a) confused ✓   b) pleased, flattered
2 **dwile**
   a) a soft ball   b) a rag or piece of cloth
3 **flonk**
   a) a player in a team   b) throw wildly
4 **jobanowl**
   a) a referee   b) a hidden camera
5 **beet**
   a) directly   b) a root vegetable
6 **driveller**
   a) a wooden pole   b) a cloth seller
7 **girting**
   a) dancing   b) facing
8 **Wonton**
   a) a hit on the face   b) a hit on the stomach
9 **Swadger**
   a) a hit on the legs   b) a complete miss

 3 **a)** Read this guide to guessing the meaning of unknown words. Choose the correct words.

We can use different methods for guessing the meaning of unknown words:

- use [1](your knowledge of the world)/descriptions to help you (e.g. *sugar beet from a nearby field*).
- look for a [2]synonym/description of the word elsewhere in the text (e.g. *dwile* and *rag*).
- look for the [3]purpose/result of something elsewhere in the text (e.g. *a 'jobanowl' to look out for cheating and keep the score*).
- look for the [4]purpose/result of something in the text (e.g. *'Swadger' – this gives zero points*).
- look for the [5]function/appearance of something (e.g. *for example, a 'Wonton' earns*).
- look for [6]pronouns/connecting words that show there is a similarity or contrast (e.g. *Even most British people will be baffled ... **But** for the inhabitants of some villages in Eastern England ...*).
- look for a [7]pronoun/connecting word that indicates whether the word relates to a person or an object (e.g. *'driveller' which has a beer-soaked 'dwile' on the end of **it***).
- look for a [8]synonym/description of how something is done to help guess the meaning of a verb (e.g. *join hands in a circle around him and start 'girting' in a clockwise direction*).

b) Which methods did you use to guess the meanings in 2?

© Cambridge University Press 2009

---

1 B **2** 2b) 3b) 4a) 5b) 6a) 7a) 8a) 9b) **3 a)** 2 synonym 3 purpose 4 result 5 function 6 connecting words 7 pronoun 8 description

3 Health idioms

1 Read the questionnaire. Do you think you are a hypochondriac?

Because of medical advice on the Internet, we are better informed about our health. However, if looking up treatment for a mouth ulcer sends you running to a doctor with a list of possible diseases, maybe you should do our not-so-serious questionnaire. If you have more 'yes's than 'no's, you may be a hypochondriac – but you probably don't need to go to the doctor to check!

Are you a hypochondriac?

1 Do you go to the doctor's if you feel **run-down**?
2 If you wake up with **pins and needles** in your arm, do you think you're about to have a heart attack?
3 Whenever you are feeling **under the weather**, do you take the day off work, just in case it's something serious?
4 When other people **are** jumping around **full of beans**, do you think to yourself "If I did that I'd probably **black out**"?
5 When you've got a cold, do you tell people you've got **full-blown** 'flu?
6 Which words sound sweeter: "Oh, poor you! You look **like death warmed up**" or "I'm glad you**'re over the worst**. You'll soon **be back on your feet**"?
7 Have you ever **thrown a sickie** because you didn't want to go to work, and then actually decided during the day that you *are* ill?
8 Do you **get the runs** if you even *think* about going abroad and eating foreign food?

VOCABULARY PLUS: PHOTOCOPIABLE

2 Match the idioms in **bold** in the questionnaire to definitions a)–k).

a) slight sharp pains, usually felt just after you have moved from being still in one position for a long time   *pins and needles*
b) become unconscious suddenly but for a short period ....
c) have a lot of energy and enthusiasm ....
d) fully developed ....
e) have experienced the worst stage of the illness and are now improving ....
f) slightly ill ....
g) be healthy again after a period of illness ....
h) tired and not healthy, especially because of working too much ....
i) told your employer you are ill when you are not so you do not have to go to work that day ....
j) have diarrhoea ....
k) look or feel very ill ....

3 Complete the sentences so they are true for you.

1 When I get run-down, I …
2 I get pins and needles if I …
3 If a friend looks under the weather I …
4 The last time I was full of beans was …
5 If someone blacks out you should …
6 The best way to avoid full-blown arguments with people is to …
7 As soon as you're over the worst of an illness, you should …
8 The first thing I want to do when I get back on my feet after an illness is …
9 The trouble with throwing a sickie is …
10 The last time I felt like death warmed up was …
11 If you have the runs, you shouldn't …

---

2 b) black out c) are full of beans d) full-blown e) are over the worst f) under the weather g) be back on your feet h) run-down i) thrown a sickie j) get the runs k) like death warmed up

4 Words used in newspaper headlines

1 What do you think these headlines are about?

(1) Camera **boom** has not **slashed** crime

(2) Cops **quiz** gang after huge heroin **haul**

(3) Shares set to **plunge** after $2bn **bid** is withdrawn

(4) Dove doctors **dash**

(5) Footy fans **brawl** on jet

(6) Greedy MPs call for huge pay **hike**

(7) Breast milk **boosts** IQ

2 Match headlines 1–7 to these first lines from newspaper articles.

a) Babies who are fed by their mothers grow up to be more intelligent than those who are bottle-fed, scientists claim. **7**

b) Detectives seized drugs with an estimated street value of over £20m at a UK port yesterday. ....

c) Politicians are demanding a 22% pay rise – saying their current salary does not compensate for the stress involved in their job. ....

d) Rock singer Candy Dove was rushed to hospital after returning home to London from a week's partying in New York. ....

e) Shares in a supermarket chain are expected to fall sharply today after it refused an improved $2.2 billion takeover approach from US store giant, Supermarty. ....

f) Terrified air passengers described how 25 drunken football supporters started a free-for-all fight on a London-bound flight. ....

g) The billions of pounds spent on CCTV equipment have failed to have an impact on crime figures, a senior police officer claimed today. ....

3 Match the words in **bold** in the headlines in 1 to definitions a)–k).

a) a period of sudden growth _boom_

b) an offer or attempt ....

c) improves or increases something ....

d) fight ....

e) police officers ....

f) run somewhere very quickly ....

g) a large amount of something that has been stolen or is illegal ....

h) an increase in the cost of something, especially a large or unwanted increase ....

i) suddenly fall in value or level ....

j) ask someone questions about something
....

k) greatly reduced ....

4 Write the first sentence of a newspaper article for each of these headlines.

1 Cops pay hike bid

....

....

2 Privileges slashed after prison brawl

....

....

3 Interest rate plunge boosts spending

....

....

4 Savers dash to withdraw funds

....

....

5 MP quizzed about expenses

....

....

Possible answers 1 Police officers are calling for a large increase in their salaries to reflect the dangers they face at work. 2 Prisoners at a high-security jail are facing sanctions after violence broke out last night in protest at overcrowded conditions. 3 High-street spending has increased by 5% following the significant drop in interest rates announced by the government last week. 4 Customers of the GCI Bank queued outside their local branches yesterday to withdraw their savings after news of the bank's difficulties broke on Tuesday. 5 A leading Member of Parliament has been interviewed about the money she paid her sister for providing her with accommodation in London.

2 b)2 c)6 d)4 e)3 f)5 g)1 **3** b) bid c) boosts d) brawl e) cops f) dash g) haul h) hike i) plunge j) quiz k) slashed **4** Possible answers

5 Phrasal verbs with *out*, *back* and *down*

1 Match sentence beginnings 1–10 to sentence endings a)–j).

1 After disappointing Christmas sales,
2 Sorry, we've **sold out** of the Xi53s,
3 We've got too many options,
4 JBS have **bought out** Howletts,
5 If we **knock down** the price to match our competitors',

a) we'll lose money and go out of business.
b) so we need to **narrow** them **down**.
c) the retail industry is starting to **bounce back**.
d) but we should get a delivery next week.
e) so I wonder if they'll change the name to JBS now.

6 The rubber belt has **worn out**,
7 The PR department is trying to **play down** the scandal,
8 Most of their problems **date back**
9 We're allowed to **dress down** on Fridays,
10 It would be good if we could **claw back**

f) and they're focusing on the new product launch.
g) so most people wear jeans instead of suits.
h) so we'll have to have it replaced.
i) some of the market share we lost last year.
j) to when Gordon was in charge of human resources.

2 Match the phrasal verbs in **bold** in 1 to definitions a)–j).

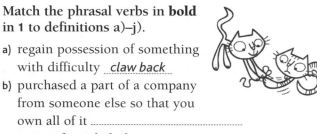

a) regain possession of something with difficulty   *claw back*
b) purchased a part of a company from someone else so that you own all of it _____
c) wear informal clothes _____
d) make a list of things smaller, by removing the things that are least important or desirable _____
e) make something seem less important or less bad than it really is _____
f) sold all of the supply that you have of something _____
g) lower _____
h) start to be successful again after a difficult period _____
i) have existed since a particular time _____
j) used so much that it has become too damaged to use any more _____

3 The phrasal verbs in 1 use the particles *out*, *back* and *down*. In these phrasal verbs, which particle has the general meaning of:

a) reducing? _____
b) returning or referring to an earlier time? _____
c) completed or finished? _____

4 a) Fill in the gaps with the correct form of the phrasal verbs from 1.

1 Never let failure stop you; just be determined to _____*bounce back*_____ .
2 In order to prioritise, I always _____ long lists of things to do.
3 It's a great idea to allow staff to _____ once a week.
4 It's best to buy expensive shoes that don't _____ quickly.
5 In my country lots of small shops have been _____ by big companies.
6 I like people who _____ their problems and concentrate on the positive.
7 If a shop has _____ of something I want, I ask them to order one for me.
8 High-street shops will never be able to _____ customers they have lost to the Internet.
9 I think most phobias _____ to childhood experiences.
10 When I need to buy something expensive, I always try to _____ the price.

b) Work in groups. Which sentences in 4a) do you agree with?

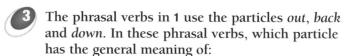

1 2d) 3b) 4e) 5a) 6h) 7f) 8j) 9g) 10i) **2** b) bought out c) dress down d) narrow down e) play down f) sold out g) knock down h) bounce back i) date back j) worn out **3** a) down b) back c) out **4** a) 2 narrow down 3 dress down 4 wear out 5 bought out 6 play down 7 sold out 8 claw back 9 date back 10 knock down

6 New words from the Internet

1 Read the advertisement for Web-Savvy, a company providing Internet solutions. How would you describe the company?

a) young ✓

b) dynamic

c) traditional

d) flexible

e) knowledgeable

f) creative

g) conservative

WEB-SAVVY
online marketing that knows its stuff!

How would you like over one billion customers? That's how many Internet users there are in this **cyberactive** world. But how can you direct your share of that traffic to *your* site?

Web-Savvy **emarketing** provides real results. We turn a **surfer** into a customer – yours! How?

- **SEO** – when you **google**, you'll be found. We can raise your **page ranking** pretty much instantly.
- **Banner ads** – be visible, be noticed, be clicked.
- **Viral advertising** – is everyone talking about you? We make your **advertainment** the one everyone wants to see.
- **Webinars** – show your product in all its glory and let your customers interact from the comfort of their own computer.

We can provide complete emarketing campaigns, from sourcing you a memorable and unique **URL** to complete technological support. Or maybe you know exactly what you want and you'd just like us to **action** it.

2 Complete the crossword with the words/phrases in **bold** from the advertisement.

ACROSS

2 The position of a website in search engine listings.

6 Encouraging people via the Internet to buy a product or service.

9 A type of advertising in which viewers like an advertisement (e.g. a video) so much that they talk about it to others.

11 Someone who uses computers widely is … .

12 Do something to achieve a particular goal.

DOWN

1 A person who searches for information or entertainment on the Internet.

3 Advertisement of a product or brand that is also entertaining.

4 Use a search engine to find information on the Internet (named after a popular search engine).

5 A process of making a website appear high in search engine listings (an abbreviation of 'search engine optimisation').

7 A website address.

8 An advertisement on a web page.

10 An interactive web-based seminar or presentation.

3 Complete descriptions 1–6 of how new vocabulary is formed with examples from 1.

1 An old word is used with a new meaning.
   (e.g. _surfer_ , _viral_)

2 A new prefix is added to an existing word.
   (e.g. _____ , _____)

3 Two existing words are joined to make a new compound. (e.g. _____ , _____)

4 Two existing words are blended to make a new word.
   (e.g. _____ , _____)

5 An abbreviation becomes more well known than the words that it stands for. (e.g. _____ , _____)

6 An existing word takes on new grammar, for example, a noun becomes a verb. (e.g. _____ , _____)

1 **a)** Look at the chart. Why do you think the number of murders in New York has fallen so dramatically in the last two decades?

b) Read the article. Were any of your ideas the same?

Cracking down on broken windows

As [1]**crime figures** cause increasing concern in our cities, the question of [2]**zero tolerance** is once again on the agenda. When such a policy was adopted in New York in the mid-1990s, it seemed to cause a dramatic reduction in violent crime. As police [3]**cracked down** on minor crimes, such as vandalism, littering and [4]**fare dodging** on the subway, the number of more [5]**serious offences**, like murder, also declined.

Zero tolerance is based on the 'broken window theory' of James Wilson and George Kelling. They suggested that a broken window in a neighbourhood gave the impression that nobody cared about it and very soon more windows would be smashed. Whereas, if the broken window was repaired quickly, this was less likely to happen. They believed that by dealing with people who [6]**flout the law** in relatively minor ways the rate of more serious crimes could also be reduced. Often, people arrested for [7]**petty theft** or public disorder were seen as those most likely to commit dangerous crimes. And it seemed to work for New York.

But did it? Critics claim that similar decreases were seen in other US cities which did not [8]**enforce the law** so strictly. They suggest that other factors such as more [9]**community policing** and increased [10]**video surveillance** has made the US a safer place to live.

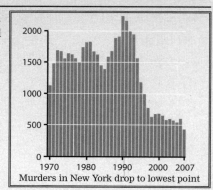

Murders in New York drop to lowest point

2 Match phrases 1–10 in the article to definitions a)–j).

a) a crime with a severe effect _5_

b) a system in which officers work with the residents of a neighbourhood to prevent crimes ....

c) make people obey rules ....

d) statistics about criminal activity ....

e) the act of dishonestly taking something which is relatively unimportant or inexpensive ....

f) intentionally disobey the rules of the country ....

g) start dealing with bad or illegal behaviour in a more severe way ....

h) travelling on public transport without paying for a ticket ....

i) the use of cameras to watch a person or place ....

j) when all criminal behaviour, even if not very serious, is punished severely ....

3 **a)** Match sentence beginnings 1–10 to sentence endings a)–j).

1 People should be arrested for fare _c_

2 The trouble with zero ....

3 The police should crack ....

4 The rapport that can be built through community ....

5 Crime ....

6 Someone who goes to prison for petty ....

7 Police should enforce the ....

8 If kids see their relatives flouting ....

9 There's too much video ....

10 Prison is the only place for people who commit serious ....

a) figures in my country have got worse recently.

b) the law, they will learn to do the same.

c) dodging on public transport.

d) law, even if it sometimes means inconveniencing innocent people.

e) policing is more valuable than arresting petty criminals.

f) down on littering in my home town.

g) surveillance in public places nowadays.

h) offences.

i) tolerance is that it can lead to police brutality.

j) theft will probably learn to be a better thief!

b) Work in groups. Which sentences in 3a) do you agree with?

8 Stress patterns in long words

 1 **a)** What do you think are the qualities of a hero? Make a list.

_____

b) Read the blog. Are your ideas the same?

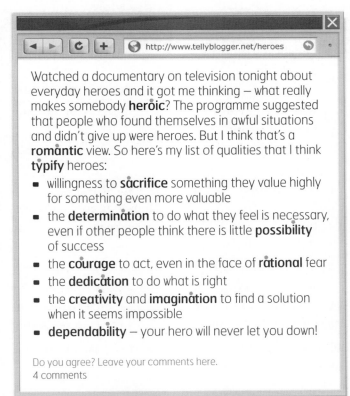

http://www.tellyblogger.net/heroes

Watched a documentary on television tonight about everyday heroes and it got me thinking – what really makes somebody **heroic**? The programme suggested that people who found themselves in awful situations and didn't give up were heroes. But I think that's a **romantic** view. So here's my list of qualities that I think **typify** heroes:

- willingness to **sacrifice** something they value highly for something even more valuable
- the **determination** to do what they feel is necessary, even if other people think there is little **possibility** of success
- the **courage** to act, even in the face of **rational** fear
- the **dedication** to do what is right
- the **creativity** and **imagination** to find a solution when it seems impossible
- **dependability** – your hero will never let you down!

Do you agree? Leave your comments here.
4 comments

 2 Fill in gaps 1–12 with the words in **bold** from the blog.

noun	verb	adjective
hero	–	1 _heroic_
romance	a)	2 ....
type	3	b) ....
sacrifice	4	c) ....
5	determine	d) ....
6	–	possible
7	–	courageous
rationalisation	e)	8 ....
9	dedicate	f) ....
10	create	g) ....
11	imagine	h) ....
12	depend	i) ....

3 Fill in gaps a)–i) in **2** with these words.

> creative   determined   imaginative   typical
> dependable   romanticise   dedicated   sacrificial
> rationalise

4 Where is the stress on words with these suffixes? Write A if the stress is on the second from last syllable (●●) or B if the stress is on the third from last syllable (●●●).

1	-tion	_A_	6 -cial	....
2	-ity	....	7 -ible	....
3	-ical	....	8 -able	....
4	-ic	....	9 -ous	....
5	-ify	....	10 -ive	....

 5 Add the stress marks to these words.

1 clarify   2 responsive   3 likeable   4 sympathetic

5 curiosity   6 incredible   7 enormous   8 logical

9 official   10 examination

 6 Answer these questions for yourself. Try to use words from **2** and **5**.

1 What are the qualities of a good student?

2 What does a good teacher need to do?

3 What do you look for in a good friend?

9 Formal and informal money expressions

1 Read the voxpops. Who thinks it's OK to borrow money? Why?

This week's hot question – is it OK to be in debt?

Jimmy Poole, builder

Debt? Ha, you're talking to the right man, mate! It's the kids, you know, they see something they want and you get it because you don't want to be **stingy**. So you end up borrowing a bit more, but then that's what the banks are there for, isn't it? Live for today, that's what I say. Hey, you couldn't lend us a **tenner**, could you?

Monty Frears, retired accountant

Borrowing money is expensive, so if people are **experiencing cash-flow problems**, they should first arrange to pay off any **outstanding debts** little by little. Then they should draw up a budget of their essential **outgoings**. Any remaining money may be used for luxury **purchases** or investment for the future.

Frances Pearson, teacher

It's all very well to say people shouldn't spend money they haven't got, but for some folks it's the only way they can live. They're **skint** most of the time because they're on benefits. Or if they are working, they get **paid peanuts**. They have to borrow a few **quid** just to feed their families. It's not like they **splash out** on expensive holidays or anything like that.

2 Fill in gaps 1–11 with words/phrases in **bold** from 1.

more formal	less formal
poor, lacking funds	¹ *skint*
²_____ _____	not having enough money to pay the bills
³_____	money you owe people
pound(s)	⁴_____
ten-pound note	⁵_____
spend money extravagantly	⁶_____
unwilling to spend money	⁷_____
on a low salary	⁸_____
⁹_____	money that has to be regularly spent
¹⁰_____	things you buy

3 **a)** Complete these sentences with words/phrases in **bold** from 1.

1 If you are _experiencing cash-flow problems_, you should inform those to whom you owe money.

2 I can't stand _____ people – you know, the ones who buy you a pencil for your birthday!

3 I'm always _____ at the end of the month.

4 I never buy really cheap clothes because the people who make them are _____ for working in awful conditions.

5 Sometimes I _____ on something really expensive to cheer myself up.

6 If a taxi costs, say, £8.50, I give the driver a _____ and tell him to keep the change.

7 If your _____ exceed your income, you should work out how to live more cheaply.

8 It is advisable to pay off _____ before starting to save.

9 I usually make major _____ on a credit card.

10 I wouldn't pay nine _____ to see a film.

b) Work in groups. Which sentences in **3a)** are true for you? Which do you agree with?

---

face2face Advanced Photocopiable   © Cambridge University Press 2009   Instructions p171

10 Idioms about success and failure

 1 Read Thomas Wonder's school report. Fill in gaps a)–e) with these grades.

| ✗ 4 6 10 10 |

Montgomery School
for Boys

Report for

| Thomas Wonder Year 10 |

Subject	Comments	Grade/10
English	Thomas has a lot of difficulty spelling. He does not seem to realise that letters have to go in a certain order to make a word. He really needs to ¹**go back to square one** and learn the basics again.	a) _1_
Mathematics	Thomas truly is a 'Wonder' at Maths. He ²**sails through** all his tests, getting 100% every time. He's on course for a very high grade in his exam next month.	b) ....
French	French is not Thomas's strongest subject, but he does try hard. He ³**gets by** in speaking but has great difficulty with written French. If he works very hard, he may ⁴**scrape through** his exam in June.	c) ....
Biology	Thomas ⁵**got off to a flying start** at the beginning of term and I was expecting great things from him. But then he got distracted by other things and he started to ⁶**fall behind**. He has great potential to pass the exam so it would be a shame to ⁷**let it slip through his fingers** for lack of concentration.	d) ....
Chemistry	Thomas ⁸**is a natural** in the science lab. He started well and his work ⁹**goes from strength to strength**. With his parents' permission, we would like to put him in for his final exam one year early. It would challenge him but we are sure he could manage it.	e) ....

2 Match idioms 1–9 in **bold** in 1 to definitions a)–i).

a) be able to deal with a situation, usually by having just enough of something you need _3_

b) begin an activity very successfully ....

c) be born with a skill or talent ....

d) fail to do something fast enough or on time ....

e) gradually become increasingly successful ....

f) miss an opportunity through lack of care or effort ....

g) narrowly succeed in something but with a lot of difficulty ....

h) start working on something from the beginning because your previous attempt failed ....

i) succeed very easily in something, especially a test or examination ....

 3 **a) Complete these questions with the correct form of the idioms in 1.**

1 Can you think of a famous person who has gone from _strength to strength_ in their career?

2 And what about someone who got off to a .... , but then disappeared from the scene?

3 Do you get stressed if you .... with your work?

4 Do you know anyone who .... through all their exams easily although they don't do much work?

5 Do you know someone who's a .... at something? Do you admire or envy them?

6 Have you ever just .... through something that you thought you'd fail?

7 Have you ever let something .... through ....?

8 How many languages can you .... by in?

9 When might going .... to .... be a positive thing?

b) Work in groups. Answer the questions in 3a) for yourself.

Instructions p171   © Cambridge University Press 2009   **face2face** Advanced Photocopiable

Help with Listening

Instructions

There are 10 Help with Listening worksheets (p189–p198). The aim of these worksheets is to help students to develop their ability to understand authentic spoken English. The worksheets use authentic recordings from the Student's Book, and focus on how fluent speakers of English structure their discourse in a variety of genres.

These Help with Listening worksheets are designed to be used in class, offering a change of pace and focus for both teacher and students. You will need to photocopy one Help with Listening worksheet for each student, and prepare the relevant Student's Book recording.

1 Monologues p189

Aim

To help students understand spoken monologues.

When to use and time

Use any time after lesson 1C. 30–40 minutes.

Preparation

You will need to play **R1.4** and refer students to R1.4, SB p148.

Procedure

1 **a)** Remind students of the five sayings from lesson 1C (*If you fly with the crows, you get shot with the crows*, etc.). **R1.4** Play the recording. Students listen and do the exercise on their own before comparing answers in pairs. Check answers with the class.

> **b)**

b) Students do the exercise on their own before comparing answers in pairs. Check answers with the class.

> 2 W
> 3 P
> 4 P
> 5 P (Pete talks about work, but not about a work relationship.)

2 Play the recording again. Students listen and do the exercise on their own before comparing answers in pairs. Check answers with the class.

> 1 basically means
> 2 basically means
> 3 what it means
> 4 this basically means
> 5 Basically

 3 Students do the exercise in pairs. Check answers with the class.

> 1 basically
> 2 It is used to introduce the explanations by giving key information about them.
> 3 It can be removed without affecting the grammar or changing the meaning.
> 4 Used in this way, *basically* is more common in spoken English.

 4 Students do the exercise on their own before checking in pairs. Check answers with the class.

> 2 So, basically, we could argue for hours about who said what, but it was a ~~basically~~ misunderstanding.
> 3 It's quite a ~~basically~~ complicated-looking machine and basically the way it works is …
> 4 It's basically a rip-off. Their promises of accountability and ~~basically~~ all that don't mean a thing.
> 5 Basically, what you do first is peel ~~basically~~ the potatoes.
> 6 It's basically a good film, but I didn't like the ~~basically~~ lead actor's performance.

 5 Put students into small groups to discuss their answers. Check answers with the class.

> 1 It can give you some idea of the content and help you predict what speakers will say.
> 2 Listening for key words/phrases can help work out the type of spoken language. *For example* might be used when someone is giving an explanation; *a few years ago* might be used when someone is telling a story.
> 3 Yes.
> 4 Usually it won't. Many words common in spoken English, such as *basically*, are redundant.
> 5 Yes. It is very helpful to recognise these words. When non-native speakers (such as Claudia) use these words, it can help make them sound fluent.
> 6 If you are having a conversation with a fluent speaker, you can ask that person once they have finished talking. Alternatively, if you hear a word in another context, you can note it down and check with a fluent speaker or your teacher later.

2 Taking part in a conversation p190

Aim

To help students develop strategies for becoming active listeners.

When to use and time

Use any time after lesson 2B. 30–40 minutes.

Preparation

You will need to play **R2.3** and refer students to R2.3, SB p149.

Procedure

 a)–b) Remind students of the holiday stories from lesson 2B (of the Galápagos Islands and Ireland). R2.3 Play the recording. Students listen and do the exercises before comparing answers in pairs. Check answers with the class.

> a) a)
> b) I went to Ireland last summer expecting to see **lush, green** hills. We thought we would be staying in a lodge that we rented from friends of **friends**. It took **18** hours of driving in terrible **rain** to get to where we were staying. The house turned out to be a **stark, modern log cabin**. The beach was half an hour's **sail** away.

2 Play the recording again. Students listen and answer the questions on their own. Check answers with the class.

> a) 3 (Melissa) b) 6 (Brendan) d) 4 (Brendan)
> e) 2 (Brendan) f) 5 (Melissa)

3 Elicit the first example where Brendan gives feedback and write it on the board. Students turn to R2.3, SB p149 and do the exercise on their own before checking in pairs. Check answers with the class.

> 1 Right, OK; Oh, OK
> 2 No rustic charm then; Which is something that you don't want to be doing in bad weather
> 3 Oh, dear.

4 Students work in pairs and complete the conversation. Point out that there is more than one possible way of completing the conversation. Ask one or two pairs to role-play their conversation for the class.

> **Possible answers**
> 1
> A So, by the time I got home it was after midday.
> B Oh, OK.
> A And I put the key in the door.
> B Right.
> A And I couldn't get it in.
> B Wouldn't fit.
> A My flatmate had changed the lock and forgotten to tell me!
> B Oh, dear!
> 2
> A I'd been expecting to go to a really smart restaurant.
> B Right.
> A So I got all dressed up.
> B Put on your best clothes.
> A And I was looking forward to a great night out.
> B OK.
> A Then I found out we were just going to a cheap and cheerful place down the road.
> B Oh, dear!

5 Put students into small groups to discuss their answers. Check answers with the class.

> c) Providing some kind of feedback shows we're interested and supports the speaker. All the strategies used by Brendan in R2.3 are useful ways of responding to someone's story.

3 Leaving things out p191

Aim

To help students develop awareness of ellipsis and substitution as natural features of spoken language.

When to use and time

Use any time after lesson 3A. 30–40 minutes.

Preparation

You will need to play part of R3.2 and refer students to R3.2, SB p150.

Procedure

 Remind students of the interviews about impostor syndrome from lesson 3A. R3.2 Play the part of the recording where Richard speaks. Students listen and choose the best description. Students compare answers in pairs. Check answers with the class.

> c)

 Students do the exercise on their own before checking in pairs. Check answers with the class.

> 1F He's only just heard about it from the interviewer.
> 2F He doesn't want to sound arrogant to the interviewer.
> 3T
> 4T

 a) Ask students to predict what will be deleted or changed. Elicit the first example and write it on the board. Play the recording again. Students listen and do the exercise on their own before checking in pairs. Check answers with the class.

> 2 Why, no ~~I haven't had any experience of it~~.
> 3 … I think I'm good enough ~~at my job~~ that most of the time …
> 4 … when I make a mistake, only I realise I've made ~~a mistake~~ **one**.
> 5 No, I don't think ~~I have this sort of self doubt~~ **so**.

b) Students do the exercise on their own before checking in pairs. Check answers with the class.

> b) 4 c) 3 d) 5 e) 2

c) Students do the exercise on their own before checking in pairs. Check answers with the class.

> 1 one 2 so

4 Students work in pairs and rewrite the conversations. Remind students to use ideas from **3** where possible.

✍ Write the conversations on the board. Elicit ideas from the class and make changes to the conversations with a different-coloured pen.

> **Possible answers**
>
> 1
>
> A Have you ever been on TV?
> B Yes, I~~'ve been on TV~~ once.
> A When was that?
> B ~~It was~~ A couple of years ago. I was interviewed on the TV news about my work.
> A Did you feel nervous?
> B No, I don't think ~~I felt nervous~~ so. It was only for a regional channel, ~~It wasn't for~~ not a national ~~channel~~ one.
>
> 2
>
> A What are you doing tonight?
> B ~~I'm~~ Going to the cinema ~~tonight~~.
> A What are you going to see ~~at the cinema~~?
> B ~~I'm going to see~~ The latest James Bond film. Have you seen it?
> A No, I haven't ~~seen it~~.
> B Would you like to come ~~to the cinema to see the film~~?
> A Yes, I would ~~like to come to the cinema~~.

5 Students work in pairs and rewrite the conversation.

✍ Write the conversation on the board. Elicit ideas from the class and make changes to the conversation with a different-coloured pen.

> **Possible answers**
>
> A **Have** you ever wanted to try another job?
> B Yes, **I have**.
> A What **job would you like to try**?
> B **(I'd like to try) being a** teacher.
> A Really? **That's** interesting!
> B **What about** you?
> A **(I'd like to try) being a** photographer.

6 Put students into small groups to discuss their ideas. Check with the class.

> **Possible answers**
>
> 1 No, the reason they do this is to make their speaking sound more natural and fluent.
> 2 Yes, there are grammar rules about this. *The Cambridge Grammar of English* has useful information on ellipsis and substitution.
> 3 No, it is very hard to listen and work out what omissions and changes fluent speakers make when they are talking. Being aware that fluent speakers make changes is enough. It is better to listen out for key content words that convey meaning.
> 4 Yes, this is a useful strategy if you are listening to a fluent speaker. It is normal for two fluent speakers to ask for clarification when they are communicating with each other.

---

4 Disagreeing p192

Aim

To highlight strategies that native speakers use to disagree with someone they know well.

When to use and time

Use any time after lesson 4A. 30–40 minutes.

Preparation

You will need to play and refer students to R4.1, SB p151.

Procedure

1 a) Remind students of Sue and Dan's discussion from lesson 4A. Play the recording. Students listen and do the exercise. Students compare answers in pairs. Check answers with the class.

> b)

b) Students do the exercise on their own before checking in pairs. Check answers with the class.

> 2 Sue   3 Dan   4 Sue   5 Sue

2 a) Play the recording again. Students listen and do the exercise on their own before checking in pairs. Check answers with the class.

> c) Both speakers are direct in expressing their opinions and use almost no language of agreement. This suggests they know each other reasonably well.

b) Students do the exercise on their own before checking in pairs. Check answers with the class.

> well

3 Students do the exercise on their own before checking in pairs. Remind students that they can see the examples in context in R4.1, SB p151. Check answers with the class.

> 1c)   2a)   3b)

4 a) Tell students to think of possible replies but not to write them. Students work in pairs using their own ideas. Encourage students to use language from **3**. Point out that there is more than one possible way of completing the conversation.

> **Possible answer**
>
> ALEX English is a really easy language to learn.
> KIM I find it quite hard, actually.
> ALEX Well, everyone speaks it, so there are lots of chances to practise.
> KIM Not everyone speaks it – not in my country!
> ALEX I think the grammar is really straightforward.
> KIM Well, I've always found it really difficult to understand.

ALEX	And it's not as though there's that much vocabulary to learn.
KIM	Well, I think there are a huge number of words to learn.

b) Students practise the conversation, taking turns to be Alex and Kim. Ask one or two pairs to role-play their conversations for the class.

--- EXTRA IDEA ---
- Introduce a new controversial topic (e.g. watching TV is a good way to relax). Ask students to discuss it in pairs or small groups using language from **3**.

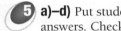 **a)–d)** Put students into small groups to discuss their answers. Check answers with the class.

> **a)** 1 Yes, if you know the other person well, for example, a friend or colleague.
> 2 Put forward contrasting ideas to counter the other person's argument.
> 3 No, typical expressions of agreement and disagreement are not always used in a discussion between two people who know each other well.
> 4 Yes, this is preferable to saying *Well, I don't agree.*
>
> **b)–c)** *Well* has a great variety of uses and is not only used as a filler in a conversation. It can signal doubt, surprise, shock and indignation.
>
> **d)** The intonation of *well* changes the way it is used by fluent speakers.

5 Talking about problems and solutions
p193

Aim
To raise awareness of and provide practice in problem–solution discourse patterns in spoken English.

When to use and time
Use any time after lesson 5B. 30–40 minutes.

Preparation
You will need to play **R5.4** and refer students to R5.4, SB p152.

Procedure

1 **a)–b)** Remind students of Claire, Will and Charlie's discussion of their career/study plans from lesson 5B. **R5.4** Play Claire's extract of the recording. Students listen and do the exercises. Students can compare answers in pairs. Check answers with the class.

> **a)** teaching, publishing, charity work
> **b)** 2a) 3a) 4b)

2 If students are unfamiliar with listening to recordings in this way, play part 1 and elicit the answer from the class. Students then do the rest of the exercise before checking in pairs. Check answers with the class.

> 1 part 3   2 part 1   3 part 2

3 Focus students on Claire's extract in R5.4, SB p152. Students work alone. Check answers with the class. If your class is strong, do this exercise as an intensive listening task and get them to listen for the words.

> 1 struggled   2 trying   3 working

4 Focus students on Will and Charlie's extracts in R5.4, SB p153. Students work in pairs and do the exercise. Check answers with the class.

> 1 **Will's extract: problem** is first signalled by *not really* (an easy decision); **solution** is first signalled by *chose*; **comment** is first signalled by *options*.
> 2 **Charlie's extract: solution** is first signalled by *I do now* (know what to do); **problem** is first signalled by *but* (that decision came after a lot of change); **solution** is restated and signalled by *and that's when*; **comment** is first signalled by *confident*.

5 Tell the class your own personal example using the pattern 'problem > solution > comment'. Invite the class to ask follow-up questions. Students then work alone to make notes on their story. Students work in pairs to tell their stories. Finally, ask students to tell the class what they found out about their partner.

6 Put students into small groups to discuss their answers. If you have a multilingual class, group different nationalities together. Check answers with the class.

> 1 Not all languages use problem–solution patterning as commonly as English. For example, Mandarin and Arabic speakers tend to talk around a problem and not mention it so directly.
> 2 People who use problem–solution patterning usually don't do so consciously.
> 3 It can help you to know what kind of information to expect next.

6 Asides p194

Aim
To raise awareness of how asides are used in spoken narratives.

When to use and time
Use any time after lesson 6A. 30–40 minutes.

Preparation
You will need to play **R6.1** and refer students to R6.1, SB p153.

Procedure

1 **a)–b)** Remind students of the four stories of strange behaviour from lesson 6A. **R6.1** Play the recording. Students listen and do the exercises. Students compare answers in pairs. Check answers with the class.

a) a)

b)

person mentioned	strange behaviour
friend, Martina	takes her two pet rabbits with her everywhere she goes
commuter	walks up and down the train looking for the perfect seat
commuters	arranged stuffed toys on the train so they could look out of the window
daughter	collects pebbles and brings them home; wears odd socks

 2 Play the recording again. Pause after each story to allow students to write their answers. Students can compare answers in pairs. Check answers with the class.

a) Not so strange in itself …
b) And the thing that I will never forget …
c) I mean, I've been travelling for two years now.
d) and you've just reminded me actually …
e) I've only just remembered this.
f) 'cos we're British …
g) It's obviously the height of fashion.

 3 Students do the exercise on their own before checking in pairs. Check answers with the class.

1 Yes, it is.
2 They comment on the story.
3 They show both. For example, a) is an example of the speaker's reaction, while d) is an example of the speaker's spontaneous thought.
4 Asides.

 4 Give the class an example that includes one or two asides. Ask students to notice your asides. Ask students to prepare their own story. Give them time to think and make notes. Ask them to tell their story to a partner. Encourage students to use asides. Highlight that the kind of aside they use does not have to be the same as those in **2** – students can invent their own. Encourage students to listen to their partner and notice what asides they use. Conduct feedback with one or two pairs and ask them what the asides were.

5 Students do the exercise on their own. They should only make notes. Put students into small groups to discuss their answers. If you have a multilingual class, group different nationalities together. Check answers with the class.

1 It is likely that asides are common in most languages.
2 No, it isn't. Point out that it is useful if students realise that fluent speakers will probably use asides when they speak.
3 In general, asides have a low tone (the pitch drops slightly). Knowing this may help students recognise an aside.

7 Opinions p195

Aim

To develop learners' awareness of language used to give opinions.

When to use and time

Use any time after lesson 7B. 30–40 minutes.

Preparation

You will need to play R7.3 and refer students to R7.3, SB p155.

Procedure

 1 **a)–b)** Remind students of the topic of state intervention from lesson 7B. Elicit the three topics that were discussed: smoking, rubbish and personal lifestyles. R7.3 Play the recording. Students listen and do the exercises before comparing answers in pairs. Check answers with the class.

a) c)

b) 1 No, he thinks it would be harmful for others.
2 Yes, because stopping them would mean too much state intervention.
3 She thinks it's fair that people pay for what they throw away. She also suggests this might be an effective way of reducing the amount of rubbish thrown away.
4 The fact that only married people are eligible for a tax exemption, which could result in people feeling pressured to get married to qualify for the tax exemption.

 2 **a)–b)** Students read the words and think about a possible order. Students compare answers in pairs. Play the recording again and check answers with the class.

1 I think that, basically, if the state intervenes, for example, to ban smoking …
2 In the case of rubbish, there clearly has to be more state intervention …
3 … when it comes to the state intervening in people's lifestyles …

 3 **a)** Students do the exercise in pairs. Check answers with the class. ✎ Elicit other expressions used to give opinions (e.g. *I believe, I understand, I'm of the opinion, In my opinion/view*) and write them on the board.

1 The first four words introduce the opinion.
2 I think that basically
3 In the case of; when it comes to

b) Students do the exercise on their own before comparing answers in pairs. Ask pairs to share one or two of their opinions with the class.

4 Give students time to think and make notes, particularly about the ideas and examples that support their opinion. Put students into small groups of three or four. Students take turns to state their opinion and then discuss each other's ideas. Indicate it is fine to disagree with their partners in the discussion. Share ideas with the class.

5 Students do the exercise on their own. They should only make notes. Put students into small groups to discuss their answers. Check answers with the class.

> 1 Yes, they normally do.
> 2 They use phrases such as the underlined examples in **2a)**, or phrases such as *I believe, I understand, I'm of the opinion, In my opinion/view*. These phrases usually come before the opinion.
> 3 Yes, otherwise the opinion could be perceived as a kind of factual claim that is not backed up by any evidence.

8 Small words p196

Aim
To raise awareness of *and* and *so* as discourse markers in spoken text, with multiple meanings.

When to use and time
Use any time after lesson 8A. 30–40 minutes.

Preparation
You will need to play **R8.1** and refer students to R8.1, SB p156.

Procedure

1 a) Remind students of Hazel Henderson from lesson 8A without eliciting too much detail about her life story. **R8.1** Play the recording until 'fell in love, married, had a family'. Students listen and do the exercise on their own before checking in pairs. Check answers with the class.

> 1T
> 2F She was born into an ordinary family.
> 3T
> 4F She hated school.
> 5T
> 6T
> 7F She worked as a hotel receptionist.
> 8F She applied for a job in a New York hotel.
> 9T

b) Give an example by playing the extract from the recording again and highlighting the first appearances of *and* and *so*. Students then do the exercise on their own before checking in pairs. Check answers with the class.

> 1 10   2 3

2 Write the first example on the board. Students do the exercise on their own before checking in pairs. Check answers with the class.

> 2d)   3a)   4e)   5b)

3 Write the first example on the board. Students do the exercise on their own before checking in pairs. Check answers with the class.

> 2a)   3b)   4a)   5e)   6b)   7c)   8d)   9c)   10a)
> 11e)   12b)

4 Put students into small groups to discuss their answers. Check answers with the class.

> 1 They are used as signposts. In general, *and* is used to indicate extra or new information is following; *so* is used to indicate a result.
> 2 Yes, it is. Although they are small words and sometimes difficult to hear, it can be useful to listen out for these words as they can help make sense of what follows, i.e. after *and* there is likely to be new information and after *so* there is likely to be a result of what has been previously mentioned.
> 3 We can write down examples of different uses in vocabulary notebooks, or look up different meanings in the *Cambridge Advanced Learner's Dictionary*.

9 Different uses of *that* p197

Aim
To raise awareness of *that* as a referring word in spoken text.

When to use and time
Use any time after lesson 9A. 30–40 minutes.

Preparation
You will need to play **R9.1** and refer students to R9.1, SB p157.

Procedure

1 a) Remind students of Cate, Maureen and Peter's discussion from lesson 9A. **R9.1** Play the recording. Students listen and do the exercise on their own before checking in pairs. Check answers with the class.

> 1 They can't buy you happiness.
> 2 Because they haven't taken advantage of the opportunities that having money provides.
> 3 He worked hard to buy a home-entertainment system, but wasn't happy with it when he finally got it.
> 4 It can make you feel miserable.
> 5 It can shorten your life expectancy.

b) Play the recording again. Students do the exercise on their own before checking in pairs. Check answers with the class.

> The same word goes in all the gaps: *that*.

2 a)–c) Students discuss the questions in pairs. Check answers with the class.

a) 1 4; 6 2 1; 2; 3; 5

b) Both examples are correct. The linking is closer in ii) where *this* is used, giving the impression that the speaker feels the idea of not having money is more strongly connected to the idea of being able to do things.

c) 1 Yes, she is.
2 The first sentence refers to just one idea in the discussion.
3 Example ii) includes *that* and sounds more natural. In this example, the speaker is referring back to one specific idea in the discussion rather than referring to the main topic that runs through the discussion.

3 Write the first example on the board and refer to the rule discussed in **2b)**. Students then do the exercise on their own before checking in pairs. Check answers with the class.

> 1 that   2 It's   3 That's   4 that's   5 it   6 that

4 Put students into small groups to discuss their answers. Check answers with the class.

> 1 *That* is used more frequently in R9.1 to refer back to an idea that has been previously mentioned in the discussion.
> 2 A strong form.
> 3 *That* used in this way is more common in discussion, where speakers refer to different ideas they have mentioned. *That* is sometimes used to refer back to previously mentioned ideas in narratives, but because narratives tend to be monologues, there is less referring between speakers.

10 Presenting information p198

Aim

To raise awareness of ways of organising information in an explanation.

When to use and time

Use any time after lesson 10C. 30–40 minutes.

Preparation

You will need to play R10.4 and refer students to R10.4, SB p159.

Procedure

1 Remind students of Bruce's ideas on language learning from lesson 10C. R10.4 Play the recording. Students listen and do the exercise on their own before checking in pairs. Check answers with the class. Write answers on the board.

>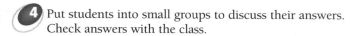
> 2 words   3 sociable   4 professional   5 magazines   6 acquire   7 films   8 effort   9 interact   10 reading and listening

2 **a)–b)** Students work in pairs to predict the order before listening to the recording again. Check answers with the class.

> a)4   b)2   c)5   e)3

3 **a)–b)** Students discuss the answers in pairs. Check answers with the class.

> **a)** 2b)   3e)   4a)   5c)
> **b)** Yes, they do. The general statements for each section are as follows:
> **reading** *What's been really useful for me is reading …*
> **listening** *I also like to listen a lot …*
> **grammar & vocabulary** *… having said that, you know, I do feel I ought to do more grammar exercises …*

4 Give the class your own personal example. Students then work alone making notes before talking in pairs, presenting their explanations. Ask two or three students to share with the class interesting things they found out about other students.

5 Put students into small groups to discuss their answers. Check answers with the class.

> 1 Yes, it is.
> 2 Students should try to listen for key content words that signal a change in topic in longer explanations. For example, when Bruce changes from giving details on classroom experience to the general statement about reading, it helps to listen to the key content word (*reading*) that signals the change.
> 3 Yes, there is flexibility in this way of presenting information. The key point is that fluent speakers usually back up a general statement with some kind of detail to support the general statement.

1 Monologues

 1 **a)** `R1.4` Listen to five people talking about sayings they like. In all the monologues, what is the speaker doing? Choose the best description.

a) describing something and explaining

b) explaining something and narrating

c) discussing something and narrating

b) Do the speakers talk about a personal relationship (P) or a work relationship (W)?

1 Claudia ..P..

2 Chris ....

3 Claire ....

4 Lynn ....

5 Pete ....

2 Listen again and notice how the speakers explain their favourite sayings. Fill in each gap with one word.

1 CLAUDIA It .... that you can't always plan ahead …

2 CHRIS … which kind of ....
.... that the less money you pay …

3 CLAIRE And ....
.... is that if you hang about with …

4 LYNN And ....
.... there's no need to bother …

5 PETE .... , different horses are involved in …

 3 Work in pairs. Answer the questions.

1 What word is used in the explanations by everyone except Claire?

2 What is this word used for in the explanations?

3 If this word is removed, are phrases 1–5 in **2** still grammatically correct?

4 Do you think this word is used more in spoken or written English?

 4 Cross out the example of *basically* which is in the wrong position.

~~basically~~   basically,
1 I'd been awake all/night and/I was exhausted.

basically,
2 So,/we could argue for hours about who said

basically
what, but it was a/misunderstanding.

basically
3 It's quite a/complicated-looking machine and

basically
/the way it works is …

basically
4 It's/a rip-off. Their promises of accountability

basically
and/all that don't mean a thing.

Basically,   basically
5 /What you do first is peel/the potatoes.

basically   basically
6 It's/a good film but I didn't like the/lead actor's

performance.

 5 Work in groups. Discuss these questions.

1 Why can it be useful to think about the type of spoken language that you listen to?

2 What can help you work this out?

3 Will fluent speakers of English use some words that are not common in written English?

4 If you don't understand these words, does it stop you from understanding the speaker?

5 Is it useful to learn these words? Why?/Why not?

6 If you want to find out about these words, what can you do?

HELP WITH LISTENING: PHOTOCOPIABLE

Instructions p182   © Cambridge University Press 2009   **face2face** Advanced Photocopiable

2 Taking part in a conversation

Real Ireland Holidays

1 **a)** **R2.3** Listen to the conversation between Melissa and Brendan. What is Melissa doing? Choose the best description.

a) telling a story and describing something

b) telling a story and explaining something

c) describing and explaining something

b) Read this summary of Melissa's holiday. Find and correct the mistakes.

I went to Ireland last summer expecting to see ~~remote,~~ *lush,* ~~green desolate~~ hills. We thought we would be staying in a lodge that we rented from friends of relatives. It took eight hours of driving in terrible wind to get to where we were staying. The house turned out to be an old run-down cottage. The beach was half an hour's drive away.

2 Listen again. Put words/phrases a)–f) in the correct order. Who says each one: Melissa or Brendan?

a) log cabin ....

b) oh, OK ....

c) but a very stark, modern .... *1 Melissa* ....

d) no rustic charm then ....

e) right, OK ....

f) primitive ....

3 Look at R2.3, p149 in the Student's Book. Read from 'We then arrived very late' to the end. What does Brendan say to:

1 give feedback?

....

2 add information to what Melissa is saying?

....

....

3 sympathise with Melissa?

....

4 Work in pairs. Complete the conversations using the ideas in brackets and language from **3**.

1

A So, by the time I got home it was after midday.

B ¹.................................... (give feedback)

A And I put the key in the door.

B ².................................... (give feedback)

A And I couldn't get it in.

B ³.................................... (add information)

A My flatmate had changed the lock and forgotten to tell me!

B ⁴.................................... (sympathise)

2

A I'd been expecting to go to a really smart restaurant.

B ⁵.................................... (give feedback)

A So I got all dressed up.

B ⁶.................................... (add information)

A And I was looking forward to a great night out.

B ⁷.................................... (give feedback)

A Then I found out we were just going to a cheap and cheerful place down the road.

B ⁸.................................... (sympathise)

5 Work in groups. When you listen to a story that someone is telling you, which of these things should you do? Choose the best answer and say why.

a) listen quietly, and tell the other person what you have understood at the end

b) listen as quietly and politely as possible

c) listen and respond in some way while the other person is talking

3 Leaving things out

 1 **R3.2** Listen to Richard talking about his work. Which personality adjectives best describe the way he sounds? Choose the best description.

a) pleasant but vague
b) arrogant and annoyed
c) confident and calm
d) courteous but cold

2 Tick the true sentences. Correct the false ones.

1 Richard has heard a lot about impostor syndrome.

....

2 He thinks sometimes it's useful to come across as being arrogant.

....

3 He admits that he occasionally makes mistakes.

....

4 He believes that people in the media are afraid of showing doubt.

....

3 **a)** Listen again. Delete or change words/phrases in 1–5 so they are the same as Richard's.

1 No, I hadn't ~~heard of it~~, not until you explained it to me.

2 Why no, I haven't had any experience of it.

3 … I think I'm good enough at my job that most of the time …

4 … when I make a mistake, only *I* realise I've made a mistake.

5 No, I don't think I have this sort of self doubt.

b) Match descriptions a)–e) to 1–5 in **3a**).

a) the past participle and the object are deleted __1__
b) a noun is replaced ......
c) a prepositional phrase is deleted ......
d) a clause is replaced ......
e) a clause is deleted ......

c) What word can be used to replace:

1 a noun? ....
2 a clause? ....

4 Work in pairs. Delete or replace words in the conversations to make them sound more natural. Try to use ideas from **3**.

1
A Have you ever been on TV?
B Yes, I've been on TV once.
A When was that?
B It was a couple of years ago. I was interviewed on the TV news about my work.
A Did you feel nervous?
B No, I don't think I felt nervous. It was only for a regional channel. It wasn't for a national channel.

2
A What are you doing tonight?
B I'm going to the cinema tonight.
A What are you going to see at the cinema?
B I'm going to see the latest James Bond film. Have you seen it?
A No, I haven't seen it.
B Would you like to come to the cinema to see the film?
A Yes, I would like to come to the cinema.

5 Work in pairs. Too much language has been removed from the conversation. Add enough to make it sound more natural.

A Ever wanted to try another job?
B Yes.
A What?
B Teacher.
A Really? Interesting!
B You?
A Photographer.

6 Work in groups. Do you agree with these statements? Why?/Why not?

1 Fluent speakers leave out some words or replace others because they are lazy.
2 It can help your listening if you know what kinds of things fluent speakers leave out or change.
3 As I listen, I should try to focus on all the changes fluent speakers make.
4 If I am listening to a fluent speaker, I can check if I am not sure what they have left out or replaced.

HELP WITH LISTENING: PHOTOCOPIABLE

© Cambridge University Press 2009 **face2face** Advanced Photocopiable

4 Disagreeing

1 **a)** 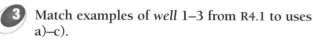 Listen to Dan and Sue discussing reality TV. Choose the best summary of their discussion.

a) Sue thinks reality TV is a fascinating insight into human nature while Dan thinks it is really boring.

b) Sue thinks reality TV is entertaining, while Dan thinks it insults viewers' intelligence.

b) Who talks about these topics first, Sue or Dan?

1 youth culture _Sue_

2 facing challenges ....

3 becoming famous ....

4 costume dramas ....

5 intellectual stimulation ....

2 **a)** Listen again. How do Dan and Sue show that they disagree? Choose the best answer.

a) They use a lot of agreeing and disagreeing expressions in their discussion (e.g. *I don't think I agree with you* ... ; *I'm not sure I share your view* ...).

b) They speak loudly and show their feelings.

c) They constantly introduce new ideas that contradict the other person's ideas.

b) What word do they both use frequently at the beginning of a statement?

3 Match examples of *well* 1–3 from R4.1 to uses a)–c).

1 SUE **Well**, I think it's fun. ....

2 DAN **Well**, I'd like to watch more sport and more comedy, frankly. ....

3 SUE **Well**, each to their own. ....

a) *Well* is used to show the speaker is thinking.

b) *Well* is used as a way to finish off a conversation.

c) *Well* is used to emphasise a point.

4 **a)** Work in pairs. Complete the conversation so that Kim disagrees with Alex. Try to use language from **3**.

ALEX English is a really easy language to learn.

KIM ....

ALEX Well, everyone speaks it, so there are lots of chances to practise.

KIM ....

ALEX I think the grammar is really straightforward.

KIM ....

ALEX And it's not as though there's that much vocabulary to learn.

KIM ....

b) Practise the conversation. Take turns to be Alex and Kim.

5 **a)** Work in groups. Discuss these questions.

When you disagree with someone you know well ...

1 ... is it OK to use direct language?

2 ... what is one possible strategy from Dan and Sue's conversation that you could use?

3 ... will they always say *Well, I don't agree*?

4 ... should you share your own ideas?

b) Do you agree with this statement? Why?/Why not?

"It is often said that *well* is used when a speaker wants to pause to think at the beginning of a sentence."

c) Can you think of or find any other uses of *well*?

d) What aspect of pronunciation helps change the way *well* is used?

Instructions p184

5 Talking about problems and solutions

 a) R5.4 Listen to Claire. What jobs has she thought about or tried?

....

b) Which is the best ending for sentences 1–4: a) or b)?

1 She has been thinking about her future …
   a) only recently. ✓
   b) for a while.

2 The reality of the working world is …
   a) difficult to imagine.
   b) easy to imagine.

3 She has been talking to different people in different jobs …
   a) to find out what's involved with each one.
   b) to find out the pay for each one.

4 She is …
   a) very keen on a publishing career.
   b) considering a publishing career.

2 There are three parts to Claire's conversation. Part 1 begins with 'Not really – it's something …'; part 2 begins with 'Well, recently, I've been …'; part 3 begins with 'Yes and no …'. Listen again and answer these questions.

1 In which part does Claire comment on her actions? ....

2 In which part does Claire talk about problems?

   ....

3 In which part does Claire suggest solutions?

   ....

3 Look at R5.4 on p152 in the Student's Book and read Claire's answers. Answer these questions.

1 What is the first word that Claire uses to indicate there is a problem? ....

2 What is the first word that Claire uses to signal a solution? ....

3 What word does the interviewer use to ask Claire for an evaluation of the solution?

   ....

4 Work in pairs. Look at R5.4 on p153 in the Student's Book and read Will and Charlie's answers. Then answer these questions.

1 Whose extract follows the pattern 'problem > solution > comment'? ....

2 Whose extract changes the pattern and describes the solution before talking about the problem?

   ....

5 Work in pairs. Follow these instructions.

1 Think of a problem you have recently had. It can be something small or important. Make notes on the solution you found for the problem and how effective it was.

2 Take turns to talk about your problem and the solution and then make your comment. Alternatively, you can talk about the solution, then describe the problem and follow up with a comment. Ask follow-up questions.

3 As you listen to your partner, make notes on what they say. When they have finished speaking, tell them what you understood was the problem, solution and comment.

6 Work in groups. Discuss these questions.

1 Do you think people from your country sometimes explain problems in a similar way in their first language?

2 Do you think they do this consciously?

3 How can being aware of this pattern help your understanding of fluent speakers of English?

HELP WITH LISTENING: PHOTOCOPIABLE

6 Asides

 a) [R6.1] Listen to four people talking about strange behaviour. Do they mix narration with a) comment or b) criticism?

b) Complete the table.

person mentioned	strange behaviour
commuter	
	collects pebbles and brings them home

2 Listen again and fill in gaps a)–g).

1 PETE I have a friend called Martina and she owns two rabbits. a) _____ _____ but she's got a habit of taking them …

… to stop the rabbits eating her books. b) _____ _____ is the first time I met her.

2 NATALIE I guess that's what he's looking for, c) _____ _____. And I've sort of …

3 ALEX … to Liverpool Street for ten years d) _____ _____ there was a couple who used … … to get them out and line them up. e) _____ _____.

KEITH That's very strange.

ALEX … to sit there just, ignoring them and nobody, you know, nobody f) _____ nobody would say anything.

4 KEITH Yeah, she wanted to put on different colour socks. g) _____ _____ .

NATALIE Oh no, wow!

 Answer these questions.

1 Is it possible to understand the story without the phrases in gaps a)–g)?

2 Do the phrases in gaps a)–g) add information to the story or do they comment on the story in some way?

3 Do these words show the speakers' reactions, the speakers' spontaneous thoughts or both?

4 What do we call this type of language?

 Work in pairs. Follow these instructions.

1 Think of something interesting or strange that happened to you recently.

2 Tell your partner this story.

3 Listen for the asides in your partner's story.

 Work in groups. Discuss these questions.

1 Do people use asides when they speak in your first language?

2 Is it necessary to try and understand asides when listening to fluent English speakers?

3 In general, do you think the intonation of asides is in a high or low tone?

Instructions p185

7 Opinions

1 **a)** R7.3 Listen to Stefano, Hiltrud and Justyna talking about state intervention. What are they doing? Choose the best description.

a) outlining arguments for and against state intervention

b) responding to different opinions on state intervention

c) stating their own opinions on state intervention

b) Answer these questions.

1 Does Stefano want people to be able to smoke inside?

2 Does he want them to be able to smoke outside?

3 Why does Hiltrud think people should pay for rubbish?

4 What current issue concerning people's lifestyles does Justyna not agree with?

2 **a)** Put these words in the correct order and add punctuation where necessary.

1 STEFANO if / I / that / the / example / state / for / to / basically / ban / smoking / think / intervenes

....

....

2 HILTRUD more / the / in / rubbish / there / of / has / case / to / be / state / clearly / intervention /

....

....

3 JUSTYNA people's / it / to / state / … when / intervening / the / in / comes / lifestyles

....

....

b) Listen and check your answers.

3 **a)** Underline the first four words in each extract in 2. Answer these questions.

1 Do these words introduce the opinion or do they give the opinion?

2 Which phrase is followed by a clause?

3 Which phrases are followed by a noun?

b) Complete the sentences with your own opinions.

1 Genetic modification? I think that, basically,

....

2 When it comes to car ownership,

....

3 In the case of care for the elderly,

....

4 The arts are inadequately funded. I think that, basically, ...

5 When it comes to building new houses,

....

6 In the case of taxes on higher-income earners,

....

4 Work in groups. Follow the instructions.

1 Think of a topic that you feel quite strongly about. Make notes and think of some details and information to back up your opinion.

2 Take turns to share your opinions and respond to your partner's ideas. Try to use the underlined phrases from **2a)**.

3 Make notes about what your partner says. Did you agree with his/her opinion?

Topic ....

Opinion ....

....

Details ....

....

5 Work in groups. Discuss these questions.

1 In a discussion, do fluent speakers normally signal that they are about to give an opinion?

2 How do they do this?

3 Should you do the same when you give an opinion?

© Cambridge University Press 2009 **face2face** Advanced Photocopiable

8 Small words

Hazel Henderson

 a) R8.1 **Listen to the first part of the recording where Eddy speaks about Hazel's background. Tick the true sentences. Correct the false ones.**

1 Eddy admires Hazel Henderson.

2 Hazel was born into a famous family.

3 She was born in the 1930s.

4 She was a hard-working student at school.

5 She left school without any kind of certificate or diploma.

6 She was not content to stay working in a dress shop.

7 Her second job was as a waitress in a hotel.

8 The hotel she worked for transferred her to New York.

9 She met her husband in New York.

b) Listen again and answer these questions.

1 Eddy uses the word *and* frequently. How many times?

2 Eddy uses the word *so* more than once. How many times?

 Match examples 1–5 to uses a)–e).

1 One person that I think is very inspirational is a woman called Hazel Henderson **and** the reason her story has struck me … __c)__

2 … her story has struck me **so** strongly … _____

3 She was born before the Second World War **and** she had a very typical upbringing … _____

4 **So**, she took a job in a hotel as a receptionist … _____

5 … **and** then realised that because hotels are around the world … _____

a) *And* is used to join two phrases or clauses together.

b) *And* introduces the next event in a narrative.

c) *And* is used to introduce a new topic or new information in a narrative.

d) *So* is used to make an adverb or an adjective stronger and means *very*.

e) *So* is used to introduce the result of a previously mentioned idea.

 Match examples 1–12 to uses a)–e) in 2.

…married, had a family. [1]**And** one day she noticed that her, her young child who would play every day in a, in a local park in New York was covered in soot [2]**and** in fact it was quite typical that she would come home very dirty, [3]**and** she'd have to put her in a bath [4]**and** scrub her to, to get this dirt off her. [5]**So**, she went to investigate where the soot was coming from [6]**and** saw that all of the equipment in the, the playground was covered in soot. [7]**And** the reason for this was because the, the quality of the air in New York was [8]**so** poor from the pollution of the cars [9]**and** also there were lots [10]**and** lots of incinerators that burnt rubbish. [11]**So**, she started to talk to some of the other mothers whose children played in the park [12]**and** they also saw this was a, a problem.

1 _c)_   2 _____   3 _____   4 _____   5 _____   6 _____
7 _____   8 _____   9 _____   10 _____   11 _____   12 _____

 Work in groups. Discuss these questions.

1 In general, how are the words *and* and *so* used in Hazel's life story?

2 Is it useful to listen for these words? Why?/Why not?

3 What can we do to help remember all these different meanings?

Instructions p187

9 Different uses of *that*

 a) **R9.1** Listen to Cate, Maureen and Peter talking about money. Answer these questions.

1 What is Maureen's attitude towards possessions?

2 Why doesn't she have any sympathy for rich people who aren't happy?

3 What was the problem with the man Peter knows who worked in the money markets?

4 How does Cate describe the feeling of being without any money?

5 Maureen suggests that living in a poor country can have a negative effect. What is that effect?

b) Listen again. Fill in the gaps in these extracts from the conversation.

MAUREEN   I know a lot of people say ¹_____ , Cate, but then they're thinking of …

MAUREEN   So, in ²_____ way, I think money really can buy you happiness.

CATE   You mean, if you don't have to worry about money, ³_____ in itself allows you to do some things ⁴_____ might contribute towards your happiness. Is ⁵_____ what you're saying, Maureen?

PETER   Well, what about things ⁶_____ don't necessarily take a lot of money …

 a) Work in pairs. Discuss these questions.

1 In which examples in **1b)** is *that* used as a relative pronoun?

2 In which examples is *that* used to refer back to an idea previously mentioned?

b) Look at these examples. Are both correct? In which example is the idea of 'not having to worry about money' linked more closely to the idea of 'allowing someone to do things'?

i) If you don't have to worry about money, **that** in itself allows you to do some of the things …

ii) If you don't have to worry about money, **this** in itself allows you to do some of the things …

c) Look at examples i) and ii) then answer questions 1–3.

i) that in itself allows you to do some of the things that might contribute towards your happiness. Is **it** what you're saying, Maureen?

ii) that in itself allows you to do some of the things that might contribute towards your happiness. Is **that** what you're saying, Maureen?

1 In the first sentence of both i) and ii), is Cate rephrasing something that Maureen has said?

2 Is the topic of the first sentence the topic of the whole discussion or just one idea in the discussion?

3 Which example sounds more natural, i) or ii)?

 Choose the best words in this extract from the second half of the conversation.

CATE   As I said earlier, I think we need *some* money. I would agree with ¹*this/that*. Yeah. And not having money can really make you miserable but …

PETER   Yeah, I've been there, worrying about where the next penny's coming from. ²*That's/It's* no joke. So yes, money can free you from worries, but the question was, can it buy you happiness? ³*This is/That's* different.

MAUREEN   For me it isn't. And it's like when they say money can't buy you health – well, ⁴*it's/that's* not true, either. You just have to look at how long people live in poor countries. I can't remember where it was, but I recently read about a place where the average life expectancy is 40 something.

PETER   I'm with you on that one.

MAUREEN   And when they say money can't buy you love? Again I think ⁵*that/it* can sometimes.

CATE   Oh, I don't know about ⁶*that/this*!

 Work in groups. Discuss these questions.

1 *That* can be used to refer back to an idea previously mentioned or as a relative pronoun. How is *that* more frequently used in R9.1?

2 Used in this way, do you think *that* will usually be pronounced with a strong or a weak form?

3 Do you think you are more likely to hear *that* used in this way in narratives or discussions?

10 Presenting information

1 **R10.4** Listen to Bruce talking about his experience of learning languages. Fill in each gap with one word.

> Grammar + Vocabulary
> - grammar ¹ _exercises_ help understand rules
> - use a dictionary + keep record of high-frequency ² _____
>
> Classroom experience
> - ³ _____ learning environment
> - instruction from a ⁴ _____
>
> Reading
> - range of ⁵ _____, novels, newspapers
> - helps you to ⁶ _____ new grammar + vocabulary
>
> Listening
> - CDs, iPod + ⁷ _____ but not dubbed ones
> - takes time + ⁸ _____
>
> Learning outside the classroom
> - ⁹ _____ with people
> - do ¹⁰ _____ by yourself

2 **a)** Work in pairs. Put the extracts a)–e) from what Bruce says in the correct order.

a) I think once you've got to an advanced level, you need to leave the classroom behind, really. I mean, language learning doesn't stop there. ......

b) I think when starting out, I found the classroom experience very helpful. ......

c) … there's a whole load of things to learn, but you have to go out and do it by yourself. ......

d) Yes, I've tried to learn various languages at different points in my life, including French, Italian, Mandarin and Arabic, all with rather different levels of success. _1_

e) I enjoy the sort of, the sociable nature of learning in a group, and being instructed by, by you know, a professional. ......

b) Listen again and check.

3 **a)** Match descriptions 1–5 to sentences a)–e) in **2a)**.

1 General statement about learning languages _d)_

2 General statement about classroom experience ......

3 Detailed statement about classroom experience ......

4 General statements about learning outside the classroom ......

5 Detailed statement about learning outside the classroom ......

b) Look at R10.4 on p159 in the Student's Book. Do the sections on reading, listening, and grammar and vocabulary follow a similar pattern of a general initial statement followed by more details?

4 Work in pairs. Follow the instructions.

1 Think about a learning experience you have had, not related to languages.

2 Make notes on something you did that was successful and helped you learn.

3 Think of some advice you would give to another person trying to learn the same thing.

4 Explain your learning experience and give advice to your partner.

5 Work in groups. Discuss these questions.

1 Bruce's explanation moves from giving general information to more detailed information. When fluent speakers explain or describe an experience, is this a typical way of presenting information?

2 What kinds of words should you listen for in this kind of explanation?

3 Is it possible that fluent speakers will give details and then follow up with a general, summarising statement?

Instructions p188

Progress Tests

Instructions

The Progress Tests (p204–p223) are designed to be used after students have completed each unit of the Student's Book. Each Progress Test checks students' knowledge of the key language areas taught in the unit. The final exercise of each Progress Test also tests students' knowledge of language taught in previous units. It is helpful for students to have done the Review section at the end of each unit before doing a Progress Test. You can also encourage students to revise for the test by reviewing the relevant Language Summary in the back of the Student's Book and by doing exercises for that unit on the CD-ROM and in the Workbook. Note that Progress Test 5 also reviews items from Units 1–4, and Progress Test 10 reviews items from the whole of the Student's Book.

- Allow students 40 minutes for Progress Tests 1–4 and 6–9, and 60 minutes for Progress Tests 5 and 10. You may wish to adjust this time depending on your class.

- Photocopy one test for each student. Students should do the tests on their own. You can either check the answers with the whole class at the end of the test or collect in the tests and correct them yourself. Keep a record of the test scores to help you monitor individual students' progress and for report writing at the end of the course.

- Progress Tests can also be given as homework for general revision.

Listening Tests

There is a listening section in Progress Tests 5 and 10 only. The corresponding recording scripts (R5.9 and R10.5) are in the Answer Key for the tests. Both R5.9 and R10.5 have two separate sections. Focus on one section of the recording at a time. Allow students time to read through the questions for that section in the Progress Test before you start. Play that section of the recording without stopping and allow students to answer the questions. Then play the recording again without stopping. Repeat this procedure for the other section.

Answer Key and Recording Scripts

Progress Test 1 p204

1   (2 marks each) 2 chatting her up 3 overheard
    4 butt in 5 wittering on 6 chatting 7 had a row
    8 will bicker 9 gossip

2   2 in 3 out of 4 out of 5 on 6 In 7 on 8 in 9 out of
    10 on

3   (2 marks each) 2 Once bitten, twice shy 3 Nothing
    ventured, nothing gained. 4 Rome wasn't built in a day.
    5 Don't make a mountain out of a molehill. 6 better
    late than never 7 One man's meat is another man's
    poison

4   (4 marks each) 2 spoke; was 3 have been going; have
    decided 4 went; were 5 hasn't had; changed 6 've been
    peeling; 've ruined 7 Has … done; has … been staring

5   2 during the last couple of weeks 3 On Saturday
    4 last night 5 Since 6 this term 7 Over the past few
    months 8 during the lesson

6   (2 marks each) 2 What makes me angry is when
    people show no respect for others. 3 It was in 2007
    that things started going wrong for Tom. 4 The person
    who left me these paintings was my great-grandmother.
    5 What happened was that the weather worsened when
    they reached the summit. 6 It wasn't until Will was 40
    that he left home. 7 It was Stuart I liked the best.

7   2 is 3 which 4 means 5 What 6 trying 7 in 8 it
    9 way 10 put 11 simply

8   3 ✓ 4 ✓ 5 since you **gave** 6 **out of** necessity
    7 **have** ever had 8 ✓ 9 I've **spoken** 10 It's **her**
    11 didn't come **was** 12 ✓

Progress Test 2 p206

1   (2 marks each) 2 bitterly disappointed 3 highly
    unlikely 4 distinctly remember 5 thoroughly enjoys
    6 firmly believed

2   (2 marks each) 2 in a charming rustic stone cottage
    3 some amazing old white houses with tiny windows
    4 a small ancient temple 5 some wonderful tiny black
    olives 6 some delicious traditional fish soup

3   2 cosmopolitan 3 meandering 4 diverse 5 rugged
    6 unique 7 golden

4   2 who 3 whose 4 – 5 where 6 which 7 – 8 who

5   (2 marks each) 2 … know the woman Tom's chatting
    to? 3 … the file you were looking for? 4 … Ben
    accused of? 5 … the party she was invited to.
    7 The family with whom we stayed were extremely
    hospitable. 8 James was unhappy about the story on
    which he was working. 9 Kate works with people in
    whom she has no interest. 10 That is the experiment
    to which I referred earlier.

6   (2 marks each) 2 the best of which 3 all of which
    4 both of whom 5 neither of which 6 none of whom

7   (2 marks each) 2 Having opened 3 opened 4 Opening
    5 Writing 6 writing 7 written 8 Having written

8   (2 marks each) 2 Cooked 3 Not wanting to 4 Not
    having lived 5 Going 6 Shot in black and white
    7 Having no food 8 Having walked 9 Looking through

9   3 ✓ 4 ✓ 5 **which/that** everyone 6 with **whom** 7 **at**
    which point 8 **which** I haven't got 9 **Having told** a lie
    10 ✓ 11 a **stunning large red** balloon 12 in touch
    with 13 ✓

Progress Test 3 p208

1   (2 marks each) 2 trusting; gullible 3 thrifty; tight-
    fisted 4 meticulous; finicky 5 generous; extravagant
    6 spontaneous; impetuous 7 courageous; reckless
    8 determined; obstinate

2 (2 marks each) 2 going down with something
3 going around 4 picked up 5 is blocked up 6 come
out in 7 to put me on 8 'll get over

3 2 economical with 3 better days 4 under … weather
5 on … bit 6 the times 7 of … handful 8 hard …
hearing 9 challenging 10 on … chilly side

4 (2 marks each) 2 wonder that 3 to understand
4 not a book 5 can't stand it when 6 it difficult to
7 concerned most of us to hear 8 appears that
9 It's obvious

5 (2 marks each) 2 Have you any idea why Jenny took
your bike? 3 I can't remember what I did with my
keys. 4 Mark asked me if I belonged to a gym.
5 I wonder why Paul didn't go to the party.
6 Look! Here comes the sun! 7 Neither can I.

6 (2 marks each) 2 Only once have I broken 3 Under
no circumstances will I support 4 Not for a minute did
I think 5 Only when … did he begin to 6 Not only
was Eva overworking 7 Seldom has there been

7 2 better 3 sort 4 Unfortunately 5 suits 6 better
7 could 8 with 9 bit 10 go 11 on 12 side 13 Quite
14 planning

8 3 like **it** that 4 **It's** no good 5 nor **does she enjoy**
6 ✓ 7 is it **we are** 8 **Trying not** to 9 in **which** case
10 What I like **is** 11 **Have you enrolled** on 12 ✓

Progress Test 4 p210

1 (2 marks each) 2 suing 3 made 4 received 5 to seek
6 is holding 7 will make/hit

2 2 man 3 pestilence(s) 4 huge 5 developments
6 village 7 enjoy 8 land 9 kids 10 rural inhabitants
11 villagers 12 entire

3 (2 marks each) 2 'll have been married 3 'll be
4 are going 5 gets 6 arrive 7 'll pick 8 'll be going

4 2 I'll be cooking 3 will have lived 4 leaves 5 is going
to fall 6 starts 7 won't be meeting 8 won't have
finished 9 are you doing 10 will always print

5 (2 marks each) 2 are unlikely to use 3 is set to do
4 is due to star 5 am not about to cook 6 is on the
verge of taking over 7 is sure to be 8 is bound to have
9 are likely to want 10 is on the brink of completing

6 (2 marks each) 2 was supposed to be 3 was to meet
4 would have 5 was about to leave 6 were not going
to worry 7 were going to be 8 wasn't supposed to hit
9 was just about to burst 10 were going to enjoy
11 wouldn't do 12 would have to be

7 3 ✓ 4 to **run** the victim's 5 **is** likely to 6 exam **the
following day** 7 **huge** problems 8 are **to** face
9 will **have finished** 10 find **it** hard 11 ✓ 12 **really**
furious 13 neither **do** I like 14 the best of **which**
15 ✓ 16 **having slept** very badly

Progress Test 5 p212

R5.9 See p199 for Listening Test instructions.

1

a) INTERVIEWER So, Theresa, you must be happy that your
exhibition is opening next week.

THERESA In some ways, yes, I am. It's great to see the
result of all my months of painting, but at this
stage I don't know how people will respond to my
work. The critics have always been enthusiastic
about it, but until I see it hanging up and being
enjoyed by others, then I'm stressed. This
exhibition might be compared unfavourably
with my previous ones, and if that happens, it's
tempting to think, that people have lost their
judgement but …

I Being a painter is a very insecure way of earning
a living, isn't it?

T Yes, it is. I mean, I'm now quite well known and
I earn a living from it, but for many painters it's
not like that. It's hard to get yourself recognised in
the art world. We've all had to work out our own
individual ways of reaching our goals and have
all had to give up going to restaurants or having
holidays, but not to paint would be unthinkable.

b) JOE I'm glad we're both going to university. I think
it'll be great.

TIM Yeah, me too. I mean, university is about people
as well as what you learn there, isn't it? It gives
you opportunities you'd never have otherwise.
And with a bit of luck you come out with a better
understanding of what you want in life and who
you are. I really want to do medicine, but whether
I turn out to be a surgeon like my father remains
to be seen.

J How long's your course?

T Five years, but then I have to do a year of
postgraduate training before I'm a registered
doctor. The cost of it all will be pretty massive,
but it's an investment. I know it's what I want to
do, so I'm prepared to put everything into it.
Everyone's told me it's intense and you don't have
much time to socialise – at least at the beginning,
which might not be that much fun.

J Sounds a bit scary to me.

2

First of all, let me tell you a bit about myself and how I
became a pilot. Well, I've had a varied career but my
present job as a commercial airline pilot is the best one I've
had. I fly passengers and cargo all round the world and see
some amazing places. Being a pilot requires a great deal of
technical knowledge and I've always been fascinated by
engines. In fact, that's what made me go for this job. That
and the fact that I knew I had to make a decision about my
working life. I'd been a secretary, a waitress and finally a
fitness instructor, which I enjoyed, but just wasn't very
exciting, so I began to explore the idea of becoming a pilot.

The more I thought about it, the keener I was to do it and get started on the training. Some of the theoretical bits of the flying exams I was able to do through a mixture of distance learning and classroom-based courses at a flying school in Scotland. And obviously I had to build up my flying hours in order to get my licence.

I work for a large airline that does both short- and long-haul flights. The advantage of flying to somewhere far away means that you get two days there to look around and recover before flying back to Heathrow Airport where we're based, and for me that's much better, even though if you're only flying from Heathrow to Madrid and back you can be home and sleeping in your own bed the same night.

Before a flight, I need to be at Heathrow at least 90 minutes before take-off as there are a series of things we need to do on the ground before boarding the plane 45 minutes before departure. With my first officer, I check the flight plan and make sure there aren't any changes to normal procedure. One thing we can never be sure of, of course, is the weather. Naturally, we have to take it into account before take-off.

There's often time to chat with the guys on the flight deck when we're up at cruising height. I know them all quite well now. Unlike me, they all have families so the conversation is usually about them. I must say crew catering is not exciting. We often don't get what the passengers get and I don't eat the same food as my co-pilot – just in case.

Up in the air, we constantly have to monitor all the instruments, and we have to be prepared to alter course if necessary. It's inevitable that on some flights we will encounter turbulence which passengers can find alarming, but it's not necessarily anything to worry about. Storms, on the other hand, can be very hazardous, and we keep away from them.

Then when we arrive at our destination …

1 (2 marks each) 1a) 2b) 3c) 4b)

2 (2 marks each) 2 fitness instructor 3 distance learning 4 long(-)haul/long 5 45 minutes 6 the weather 7 food 8 turbulence

3 2 inter 3 counter 4 under 5 pseudo 6 over 7 semi 8 under

4 2 make 3 not to take 4 being 5 working 6 to find 7 to apply 8 not doing 9 having 10 to focus 11 living 12 to finance 13 have to

5 (2 marks each) 2 doing; carrying out 3 have; get 4 did; got 5 took; sat 6 do; get

6 (2 marks each) 2 eyes in 3 career ladder 4 stuck … rut 5 dead-end 6 against … clock 7 high-powered 8 self-employed 9 take … easy 10 team player

7 2 – 3 myself 4 himself 5 ourselves 6 yourselves 7 itself 8 – 9 yourself 10 – 11 themselves

8 2 Ann 3 All 4 saying 5 with 6 on 7 Not 8 mention 9 By 10 about 11 got 12 there

9 3 to **each other** 4 snowed **under** 5 ✓ 6 with **her** 7 **on** a regular basis 8 I'll **be lying** 9 her **charming Spanish** 10 **put** you on 11 ✓ 12 **has it** become

Progress Test 6 p214

1 2 top 3 branch 4 plain 5 heavy 6 odd 7 flat 8 heavy 9 branch 10 flat 11 plain 12 top

2 (2 marks each) 2 take it or leave it 3 pick and choose 4 in leaps and bounds 5 sick and tired 6 over and over again 7 on and off 8 part and parcel 9 hit and miss

3 (2 marks each) 2 did … drag 3 hissed 4 to storm out 5 leapt up 6 nudged 7 Grabbing

4 2 deal 3 than 4 more 5 better 6 less 7 as 8 nowhere 9 no 10 not 11 as

5 (2 marks each) 2 pretty much the same as 3 loads more people than 4 decidedly less safe than 5 way higher than 6 somewhat smaller than 7 anywhere near as funny as 8 marginally more expensive than

6 (2 marks each) 2 reasonably 3 badly 4 well 5 lately 6 high 7 temporarily 8 academically 9 happy

7 (2 marks each) 2 I'll probably go; there any more 3 ✓; has always been 4 the violin beautifully; ✓ 5 completely mystifying; doesn't quite 6 ✓; even enjoy

8 3 I've **hardly spoken** 4 ✓ 5 house **more** or less 6 **highly** qualified 7 ✓ 8 **talk** shop 9 **team** player 10 **would** be taken up 11 ✓ 12 went on **to found** 11 to **issue** a press release

Progress Test 7 p216

1 (2 marks each) 2 got away with 3 getting at 4 got into 5 got round 6 get through to 7 get his own back on

2 2 onset 3 breakdown 4 get-together 5 Kick-off 6 downpour 7 outlook 8 outcry

3 2 fly 3 bright 4 freeze 5 flood 6 warm 7 grill 8 dawn

4 (2 marks each) 2 wash; shrinks 3 might have come; had 4 hadn't parked; wouldn't have got 5 won; I'd 6 is; 'll have

5 (2 marks each) 2 the river to rise; would be flooded 3 wouldn't be; had slept 4 had planned; wouldn't be panicking 5 the performance be cancelled 6 didn't have; would have come 7 we not called; wouldn't be

6 (2 marks each) 2 has been practised 3 was known 4 is credited 5 was taken 6 has been found 7 is done 8 are choreographed 9 be completed 10 will be enjoyed

7 (2 marks each) 2 is expected to be 3 was believed to have been destroyed 4 is … argued 5 is thought to be making 6 is rumoured to be leaving 7 has been predicted that 8 are estimated to be over 10,000 people going

8 2 falling 3 falling 4 rising 5 falling 6 falling

9 3 found **to be false** 4 ✓ 5 **wouldn't** go 6 **There** appears 7 the same **as** 8 **probably won't** be 9 ✓ 10 occupy **myself**

Progress Test 8 p218

1 (2 marks each) 2 found time 3 had time to spare
4 are … giving me a hard time 5 took his time over
6 have no time for

2 (2 marks each) 2 Whoever left the door unlocked
mustn't do it again. 3 Whatever you've done, I forgive
you. 4 However hard I practise, I will never become
a great guitarist. 5 Wherever he goes, Rob takes lots of
photos. 6 Whoever told you about Emma is wrong.
7 Whenever I see Anya she's always smiling.
8 Whichever number you ring, you'll get through to
me. 9 Please ask for the name and address of whoever
phones. 10 However did you manage to carry all that
shopping home! 11 I tried to include whatever was
relevant in my essay. 12 Just buy whichever of them
you like.

3 2 widely 3 widen 4 rationally 5 rationalise
6 disturbance 7 remarkable 8 courageous 9 possibility
10 sympathetic 11 survival 12 dependent/dependable
13 failure 14 talented 15 pride 16 cowardly 17 division
18 happiness 19 recovery 20 creative 21 excitement

4 (2 marks each) 2 was watching 3 hadn't chosen
4 could remember 5 I had 6 had brought
7 would stop

5 2 hadn't 3 didn't/wouldn't 4 could 5 had 6 would
7 weren't 8 doesn't 9 won't/don't 10 did 11 don't

6 (2 marks each) 2 stay 3 to stop 4 to do 5 I didn't
cook 6 we went 7 you'd asked 8 Jo decided 9 she
thought

7 3 **There's** no time 4 whichever **of** our 5 sooner **book**
6 ✓ 7 the government **listened** 8 sounded **strange**
9 ✓ 10 is **understood** 11 ✓ 12 ✓

Progress Test 9 p220

1 2 cost a fortune 3 cost-effective 4 priceless 5 price tags
6 overpriced 7 reasonably priced

2 2 led 3 conscious 4 proof 5 free 6 minded 7 ish
8 related

3 (2 marks each) 2 economic superpower
3 gender discrimination 4 mass-produced
5 record levels 6 earth's resources 7 economic growth
8 renewable energy

4 (2 marks each) 2 is going 3 has been sending 4 stayed
5 went 6 doesn't know 7 speak 8 has been camping
9 heard 10 was setting 11 hasn't visited 12 's enjoying
13 doesn't want

5 (2 marks each) 2 do … come 3 expect 4 'm having
5 looks 6 are … seeing 7 are coming 8 'm expecting
9 is looking 10 have

6 2 the 3 – 4 the 5 a 6 the 7 a 8 an 9 an 10 an 11 –
12 the 13 –

7 2 one 3 one 4 a 5 little 6 quite a few 7 Very few

8 2 leaving that aside for a moment 3 First of all
4 To go back to 5 So to sum up 6 let's move on to
7 And finally

9 3 I **weigh** 60 kg 4 ✓ 5 the **housing** market 6 in
hospital 7 rather **live** 8 ✓ 9 I **didn't** find

Progress Test 10 p222

[R10.5] See p199 for Listening Test instructions.

1

INTERVIEWER Colin, this TV series you've made, it's all about
singing, isn't it?

COLIN Yes, we wanted to show how wonderful singing with
other people is and how much fun it is. In fact, singing
in the UK is second only to sport in the number of
people involved in it. Someone's estimated that there
are over 25,000 choirs and half a million singers in this
country. That shouldn't really be a surprise. It is, after
all, a free and immediate way to get across what you're
feeling. It improves your fitness – it increases lung
capacity and gives you better posture. And nothing
beats the sheer joy you get from singing with a group
of friends.

I   And for the programme you trained a group of novice
singers to sing in a choir.

C   Right. We called ourselves Abacus, and the series
follows the choir's progress from the auditions through
rehearsals up to our performance in the competition
'Champion Choir'.

I   And how did you do?

C   Well, I don't want to give too much away, but
we did very well. The singers' timing improved hugely,
as did their confidence. But what's given me the most
pleasure is the fact that many of them say that singing
is a necessary part of their lives now. You know, I've
always worked with professional musicians, and these
people aren't. They've got jobs and busy lives outside
singing, so working with them in the choir was a great
experience for me.

I   Can everybody sing?

C   Ahhh, yes we can all sing in that we've all got the
physical equipment to do it. As children we do it
naturally but we can't seem to keep that up, you know,
singing with the same freedom and lack of
embarrassment. The other day, for example, I asked
this 30-year-old guy to sing a line from his favourite
song and, like most people, he tried to sing it in the
style of the artist who'd recorded it. When I eventually
got him to sing something in his own real voice, he
clearly felt as if he'd revealed a side of himself that was
meant to be private. But that's what you have to do –
and it's scary.

I   So what is it about singing in a choir that's so good?

C   I guess if you asked most choral singers they'd say you
can hide better in a group. It's not the end of the world
if you sing a wrong note, as the collective sound will

probably drown it. When you're in a choir, you get to sing lots of different kinds of music – some of it may not be to your own personal taste but somehow when you're doing it in a group, it doesn't seem to matter as much. The job of singing takes over.

I   And what about you? Do you have any plans for future choirs?

C   Yes, I want to form a choir of teenagers. Now with them, I know I won't be able to get away with the methods I've adopted with Abacus. People tell me they won't listen to me but I'm confident we'll be able to work together. What the end result will be is anyone's guess, but it'll be exciting.

2

Speaker 1
To be honest, I haven't worked out how I feel yet and what might happen – a new career perhaps? I only sent it in because Dave made me. It was one of a series I'd taken of water on our holiday last year and it was quite an unusual interpretation according to the judges. Dave thinks my success is all down to him. Maybe there wasn't much competition – who knows?

Speaker 2
I only took it up so I could play something with my kids. They'd learnt it at school but I had to start from scratch, and it's not easy. At first, it took me ages to remember the rules about how each piece can move and I was very hesitant, which must have annoyed everyone. So I think it's quite a triumph to win a prize at my age – I beat loads of younger people. My kids can't believe it.

Speaker 3
I was stuck for what to do for my end-of-year project at college. Then I happened to see a photo in a magazine of a woman wearing an interesting dress and I thought I could use that and add my own touches to it. I've never told anyone that's what I did. It's not something you boast about, especially after it won a prize and was seen by everyone in college. As a result of winning, my future is looking full of promise.

Speaker 4
I was reading a magazine in the garden one day and came across the competition. I'd had some things swirling about in my head for ages so I just put it all down and sent it off. I'd no idea whether it was any good or not so imagine how I felt when I saw it printed in a magazine a few months later. Nobody had told me I'd won so I rang them up and asked them to send me any comments from the judges because I thought it would be useful to know what they thought.

1   (2 marks each) 1b) 2a) 3a) 4b) 5c)

2   (2 marks each) 1d) 2b) 3a) 4e) 5f) 6b) 7e) 8c)

3   2 clear 3 strong 4 dark 5 rough 6 gentle 7 sour 8 weak 9 opaque 10 patterned 11 heavy

4   2 was 3 are 4 are 5 is 6 was 7 is 8 were 9 is 10 were 11 is

5   (2 marks each) 2 should have told 3 was able to fix 4 didn't need to work 5 will try 6 wouldn't come 7 should/ought to go 8 mustn't/can't/aren't allowed to smoke 9 had to send 10 needn't have got up 11 could swim

6   (2 marks each) 2 must have got 3 might be working 4 may have forgotten 5 must be 6 wouldn't have known 7 can't have left 8 'll be lying 9 could be switched 10 shouldn't be

7   3 **low** building 4 ✓ 5 you **to** give 6 ✓ 7 ✓ 8 What **happens is** 9 **economic** decline 10 but **do you see** 11 in **plenty of** time 12 **did he realise** how cold 13 ✓ 14 for **myself** 15 **As a rule** I buy/the market **as a rule** 16 ✓ 17 will **have been** 18 ✓

PROGRESS TESTS: ANSWER KEY

Progress Test 1 40 minutes

Name .... Score │100│

 1 Fill in the gaps with the correct form of these verbs.

> ~~grumble~~ gossip butt in overhear have a row
> witter on chat her up bicker chat

1 Anna never _grumbles_ about all the extra work she has to do.
2 Luke thought Claire looked gorgeous and spent all evening ....
3 On the train yesterday, Jo .... a woman talking about losing her job.
4 David, you can't just .... when someone else is talking!
5 I couldn't stop .... about my cat even though nobody looked interested.
6 Andrea had a great time at the party .... to an old friend.
7 After Mike and his mother .... , they didn't speak for days.
8 Give *both* kids a toy to play with otherwise they .... about it all morning.
9 I find it hurtful when people .... about me.

│16│

2 Fill in the gaps with *in*, *on* or *out of*.

1 I'm _on_ good terms with my ex-boss.
2 My enthusiasm for exercise goes .... phases.
3 The demonstration gradually got .... control and became a riot.
4 I'm completely .... my depth when it comes to discussing philosophy.
5 Jo and Sam found it hard to agree as they were not .... the same wavelength.
6 .... the long run it's better to be honest.
7 I see my grandma three times a week .... average.
8 Shani doesn't have much .... common with her work colleagues.
9 Ian corrects everything his wife says .... habit.
10 Did Natalie say those hurtful things .... purpose?

│9│

3 Fill in the gaps with the complete sayings.

> ~~Actions speak ...~~ Rome wasn't ... Better late ...
> Don't make a mountain ... Once bitten, ...
> One man's meat ... Nothing ventured, ...

1 John's promises sound good, but _actions speak louder than words_ , don't you think?
2 Emma's not going rock-climbing again after her bad experience. .... , she says.
3 Ben was anxious about asking Gina out but then he thought ".."
4 You have to learn some basic cooking techniques before you tackle a four-course meal for 30 people. Remember, ...
5 Why are you so worried? They were only cheap. You can easily get another pair of gloves.
....
6 Ah, ... What kept you? We've been waiting ages.
7 Modern art does nothing for me but Tim really loves it. .... , I guess.

│12│

 4 Complete the sentences with the correct form of the verbs in brackets. Use the **Present Perfect** or **Past Simple**.

1 What time _did_ you _have_ (have) dinner, or _haven't you eaten_ (not eat)?
2 The last time I .... (speak) to Kate she .... (be) really excited about going abroad.
3 James and Nikki .... (go) out for ages and now they .... (decide) to get married.
4 We .... (go) swimming every day when we .... (be) on holiday.
5 Dan .... (not have) much exercise since he .... (change) jobs last month.
6 I'm crying because I .... (peel) onions. I bet I .... (ruin) my make-up.
7 Look at Paul! .... he .... (do) any work today or .... he .... (stare) out of the window all morning?

│24│

Choose the correct time expressions.

1 Nobody's given me any feedback *last week* / *up to now*.

2 Lucy's been away a lot *during the last couple of weeks* / *two weeks ago*.

3 *On Saturday* / *This is the first time* Erica played tennis with us.

4 Why didn't you phone me *last night* / *so far*?

5 *Once* / *Since* Dimitri came to this country, he's been learning the language.

6 How much have you done *this term* / *yet*?

7 *Over the past few months* / *In 2005* Mark has lived in Spain.

8 Kenji was ill *during the lesson* / *until now*. `7`

 Rewrite these sentences starting with the words in brackets.

1 Eva falls asleep in front of the TV every night. (What) *What Eva does is fall asleep in front of the TV every night.*

2 It makes me angry when people show no respect for others. (What) _____

3 In 2007, things started going wrong for Tom. (It) _____

4 My great-grandmother left me these paintings. (The person) _____

5 The weather worsened when they reached the summit. (What happened) _____

6 Will didn't leave home until he was 40. (It) _____

7 I liked Stuart the best. (It) _____ `12`

7 **Fill in the gaps in the teacher's welcoming speech with these words.**

| ~~what~~ means which way simply in is it |
| put trying what |

Welcome to the pottery course. Before we start, I'd like to run through some things with you. As you can see, the room is quite small and ¹ *what* that means ² _____ we all have to work tidily. Unfortunately, we don't have enough wheels for all of you to be working at the same time, ³ _____ basically ⁴ _____ that you'll have to take it in turns.

Now, clay. Take some from the bench. If you don't like what you make, please don't put the clay back on the bench. It goes in the bin by the door. ⁵ _____ I'm ⁶ _____ to say is it's important not to mix up new and old clay. Clay must be kept in a workable condition, ⁷ _____ other words, don't let it get too dry. Making a pot on a wheel can take a bit of practice, or to put ⁸ _____ another ⁹ _____ , don't expect miracles too soon. Health and safety rules in a pottery studio are complicated, but to ¹⁰ _____ it ¹¹ _____ , work tidily. Anyway, let's get started. `10`

8 **Tick the correct sentences. Change the incorrect ones.**

1 Sometimes it's uncomfortable to make ~~an~~ eye contact with a stranger.

2 What I mean by that is it's better not to discuss it until you know the facts. ✓

3 When you travel, you come into contact with all kinds of interesting people.

4 We can go for a walk after we've had our meal.

5 I've worn this jumper a lot since you've given it to me.

6 Kate emigrated not from choice but in necessity.

7 This particular dictionary is the best one I ever had.

8 As soon as I heard the news, I rang my mum.

9 I'll email you once I spoke to Matt.

10 It's she that wrote it – not me.

11 The reason why Elliot didn't come is because he was ill.

12 The thing I love most about Jack is his optimism. `10`

Progress Test 2 40 minutes

Name .... Score 100

1 Fill in the gaps with words from both boxes.

| absolutely distinctly |
| firmly highly |
| thoroughly bitterly |

| impossible remember |
| disappointed believed |
| unlikely enjoys |

1 It's _absolutely impossible_ for Adam to come.
2 Matt was .... by his team's defeat.
3 It's .... that we'll ever have a better holiday.
4 I .... the first time I saw Niagara Falls.
5 Joe .... his job as a pilot.
6 Jane's father .... that she would succeed in her career. [10]

2 Put the words in the correct order.

On our holidays we stayed

1 an / Greek / idyllic / on / island
   on an idyllic Greek island

2 stone / a / charming / in / cottage / rustic
   ....

we saw

3 houses / some / white / with tiny windows / old / amazing
   ....

4 ancient / a / temple / small
   ....

and we ate

5 black / some / wonderful / olives / tiny
   ....

6 fish / soup / traditional / delicious / some
   .... [10]

3 Complete these adjectives.

Are you searching for an ¹ _unspoilt_ region of the United Kingdom? Try one of the islands off the west coast of Scotland! They are a world away from the ²c........... life of the capital city, Edinburgh. There's not much to do on them except follow the ³m........... paths around the coast and marvel at the ⁴d........... population of seabirds. There is a great variety of scenery to enjoy. Some of the coastline of the Isle of Rum, for example, is quite ⁵r..........., whereas other parts are more gentle. The local people believe their ⁶u........... landscape with its ⁷g........... beaches and spectacular scenery provides an unforgettable experience for any visitor. [6]

4 Fill in the gaps with *who, that, which, whose* and *where* if necessary. Put – if no word is needed.

JAN   I saw a great film last night.
MARK Me too. Was it the one ¹ _that/which_ won the Oscar?
JAN   No, it was called *Mountain*. It was directed by a woman ² .... has never made a film before.
MARK What's it about?
JAN   A guy ³ .... memory disappears and—
MARK Yes, I've seen it! It's the one ⁴ .... I was telling you about last month.
JAN   Was it? Sorry, I forgot. I just loved it. It was shot in the place ⁵ .... I used to go on holiday as a kid.
MARK Really? It has Angie Curtis in, ⁶ .... is the reason ⁷ .... I enjoyed it.
JAN   I don't understand this Angie Curtis thing. Phil, ⁸ .... works in my office, is mad about her too. [7]

5 Complete the sentences so the preposition is at the end.

1 I work with some young people. I like them.
   I like _the young people I work with._
2 Tom's chatting to a woman. Do you know her?
   Do you .... ?
3 You were looking for a file. Is this the one?
   Is this .... ?
4 Ben was accused of something. What was it?
   What was .... ?
5 Lucy was invited to a party. She enjoyed it.
   Lucy enjoyed ....

Rewrite the phrases in **bold** using a preposition + *which* or *whom*.

6 This is the house **which Mozart was born in**.
   This is the house in which Mozart was born.
7 The family **that we stayed with** were extremely hospitable.
   ....
8 James was unhappy about the story **that he was working on**.
   ....
9 Kate works with people **who she has no interest in**.
   ....
10 That is the experiment **that I referred to earlier**.
   .... [16]

6 Fill in the gaps with *neither, both, the best, none* or *all + of which/whom.*

1 There are two books on the floor, _neither of which_ belongs to me.

2 The album has great tracks on it, ... is 'Calling You'. It's magic.

3 In the evening we sang a lot of songs, ... we'd learnt together at school.

4 I have two brothers, ... live in Canada.

5 Rob suggested meeting on Friday or Saturday, ... were convenient for me, unfortunately.

6 Leah talked to various people at the party, ... she particularly liked.

[10]

7 Complete these sentences with a present, past or perfect participle.

open

1 Meg felt very proud, _opening_ her own shop.

2 .... all his presents, my son promptly burst into tears.

3 Caves restaurant, ... in 1967, is still popular with students.

4 .... the door, I felt a sudden blast of heat.

write

5 .... to Josh, Donna remembered all the good times they had had.

6 I had a busy morning, ... lots of emails.

7 Carefully .... in Gothic script, the manuscript made fascinating reading.

8 .... my report on the situation, I decided I needed a break.

[14]

8 Rewrite the phrases in **bold** using a present or past participle clause.

1 **Because we didn't like** indie music, we left the gig before the end.
   Not liking indie music, we left the gig before the end.

2 **If it's cooked** slowly at a low temperature, it will be very tender.
   .... slowly at a low temperature, it will be very tender.

3 **I didn't want to** appear anxious so I didn't ask Max about his interview.
   .... appear anxious, I didn't ask Max about his interview.

4 **Because Anna hadn't lived** in a hot country before, she was unprepared for the humidity.
   .... in a hot country before, Anna was unprepared for the humidity.

5 **As I was going** into the supermarket, I tripped over a basket.
   .... into the supermarket, I tripped over a basket.

6 **Because the film is shot in black and white**, it feels quite sinister.
   .... , the film feels quite sinister.

7 We decided to eat out **as we had no food** in the fridge.
   .... in the fridge, we decided to eat out.

8 **Because Tess had walked** home in uncomfortable shoes, her feet were hurting.
   .... home in uncomfortable shoes, Tess's feet were hurting.

9 Matt **looked through** the window and saw a fox in the garden.
   .... the window, Matt saw a fox in the garden.

[16]

9 Tick the correct sentences. Change the incorrect sentences.

                    really
1 Fortunately, the dog was ~~entirely~~ friendly.

2 The village still had many quaint thatched cottages. ✔

3 Ray deeply regrets not trying harder at school.

4 The hotel was slightly further from the centre than I'd expected, but it was fine.

5 You must watch that new series on TV what everyone is talking about.

6 The person with who he had the closest relationship was his brother.

7 The delegates moved on to discuss the budget requirements, in which point I left.

8 Madonna's first album, that I haven't got, is meant to be her best.

9 Telling a lie, Rosie then felt guilty.

10 Sitting on the train, Ben thought about Sarah.

11 A large stunning red balloon floated over the water.

12 Are you still in touch to your old friends?

13 This is the second time I've been skiing.

[11]

Answer Key p199   © Cambridge University Press 2009   **face2face** Advanced Photocopiable

Name .... Score │100│

1 Complete the table with positive and negative character adjectives.

Someone who....	+	–
1 is certain of their abilities	_confident_	_arrogant_
2 believes that other people are good	t.................	g.................
3 is careful with money	t.................	t.................
4 pays great attention to detail	m.................	f.................
5 is happy to spend money	g.................	e.................
6 does things in a natural, often sudden way	s.................	i.................
7 has the ability to control their fear	c.................	r.................
8 wants to do something very much	d.................	o.................

│14│

2 Fill in the gaps with the correct form of these phrasal verbs.

~~swell up~~   block up   put sb on   get over
come out in   pick up   go down with sth   go around

SUE   Oh, Fran, your face looks a bit ¹ _swollen up._
FRAN   I don't feel very well. I think I must be
       ² ....
SUE   Well, there's a nasty infection
       ³ .... at the moment. My
       15-year-old ⁴................................. something
       at school last week.
FRAN   I can't breathe. My nose ⁵.................................
       and I've ⁶................................. a rash on my
       chest.
SUE   Sounds familiar. You'd better go to the doctor.
FRAN   I don't want him ⁷.................................
       antibiotics.
SUE   Why not? You ⁸................................. whatever
       it is much quicker.
FRAN   I guess so, but I just don't like antibiotics.

│14│

3 Complete the euphemisms.
1 an old person: a _senior_ _citizen_
2 not tell the truth: be .... the truth
3 be old and in bad condition: see ....
4 be or feel ill: be/feel .... the ....
5 getting old: getting .... a ....
6 old-fashioned: behind ....
7 a lot to look after: a bit .... a ....
8 a bit deaf: a bit .... of ....
9 very difficult: ....
10 cold: a bit .... the ....

│9│

4 Complete the sentences.
1 James was shocked when he realised that the police were looking for him.
   It _shocked James to realise_ that the police were looking for him.
2 Sofia practised every day, so naturally she won the tournament.
   It's no .... Sofia won the tournament as she practised every day.
3 I don't understand why Chloe doesn't express her ideas more.
   It's hard .... why Chloe doesn't express her ideas more.
4 I read the book and I wouldn't recommend it.
   It's .... I'd recommend.
5 Our dog can't stand us tickling her ears.
   Our dog .... we tickle her ears.
6 To cut down on caffeine is difficult.
   I find .... cut down on caffeine.
7 Most of us were concerned when we heard that our company was relocating.
   It .... that our company was relocating.
8 Apparently, eating chocolate is sometimes good for you.
   It .... eating chocolate is sometimes good for you.
9 Everyone must follow the emergency procedure. That's obvious.
   .... that everyone must follow the emergency procedure.

│16│

208

(Answer Key p199)

5 Rewrite the sentences using the words in brackets.

1 What time are you leaving? (you know)
   Do you know what time you are leaving?

2 Why did Jenny take your bike? (you any idea)
   ....

3 What did I do with my keys? (can't remember)
   ....

4 Mark asked me, "Do you belong to a gym?" (if)
   ....

5 Why didn't Paul go to the party? (wonder)
   ....

6 Look! The sun! (comes)
   ....

7 A I can't go to Jack's party.
   B I can't either. (neither)
   B ....

   [12]

6 Fill in the gaps with these words/phrases and the correct form of the verbs.

| ~~Rarely~~   Only once   Not for a minute   Seldom |
| Under no circumstances   Not only   Only when |

1 You hardly ever see professional athletes eating junk food.
   Rarely do you see professional athletes eating junk food.

2 I've only broken my leg once when skiing.
   .... my leg when skiing.

3 I will not support John's proposal under any circumstances.
   .... John's proposal.

4 I never thought I'd enjoy jogging, but I do.
   .... I'd enjoy jogging, but I do.

5 It wasn't until Greg gave up eating fatty foods that he began to feel better.
   .... Greg gave up fatty foods
   .... feel better.

6 Eva wasn't just overworking, she was also taking no exercise.
   .... , she
   was also taking no exercise.

7 There has not often been so much interest in health issues.
   .... so
   much interest in health issues.

   [12]

7 Fill in the gaps in the conversations with these words.

| ~~could~~ go better side planning sort suits |
| could unfortunately on quite better bit with |

JO   What did you think of the film?
SEB   Well, it ¹ *could* have been ² ....
JO   The ending was a bit feeble, wasn't it?
SEB   Yeah, the whole thing was ³ .... of left unresolved.
JO   Coming for a coffee?
SEB   Not tonight. ⁴ .... , I've got to go back to work.

LENA Do you like my hair longer like this?
JULIE Well, actually, I think shorter hair ⁵ .... you ⁶ ....
LENA Really? Perhaps it ⁷ .... do ⁸ .... being a ⁹ .... shorter at the front.
JULIE Yeah, I'd ¹⁰ .... for a shorter fringe if I were you.

MAX   Do you fancy going for something to eat?
TOM   Good idea, but not to the Grill House. The last steak I had there was definitely ¹¹ .... the tough ¹² ....
MAX   OK. ¹³ .... honestly, I think they overcharge anyway, so how about the Thai on the High Street?
TOM   Fine. Oh, I was ¹⁴ .... to meet Tony tonight. Is it OK if I invite him along?
MAX   Sure, no problem.

   [13]

8 Tick the correct sentences. Change the incorrect sentences.

                    goes my money.
1 There ~~my money goes~~.
2 I've had better meals. ✓
3 I don't like that he's a bad loser.
4 There's no good asking Alex.
5 Claire doesn't eat much fruit and nor she enjoys vegetables.
6 There aren't any tickets, are there?
7 Which film is it are we going to?
8 Not trying to laugh, Gina asked a question.
9 The front door may be locked, in that case go to the neighbours for a key.
10 What I like it's having lunch with my friends at the weekend.
11 Did you enrol on any courses yet?
12 I completely agree with you.

   [10]

Answer Key p199   © Cambridge University Press 2009   face2face Advanced Photocopiable

Name .... Score ☐ 100

1 Fill in the gaps with the correct form of these verbs.

| ~~issue~~ hold sue seek receive hit make |

Gloria Gray's agent ¹ _issued_ a press release yesterday in which it was announced that the singer would be ² .... a magazine for libel over a recent article about her. The news of her intentions ³ .... the front page of the tabloids the following day, and astonishingly even ⁴ .... a lot of coverage in the quality press. Most of the articles were critical of Gray's seeming desire ⁵ .... publicity for everything she does. The tone of the articles has not pleased the singer and she ⁶ .... a press conference tomorrow to explain her reasons for going to court. No doubt this ⁷ .... headlines, and so we go on.

☐ 12

2 Complete the table with near synonyms.

humans	¹p_eople_	²m............
disease	³p............	
large	⁴h............	
improvements	⁵d............	
a settlement	a ⁶v............	
like	⁷e............	
the countryside	the ⁸l............	
children	⁹k............	
country folk	¹⁰r............	¹¹v............
	i............	
whole	¹²e............	

☐ 11

3 Complete the sentences with the correct future form of the verbs in brackets.

ANN   You look as if you're in a hurry, Meg.

MEG   Yes, I've got to get the train at five.
I ¹_'m going to see_ (see) my parents. It's their wedding anniversary tomorrow. They ² .... (marry) for 40 years.

ANN   Fantastic. Give them my love.

MEG   Thanks.

ANN   When do you think you ³ .... (be) back?

MEG   Monday evening. Why?

ANN   Ed and I ⁴ .... (go) to the cinema on Monday. Do you want to come with us?

MEG   Well, my train ⁵ .... (get) in at six. I could go straight to the cinema as soon as I ⁶ .... (arrive).

ANN   I tell you what. I ⁷ .... (pick) you up at the station. I ⁸ .... (go) past the station on my way to the cinema anyway.

MEG   Well, if you're sure, that's great. Thanks.

☐ 14

4 Choose the correct future form.

1 I don't feel very well. I think *I'll be/ I'm going to be* sick.

2 Don't ring me at 6.00 tonight. *I'll cook/I'll be cooking* dinner then. Ring later.

3 At the end of this month, David *will have lived/is going to live* in the same house for 30 years.

4 As soon as Emma *leaves/is going to leave* college, she expects to get a job.

5 That child *is going to fall/is falling* in the river if he leans over any more.

6 The film's on at the Vue cinema and it *will start/ starts* at 8.00.

7 I *won't be meeting/won't meet* Rob as usual this week. He's away on business.

8 Claire *won't have finished/isn't finishing* work before 7.00 so we can't meet her before then.

9 What *are you doing/do you do* for lunch today?

10 Until people lose interest in celebrities, magazines *are always printing/will always print* gossip about them.

☐ 9

face2face Advanced Photocopiable   © Cambridge University Press 2009   Answer Key p200

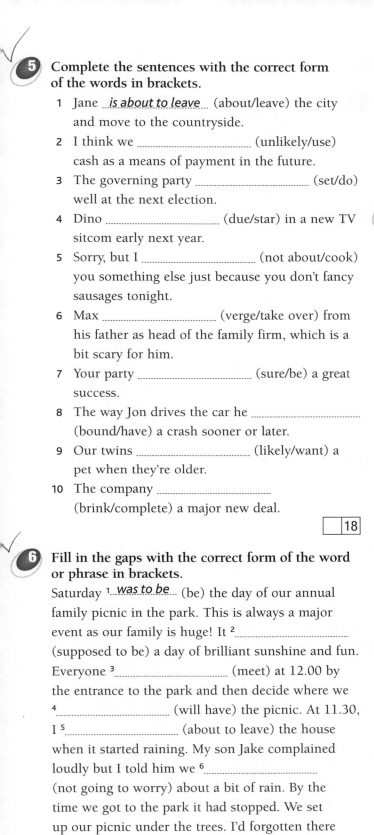

5 **Complete the sentences with the correct form of the words in brackets.**

1 Jane __is about to leave__ (about/leave) the city and move to the countryside.

2 I think we _____ (unlikely/use) cash as a means of payment in the future.

3 The governing party _____ (set/do) well at the next election.

4 Dino _____ (due/star) in a new TV sitcom early next year.

5 Sorry, but I _____ (not about/cook) you something else just because you don't fancy sausages tonight.

6 Max _____ (verge/take over) from his father as head of the family firm, which is a bit scary for him.

7 Your party _____ (sure/be) a great success.

8 The way Jon drives the car he _____ (bound/have) a crash sooner or later.

9 Our twins _____ (likely/want) a pet when they're older.

10 The company _____ (brink/complete) a major new deal.

[ ]18

6 **Fill in the gaps with the correct form of the word or phrase in brackets.**

Saturday ¹ __was to be__ (be) the day of our annual family picnic in the park. This is always a major event as our family is huge! It ² _____ (supposed to be) a day of brilliant sunshine and fun. Everyone ³ _____ (meet) at 12.00 by the entrance to the park and then decide where we ⁴ _____ (will have) the picnic. At 11.30, I ⁵ _____ (about to leave) the house when it started raining. My son Jake complained loudly but I told him we ⁶ _____ (not going to worry) about a bit of rain. By the time we got to the park it had stopped. We set up our picnic under the trees. I'd forgotten there ⁷ _____ (going to be) so many kids. It was difficult to keep an eye on them all. I had to tell Jake he ⁸ _____ (not supposed to hit) his cousin Marta with a bat. Marta ⁹ _____ (just about to burst) into tears when her mother gave her some chocolate

cake. It began raining a bit, but we decided we ¹⁰ _____ (going to enjoy) ourselves and we played some good games. However, we decided we probably ¹¹ _____ (will not do) a picnic again – it ¹² _____ (will have to be) an indoor event.

[ ]22

7 **Tick the correct sentences. Change the incorrect sentences.**

    I'll

1 I̶ let you know when I hear from them.

2 Do you read the tabloids? ✓

3 Andy's tennis coach feels that he's on the point of giving up.

4 The paper decided not to hold the victim's story.

5 The president was likely to cancel next week's visit to the US.

6 Dan was quite anxious because he had an important exam tomorrow.

7 There were a number of large problems to deal with on my return.

8 We understand that the arrested men are face trial before being deported.

9 My course will finish by the end of July.

10 Most of Jane's friends find hard to understand her decision.

11 Only when I recovered did I realise how ill I'd been.

12 Jack was very furious about the way his story was reported in the paper.

13 I don't like soap operas and neither I like reality shows.

14 There were loads of good films at the festival, the best of whom was an Iranian one.

15 Grandad's not deaf – just a bit hard of hearing.

16 We were tired, sleeping very badly.

[ ]14

1 R5.9 **Listen to an interview with a successful painter, Theresa Garrett. Choose the correct answers.**

1 When Theresa has a new exhibition she feels …
   a) anxious about the public reaction. b) critical of the work she has produced. c) disappointed that the paintings are finished.

2 Theresa says that being a painter …
   a) is not a well-regarded job. b) involves making sacrifices. c) can be a lonely life.

Listen to a conversation between two friends about going to university. Choose the correct answers. (Tim is the second speaker.)

3 Tim thinks that going to university …
   a) guarantees you a good job afterwards.
   b) enables you to meet a wide variety of people.
   c) allows you to find out more about yourself.

4 What does Tim say about the course he's going to do?
   a) There will be boring parts to it. b) It will be hard work. c) The financial aspect of it is worrying.

[8]

2 **Listen to Sarah White giving a talk to a group of students about her job as an airline pilot. Fill in the missing information.**

Sarah's love of [1] _engines_ led her to become a pilot.
It was while Sarah was working as a [2] _____
that she decided to change careers.
Sarah combined [3] _____
and attending classes in order to pass her flying exams.
Sarah prefers [4] _____ flights.
Sarah doesn't get on the plane until [5] _____ before take-off.
According to Sarah, the factor most likely to cause a change of plan is [6] _____ .
For safety reasons, the [7] _____ that Sarah has is different.
Sarah says that during a flight, [8] _____ cannot always be avoided.

[14]

3 **Complete the words with prefixes.**

1 You're in danger of _over_doing the flattery. Just relax and be natural.

2 I don't have much social _____action at work because we all work on our own.

3 The honey really _____acts the sourness of the lemon, doesn't it?

4 I was late because I _____estimated the time it would take to get there.

5 The article included a lot of _____-scientific research which was completely unreliable.

6 David _____heard someone on the phone talking about redundancy plans.

7 The chairs were arranged in a small _____-circle facing the teacher.

8 We had _____floor central heating installed which felt very luxurious.

[7]

4 **Complete the text with the correct form of the verb in brackets.**

I stopped [1] _working_ (work) two months ago so everyone tells me I'd better [2] _____ (make) an effort to find another job. I've decided [3] _____ (not/take) an office job because I don't like [4] _____ (be) inside all day. I don't mind [5] _____ (work) outside so maybe I could try [6] _____ (find) a job with the Parks Department. My friends are encouraging me [7] _____ (apply) but I think they'll want someone who's qualified. I really regret [8] _____ (not/do) horticulture at college when I had the chance. Maybe I'll end up [9] _____ (have) to go back to college and this time I'll need [10] _____ (focus). It'll mean [11] _____ (live) at home again because I couldn't manage [12] _____ (finance) my study and living expenses. I'd rather not [13] _____ (have to) ask my parents but I know they'll help me.

[12]

5 **Choose the two verbs that collocate.**

1 Ella (got)/achieved/(obtained) a place at the best art college in the country.

2 Jacob spent years doing/carrying out/gaining research into earthworms.

3 Did you have/get/do a good education?

PROGRESS TESTS: PHOTOCOPIABLE

4 She *did/got/achieved* a degree in applied physics.

5 I *carried out/took/sat* my final exam last week.

6 Our students don't have the opportunity to *do/get/take* work experience.

[ ] 10

 Complete these words/phrases connected to work.

1 ordinary, not special: r*un*-of-the-m*ill*

2 be very busy doing something: be up to your e_____ i_____ sth

3 the sequence of job positions progressing upwards: the c_____ l_____

4 too fixed in one particular activity: s_____ in a r_____

5 a job where there's no chance of progressing: a d_____-e_____ job

6 do something as fast as possible, before a certain time: a_____ the c_____

7 having a very important job: h_____-p_____

8 having your own business: s_____-e_____

9 relax and not use too much energy: t_____ it e_____

10 someone who's good at working with others: a t_____ p_____

[ ] 18

7 Fill in the gaps with a reflexive pronoun. Put – if no word is possible.

1 I was occupied ____–____ with the children for the whole afternoon.

2 Do you feel _____ at home here?

3 I didn't buy any of the food. I made it all _____ .

4 Did you speak to Sam _____ or to his assistant?

5 We had to exert _____ to make conversation with our boring neighbours.

6 Prepare _____ for a big surprise! I've got something for you both!

7 I like the house _____ but not the location.

8 Relax _____ and you'll feel the tension in your shoulders disappearing.

9 Did you put these shelves up _____ ?

10 You must try and concentrate _____ on what we're discussing.

11 Everybody really enjoyed _____ at the party.

[ ] 10

8 Fill in the gaps in these conversations using these words.

~~look~~	by	got	not	about	Ann	there
saying	with	all	mention	on		

TOM   You ¹ *look* shocked, ²_____ .

ANN   I can't believe you think we shouldn't teach foreign languages in school.

TOM   ³_____ I'm ⁴_____ is there's little point forcing people until they're ready.

ANN   Oh, well, I'm ⁵_____ you ⁶_____ that. But that's true for everything, not just languages.

SUE   The food last night was brilliant.

ZOE   ⁷_____ to ⁸_____ the wine and the company.

SUE   ⁹_____ company you mean Jack?

ZOE   Yes. I think he's really special, don't you?

DAN   There's no point asking John for his opinion. He hasn't got one.

MAX   Oh, I don't know ¹⁰_____ that. I think he's just a quiet person.

DAN   If that's the case why did he spend two hours telling me about his new dog?

MAX   Ah, you've ¹¹_____ me ¹²_____ . Maybe he's just dull.

[ ] 11

 Tick the correct sentences. Change the incorrect ones.

              to work

1 Wouldn't you prefer ~~working~~ in a small company?

2 For the work she does, Nadia feels she is underpaid. ✓

3 Rosie and I had offices next door to ourselves.

4 We're completely snowed on so we need to take on extra staff.

5 It was meant to be a joke – I'm sorry if I offended you.

6 Lucy always took her cat with herself when she went away.

7 Adam told lies in a regular basis.

8 I'll lie on a beach this time next week. I can't wait.

9 Spending time with her Spanish charming godson was a real pleasure for Julia.

10 The hospital took you on a light diet for a reason, you know.

11 The elections are on November 6th.

12 Only recently it has become clear how fast the glaciers are melting.

[ ] 10

Answer Key p200   © Cambridge University Press 2009   **face2face** Advanced Photocopiable

Progress Test 6 40 minutes

1 Fill in the gaps with these words. Use each word twice.

| ~~odd~~ plain flat heavy branch top |

1 What was the matter with Sam last night? His behaviour was very _odd_.
2 The view from the _____ of the mountain was breath-taking.
3 The Manchester _____ of my favourite department store is closing down.
4 I like my food _____ , not drowning in sauces.
5 Dan used to be a _____ smoker.
6 Alice wore _____ gloves as a matter of choice.
7 This mineral water is _____ because someone left the top off the bottle.
8 The _____ rain forced us to abandon our trip.
9 One _____ of our family is in Canada.
10 Have you got a big _____ dish to put the sandwiches on?
11 When Jan saw her friends' glamorous clothes, she felt ashamed of her _____ dress.
12 Jason is one of the country's _____ golfers.

[11]

2 Rewrite the words or phrases in bold using word pairs.

1 This gig could **make** Josh **a success or a failure**.
make or break
2 I quite like opera but actually I can **live without it**. _____
3 A good professional footballer can usually **decide** which team he wants to play for.
_____
4 David's cooking skills have come on **rapidly** in recent months. _____
5 Aren't you **fed up** of listening to Will's jokes?
_____
6 We rehearsed the opening ceremony **many times** in order to get it perfect. _____
7 I've been writing a novel **from time to time** for years. _____
8 Dealing with dangerous people is **an inescapable part** of a police officer's life. _____
9 The service here is very **unpredictable**.
_____

[16]

3 Complete the text with the correct form of these verbs.

| ~~cajole~~ nudge storm out hiss drag leap up grab |

Jack didn't want to go to Alison's party but I
[1] _cajoled_ him into coming with me. Unfortunately it turned out to be awful. There were hardly any people and the food was dreadful.
"Why [2] _____ you _____ me here?" he
[3] _____ in my ear.
"We'll stay half an hour and then go," I replied.
I knew Jack was likely [4] _____ if he got bored and in fact half an hour later, Jack [5] _____ and walked to the door. The woman I was talking to
[6] _____ me and said something about Jack being in a hurry. [7] _____ my handbag, I said goodbye to Alison and rushed out. We then went to a restaurant to recover from the experience.

[12]

4 Fill in each gap with one word.

On your bike!
There has been a big change in the way we are getting to work. We are becoming [1] _far_ less dependent on our cars and using bikes much more. We've realised that it's a great
[2] _____ cheaper to cycle to work [3] _____
to drive. And of course, the [4] _____ we leave our cars at home the [5] _____ it is for the environment. It can be quicker too. You're much [6] _____ likely to get held up by traffic because you can go in the cycle lanes. I got to work twice [7] _____ fast last week, and I was
[8] _____ near as stressed as when I drove. It's good to start the day with some exercise too. I
[9] _____ longer feel tired when I get to work – instead I feel energised. Of course you have to be careful, but cycling is [10] _____ nearly as dangerous [11] _____ you may think, provided you wear protective clothing and stay alert.
So what has brought about this change of

[10]

5 Complete these sentences using the ideas in brackets to make comparisons.

1 Most men are _a good deal_ _less interested_ in shopping for clothes _than_ women. (a good deal/interested)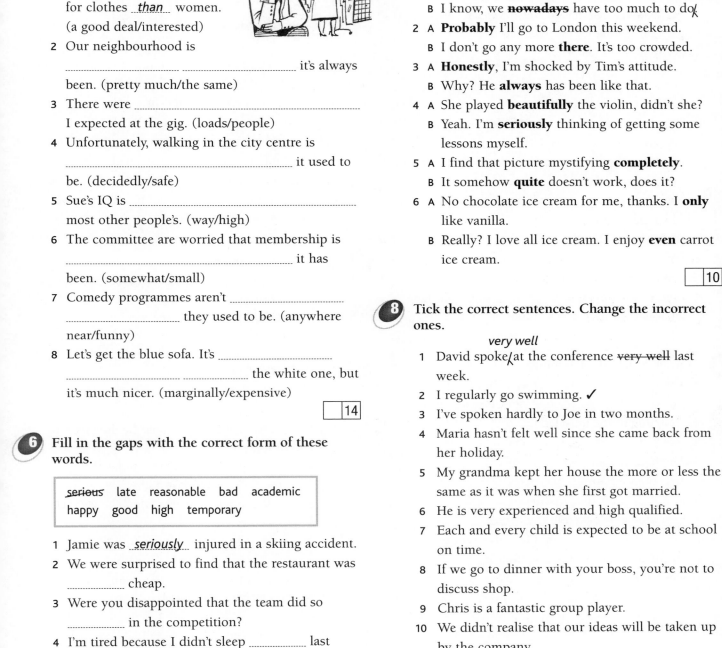

2 Our neighbourhood is _____ _____ it's always been. (pretty much/the same)

3 There were _____ I expected at the gig. (loads/people)

4 Unfortunately, walking in the city centre is _____ it used to be. (decidedly/safe)

5 Sue's IQ is _____ most other people's. (way/high)

6 The committee are worried that membership is _____ it has been. (somewhat/small)

7 Comedy programmes aren't _____ _____ they used to be. (anywhere near/funny)

8 Let's get the blue sofa. It's _____ _____ the white one, but it's much nicer. (marginally/expensive)

[ ] 14

6 Fill in the gaps with the correct form of these words.

| ~~serious~~ late reasonable bad academic |
| happy good high temporary |

1 Jamie was _seriously_ injured in a skiing accident.

2 We were surprised to find that the restaurant was _____ cheap.

3 Were you disappointed that the team did so _____ in the competition?

4 I'm tired because I didn't sleep _____ last night.

5 Have you seen Zoe _____?

6 Everyone held their arms up _____ and swayed with the music.

7 The museum is _____ closed for renovations.

8 Nina is not as well qualified _____ as you are.

9 Tom sounded very _____ when he told us about his engagement to Lucy.

[ ] 16

7 Tick the adverbials shown in **bold** that are in a correct position. Change the incorrect ones.

1 A **Sometimes**, it's hard to find the time to see friends. I'm so busy. ✓

   B I know, we **nowadays** have too much to do. _nowadays_ ✗

2 A **Probably** I'll go to London this weekend.

   B I don't go any more **there**. It's too crowded.

3 A **Honestly**, I'm shocked by Tim's attitude.

   B Why? He **always** has been like that.

4 A She played **beautifully** the violin, didn't she?

   B Yeah. I'm **seriously** thinking of getting some lessons myself.

5 A I find that picture mystifying **completely**.

   B It somehow **quite** doesn't work, does it?

6 A No chocolate ice cream for me, thanks. I **only** like vanilla.

   B Really? I love all ice cream. I enjoy **even** carrot ice cream.

[ ] 10

8 Tick the correct sentences. Change the incorrect ones.

1 David spoke at the conference ~~very well~~ last week. _very well_

2 I regularly go swimming. ✓

3 I've spoken hardly to Joe in two months.

4 Maria hasn't felt well since she came back from her holiday.

5 My grandma kept her house the more or less the same as it was when she first got married.

6 He is very experienced and high qualified.

7 Each and every child is expected to be at school on time.

8 If we go to dinner with your boss, you're not to discuss shop.

9 Chris is a fantastic group player.

10 We didn't realise that our ideas will be taken up by the company.

11 The president is to open the new stadium on Friday.

12 After their first success, they went on founding two other successful businesses.

13 The company had to make a press release to explain the ongoing situation.

[ ] 11

1 Fill in the gaps with the correct form of these phrases.

> ~~get round to~~   get (my, your etc.) own back on
> get into   get through to   get round
> get away with   get at

1 We must __get round to__ having a burglar alarm installed some time.

2 When she was younger, Jo regularly stole sweets and always _____ it.

3 I'm not _____ you, honestly. I'm just trying to explain how I feel.

4 Nick _____ petty crime at a very early age.

5 The regulations can easily be _____ if we study them carefully.

6 Jenny, how can I _____ you that your behaviour is unacceptable?

7 Fred was determined to _____ his colleague who had wrongly accused him of fraud.   ☐ 12

2 Complete the phrasal nouns.

1 The council is facing a s__etback__ in their plans.

2 The o_____ of the disease is marked by a stiffening of the muscles.

3 Stress at work caused Jim's nervous b_____ .

4 The high school class of '98 had a g_____ in an Italian restaurant.

5 K_____ for the cup final is at 3.00.

6 Everyone got soaked in the d_____ .

7 My whole o_____ on life is different now.

8 Surprisingly, there was no public o_____ when the government raised taxes.   ☐ 14

3 Write these metaphors.

1 attack: __storm__

2 pass very quickly: f_____

3 clever and quick to learn: b_____

4 stop moving and become still: f_____

5 fill a place in large numbers: f_____

6 affectionate and friendly: w_____

7 ask someone a lot of questions: g_____

8 begin to be understood by somebody: d_____   ☐ 7

4 Choose the correct conditional form.

1 We (wouldn't feel)/didn't feel so cold if we (could)/would close the window properly.

2 If you *will wash/wash* wool at a high temperature, it *shrinks/would shrink*.

3 I *might have come/might come* to the festival with you if I *would have/had* known about it in time.

4 If you *hadn't parked/wouldn't have parked* here, *we wouldn't have got/didn't get* a £50 fine.

5 I know it's an impossible dream but if I *won/win* the competition, *I'd/I'll* have a real chance of becoming a singer.

6 If there *is/will be* a ban on cars in the city, *we'll have/we have* to walk to work.   ☐ 10

5 Complete the sentences.

1 I regret having a day off last week because now I have to work.
If I __hadn't had__ a day off last week, __I wouldn't have to__ work now.

2 It's unlikely that the river will rise any more, but we'll be flooded if it does.
Were _____ any more, we _____ .

3 Joe is really tired today because he didn't sleep well last night.
Joe _____ so tired today if he _____ well last night.

4 I didn't plan things properly, which is why I'm panicking now.
If I _____ things properly, I _____ now.

5 In the event of the performance being cancelled, you will receive a full refund.
Should _____ , you will receive a full refund.

6 Sarah's got exams next week, which is why she didn't come out with us on Friday.
If Sarah _____ exams next week, she _____ out with us on Friday.

7 We called the police and as a result the suspects are at the police station now.
Had _____ the police, the suspects _____ at the police station now.   ☐ 12

6 Complete the text with the correct passive form of the verbs.

Skipping, which ¹ _is_ also _called_ (call) jump rope, is a wonderful form of exercise. It ² _____ (practise) for centuries around the world by children and adults. A form of skipping ³ _____ (know) in China, Ancient Egypt and Ancient Greece but it is the Netherlands that ⁴ _____ (credit) with having originated the modern form in the 1600s. It ⁵ _____ (take) to North America by the Dutch and became popular there.

Today, athletes use skipping as part of their fitness programmes because it ⁶ _____ (find) to provide an aerobic workout and to develop footwork skills.

Skipping ⁷ _____ (do) at a competitive level too. In freestyle competitions, skipping routines ⁸ _____ (choreograph) to music; during speed events as many jumps as possible must ⁹ _____ (complete) within a certain amount of time.

Enthusiasts for the sport talk about its many benefits and hope that it ¹⁰ _____ (enjoy) by people of all ages for many years to come.

☐ 18

 7 Rewrite the sentences using impersonal report structures.

1 We know that thieves operate in this area.
Thieves _are known to operate_ in this area.

2 People expect that there will be a big increase in the amount of car crime.
There _____ a big increase in the amount of car crime.

3 The fire service believed that the building had been destroyed by a gas explosion.
The building _____ _____ by a gas explosion.

4 Sometimes people argue that chewing gum helps them concentrate.
It _____ sometimes _____ that chewing gum helps people to concentrate.

5 People think that David Beckham is going to make an appearance here next week.
David Beckham _____ an appearance here next week.

6 There are rumours that John is leaving.
John _____ .

7 Economists have predicted that there will be many job losses in the coming months.
It _____ there will be many job losses in the coming months.

8 At a rough estimate, over 10,000 people are going to Saturday's concert.
There _____ _____ to Saturday's concert.

☐ 14

8 Choose the usual intonation pattern for these questions.

1 A It's a beautiful day today, isn't it?   *rising/ (falling)* tone
  B Yes, lovely.

2 A What's your email address?   *rising/falling* tone
  B nabb@hotmail.com

3 A So you want it, do you?   *rising/falling* tone
  B Yes, it *is* mine, after all.

4 A Isn't this the place where you were born?   *rising/falling* tone
  B Yes, that's right.

5 A Why me?   *rising/falling* tone
  B Because you're the one who left the mess.

6 A I know Jan lives in Spain now, doesn't she?   *rising/falling* tone
  B Yes, and loves it.

☐ 5

9 Tick the correct sentences. Change the incorrect ones.

                input
1 It was your valuable ~~output~~ to the project that enabled us to secure the contract.

2 It seems that Sam doesn't like the new house. ✓

3 The rumour about the closure of the car factory was found false.

4 I'd like to change the décor if I'm going to live in this flat for a long time.

5 If everyone were to object, then we didn't go ahead with his idea.

6 It appears to be no update planned for our software system.

7 Living in London costs much the same like living in New York.

8 I won't probably be at work tomorrow.

9 I'm looking forward to doing my work experience.

10 I can occupy me with knitting for hours.

☐ 8

PROGRESS TESTS: PHOTOCOPIABLE

1 Fill in the gaps with the correct form of these phrases.

> ~~have time to kill~~   take (my/your/etc.) time over
> give sb a hard time   find time   have time to spare
> have no time for

1 Josie __*had time to kill*__ before her plane left, so she had a meal in a restaurant.

2 Although Sam worked very long hours, he somehow _____ to study for another degree.

3 I remember that if ever my gran _____ , she'd always be working in the garden.

4 I've decided not to go, so why _____ you _____ about it?

5 My father-in-law always _____ things and refused to be rushed.

6 I really _____ people who don't take climate change seriously. [10]

2 Rewrite the sentences. Where possible, begin with the word in brackets.

1 I don't know what made you buy those shoes. (whatever)
   Whatever made you buy those shoes!

2 I don't know who left the door unlocked, but they mustn't do it again. (whoever) _____

3 It doesn't matter what you've done, I forgive you. (whatever) _____

4 I will never become a great guitarist even though I practise hard. (however) _____

5 Rob takes lots of photos in every place he goes to. (wherever) _____

6 I don't know who told you about Emma, but they're wrong. (whoever) _____

7 It doesn't matter when I see Anya, she's always smiling. (whenever) _____

8 It doesn't matter which number you ring, you'll get through to me. (whichever) _____

9 Please ask for the name and address of anyone who phones. (whoever) _____

10 I can't believe you managed to carry all that shopping home! (however) _____

11 I tried to include anything that was relevant in my essay. (whatever) _____

12 Just buy any of them that you like. (whichever) _____ [22]

3 Complete the tables with nouns, verbs, adjectives and adverbs.

adjective	adverb	verb
clear	clearly	1 *clarify*
wide	2	3
rational	4	5

verb	noun	adjective
disturb	6	
remark		7
	courage	8
	9	possible
	sympathy	10
survive	11	
depend		12
fail	13	
	talent	14
	15	proud
	coward	16
divide	17	
	18	happy
recover	19	
create	creation	20
excite	21	excited

[20]

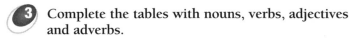

4

Fill in the gaps in this conversation with the correct form of the verbs in brackets.

LIZ   What's the matter?

ZOE   I wish we ¹ _were_ (be) back home. I wish I ² _____ (watch) telly in my bedroom!

LIZ   Why? Don't you like it here?

ZOE   Not really. It's not a very nice hotel, is it? I wish we ³ _____ (not/choose) this one.

LIZ   I think it's OK. It's not five-star, but it's all right.

ZOE   If only I ⁴ _____ (can remember) the name of the hotel Greg recommended, we could go there. I wish I ⁵ _____ (have) the brochure he gave me. If only I ⁶ _____ (bring) it! Then we could get out of here and go somewhere nice!

LIZ   Zoe! I wish you ⁷ _____ (stop) complaining! Let's try and enjoy ourselves!

[12]

5

Complete the sentences.

1 I wish I wasn't scared of spiders but I _am_ .

2 I'm sorry I said that. I wish I _____ .

3 I think it's awful that you watch so much TV. I wish you _____ .

4 I regret not being able to ski. I wish I _____ .

5 It's a pity I haven't got a car. I wish I _____ .

6 You won't eat vegetables, will you? I wish you _____ .

7 I'm sorry you're going away. I wish you _____ .

8 If only Joe lived nearer me but he _____ .

9 If only people would support their local team more but they _____ .

10 I wish you hadn't told her but you _____ .

11 If only I played the guitar instead of the violin but I _____ .

[10]

6

Fill in the gaps with the correct form of the words in brackets.

1 A Hurry up! It's time ¹ _we left_ (we/leave). We're going to be late.

B I wish we didn't have to go. I'd much rather ² _____ (stay) at home.

2 A It's time ³ _____ (stop) stretching and move on to push-ups.

B I don't feel warmed up yet. I'd prefer ⁴ _____ (do) a few more stretches.

3 A Would you prefer it if ⁵ _____ (I/not cook) dinner tonight?

B If I'm honest, I'd sooner ⁶ _____ (we/go) out for a pizza.

4 A I'd rather ⁷ _____ (you/ask) me before you borrowed it.

B Sorry. I forgot.

5 A It's high time ⁸ _____ (Jo/decide) what she wants to do.

B Why? I'd rather ⁹ _____ (she/think) about it carefully.

[16]

7

Tick the correct sentences. Change the incorrect ones.

        sympathetic
1 It's hard to be ~~sympathy~~ when Matt is so stubborn about things.

2 For the time being, Tom is working in his parents' shop. ✓

3 Tomorrow will be too late. It's no time like the present.

4 I hope you'll be very pleased whichever our products you decide to use.

5 I'd sooner to book the tickets now than wait till next week.

6 I'd have much preferred it if you'd never mentioned going on holiday.

7 Isn't it about time the government listen to public opinion?

8 The music sounded strangely to her.

9 It's taken me ages to get round to replying to Lee's email.

10 Leonardo da Vinci is understand to have invented a primitive helicopter.

11 It appears that the climbers left without saying where they were going.

12 If you should have any problems with it, come back to us.

[10]

219

1 Fill in the gaps with these words/phrases.

> cost of living cost-effective over-priced
> priceless cost a fortune reasonably priced
> price tags

I don't earn much but the ¹ _cost of living_ here is quite
low so I decided to join a gym as a way of getting fit.
Some gyms ² _____ but I hoped to find
one that wasn't too expensive. I thought joining a gym
would be ³ _____ in the long run. I
mean, good health is ⁴ _____ , isn't it?
Anyway, I found a gym and joined for six months.
Then I went into the gym's shop to get some clothes.
When I saw the ⁵ _____ on the outfits I
realised they were grossly ⁶ _____ and
it'd be cheaper to find some ⁷ _____
shorts and T-shirts in a department store. I found
some nice stuff, so now I'm ready to get fit!

☐ 6

2 Complete the words with suffixes.

1 The study by Professor Davis is note_worthy_
because it is the first to look at this topic.

2 Two members of a Swiss-_____ expedition
are missing.

3 Emma is very health-_____ and never eats
ready-made meals.

4 All the important papers were stored in a
fire_____ cabinet.

5 The gymnast gave an error-_____
performance and was awarded top marks.

6 Not being particularly money-_____ , Jan
didn't want a better-paid but more stressful job.

7 She can be very child_____ at times and
difficult to live with.

8 Rob is suffering from a stress-_____ illness.

☐ 7

3 Write the news and economics collocations.

1 economic help provided to countries abroad:
o_verseas_ a_id_

2 a country which has very great economic power:
e_____ s_____

3 different treatment of somebody because of being
male or female: g_____ d_____

4 something which is made cheaply and in large
numbers: m_____-p_____

5 higher levels than ever achieved before:
r_____ l_____

6 the useful possessions or qualities of the earth:
e_____ r_____

7 an increase in a country's capacity to produce
goods, etc.: e_____ g_____

8 energy which can be produced as quickly as it is
used: r_____ e_____

☐ 14

4 Fill in the gaps with the correct form of the verbs
in brackets.

I¹ _'ve been working_ (work) for a travel magazine for
three months and I've made friends with one of my
colleagues, Jessica. At the moment, she ² _____
(go) around Sweden researching an article and she
³ _____ (send) me emails and text
messages since she got there. First she
⁴ _____ (stay) in Stockholm for a few
days and ⁵ _____ (go) to quite a few
clubs and restaurants. She ⁶ _____ (not
know) any Swedish but lots of people
⁷ _____ (speak) English. For the past
three days she ⁸ _____ (camp) in the
wilderness with a travel company and she's having a
great time there. The first night they were there she
⁹ _____ (hear) wolves! She said they
began howling just as the sun ¹⁰ _____
(set) and carried on all night. She said so far she
¹¹ _____ (not visit) any of the islands,
but she's going to sail around some of them next
week. Obviously she ¹² _____ (enjoy) her
trip very much and probably ¹³ _____
(not want) to come back to the office.

☐ 24

5 Fill in the gaps with the correct form of these
verbs. Use each verb once in the Present Simple
and once in the Present Continuous.

> have look expect see come

1 _Do_ you _see_ why we had to close?

2 Which part of Italy _____ you _____ from?

3 I .... you'll have to pay a fortune for a seat on the front row.

4 I .... a problem with this lid. Can you try and get it off?

5 That restaurant .... nice.

6 When .... you .... Ed next?

7 People .... from all over the country for our wedding next month.

8 I .... a letter from the bank about my overdraft any day now.

9 The IT department .... at a new computer system for the office.

10 Some friends of mine .... a house by the sea that I go to occasionally.

| 18 |

6 Complete the text with *a(n)*, *the* or no article (–).

Muhammed al-Idrisi – Moroccan cartographer
Muhammed al-Idrisi was one of ¹ *the* finest cartographers of ² ...... Middle Ages. Born in 1099 in ³ ...... Morocco, he spent much of his youth travelling. He was invited to Sicily by ⁴ ...... Norman king, Roger II, who wanted him to create ⁵ ...... map of the world that would bring together all the knowledge the Greek and Arab mapmakers had accumulated. After 15 years' work, al-Idrisi finally carved ⁶ ...... map onto ⁷ ...... large silver disc. He also wrote ⁸ ...... accompanying geographical guidebook, which is arguably ⁹ ...... even greater achievement. During ¹⁰ ...... uprising in Sicily, al-Idrisi escaped to ¹¹ ...... North Africa. His guidebook was published in Arabic in 1592 but it wasn't until ¹² ...... 17th century that it became accessible to ¹³ ...... speakers of other languages.

| 12 |

7 Choose the correct words or phrases.

1 I wish there was *fewer*/(*less*) traffic here.

2 James left home *a/one* day in June.

3 There's only *a/one* biscuit left.

4 Have you got *a/one* screwdriver I could borrow?

5 Josh is so busy at work that he has *a little/little* time to spend with his family.

6 I've been to Spain *few/quite a few* times so I know it quite well.

7 *Very few/A very few* tourists visit my town as it's very remote.

| 6 |

8 Fill in the gaps in this speech with these phrases.

~~let's start by~~   first of all   so to sum up
leaving that aside for a moment   and finally
to go back to   let's move on

Welcome, everyone, to tonight's meeting.
¹ *Let's start by* thanking Jack for all his fund-raising. However, I'm afraid that members are not paying their subscriptions on time. But
² .... , I'd like to ask what you think about a recruitment drive. As you know, membership numbers are down. I think there are a couple of things we can do about this.
³ .... , we could improve our marketing, and secondly we could make the club more attractive. Liz, you have some ideas about that, I think. ⁴ .... the late payment of subscriptions, I'd be grateful for any suggestions for dealing with this. Perhaps a discount of some kind?
⁵ .... , we need to attract more members and make everyone pay their subscriptions promptly.
OK, ⁶ .... to this summer's events. We have four big tournaments which Graham will tell you about later.
⁷ .... , let me pass on the news that Diane is doing well after her operation and hopes to be with us next time.

| 6 |

9 Tick the correct sentences. Change the incorrect ones.

Are you thinking
1 ~~Do you think~~ of looking for a new job?

2 Have you worked out the cheapest way of getting to London? ✓

3 I'm weighing 60 kg at the moment.

4 These blankets are both warm and washable.

5 The house market is booming.

6 Zoe's still in the hospital but she's much better.

7 Aren't you lonely? Wouldn't you rather living with your sister?

8 The upshot of the meeting was that we had to renegotiate the contract.

9 I wish I wouldn't find Marcus so irritating.

| 7 |

PROGRESS TESTS: PHOTOCOPIABLE

Answer Key p202   © Cambridge University Press 2009   **face2face** Advanced Photocopiable

1   **Listen to Colin Judge, who is a choir master, talking about singing. Choose the correct answer.**

1   What does Colin say about singing?

a) It's as beneficial as sport.   b) It's an easy way of expressing yourself.   c) Its popularity is growing.

2   Colin says he is very pleased with Abacus because …

a) they want to continue singing.   b) they've worked so hard.   c) they've achieved their goals.

3   Colin believes that when adults want to sing they should …

a) find their own individual style.   b) sing as they did when they were younger.   c) imitate someone else's voice.

4   According to Colin, why do people enjoy choral singing?

a) They can produce a powerful sound together.

b) They can get away with making some mistakes.

c) They can sing a wider range of music.

5   What does Colin say about his next possible project?

a) It will pose discipline problems.   b) It will be similarly successful.   c) It will need a new approach.

[10]

2   **Listen to four people talking about the experience of winning something.**

Task 1

Match speakers 1–4 to topics a)–f).

1   Speaker 1 ....   a) award-winning design

2   Speaker 2 ....   b) chess competition

3   Speaker 3 ....   c) tennis tournament

4   Speaker 4 ....   d) photography competition

                       e) prize-winning short story

                       f) cookery competition

Task 2

What does each speaker feel about the experience? Match speakers 1–4 to feelings a)–f).

5   Speaker 1 ....   a) disappointed with the lack

6   Speaker 2 ....   of rivals

7   Speaker 3 ....   b) proud of the achievement

8   Speaker 4 ....   c) surprised to be a winner

                       d) confused by the judges' comments

                       e) embarrassed at how it was done

                       f) unsure of what it could lead to

[16]

 3   **Write antonyms for the words in bold.**

1   **rich** food → ..*plain*.. food

2   a **vague** idea → a .... idea

3   a **vague** possibility → a .... possibility

4   **light** blue → .... blue

5   **calm** sea → .... sea

6   an **aggressive** manner → a .... manner

7   a **sweet** taste → a .... taste

8   **strong** tea → .... tea

9   **clear** glass → .... glass

10   a **plain** scarf → a .... scarf

11   a **light** meal → a .... meal

[10]

4   **Fill in the gaps with the correct singular or plural form of *be*.**

1   Reading novels ..*is*.. great escapism for me at the moment.

2   The TV news .... very depressing last night.

3   It's OK, the police .... on their way.

4   A thousand people .... in emergency accommodation at the moment.

5   Eight kilometres .... a long way to walk to school if you're only 12 years old.

6   What concerned us most .... the enormous number of people needing medical treatment.

7   If everyone .... in agreement, then let's move on.

8   A couple of golden eagles .... seen in the area last week.

9   Economics .... not something I know much about.

10   Joe's cat and dog .... looked after by his neighbour while he was away.

11   Their team .... much better now than last season.

[10]

 face2face Advanced Photocopiable   © Cambridge University Press 2009   (Answer Key p202)

5 Complete the sentences with a modal verb and the correct form of the verb. Sometimes more than one modal is possible.

1 I was regularly taken to the zoo by my father when I was small.

My father _would take_ me to the zoo regularly when I was small.

2 It was wrong of Kate not to tell you the news.

Kate _____ you the news.

3 Fortunately Fred had the necessary skill to fix our car which had broken down.

Our car broke down but fortunately Fred

_____ it.

4 It wasn't necessary for Nick to work as he had loads of money.

Nick had loads of money so he _____

_____

5 It's typical of Ella to try to assemble something before she's read the instructions.

Ella _____ to assemble something before she's read the instructions.

6 Josh refused to come running with me.

Josh _____ running with me.

7 It'd be a good idea if you went to the dentist.

I think you _____ to the dentist.

8 Smoking is not allowed in here.

You _____ in here.

9 It was obligatory to send three photos.

I _____ three photos.

10 The flight was delayed for five hours so getting up early was a waste of time.

I _____ early because the flight was delayed for five hours.

11 Oliver had the ability to swim really well when he was ten years old.

When he was ten years old, Oliver _____

_____ really well.

[20]

6 Choose the correct modal verbs and fill in the gaps with the correct form of the verbs in brackets.

ZOE   I wonder why Luke isn't here yet. He ¹(should)/could _be_ (be) here by now.
He ²must/can't _____ (get) stuck in traffic.

BEN   Or he ³might/should _____ (work) late.

ZOE   Did you tell him we'd changed the time to 8.30 instead of 9.00?

BEN   Yes – but he ⁴can/may _____ (forget). He's been really busy. Did you know he's got his promotion?

ZOE   No! That's brilliant. He ⁵must/could _____ (be) really pleased. I wonder why he didn't tell me when I spoke to him on Tuesday.

BEN   He ⁶mustn't/wouldn't _____ (know) about it then. They only told him yesterday.

ZOE   Oh, right. Anyway, I'm going to call him to see what's happened. Oh, where's my mobile? I ⁷can't/mustn't _____ (leave) it at home because I used it this morning.

BEN   It ⁸'d/'ll be _____ (lie) on your desk, I bet. You're always leaving stuff at work.

ZOE   Could I use yours then?

BEN   Yeah, but remember his mobile ⁹could/can _____ (switch) off if he's in the car.

ZOE   You're right, it is. Let's order something to eat. He ¹⁰shouldn't/wouldn't _____ (be) too much longer.

[18]

7 Tick the correct sentences. Change the incorrect ones.

1 I might ~~can~~ come if I finish early.

2 Jo lost her voice but still managed to teach. ✓

3 It was a short building with only two floors.

4 The public are interested in celebrities.

5 Ought you give him a ring if you're worried?

6 My dad would always read to me when I was little.

7 It wouldn't have been safe to have gone alone.

8 What happens it is that I get too tired and can't concentrate.

9 There has been a general economical decline in the past two years.

10 I know it's complicated but are you seeing what I mean?

11 If we leave now, we'll arrive in a lot of time to see the film.

12 Not until Jamie went outside he realised how cold it was.

13 Taught by someone who's enthusiastic, maths can be fun.

14 I bought a coat for me in the sales.

15 I buy my vegetables as a rule from the market.

16 Ed has had many setbacks in his career.

17 By the end of this week the government will be in power for three years.

18 Whatever is that you're wearing!

[16]

Acknowledgements

Nick Robinson would like to thank Andrew Reid for inviting him to be involved in writing this book and Brigit Viney for her thoughtful, insightful editing and good humour throughout the writing and production process. Thanks also to Anna for her constant support.

Lindsay Warwick would like to say a huge thank-you to the following people: the in-house team at Cambridge University Press, to Andrew Reid and Brigit Viney, for fab feedback, support and ideas; Kerry Powell and Anna Gebka-Suska for suggestions at a particularly exhausting time; colleagues and students at Bell International from whom I constantly learn loads; the IOW girlies for their much-valued friendship despite my lack of visits; the Rice family, who make life more interesting; my family, Mal, David and Leigh, for their love, friendship and intrepid travels; and finally Alex, for making me laugh and for always sharing his chocolate.

Johanna Stirling would like to thank all of the face2face editorial team for their positive support and encouragement. She would also like to thank all those who have said 'Yes, you can' throughout her career and the wonderful array of learners, trainees and colleagues who have taught her so much. Special thanks to Daryl for all his love, support and exceptional patience that make the impossible possible.

Craig Thaine would like to thank Andrew Reid and Brigit Viney for their expert editorial support. He would also like to thank Steven Shuttleworth for his listening and comprehension.

Helen Naylor would like to thank Brigit Viney for her amazing support and dedication.

Jan Bell and **Gillie Cunningham** would like to thank all those involved in the writing and production of this book for all their hard work and creativity.

The authors and publishers are grateful to the following contributors:

pentacorbig: cover and text design and page layout
Hilary Luckcock: picture research

The authors and publishers are grateful to the following for their permission to reproduce copyright material:

The Council of Europe for the table on p15 from the *Common European Framework of Reference for Languages: Learning, teaching, assessment* p27 (2001) Council of Europe Modern Languages Division, Strasbourg, Cambridge University Press. Copyright of the text is held by The Council of Europe exclusively. ©Council of Europe. Reprinted with permission. New York City Police Department for the reillustrated graph and statistics on p178 'Homicides Approach a New Low'. Reproduced by kind permission of the New York City Police Department.

The publishers are grateful to the following for their permission to reproduce copyright photographs:

Key: l = left, c = centre, t = top, b = bottom

Alamy Images/©Ian Francis for p175, ©Blend Images for p180(l), /©UpperCut Images for p180 (c), /©Blend Images for p180 (r), /©Blend Images for p189, /©nagelstock.com for p190, /©David Sutherland for p197, /©David Ball for p198, / ©David R Frazier Photolibrary for p212; Bubbles Photo Library for p181; Corbis /©Jason Hawkes for p157; George Kourounis for p159 (t); Getty Images for p217; Guinness World Records for p159 (b); Photolibrary/©Bernd Kohlhas for p138,/©S Nicolas for p155 (b), /©Digital Vision for p177; Punchstock/©Photographers Choice for p155 (t), /©Stockbyte for p193; Richard Gibb for p191; www.hazelhenderson.com for p196.

The publishers would like to thank the following illustrators:

Fred Blunt (New Division), Kate Charlesworth, Dirty Vectors, Mark Duffin, Andy Hamilton (Illustration), Graham Kennedy, Simon Williams (Illustration)